# THE DRAMA OF REVOLT

ANGLICA GERMANICA SERIES 2

*Editors:* LEONARD FROSTER, S. S. PRAWER *and* A. T. HATTO

*Other books in the series*

D. Prohaska: Raimund and Vienna: A Critical Study of Raimund's plays in their Viennese Setting

D. G. Mowatt: Friderich von Hûsen: Introduction, Text, Commentary and Glossary

C. Lofmark: Rennewart in Wolfram's 'Willehalm': A Study of Wolfram von Eschenbach and his Sources

A. Stephens: Rainer Maria Rilke's 'Gedichte an die Nacht'

M. Garland: Hebbel's Prose Tragedies: An Investigation of the Aesthetic Aspects of Hebbel's Dramatic Language

H. W. Cohn: Else Lasker-Schüler: The Broken World

J. M. Ellis: Narration in the German Novelle: Theory and Interpretation

# THE DRAMA OF REVOLT

## A CRITICAL STUDY OF GEORG BÜCHNER

## MAURICE B. BENN

*Formerly Associate Professor of German in the
University of Western Australia*

CAMBRIDGE UNIVERSITY PRESS

CAMBRIDGE

LONDON · NEW YORK · MELBOURNE

Published by the Syndics of the Cambridge University Press
The Pitt Building, Trumpington Street, Cambridge CB2 1RP
Bentley House, 200 Euston Road, London NW1 2DB
32 East 57th Street, New York, NY 10022, USA
296 Beaconsfield Parade, Middle Park, Melbourne 3206, Australia

© Cambridge University Press 1976

First published 1976

Printed in Great Britain at the
University Printing House, Cambridge
(Euan Phillips, University Printer)

*Library of Congress Cataloguing in Publication Data*
Benn, Maurice Bernard, 1914–1975
   The drama of revolt.
   (Anglica Germanica: Series 2)
   Bibliography: p.
   Includes index.
   1. Büchner, Georg, 1813–1837 – Criticism and
interpretation. I. Title. II. Series.
PT1828.B6B37     831'.7     75–3974
ISBN 0 521 20828 9

# CONTENTS

v

# CONTENTS

## PLATES

(between pages 104 and 105)

I   *Christ at Emmaus*, by Carel von Savoy (Reproduced by permission of the Director of the Hessisches Landesmuseum, Darmstadt)

II   Rolf Boysen as Danton, Louise Martini as Marion (Reproduced by permission of the photographer, Rosemarie Clausen)

III   Karl Streck and Julia Costa as Leonce and Lena (Reproduced by permission of the photographer, Pit Ludwig)

IV   Wolfgang Reinbacher as Woyzeck, Elisabeth Endriss as Marie (Reproduced by permission of Elisabeth Endriss and the photographer, Daisy Steinbeck)

# ACKNOWLEDGEMENTS

My thanks are due to Professor Eric Herd of the University of Otago, who kindly read this work in typescript and suggested a number of corrections, and to Professor Leonard Forster for his friendly advice and encouragement. I should like to make it clear, however, that they do not necessarily share the views I have expressed, and that the responsibility for errors and deficiencies is entirely mine.

I would also like to thank Fräulein Elisabeth Endriss of Munich – the best actress I have seen in the part of Marie – for the present of the picture of a scene from the admirable production of *Woyzeck* by 'Die Brücke' (plate IV); also Professor K.-H. Hahn and his staff of the Goethe–Schiller Archive, Weimar, and Stadtinspektor Immo Beyer of Darmstadt for the facilities they so helpfully placed at my disposal.

Finally I wish to acknowledge the valuable assistance I have received from the Australian Research Grants Committee and the subsidy contributed by the University of Western Australia.

M.B.B.

1975

The editors and publishers of *Anglica Germanica* record with regret that Maurice Benn died while this book was in the press, on 31 May 1975. This book is therefore the memorial of a distinguished Germanist.

# NOTE

Throughout this book Büchner's writings have been quoted from the edition by Werner R. Lehmann, *Georg Büchner, Sämtliche Werke und Briefe* (Christian Wegner Verlag, Hamburg; vol. 1, 1967, vol. 2, 1971).

# 1. INTRODUCTION

Many of the world's finest artists, including even some of the great tragic dramatists – Sophocles, Shakespeare, Racine – seem to set out from a position of acquiescence in the spirit of their times, from an acceptance of the institutions, customs and beliefs of their society. They are content at first to express themselves in the established artistic forms of their age, and the innovations they effect, whether in ideas or in artistic techniques, emerge gradually in the course of an organic development. But there are others who are rebels from the beginning, who are antagonized from the very outset by what they feel to be false, cruel or absurd in society, art, religion, the whole condition of mankind. Georg Büchner is one of the most distinguished of these artists in revolt. He is a rebel, first of all, in a political sense, for a brief but significant period deeply and dangerously involved in a conspiracy to overthrow the government of his country. But he is equally a rebel in all the other spheres of his activity, in his philosophical speculations, in his aesthetic theories, in his practice as a dramatist.[1]

This does not mean that his work is purely negative and destructive. Revolt implies positive values which the rebel seeks to vindicate even if he is not fully conscious of them, even if he only becomes aware of them in the moment of their violation. And Büchner's many-sided activity will accordingly be found to have its positive as well as its negative aspects. In each of its spheres that activity conforms broadly to the same pattern: falsehood is rejected for the sake of truth, evil for the sake of good. But the truth and good upheld are not independent of the falsehood and evil combated but are to some extent conditioned by these. And the initial movement of thought and action is negative rather than positive: there is a much more immediate awareness of what must be rejected than of what might possibly be accepted.

A brief comparison with Hölderlin may help to clarify Büchner's attitude. In a sense Hölderlin too was a rebel. We know how strongly he sympathized with the French Revolution; and two of his major works, *Hyperion* and *Empedokles*, are centrally concerned with revolution and revolt, the former with the revolt of the Greeks against the Turks, the latter with the revolutionary renewal of the city-state of Agrigentum. But Hölderlin, as befits a hymnic poet, is essentially a poet of praise ('Beruf ist mirs, zu rühmen Höhers').[2] His whole life and thought are governed by a vision of ideal beauty, and his poetry dwells long and lovingly on that vision. In his elegiac poetry he is concerned to keep alive the memory of it, in his hymnic poetry to prophesy its recurrence. If he can fall into despair it is because he sometimes loses sight of it. If he is moved to revolt it is because the reality of his time negates it. But always that highly positive vision remains the beginning and end of his aspirations. With Büchner it is quite otherwise. Büchner never lets his thoughts dwell on an ideal vision. It is characteristic of him to set out from a repellent reality and only with difficulty, fitfully and imperfectly, to descry the beauty that may possibly emerge from it. His deepest experience is not the enthusiasm for beauty but the pitying insight into suffering. He is not a poet of praise but a poet of revolt.

Evidently both attitudes have their positive and negative aspects; but in the one the positive give rise to the negative, in the other the negative to the positive. And this difference involves characteristic differences of emphasis, of approach, of style and tone.

Of the two attitudes it is no doubt Büchner's rather than Hölderlin's that is most in accordance with twentieth-century habits of thought; and this may well be one of the reasons for the intense interest which Büchner continues to excite and the immense influence he has had upon contemporary drama. It is true that Albert Camus, the writer of the twentieth century who has most earnestly and methodically studied the phenomenon of metaphysical, political and aesthetic revolt, begins his *L'Homme révolté* with a quotation from Hölderlin and makes no mention whatever of Büchner. Camus had indeed much in common with Hölderlin: the striving for measure and moderation, the sense of loyalty to the earth, the enthusiasm for Greece, 'la pensée solaire'. But Camus's thought is nevertheless more deeply akin to Büchner's than to Hölderlin's. Both in *Le Mythe de Sisyphe* and in *L'Homme révolté* Camus sets out from the experience of the absurdity, cruelty and injustice of the world and seeks to arrive at positive values by an analysis of the revolt which that experience may excite or imply.[3] His analysis will provide us with a number of useful insights in the following study of Büchner's revolt. But there will be no need to accept all of Camus's theses nor to make Büchner conform to any preconceived pattern. It must be our task simply to investigate the phenomenon of revolt as we find it in Büchner's life and work, to pursue the investigation freely wherever it may lead, and to see how far it will take us in the interpretation of his plays.

# 2. POLITICAL REVOLT

Büchner was a scientist, and his scientific habit of thought largely
determined his views even in matters which are not usually
regarded as scientific. A tendency to revolt is inherent in modern
science in so far as it depends on scepticism, the questioning of
authority, the determination to rely entirely on exact observation
and demonstration; and it is not surprising that Büchner, with
his early and thorough training in medicine and biology, should
have been imbued with this scientific scepticism and should have
evinced it persistently in every field of his intellectual activity.
This was well expressed by Karl Gutzkow on hearing of Büchner's
later decision to abandon medicine:

It appears you want to forsake medicine, and I am told your father will not be
pleased. Don't be unjust to this discipline, for I believe you owe to it your
greatest strength, I mean your extraordinary freedom from prejudices and
prepossessions, I might almost say: your autopsy, which is evident in everything
you write. If you approach the German philosophers so unceremoniously the
effect will certainly be novel.[1]

This 'autopsy', this scientific insistence on seeing and thinking
for oneself, might well have been sufficient, when applied to
politics in the Germany of the 1830s, to incline Büchner to
radicalism. It might well have disposed him to question the
justifiability, the endurability of the established political order in
Hesse, even if the general atmosphere of the time had been less
favourable to revolutionary tendencies. In fact these tendencies
were very strong in a Germany politically dominated by the
policies of Metternich and economically depressed by agricultural
failures and oppressive taxation. The tradition of the French
Revolution was still influential, especially in the Grand-Duchy of
Hesse which in 1813 had fought on the side of Napoleon. Büchner's father had been a physician with the Dutch troops in

4

Napoleon's army, and though of a cautious disposition and in later life increasingly conservative, still took a lively interest in the Revolution during Georg's boyhood. According to Georg's brother Wilhelm, his father

had the greatest sympathy with the progressive movement, and among the reading he most enjoyed was the periodical *Unsere Zeit* by which he could repeat and supplement the events he had earlier witnessed and lived through. It was often read in the evenings and we all followed it with the liveliest interest. A very free spirit prevailed in our family, and it is quite possible that these readings had a particular influence on Georg and may well have been the origin of *Dantons Tod*.[2]

These early political interests were of course intensified by the insurrection in Paris of July 1830, which spread waves of revolutionary excitement throughout Europe.

It was about this time, towards the end of his attendance at the Darmstadt *Gymnasium*, that Büchner wrote the school essays and orations which are the earliest expressions we have of his political sentiments. They show him to be already an enthusiastic champion of the principles of the French Revolution, which he glorifies with a romantic idealism akin to that of Fichte or the youthful Schiller. In a speech delivered in the *Gymnasium* on 29 September 1830 he undertakes to justify the suicide of Cato and seizes the opportunity to express an enthusiasm for freedom worthy of Schiller's Marquis Posa:

Den Fall seines Vaterlandes hätte *Kato* überleben können, wenn er ein Asyl für die andre Göttin seines Lebens, für die *Freiheit*, gefunden hätte. *Er fand es nicht.* Der Weltball lag in Roms Banden, alle Völker waren Sclaven, frei allein der Römer. Doch als auch dieser endlich seinem Geschicke erlag, als das Heiligtum der Gesetze zerrissen, als der Altar der Freiheit zerstört war, da war *Kato* der *einzige* unter Millionen, der *einzige* unter den Bewohnern einer Welt, der sich das Schwert in die Brust stieß, um unter Sclaven nicht leben zu müssen; denn Sclaven waren die Römer, sie mochten in goldnen oder ehernen Fesseln liegen – sie waren *gefesselt* . . . *Und war auch Rom der Freiheit nicht werth, so war doch die Freiheit selbst werth, daß Kato für sie lebte und starb.* (2, 29)

Together with the zeal for liberty, there is the idealistic hero-worship to which Cato appears as 'the representative of Roman greatness, the last of a bygone race of heroes, the greatest man of his time', his name a synonym for stoical Roman virtue, his suicide a monument in the hearts of men, triumphing over death and corruption, standing immovable amidst the weltering stream of eternity. The rather high-flown eloquence of the young Büchner's style is still far removed from his later sardonic curtness, yet there is already a sincerity and resonance in it which make the speech something more than a mere academic exercise. In another product of this early period, the essay 'Heldentod der vierhundert Pforzheimer', Büchner for the first time refers directly to the great French Revolution, and he makes no secret of his sympathy with it. He sees it as the bloody but just war of extermination which avenged the centuries of atrocities that shameful tyrants had inflicted on their subjects, and in words that anticipate Marx's dictum 'revolutions are the locomotives of history' asserts that the French 'war of liberation' had advanced the development of mankind by more than a century.

The chief claim to glory that he can concede to Germany, the only consideration that enables him to say with pride 'I am a German', is the fact that the German Reformation had made possible the French Revolution, that in the great struggle of mankind against its oppressors the Reformation had been the first Act, just as the Revolution was the second:

> sowie einmal der Gedanke in keine Fesseln mehr geschlagen war, erkannte die Menschheit ihre Rechte und ihren Werth und alle Verbesserungen, die wir jetzt genießen sind die Folgen der Reformation, ohne welche die Welt eine ganz andre Gestalt würde erhalten haben, ohne welche, wo jetzt das Licht der Aufklärung strahlt, ewiges Dunkel herrschen würde, ohne welche das Menschengeschlecht, das sich jetzt zu immer freieren, zu immer erhabneren Gedanken erhebt, dem Thiere gleich, seiner Menschen-Würde verlustig seyn würde. (2, 9)

Fichte, in his *Reden an die deutsche Nation* (VII), had maintained that it was the distinguishing mark of a German to believe in an 'infinite capability of improvement, an eternal progress of our race'.[3] It is evident that the young Büchner fully shares this 'German' conviction. No less than Fichte, Hegel and so many other Germans in the period of romanticism and idealism he thinks of history as a grand development towards an ever greater degree of enlightenment, an ever higher state of spiritual and intellectual freedom. And as he shares Fichte's and the idealists' belief in progress, so the expressions *Franken* for 'French', *teutsch* for 'German' suggest that he is also influenced by the inflamed nationalism of Fichte, Arndt, Jahn and other romantic patriots.

There is clearly an element of conformity in Büchner's early political views. He has not yet attained an independent position, but is being carried along by the great tide of revolutionary sentiment that was sweeping through the Europe and Germany of his time. As he approaches maturity his revolutionary spirit becomes much more critical and corrosive, and the idealistic form of political opposition to which he himself had formerly adhered becomes a prime object of his attack. The change becomes evident during his first period in Strasbourg, where he was studying medicine. We hear of his being a regular visitor to the students' club 'Eugenia' and of his speaking at the session of 24 May 1832 'in rather too glaring colours about the corruption of the German governments and the brutality of the students at many Universities, especially Giessen and Heidelberg'.[4] We also know that in the course of 1833 he must have had occasion to observe the activities of the Strasbourg branch of the conspiratorial revolutionary organization *Société des droits de l'homme et du citoyen*.[5] But the revision of his political views and the rejection of his earlier idealistic assumptions seem to have been induced above all by his observations and reflections on the Frankfort putsch of 3 April 1833. On that day some fifty conspirators, including a number of students, attempted to storm the military guardhouses in Frankfort, hoping thereby to start a revolution that would spread over all Germany. A few of the insurrectionists and of the soldiers were killed, there followed many arrests and intensified measures of repression against the universities. But the population as a whole remained completely unmoved. The hoped-for revolution did not occur. Replying to his anxious parents, who suspected him of complicity in the Frankfort plot, Büchner sought to allay their fears, but expressed full approval in principle of the use of force in the struggle against absolutism:

Meine Meinung ist die: Wenn in unserer Zeit etwas helfen soll, so ist es *Gewalt.*
Wir wissen, was wir von unseren Fürsten zu erwarten haben. Alles, was sie
bewilligten, wurde ihnen durch die Nothwendigkeit abgezwungen . . . Man wirft
den jungen Leuten den Gebrauch der Gewalt vor. Sind wir denn aber nicht in
einem ewigen Gewaltzustand? Weil wir im Kerker geboren und großgezogen
sind, merken wir nicht mehr, daß wir im Loch stecken mit angeschmiedeten
Händen und Füßen und einem Knebel im Munde. Was nennt Ihr denn *gesetzlichen*
*Zustand?* Ein *Gesetz,* das die große Masse der Staatsbürger zum frohnenden Vieh
macht, um die unnatürlichen Bedürfnisse einer unbedeutenden und verdorbenen
Minderzahl zu befriedigen? Und dies Gesetz, unterstützt durch eine rohe
Militärgewalt und durch die dumme Pfiffigkeit seiner Agenten, dies Gesetz ist
eine ewige, rohe Gewalt, angethan dem Recht und der gesunden Vernunft, und
ich werde mit *Mund* und *Hand* dagegen kämpfen, wo ich kann. Wenn ich an
dem, was geschehen, keinen Theil genommen und an dem, was vielleicht geschieht, *keinen Theil* nehmen werde, so geschieht es weder aus Mißbilligung, noch
aus Furcht, sondern nur weil ich im gegewärtigen Zeitpunkt jede revolutionäre
Bewegung als eine vergebliche Unternehmung betrachte und nicht die Verblen-
dung Derer theile, welche in den Deutschen ein zum Kampf für sein Recht bereites
Volk sehen.

(*An die Familie,* Straßburg, den 5. April 1833, 2, 416)

Almost the whole of Büchner's mature political creed is con-
tained explicitly or implicitly in this letter. There is already the
anticipation of the Marxist view that the State, the law, the armed
forces, are merely the instruments by which a corrupt ruling class
secures its supremacy and reduces the masses of the people to the
condition of beasts of burden; and to Büchner, with his strongly
developed sense of pity and justice, this state of affairs is intolerable. He can see no possibility of peaceful reform. The constitutions which had been granted in some of the German states,
including Hesse-Darmstadt, constitutions carefully insulated
against democracy by a complex system of indirect voting and a
narrowly limited franchise, seem to him simply absurd; and the path
of legal reform being thus closed, he can only advocate the resort
to force. A few years before Ludwig Börne had argued similarly:

Moderation is only regarded as weakness, which provokes arrogance, and respect
for the law as stupidity, which provokes trickery . . . Sword against sword . . . force
must decide. You may conquer us, but you will no longer deceive us.[6]

And Theodor Schuster was soon to exclaim: 'You won't hear of
social reform. Then bow to social revolution!'[7]

Büchner was evidently not alone in feeling that nothing would

8

avail in his time except force. But in adopting this view he was abandoning the tradition of German idealism to which he had adhered in his boyhood. To the classical Goethe and Schiller, with their concern for culture, their trust in the gradual education and refinement of society, their hope for political reforms voluntarily conceded by the ruling élite, nothing could be more abhorrent than violent insurrection. And to Hegel, with his mystical view of the State as 'the realization of freedom', as 'the progress of God in the world',[8] Büchner's view of it as a vast instrument of oppression hypocritically condemning violence while actually subjecting the people to perpetual coercion, would have been equally unacceptable.

So far Büchner agrees in principle with the Frankfort insurrectionists; and he is prepared, like them, to struggle against despotism with all the means at his disposal. But in one respect he differs from them: he cannot share the view they had held that the German people was ripe for revolution. And it is on this question – the question of the role of the people in a possible revolution, the degree of their preparedness and the means by which their active participation might be ensured – that his reflections are now evidently concentrated. For he returns to this problem in a letter written some two months after the Frankfort affair:

Ich werde zwar immer meinen Grundsätzen gemäß handeln, habe aber in *neuerer* Zeit gelernt, daß nur das nothwendige Bedürfniß der großen Masse Umänderungen herbeiführen kann, daß alles Bewegen und Schreien der *Einzelnen* vergebliches Thorenwerk ist. Sie schreiben, man liest sie nicht; sie schreien, man hört sie nicht; sie handeln, man hilft ihnen nicht. – Ihr könnt voraussehen, daß ich mich in die Gießener Winkelpolitik und revolutionären Kinderstreiche nicht einlassen werde. (*An die Familie*, Straßburg, im Juni 1833, 2, 418)

The Frankfort putsch having miscarried owing to its failure to gain the support of the people, Büchner draws the obvious conclusion that any future rising will be equally unsuccessful unless the involvement of the people can be secured. It was useless, as he later explained to August Becker, to pit a handful of undisciplined liberals against the well-equipped armies of the

German governments. A revolution can only be carried out by the masses of the people, who by sheer weight of numbers must overwhelm and crush the military.[9] But – and this is the new insight which Büchner had gained and to which he henceforth steadfastly adhered – it was only 'the essential needs' of the masses that could possibly move them to revolutionary action. They were concerned only about their material interests, and indeed could not afford to be concerned about anything else. 'With all our prejudice in their favour', Becker reports Büchner as saying, 'we must admit that they have acquired a rather ignoble outlook and are accessible to almost nothing but what concerns their pocket.'[10] Ignoble or not, it was a very intelligible attitude, and Büchner could not refuse it his sympathy: 'the material pressure', he told Becker, 'under which a great part of Germany was suffering, was just as sad and disgraceful as the intellectual pressure; and the fact that this or that liberal was not free to publish his thoughts wasn't nearly so deplorable in his eyes as the fact that many thousands of families didn't have the wherewithal to grease their potatoes.'[11]

The revolution which Büchner envisaged was therefore primarily a social revolution and only secondarily a political one. And he was led by the logic of his position to adopt a revolutionary strategy which, if not entirely new for France, was certainly new for Germany. Recognizing the exclusive preoccupation of the people with their economic needs, Büchner perceived the futility of a revolutionary propaganda which canvassed political and constitutional questions – freedom of the press, the ordinances of the Federal Diet, the Vienna Congress, etc. – which could be of no immediate concern to the masses, least of all to the peasantry which constituted the overwhelming majority of Hesse's population. For the same reason he later commented derisively on the writers of Young Germany, who imagined they could decisively influence the course of events by means of journalism and *belles lettres* addressed to the educated classes of society:

Die Gesellschaft mittelst der *Idee*, von der *gebildeten* Klasse aus reformieren? Unmöglich! Unsere Zeit ist rein *materiell*, wären Sie je directer politisch zu Werk gegangen, so wären Sie bald auf den Punkt gekommen, wo die Reform von selbst aufgehört hätte. Sie werden nie über den Riß zwischen der gebildeten und ungebildeten Gesellschaft hinauskommen. (*An Gutzkow*, Straßburg, 1836, 2, 455)

In Büchner's view an effective revolutionary propaganda must address itself directly to the masses of the people, and deal first and foremost with their economic grievances. It must appeal to their material interests, show them how they are being plundered and exploited by an unjust system of taxation, take advantage of their depressed economic condition to generate the force that might lift them out of it, make poverty itself the means to overcome poverty. And it must do this quickly. For if the German kings and princes should have the sense to disband their costly standing armies, to reduce the luxury of their courts and the ruinous burden of their overgrown bureaucracies – if they should follow the example of Metternich, whose Austrians were 'well nourished and content', who had 'smothered their revolutionary spirit in their own fat'[12] – the cause of revolution would be lost in Germany.

One sees that Büchner, like Marx, expected the revolution to be brought about by an intensification of misery. But, unlike Marx, he saw no reason to suppose that an intensification of misery was inevitable. On the contrary, he believed it to be largely a matter of chance. A skilful minister such as Metternich might be able to prevent it. On the other hand, an exceptionally foolish and selfish prince, a particularly expensive mistress, an unusually bad harvest, might be sufficient to precipitate it. Hence the grim prayer of his second Strasbourg period, a period of severe financial stringency for Büchner:

Ich wollte, es ginge der ganzen Nation wie mir. Wenn es einmal ein Mißjahr gibt, worin nur der Hanf geräth! (*An Gutzkow*, Straßburg, 1835, 2, 436)

And the similar reflections of a still later letter:

Das Verhältniß zwischen Armen und Reichen ist das einzige revolutionäre Element in der Welt, der Hunger allein kann die Freiheitsgöttin und nur ein Moses, der uns die sieben ägyptischen Plagen auf den Hals schickte, könnte ein Messias werden. Mästen Sie die Bauern, und die Revolution bekommt die

II

Apoplexie. Ein *Huhn* im Topf jedes Bauern macht den gallischen *Hahn* verenden. (*An Gutzkow*, 1835, 2, 441)

Prosperity could neutralize even the most astute revolutionary propaganda, and prosperity or destitution was largely beyond human control. It is evident that, with the perception of the dependence of the revolution on the 'essential needs' of the people, Büchner was already virtually committed to the political 'fatalism' expressed in the most famous of his letters, 'fatalism' being understood as an irresistible and inscrutable necessity in historical events. But in the first Strasbourg period it is not yet a 'horrifying fatalism'. It was only in the course of further studies of the great French Revolution pursued in the winter of 1833–4 that the cruelty and horror of history was fully brought home to Büchner. The famous letter to Minna Jaegle in which he describes this experience is important in many connexions but must be quoted here for its special relevance to his political views:

Ich studierte die Geschichte der Revolution. Ich fühlte mich wie zernichtet unter dem gräßlichen Fatalismus der Geschichte. Ich finde in der Menschennatur eine entsetzliche Gleichheit, in den menschlichen Verhältnissen eine unabwendbare Gewalt, Allen und Keinem verliehen. Der Einzelne nur Schaum auf der Welle, die Größe ein bloßer Zufall, die Herrschaft des Genies ein Puppenspiel, ein lächerliches Ringen gegen ein ehernes Gesetz, es zu erkennen das Höchste, es zu beherrschen unmöglich. Es fällt mir nicht mehr ein, vor den Paradegäulen und Eckstehern der Geschichte mich zu bücken. Ich gewöhnte mein Auge ans Blut. Aber ich bin kein Guillotinenmesser. Das *Muß* ist eines von den Verdammungsworten, womit der Mensch getauft worden. Der Ausspruch: es muß ja Aergerniß kommen, aber wehe dem, durch den es kommt, – ist schauderhaft. Was ist das, was in uns lügt, mordet, stiehlt? Ich mag dem Gedanken nicht weiter nachgehen. Könnte ich aber dies kalte und gemarterte Herz an deine Brust legen!

(*An die Braut*, Gießen, nach dem 10. März 1834, 2, 425)

We have seen Büchner, in the first Strasbourg period, breaking away from the tradition of German classicism by his advocacy of violent revolution; breaking away from liberalism and constitutionalism by his insistence on the economic interests of the people. Now, in Giessen, we see him revolting against the idealist conception of history which had guided the revolutionary hopes of his youth. There is no longer any trace, here, of Fichte's belief in the 'eternal progress of our race'. Hegel's historical 'theodicy',

Saint-Simon's utopianism – chiliastic dreams which were widely entertained in the 1830s – have become merely absurd to him. He is driven to a historical pessimism which is at variance not only with the prevailing ideas of his time but with the whole tenor of European thought since the Enlightenment. Unlike Hegelianism and its materialistic offshoot Marxism, Büchner's political theory does not involve the assumption of an intelligible pattern to which the course of history is supposed to conform. When he struggled against despotism and the exploitation of the poor he did not imagine that he was obeying the behest of the *Weltgeist* or contributing to the necessary realization of the dialectical process. He acted from an elementary sense of justice, and his abstract, unhistorical insistence on natural rights seems to have more in common with eighteenth century rationalism than with the romantic views of history which had prevailed in Germany since Herder:

Ich glaube, man muß in socialen Dingen von einem absoluten *Rechts*grundsatz ausgehen, die Bildung eines neuen geistigen Lebens im *Volk* suchen und die abgelebte moderne Gesellschaft zum Teufel gehen lassen.

*(An Gutzkow, 1836, 2, 455)*

The terrible insight which Büchner owed to his renewed study of the French Revolution in Giessen was the realization that natural justice is in no way vindicated by history, that, far from conforming to an intelligible and beneficent plan, the course of history is governed by laws which one can at best hope to understand but never to control and which condemn mankind to infinite, aimless, inexorable suffering. The attempt to wrestle with these adamantine laws merely exposes the impotence of mankind. One becomes aware of an appalling equality in human nature, all alike subject to unaccountable violence, all alike driven by forces for which they are not responsible but which crush them under a sense of guilt, all alike merely foam on the waves, puppets ruled by an inhuman fate.

One sees how Büchner's abandonment of the idealist belief in the inevitability of progress, and in mankind as the agent of such progress, necessarily entails the abandonment of the idealist

13

hero-worship to which formerly he himself – following Schiller, Fichte and the romantics – had been addicted and which had inspired his schoolboy oration on Cato Uticensis. His grimly realistic view of history marks a new stage in that process of dethroning man from his supposedly central position in the grand scheme of the universe which had begun with the Copernican revolution and was soon to be completed by Darwinism. But Büchner already feels that the great scientific development which was resulting in this shattering revision of human pretensions would ultimately involve a more sober appreciation of the limits of science itself, as the product and instrument of weak humanity. He is far from believing that human knowledge could ever be adequate to the task of reshaping the destiny of the world. If in some respects we have been able to recognize in Büchner's political principles a certain affinity with Marxism, here we must register a profound difference: though Büchner could claim to be a scientist with at least as good a right as Marx, he did not derive from science anything even remotely approaching the confidence (or hubris?) that enabled Marx to say: 'The philosophers, in their various ways, have only *interpreted* the world; it is our task to *change* it.'[13]

But now we are confronted with the most extraordinary paradox in Büchner's life. Apparently in the very same month in which he wrote that famous letter to Minna Jaegle expressing his horror at the course and outcome of the French Revolution and his profound sense of the futility of all political effort – in that same month, March 1834, Büchner for the first time embarked on conspiratorial revolutionary activity! It was then that, following the example of the *Société des droits de l'homme et du citoyen*, he founded in Giessen a secret revolutionary society called the 'Society of Human Rights' (*Gesellschaft der Menschenrechte*), a further branch of which he founded about a month later in Darmstadt. How is it possible to explain this apparent contradiction between Büchner's thoughts and actions?

We can dismiss at once the absurd suggestion of some German scholars that Büchner was driven to action by an ungovernable desire for personal prestige (*Geltungsbedürfnis*).[14] It is difficult to see what prestige, or indeed what personal advantages of any kind, he could have expected to gain by the dreadfully dangerous adventure he was entering upon. He knew that students and citizens suspected of complicity in the Frankfort plot were still in the prison at Friedberg or were being kept elsewhere in prolonged solitary confinement without a trial while their 'crimes' were being investigated, a fate that to Büchner always seemed more terrible than death:

Die Unglücklichen! Wie wird das enden? Wohl wie in Frankfurt, wo Einer nach dem Andern stirbt und in der Stille begraben wird. Ein Todesurtheil, ein Schaffot, was ist das? Man stirbt für seine Sache. Aber so im Gefängniß auf eine langsame Weise aufgerieben zu werden! Das ist entsetzlich![15]

*(An die Familie*, 16. Juli 1835, 2, 442)

He knew that this was the penalty for unsuccessful conspiracy and that, if he should have to pay it, it would destroy not only himself but also the happiness of his parents and of his fiancée. In the letter to Minna of March 1834 (2, 427) he can see no prospect for himself but a stormy life, perhaps soon to be spent in exile.

And still Büchner could not be deterred from engaging in the dreadful enterprise. He has himself indicated the true reasons for his decision:

Ich war [in Gießen] in Aeußeren ruhig, doch war ich in tiefe Schwermuth verfallen; dabei engten mich die politischen Verhältnisse ein, ich schämte mich, ein Knecht mit Knechten zu sein, einem vermoderten Fürstengeschlecht und einem kriechenden Staatsdiener-Aristokratismus zu Gefallen.

*(An die Familie*, im April 1834, 2, 429)

To a man like Büchner who had admired the revolutionary courage of the French, who had deplored the political apathy of the Germans, it was impossible without the most painful sense of shame to submit tamely to the despotism prevailing in Hesse, to consent without a struggle to be 'a slave among slaves'. And in addition to this feeling of degradation, there was his deep sympathy with the physical suffering of the impoverished masses of the population.

It is difficult to estimate precisely how severe those sufferings were. In considering this question we must not limit our attention to the Grand-Duchy of Hesse, for the revolution that Büchner envisaged was not to be confined to that petty state but was to affect all Germany. As Büchner was living in Hesse it was of course there that he had to conduct his political activity; but he was well aware – the point is explicitly made in *Der Hessische Landbote* (2, 52) – that any serious revolutionary movement in one of the smaller German states would immediately be crushed by the intervention of one or both of the two dominant powers, Prussia and Austria; that, consequently, a successful revolution could only be an all-German revolution, or one that at least included Prussia. And we have the testimony of his brother Wilhelm that this was in fact the kind of revolution he was hoping for; he was hoping that it might be possible 'to proclaim a homogeneous republic',[16] a republic in which there would be no domination of one German state by another but in which all the monarchical dynasties in all the German states would have been swept away. It was therefore necessary for Büchner to consider the condition of the people in Germany as a whole, not only in Hesse; and indeed it is in terms of the whole nation that he was accustomed to think (cf. his remark already quoted about 'the material pressure under which a great part of Germany was suffering' and his reflections on the need to win over the people before the *princes* (plural) had time to forestall the revolution).[17]

What, then, was the economic condition of the majority of the German people in the 1830s? Some indication is given by the fact that, as late as 1839, a law was introduced in the Prussian Rhineland to prohibit the employment of children under ten years of age and to restrict the labour of other children to ten hours a day! Before the introduction of that law, children in the textile factories had been working up to thirteen hours a day, and there had been instances of suicide among them.[18] Börne mentions the thousands of Germans who were emigrating to America year by year 'to still their hunger in a foreign continent'; he mentions the poor cottagers in the Spessart who were happy if they were starved of potatoes for no more than three days of the week; and he tells of the unhappy wretches in Hanover who, on exceptionally cold nights – 'cold enough to make their tears turn to ice' – were allowed to throw straw on the stone floors of the royal stables, across the running gutters, and to sleep among the horses till the morning.[19]

As for the conditions prevailing particularly in Hesse, according to Franzos –

In Upper Hesse and in Rhine Hesse elemental catastrophes (famines, floods) combined with intolerably severe taxation to produce such a sudden and general impoverishment that thousands emigrated to America, while the others who could not or would not emigrate sat with folded hands in dull defiant depair. The State, itself in perpetual financial difficulties, could offer no help and sought to stifle the cry of distress by muzzling the chambers of deputies.[20]

It was conditions such as these which, in Upper Hesse in the autumn of 1830, had led to 'the blood-bath of Södel', a brief rising of the impoverished peasants provoked by crushing tolls and imposts and brutally suppressed by the military. And though it may be true, as Viëtor asserts,[21] that the state of the peasantry in Hesse had improved somewhat since 1830 and was less miserable than that of their Bavarian and Württemberg brothers, the general economic conditions prevailing in Germany suggest that it must still have been miserable enough. The words of one of the citizens in *Dantons Tod* (I. ii. 13) 'our life is murder by hard labour' may well have been suggested to Büchner by his observation of the life of the poor in his own country. It was this observation above all that drove him to his political activism. As August Becker was afterwards to say of him: 'The foundation of his patriotism was really the purest pity and a noble feeling for everything beautiful and great.'[22] Pity is the dominant force in Büchner's politics. 'I still hope', he wrote to his parents, 'that I have directed more pitying glances at suffering, oppressed figures than I have uttered bitter words to cold aristocratic souls' (*Ich hoffe noch immer, daß ich leidenden, gedrückten Gestalten mehr mitleidige Blicke zugeworfen, als kalten, vornehmen Herzen bittere Worte gesagt habe* – 2, 423). And even after his flight from

Germany, when he was no longer actively engaged in politics, the thought that for the majority of mankind even the most trifling pleasures were unattainable luxuries could make him very bitter (cf. his letter of 1 January 1836, 2, 452).

It is evident that Büchner had powerful enough reasons for *wishing* to change the political and economic condition of the Hessians and of the Germans in general; but that he should actually have plunged into a revolutionary conspiracy for this purpose may nevertheless seem inconsistent with that deep sense of the 'fatalism' of history and of the futility of political endeavour expressed in the letter to Minna of March 1834. Logically, there certainly is a contradiction here; psychologically, Büchner's attitude is understandable. Certainly, if human beings are merely 'foam on the wave', it is absurd that they should try to change the direction of the wave; if they are merely puppets at the mercy of inexorable laws, it is absurd that they should try to revolutionize the whole order of society. But in that case it is equally absurd that they should love and hate, honour and despise, seek the truth and combat falsehood; it is absurd that they should do anything whatever. From this strictly logical point of view there was even an absurdity in Büchner's letter itself: the act of writing it was inconsistent with its contents. But it is impossible to live on this basis. If Büchner was to continue to exist, not only politically but in any sense whatever, it was necessary for him to forget or ignore those deadly insights or interpret them in a way that would make them compatible with hope. Very probably, like his hero Danton, he could maintain himself in no fixed position but wavered uncertainly between hope and despair. The sense of futility and impotence in the face of overpowering historical forces must always have haunted him, threatening to paralyse him with its hopelessness; and it must have been a great disadvantage to him, as a political activist, that, unlike Marx, he could never assume that history was necessarily on his side. But he may also have felt – and he had every reason to cherish this thought – that his historical insights were capable of an interpretation that did not exclude the possibility of meaningful political action. What his study of the French Revolution had brought home to him with such crushing force was the impossibility of prevailing against the tide of history when it is set against you. But what if it should be running in your favour? Would it be equally ridiculous *then* to try to take advantage of it, to prepare the people to take advantage of it? When, in Büchner's play, Danton is committed to the Luxembourg, he says to Tom Paine whom he meets there among the prisoners:

Was Sie für das Wohl Ihres Landes gethan, habe ich für das meinige versucht. Ich war weniger glücklich, man schickt mich auf's Schafott . . . (III. i. 50)

Büchner elsewhere lets Danton express the same view of the 'horrifying fatalism' of history as he himself had expressed in the letter to Minna, but notwithstanding that tragic insight Danton evidently feels – and here again we may suppose him to be speaking for Büchner – that fate need not be so unkind to everybody as it had been to him. If the democratic revolution had failed in France, it had succeeded in America. And we shall find evidence to prove that in his own revolutionary activity Büchner was guided not only by the example of France but also by the example of certain other countries, particularly the United States and Switzerland, where democracy had been more successful. How could he know for certain whether a German revolution might not be destined to follow the more fortunate rather than the less fortunate pattern? It is of course easy for us, with the advantage of hindsight, to deride his hopes. Probably he was himself only too acutely aware of their fragility. But he had to make sure. And indeed this was the main purpose of his conspiracy. It was not to start a revolution directly and immediately; it was rather to test the temper of the population and to prepare the necessary revolutionary organization against the eventuality that the people should show themselves ready for a rising. This was clearly stated by August Becker to have been the purpose of Büchner's *Hessischer Landbote*:

The pamphlet he had written was designed only to serve the preliminary purpose of sounding the temper of the people and of the German revolutionaries. When he afterwards heard that the peasants had handed over most of the copies they had found to the police, when he learned that even the patriots had pronounced against his pamphlet, he abandoned all his political hopes of a new order of things.[23]

Büchner was of course aware that previous political pamphlets and broadsheets had completely failed to excite the interest of the people and to gain that massive popular support which, as we have seen, he had recognized to be a precondition of successful revolution. But we have also seen that Büchner believed himself to be in possession of the key to that mass support: the appeal to the *material interests* of the poor and exploited multitude. The peasants may have failed to respond to the largely irrelevant propaganda of the liberals and constitutionalists; but what would their reaction be to a propaganda that was not irrelevant, a propaganda that touched their most vital concerns, their most pressing needs? If, according to the letter to Minna, the most we can hope to do is to *understand* the 'iron law' of history, not to control it, we must not forget that Büchner believed himself to have at least partly penetrated the secret of that 'iron law': he believed he understood better than most of his German contemporaries the conditions under which revolutions are possible. And, like a true scientist, he resolved to put his knowledge to the test.

### 'DER HESSISCHE LANDBOTE'

*Der Hessische Landbote*, published in 1834 (the first edition in July, the second in November), was the joint production of Büchner and of Ludwig Weidig, the brave and ill-fated liberal propagandist who had been engaged for many years in an underground struggle against the oppressive absolutist régime in the Grand Duchy of Hesse. Weidig was described by Becker as being in every respect the antithesis of Büchner:

He [Weidig] observed the principle that even the slightest spark of revolution had to be fostered if there was at some time to be a fire: among the republicans he was a republican, among the constitutionalists a constitutionalist.[24]

This policy of Weidig's has seemed to some critics more realistic than Büchner's. Hans Magnus Enzensberger says of Weidig:

In spite of all his romantic enthusiasm for the good old times he was a realist who understood more about the future of the bourgeoisie than Büchner, in fact almost as much as Engels who twelve years later adopted Weidig's tactic of the grand coalition in the service of a new strategy.[25]

But we must try to appreciate Büchner's point of view, we must try to understand why 'the grand coalition' advocated by Weidig and later by Engels could only appear to Büchner to be an *unrealistic* revolutionary policy. As we have seen, Büchner was convinced – and no doubt rightly – that a revolution could only succeed by enlisting the support of the masses of the people, and he was also convinced that their support could only be secured by appealing to their economic interests. It was therefore not open to him to play down the differences between the rich and the poor, but on the contrary he had to open the eyes of the impoverished population to the full extent of the economic exploitation to which they were being subjected. The difference between rich and poor being 'the only revolutionary element in the world',[26] the attempt to gloss over that difference could not result in the grand oppositional coalition that Weidig was hoping for. The effect would be quite the contrary: the masses of the people would have no further interest in the matter, and the revolution would become the exclusive concern of a handful of wealthy liberals and intellectuals who had neither the massive strength required to overcome the military power of the government, nor the will to serve any interests but their own. The fact that Büchner was prepared to join forces with Weidig is sufficient proof that he too wished for the widest possible co-operation – but not at the price of sacrificing the interests of the people or of stultifying the revolution by forfeiting their support. Nevertheless, the divergent policy of Weidig drew him farther from his projected course than he had bargained for. In particular it resulted in a revision of his pamphlet, *Der Hessische Landbote*, which made it impossible for him to recognize it as his own. Before *Der Hessische Landbote* can be accepted as an expression of Büchner's revolutionary principles and strategy, we must try to free it from the additions and alterations which Weidig is known to have made in it. According to August Becker, Weidig's revised version differs from Büchner's original 'in that the expression "the aristocrats" [*die Vornehmen*] is substituted for "the rich" and the attacks on the so-called liberal party are omitted, being replaced by other considerations which are concerned only with the effectiveness of the constitution ... The Biblical passages and the whole of the conclusion are by Weidig.'[27] Becker further informs us that the title and preface were likewise contributed by Weidig.[28]

If we mentally undo these alterations of Weidig's and imagine *Der Hessische Landbote* in its original form, we shall find it perfectly conformable to Büchner's conception of effective revolutionary propaganda.

Büchner wastes no time on the problems dear to the hearts of the liberals and constitutionalists – the question of the freedom of the press, the question of the unification of Germany. He concentrates from the outset on the 'one revolutionary element in the world':

Das Leben der Reichen ist ein langer Sonntag: sie wohnen in schönen Häusern, sie tragen zierliche Kleider, sie haben feiste Gesichter und reden eine eigne Sprache; das Volk aber liegt vor ihnen wie Dünger auf dem Acker ... Das Leben des Bauern ist ein langer Werktag; Fremde verzehren seine Äcker vor seinen Augen, sein Leib ist eine Schwiele, sein Schweiß ist das Salz auf dem Tische des Reichen. (2, 34–6.)

This is followed and supported by a statistical demonstration of the cost to the impoverished people of maintaining a court and state apparatus which had no other function than to oppress and exploit them. Büchner shows how the money extorted from the people by direct and indirect taxes of various kinds – money for which the 700,000 inhabitants of Hesse had to 'sweat, groan and hunger' – was used to pay for the maintenance of the ducal court, the courts of law, an enormous bureaucracy, the armed forces. The Grand Duke is the head of the leech crawling over the people, the ministers are its teeth and the officials its tail. The hungry bellies of the Duke's favourites are the cupping-glasses with which he drains the life-blood of the people. As for the courts of law, justice in Germany has for centuries been the whore of the German princes. The path to its tribunals must be paved with silver, its verdicts purchased at the price of penury and degradation. The bureaucracy is the officious agent of this institutionalized extortion; the military the instrument by which it is enforced:

Für das Militär wird bezahlt 914,820 Gulden . . . Für jene 900,000 Gulden müssen eure Söhne den Tyrannen schwören und Wache halten an ihren Pallästen. Mit ihren Trommeln übertäuben sie eure Seufzer, mit ihren Kolben zerschmettern sie euch den Schädel, wenn ihr zu denken wagt, daß ihr freie Menschen seyd. Sie sind die gesetzlichen Mörder, welche die gesetzlichen Räuber schützen, denkt an Södel! Eure Brüder, eure Kinder waren dort Brüder- und Vatermörder. (2, 40)

The constitutions of the German states are described as empty straw from which the princes have threshed out the grain for themselves – the electoral laws as perpetual violations of the political and human rights of the majority of Germans. What was one to think, for example, of the constitution of the Grand-Duchy of Hesse where only the wealthiest people were eligible for election and where the power of the Duke was virtually unlimited? Such a constitution was 'a wretched pitiful thing'. Büchner contrasts with it the declaration of the Rights of Man in the great Revolution of 1789:

'Keiner erbt vor dem andern mit der Geburt ein Recht oder einen Titel, keiner erwirbt mit dem Eigenthum ein Recht vor dem andern. Die höchste Gewalt ist in dem Willen Aller oder der Mehrzahl. Dieser Wille ist das Gesetz, er thut sich kund durch die Landstände oder die Vertreter des Volks, sie werden von Allen gewählt, und Jeder kann gewählt werden.' (2, 46)

Gustav Klemm, a member of the Society of Human Rights who afterwards turned traitor, testified that it was a principle of Büchner's secret society to regard all wealth as the property of the community ('"Alles Vermögen ist Gemeingut" wurde doziert').[29] But this principle is nowhere expressed in *Der Hessische Landbote*. The pamphlet contains no plans for the organization of a socialist economy; there is no anticipation of the Marxist demand for the abolition of private capital, for the common ownership of the land; there is no endorsement even of the Saint-Simonist denial of the right to inherit property. On the contrary, the sentence quoted from the declaration of human rights which Büchner holds up as the ideal to be pursued: 'nobody acquires by property a right before another' clearly implies the recognition of the right to private property, while at the same time demanding that its possession should not entail rights denied to other citizens. Büchner's aim, in short, was not to abolish private property but to neutralize its political influence. That this was really his standpoint is confirmed by the testimony of two witnesses who had been members of his organization, Adam Koch and August Becker. Koch's evidence before a court of the German Confederation shows that – in exact conformity with the passage last quoted from *Der Hessische Landbote* – the only formality to which new members of the 'Gesellschaft der Menschenrechte' were subjected was the reading aloud by Büchner of the French declaration of human rights; and, as Viëtor remarks, that declaration, in each of the three versions in which it was formulated during the French Revolution, expressly recognized the right to private property.[30] Even more significant is Gustav Becker's recollection of a quarrel between Weidig and Büchner on the question of property qualifications for the franchise:

Büchner was of the opinion that in a just republic, as in most of the North American States, every one must have a vote irrespective of income or property, and maintained that Weidig, who thought that in that case mob rule would result as in France, had a wrong view of the German people and of our age. Büchner expressed himself very strongly in the presence of Zeuner about this élitism [*Aristokratismus*] of Weidig, as he called it, and Zeuner later committed the indiscretion of repeating his words to Weidig. The result was a quarrel between Weidig and Büchner which I tried to allay and which was the cause of my remembering these details.[31]

We have already noticed the allusion in *Dantons Tod* to the success of the American revolution. Here, in Becker's recollection of the quarrel with Weidig, we find additional evidence that Büchner's political views were based partly on his observations of the American experience. The French 'déclaration des droits de l'homme', which had such an important place in his political thinking, was after all derived from the American Bill of Rights – to this extent Büchner's revolutionary activity was influenced by the Anglo-Saxon tradition of freedom. And he was evidently well informed, not only about the American revolution in the eighteenth century, but about the further development of American democracy in his own time. Like De Tocqueville, the first part of whose famous book appeared only a year after *Der Hessische Landbote*, he sees America as a country whose 'institutions are democratic, not only in their principle but in all their consequences', where the people is 'the real driving power'.[32] And he has quite rightly noticed the recent constitutional changes in most North-American states which had led to the abolition of property qualifications for the suffrage.[33] This is the point to which Büchner attached the greatest importance and on which he refused to yield an inch to Weidig. For he was convinced that only universal suffrage could save Germany from having to repeat the unhappy experience of France, where the July Revolution of 1830 had merely led to the establishment of a plutocracy, a capitalists' paradise, while the people were left to rot in destitution. If *that* was to be the result of the revolution, Büchner thought, it would be better to leave things as they were:

He often said about the constitutionalists: If these people should succeed in overthrowing the German governments and introducing a general monarchy or even republic, we would get a plutocracy [*Geldaristokratismus*] as in France, and it would be better if things were to remain as they were.[34]

That 'plutocracy' in France was based, as Büchner well knew, on a political system in which authority was vested partly in the King and partly in a chamber of deputies elected by the well-to-do. A similar 'plutocracy' in Germany could be prevented only by denying to the wealthier classes such a domination of the electorate and securing for the unmoneyed masses a political power proportionate to their numbers.

Büchner's view remained unchanged when he had an opportunity to observe at first hand a genuine democracy – on his arrival in Switzerland late in 1836. He wrote then to his parents:

Ihr werdet überrascht sein, wenn Ihr mich besucht; schon unterwegs überall freundliche Dörfer mit schönen Häusern, und dann, je mehr Ihr Euch Zürich nähert und gar am See hin, ein durchgreifender Wohlstand; Dörfer und Städtchen haben ein Aussehen, wovon man bei uns keinen Begriff hat. Die Straßen laufen hier nicht voll Soldaten, Accessisten und faulen Staatsdienern, man riskirt nicht, von einer adligen Kutsche überfahren zu werden; dafür überall ein gesundes, kräftiges Volk, und um wenig Geld eine einfache, gute, rein *republikanische* Regierung, die sich durch eine *Vermögenssteuer* erhält, eine Art Steuer, die man bei uns überall als den Gipfel der Anarchie ausschreien würde. (2, 462)

Büchner does not complain because Switzerland is not a 'socialist' country, he does not lament its failure to abolish private property or private capital. On the contrary, he is delighted to find here the fulfilment of his chief political purposes: 'a purely republican form of government' and, thanks to this, widespread economic welfare and the elimination of crass social inequalities. In Switzerland, as in the United States, property qualifications for the franchise had disappeared almost everywhere after 1830,[35] and the democratic administration of the State was not only inexpensive, but could be made to serve the economic interests of the people as a whole, by such means, for example, as the property tax mentioned by Büchner.

Büchner has sometimes been called the first German socialist, and with some justification in view of his overriding concern for the poorest sections of the community. But evidently he did not rely on any socialistic economic arrangement for the amelioration of the lot of the poor. He relied on two things: (1) the savings that could be effected by eliminating the enormous costs of a princely court, a parasitic bureaucracy and a large standing army; (2) the establishment of a genuinely democratic system of government which, because it derived its power from the people, would be subservient to the economic welfare of the majority, not to the interests of a privileged minority.

There was surely nothing very unrealistic or extravagant about such ideas. Büchner was merely demanding for Germany the political and economic conditions which he had reason to believe already existed in some of the most advanced countries elsewhere. His proposals have not lost their relevance even to-day. We still feel that genuine representative democracy and the elimination of unnecessary charges on the State are important factors in the prevention or alleviation of poverty. True, we would be far from considering them a sufficient answer to the complex problems of a modern industrial society. But it was not Büchner's task to provide solutions for problems that had not yet arisen. He was not offering a panacea for all future social evils. He was not sketching a utopia or promising the millennium. The chiliastic note is sounded only very briefly in *Der Hessische Landbote*, and then, it would seem, only by Weidig – nowhere in the passages that are quite certainly by Büchner.[36]

Just as the content of *Der Hessische Landbote* is designed to appeal to the most urgent material interests of the people, so its form and style are determined by the need to make that appeal effective, to bring it home to the people with the utmost force and clearness. It begins with a declaration of war: 'Peace to the cottages! war on the palaces!' (*Friede den Hütten! Krieg den Pallästen!*), and it is in fact a weapon which Büchner strives to wield with maximum effect in his desperate struggle against the repressive forces of the State. Though it contains statistical and historical information and offers reasoned arguments, its attitude is essentially exhortatory, not theoretical; much of it, consequently, is written in the second person plural. In this respect it differs strikingly from Marx's *Communist Manifesto*. There we find one famous sentence in the second person plural: 'Proletarians of all lands unite!' (*Proletarier aller Länder, vereinigt euch!*). But that is the only sentence in the whole of the Communist Manifesto that is addressed directly to the people. Otherwise Marx uses the second person plural only to address the bourgeoisie, to taunt and confute the enemies of the proletariat. In general the *Communist Manifesto* speaks *about* the working classes but not *to* the working classes; it is essentially theoretical, unfolding a comprehensive view of the development of society and of its future destiny. And though the greatness of the issues involved lend an urgency and pregnancy to Marx's style, his philosophical, intellectual attitude occasionally shows itself in complex expressions and intricate sentence structures not easily intelligible to the uneducated:

Wenn das Proletariat im Kampfe gegen die Bourgeoisie sich notwendig zur Klasse vereint, durch eine Revolution sich zur herrschenden Klasse macht und als herrschende Klasse gewaltsam die alten Produktionsverhältnisse aufhebt, so hebt es mit diesen Produktionsverhältnissen die Existenzbedingungen des Klassengegensatzes, der Klassen überhaupt, und damit seine eigene Herrschaft als Klasse auf.

Such a sentence would be inconceivable in *Der Hessische Landbote*. Büchner addresses himself immediately to the people, in language of stark simplicity, in short paratactic sentences of fierce directness:

'Im Namen des Großherzogs'. Dies ist ihr Feldgeschrei, wenn sie euer Geräth versteigern, euer Vieh wegtreiben, euch in den Kerker werfen. Im Namen des Großherzogs sagen sie, und der Mensch, den sie so nennen, heißt: unverletzlich, heilig, souverain, königliche Hoheit. Aber tretet zu dem Menschenkinde und blickt durch seinen Fürstenmantel. Es ißt, wenn es hungert, und schläft, wenn sein Auge dunkel wird. Sehet, es kroch so nackt und weich in die Welt wie ihr und wird so hart und steif hinausgetragen wie ihr, und doch hat es seinen Fuß auf eurem Nacken. (2, 42)

And since it is mostly peasants that Büchner is addressing, he takes care to do so in terms that will be familiar to them, drawing his images from the daily life of the country folk. The people lie prostrate before the rich 'like dung on the field'. The rich man takes the corn, the peasant is left with the stubble. The diets are 'cumbersome waggons which may once or twice be shoved across the path of princely and ministerial rapacity but out of which one will never build a firm citadel for liberty'. The people stands naked and cowering before its well-dressed masters: 'they lay their hands on its loins and shoulders and calculate how much it can still carry, and if they are merciful it is only as one spares a beast of burden which one doesn't wish to overload'. Marx's tropes have an assured and witty cheerfulness:

Der christliche Sozialismus ist nur das Weihwasser, womit der Pfaffe den Ärger des Aristokraten einsegnet.
    Den proletarischen Bettlersack schwenkten sie als Fahne in der Hand, um das Volk hinter sich her zu versammeln. Sooft es ihnen aber folgte, erblickte es auf

ihrem Hintern die alten feudalen Wappen und verlief sich mit lautem und unehrerbietigem Gelächter.

But Büchner's savage indignation expresses itself in a fiery eloquence comparable with that of Milton's sonnet on the Piedmont massacre or Shelley's Mask of Anarchy:

Geht einmal nach Darmstadt und seht, wie die Herren sich für euer Geld dort lustig machen, und erzählt dann euern hungernden Weibern und Kindern, daß ihr Brot an fremden Bäuchen herrlich angeschlagen sey, erzählt ihnen von den schönen Kleidern, die in ihrem Schweiß gefärbt, und von den zierlichen Bändern, die aus den Schwielen ihrer Hände geschnitten sind, erzählt von den stattlichen Häusern, die aus den Knochen des Volks gebaut sind; und dann kriecht in eure rauchigen Hütten und bückt euch auf euren steinichten Aeckern, damit eure Kinder auch einmal hingehen können, wenn ein Erbprinz mit einer Erbprinzessin für einen andern Erbprinzen Rath schaffen will, und durch die geöffneten Glasthüren das Tischtuch sehen, wovon die Herren speisen, und die Lampen riechen, aus denen man mit dem Fett der Bauern illuminirt. (2, 44)

Büchner's political principles and activity, and particularly *Der Hessische Landbote*, have been severely criticized, both from the Right and from the Left. Treitschke described *Der Hessische Landbote* as 'a masterpiece of unscrupulous demagogic eloquence',[37] and this judgement continues to haunt the bourgeois academic literature on Büchner right up to our own day. Karl Viëtor speaks of Büchner's 'demagogic caprioles';[38] A. Bartels describes Büchner as 'utterly unscrupulous';[39] Werner Lehmann, editor of the new standard edition of Büchner's works, repeats with full approval the damning words of Treitschke.[40] That Treitschke, of all people, should have been the originator of the charge of demagogy so persistently levelled at Büchner, is sufficient reason for regarding this charge with suspicion. For Treitschke is a perfect specimen of the type of man who continually accuses other people of being demagogic while engaging in the most pernicious demagogy himself. He describes the unfortunate participants in the Frankfort putsch as 'demagogues';[41] he accuses Börne of indulging in 'senseless demagogic ranting';[42] he refers to Paris as the 'academy of demagogy on the Seine'.[43] Yet what demagogy could be more contemptible, or more dreadful in its consequences, than Treitschke's notorious

words in the *Preussische Jahrbücher* of November 1879: 'the Jews
are our misfortune!' (*die Juden sind unser Unglück!*)? Is it not
demagogy to say of Heine:

He possessed what the Jews have in common with the French, the charm of vice
which can lend a momentary fascination even to what is base and disgusting;[44]

or to repeat – and extol as honourable and courageous – the words
of that 'procurator of the German Federation',[45] Wolfgang
Menzel:

International Jewry subverts and destroys all our conceptions of shame and
morality, and if the deluded rabble of the Middle Ages falsely accused the Jews
of poisoning the wells that old accusation must now be renewed with full justification in the domain of literature.[46]

And while accusing Büchner of unscrupulousness, what master-
pieces of distortion and falsification Treitschke himself achieves!
To give colour to the lie that Börne had no feeling for his native
country, he quotes Börne's words: 'I am as much a Frenchman as
a German', but fails to quote the first half of the same sentence:
'I love Germany more than France because it is unfortunate and
France is not.'[47] He cites the *odium humani generis* of Tacitus as if
Tacitus had been referring to the Jews, when in fact it was the
Christians whom Tacitus was accusing of 'hatred of the human
race'![48] It is evident that Treitschke's judgement on such matters
is not to be trusted, and that the charge of demagogy which he
makes against Büchner comes from him with a very ill grace.
Considering the poisonous context of Treitschke's words, one
can only wonder how Lehmann – in the second half of the twentieth century! – could still bring himself to quote them. If he
wished to accuse Büchner of demagogy he could have done so
without appealing to that disreputable authority. But, of course,
sometimes 'the devil can speak truth', and the fact that Treitschke
was himself one of the world's worst demagogues does not suffice
to disprove the charge against Büchner. We must consider to
what extent it is justified.

There is firstly the fact that Büchner may have allowed Weidig
to express in *Der Hessische Landbote* religious sentiments,

chiliastic hopes and promises, which he himself could not sincerely share. His opinion that 'the sacred rights of man' should be expressed in 'the simple images and idioms of the New Testament'[49] did not *necessarily* involve insincerity – he may have felt that this was merely the most readily intelligible way of conveying the truth to the people – but, influenced apparently by Fichte and by Voltaire's *Mahomet*, Büchner seems to have believed that no revolution could succeed without some form of *religious fanaticism*.[50] As he later wrote to Gutzkow:

Und die große Klasse selbst? Für sie gibt es nur zwei Hebel: materielles Elend und *religiöser Fanatismus*. Jede Parthei, welche diese Hebel anzusetzen versteht, wird siegen. Unsere Zeit braucht Eisen und Brot – und dann ein *Kreuz* oder sonst so was. (2, 455)

Thus Büchner found himself in the dilemma of either having to abandon the revolution which he believed to be necessary for the welfare of the people, or deliberately using as an instrument of revolution a religious fanaticism which his own sceptical and pessimistic Weltanschauung prevented him from sharing. It would seem almost inevitable that from this basic contradiction a certain insincerity in Büchner's relation to the people, and consequently demagogy, must follow. But as we do not know for certain which, if any, of the religious passages in the *Landbote* were written by Büchner, nor how far, if at all, he approved of those inserted by Weidig, it is impossible to say with certainty whether or not Büchner was actually guilty in his pamphlet of the demagogic exploitation of religious sentiment.

It may secondly be alleged that in *Der Hessische Landbote* we occasionally find passages that may have been true of Germany in general but were hardly true of Hesse in particular. Büchner was no doubt sincerely convinced that the autocratic rulers of Germany were, as a class, luxurious and corrupt, and in the neighbouring states of Bavaria and the Electorate of Hesse-Cassel he could find striking instances to illustrate his point.[51] But his picture of the Grand-Duke's court at Darmstadt – 'the princely mantle is the carpet on which the ladies and gentlemen of the court and aristocracy roll over each other in their lust' (*Der Fürsten-*

*mantel ist der Teppich, auf dem sich die Herren und Damen vom Adel und Hofe in ihrer Geilheit übereinander wälzen* – [2, 44]) – is certainly overdrawn and unjust. As Viëtor remarks, Ludwig II of Hesse was 'decent in character'; though it should be remembered that this 'decent character' had as crown prince incurred debts amounting to two million gulden which, on his accession, he expected his impoverished country to pay for him.

There are other objections that can be made to Büchner's account of conditions in Hesse, and not all of them can be invalidated. But it is nevertheless rather absurd to accuse him, as Lehmann does, of stating only the case *against* the government and not also the case *for* it: 'he wants to prevent the *pro* and *contra* from being weighed against each other, he will have only the *contra*'.[52] We must remember that Hesse was what we would now call a police state. Every publication was subject to a rigorous censorship which permitted no serious criticism of the Duke and his government. Under these circumstances no open and equal discussion of the *pro* and *contra* was possible. It was only the *pro* that could legally be presented to the people and was in fact being presented every day in the publications sanctioned by the State. Can Büchner be blamed, in such a situation, for presenting only the *contra*, the side of the question which the public would otherwise *not* be allowed to hear? Can he be blamed for failing to maintain a balanced judicial attitude in a debate in which the mere fact of his participation could be punished as high treason; in which the mere possession of a printed copy of his words could entail, if detected, prolonged imprisonment without trial; in which Weidig was actually destined to pay with his life for the part he had played? If Büchner, in this unequal struggle in which all the power was on the government's side and all the danger on his, confined himself to publicizing the case against the autocracy, is that sufficient grounds for accusing him, as Lehmann does, of ideological lying? –

Büchner the agitator balances like a dancer on the rope that stretches between truth and falsehood. He consciously presents a partial truth as the whole truth and thereby degrades it to an ideological lie.[53]

That is not a fair comment on *Der Hessische Landbote*. Büchner had a moral right to champion the cause of democracy and to demand justice for the poor. He was not bound to state the case for absolutism and inequality. And though it must be conceded that occasionally, in the heat of the discussion, he has been guilty of a false or unfair statement, his argument as a whole is sound and true. Franzos, while frankly acknowledging those occasional distortions but also recognizing the far weightier respects in which Büchner must be admitted to have been right, concludes that 'by and large, Büchner did no injustice to the State of 1834!'[54]

Other critics have objected that Büchner's political and economic views were rather primitive. And it is of course true that he was much less well informed about economics than Marx or even than Saint-Simon. He was a poet and a biologist, not an economist. Nor would an elaborate economic theory such as Marx was to offer have been relevant to his purposes. For he was not concerned with the economic analysis of all the past history of society and, on the basis of that analysis, with a prognosis and strategy for the later phases of capitalism in general. His aim was a more modest one: to secure for the Germany of his time the political and economic advantages which he believed to have been already achieved elsewhere. In a stricter sense of the word than would be applicable to Marx he was a *social-democrat*. Passionately committed to the amelioration of the lot of the poor, it was primarily by political means, by the establishment of a genuine democracy, that he hoped to achieve that essential economic purpose; whereas Marx, convinced that economic conditions were the main determinant of social and political change, tended to neglect political institutions and safeguards in a manner which has had disastrous consequences in the twentieth century.

Nowadays, however, the influence of Marxism is all-pervasive. Contemporary thinking on the theory and practice of revolution is almost always influenced by Marxist concepts and based, consciously or unconsciously, on Marxist assumptions. We have almost forgotten that there was also a non-Marxist revolutionary tradition, a tradition older than Marxism. Thus Enzensberger

declares it to have been Büchner's error to have relied on the
peasants and to have mistaken them for a class capable of a great
social upheaval,[55] and Honigmann speaks of Büchner's attempt
to base the revolution on the conservatively minded peasants as
'an idea that seems absurd to us to-day'.[56] But are peasants *always*
conservatively minded, and isn't Honigmann's sense of absurdity
merely an unconscious expression of the Marxist assumption that
the only effective revolutionary class is the industrial proletariat?
Lenin himself, though adhering to the orthodox Marxist principle
that only the class-conscious socialist proletariat could be 'the
grave-digger of the modern social system', nevertheless recognized that in 1905 the great mass of the Russian people 'consisting
mainly of the peasantry, showed in the revolution how great was
its hatred of the old, how keenly it felt all the inflictions of the
modern régime, how great within it was the spontaneous yearning
to be rid of them and to find a better life'.[57] Had there not been
the great peasants' revolt in Germany in the times of the Reformation? the continual uprisings of the French peasantry in the
seventeenth and eighteenth centuries? the revolt of the peasants
at Södel only a few years before the appearance of the *Landbote*?
Enzensberger, though feeling that Engels in his essay 'Der status
quo in Deutschland' estimated the capabilities of the German
peasants more accurately than Büchner, nevertheless points out
that 'the revolutions in China, Algeria, Cuba and Vietnam, that
is to say, all the victorious revolutions of the mid-twentieth
century, have been peasant revolutions'.[58] The industrial proletariat, on the other hand, at least in the economically most
advanced countries, have generally stood for gradual reform
rather than for revolution.

But the most persistent objection which Marxist critics have
made to Büchner's politics centres on his pessimism, his 'fatalism',
his abandonment of the idealist belief in inevitable progress which
in his early youth he had shared with Fichte and Hegel. The
Marxists regard this nihilism as evidence of Büchner's lack of historical understanding, of his ignorance of Hegelian dialectic, of
his failure, in short, to reach the superior standpoint of Marx.

Thus Georg Lukács compares Büchner unfavourably with the great French democratic revolutionary Blanqui who, having the advantage of a longer life-span than Büchner, was able to progress from 'the poor' to 'the proletariat', from Babeuf to the recognition of Marxism.[59] And Hans Mayer writes in connexion with Büchner's determinism, resignation and 'lack of historical sense':

Here the penalty is paid for ignorance of Hegel's dialectic – and for the backwardness of social circumstances in Germany. From his vantage point on the rock of atheism Marx could descry a promised land, Büchner only a vast desert of hopeless misery.[60]

But to most observers in the latter half of the twentieth century it must seem at least doubtful whether Marx's standpoint was really superior to Büchner's, whether, as compared with Büchner, Marx really represented the more advanced position. As the years go by the optimism of the Marxists becomes more and more threadbare, their belief in inevitable progress more and more untenable. The Marxist faith in the future was not a fresh contribution to European thought; it was taken over directly from Hegel's romantic conception of history as a grand theodicy, and had its remoter origin in Hebrew–Christian Messianism. Its essentially religious character is reflected even in the detail of Marxist phraseology – for example in Hans Mayer's claim that Marx had a vision of 'a promised land' – and more deliberately implied in Marx's promise to replace the illusions of religion with a state of society in which illusions can be dispensed with, a promise which not only commits Marxism to rivalry with religion, man to rivalry with God, but which could only be fulfilled in an order of society approximating to an earthly paradise.[61]

In breaking with this tradition and with all the other forms of chiliasm and utopianism so rife in the Europe of his time, Büchner was more radical than Marx. It was his most distinctive contribution to political thought. In most other respects Büchner's politics conform to well known principles and practices of revolutionary democracy. But in his clear and deep realization of the absurdity of utopianism, in his appreciation of mankind's inescapable subjection to the inscrutable and inflexible laws of

35

history, he set himself apart from his contemporaries and anticipated some of the most bitter and irrefragable insights of the twentieth century. For if anything has become clear to us it is that political activity cannot be based on the assumption that any power, material or ideal, is operating with invincible efficacy for the gradual betterment of the human condition. There may be periods of expansion or contraction, phases of development that legitimately call for a thorough renewal of the social and political order, for reform or revolution. But there can be no ideal state of society. Political activity can only be a labour of Sisyphus – an *absurd* endeavour in so far as it can never be entirely successful, yet a *necessary* endeavour since it admits the possibility of a partial and temporary success. This is precisely Büchner's standpoint, and in adopting it he was not only sounder than Marx but also more modern.

## BÜCHNER'S LATER POLITICAL ATTITUDE

*Der Hessische Landbote* was, as we have seen, an experimental work. It was designed to test the temper of the people, to determine how far they were ready for revolution. Büchner was soon forced to recognize that the experiment was a failure. Becker, in a passage of his deposition already quoted,[62] suggests that the *Landbote* was most unfavourably received by the people to whom it was addressed: the peasants handed over their copies to the police and patriots condemned the pamphlet, a reaction which induced Büchner to abandon all his political hopes. Weidig, on the other hand, claimed to have talked to peasants who had been deeply impressed by the *Landbote*, and the truth of the claim is indicated by the fact that he thought it worth while to bring out a second, modified, edition in November 1834. But there is probably some truth in Becker's account of the matter also, and it is safe to assume that the public response to Büchner's propaganda was not generally enthusiastic. He must have been discouraged, moreover, by the arrest of Minnigerode on 1 August 1834 and by the obvious danger to his associates and himself which that catastrophe implied. By the end of the year he seems to have become quite convinced that, apart from attempting to liberate Minnigerode, there was nothing to be done and nothing to be hoped for in Germany. In July 1835 he writes to his brother Wilhelm:

Ich würde Dir das nicht sagen, wenn ich im Entferntesten jetzt an die Möglichkeit einer politischen Umwälzung glauben könnte. Ich habe mich seit einem halben Jahre vollkommen überzeugt, daß Nichts zu thun ist und daß Jeder, der *im Augenblicke* sich aufopfert, seine Haut wie ein Narr zu Markte trägt. Ich kann Dir nichts Näheres sagen, aber ich kenne die Verhältnisse, ich weiß, wie schwach, wie unbedeutend, wie zerstückelt die liberale Partei ist, ich weiß, daß ein zweckmäßiges, übereinstimmendes Handeln unmöglich ist, und daß jeder Versuch auch nicht zum geringsten Resultate führt. (2, 440)

After his flight from Germany on 9 March 1835 Büchner took no further active part in politics.

Does this mean that his political views had undergone a radical change since the writing of the *Landbote* some ten months earlier? Lehmann interprets it so; he maintains that in the period between the *Landbote* and *Dantons Tod* – that is, between May 1834 and January–February 1835 – Büchner decisively modified his political principles and adopted in *Dantons Tod* a critical, hostile attitude to the revolutionary agitation of the *Landbote*.[63]

This is to misinterpret both works and to ascribe to Büchner a much deeper change of heart than the evidence warrants. Lehmann, it seems to me, does a great injustice to Büchner by insisting on the alleged likenesses and ignoring the obvious differences between the Robespierre of *Dantons Tod* and the author of the *Landbote*. Superficially considered, the fierce brevity of the *Landbote* may resemble the laconic abruptness of Robespierre's orations, but only – to apply more justly an image that is ironic on the lips of Robespierre – 'as the sword of the heroic liberator resembles the sabre of the tyrant's myrmidon'. Robespierre, at least in Büchner's representation, is not concerned to alleviate the suffering of the people. He is concerned to establish his own dictatorial power; and to achieve this purpose he is prepared to slander and murder, not only the enemies of the republic, but its best and truest friends. It would be serious misrepresentation to suggest that Büchner, even in the utmost heat of his struggle against German absolutism, was ever in the slightest degree guilty of such infamy. We have found no reason to doubt the essential honesty of his purpose, the substantial truth of his message. And just as the *Landbote* is falsified by the suggestion that its author was comparable with Robespierre, so we shall find, in the chapter devoted to this play, that *Dantons Tod* is falsified by being interpreted as a recantation.

Lehmann argues that Büchner's letter to his fiancée of March 1834, the letter in which he speaks of 'the horrifying fatalism of history', indicates 'a decisive change in Büchner's thinking', a change in which he suddenly perceives the irrationality of the revolutionary rationalism represented by the Jacobinism of Robespierre and by the 'demagogy' of his own *Landbote*.[64] But that letter was written *before* the *Landbote*, and the assertion that it reveals a complete reversal of Büchner's views is therefore inconsistent with Lehmann's earlier contention that the decisive change in Büchner's political attitude occurred between the *Landbote* and *Dantons Tod*. Moreover, if the letter of March 1834 indicates a clear recognition of the absurdity of revolutionary rationalism, how was it possible for Büchner immediately thereafter to plunge into the revolutionary activity of the Society for Human Rights? Evidently his insight into 'the horrifying fatalism' of history did not necessarily imply, for him, the futility of revolutionary activity. And, consequently, when that insight is again expressed in *Dantons Tod* it does not necessarily imply condemnation of the revolutionary activity of the intervening period.

That there had in fact been no decisive change in Büchner's political views is proved by the letters which he wrote *after* *Dantons Tod*. We have already noticed the letter of March 1835 in which he is still praying for 'a failure of all the crops except hemp!' and the still later letters in which he insists on the principle underlying the *Landbote* that 'the relation between the rich and the poor is the only revolutionary element in the world'; in which he extols the 'purely republican government' of Zurich;

in which he describes so bitterly the ragged, freezing children at the Christmas fair who were standing with wide open eyes and sad faces in front of the wondrous things made out of water and flour, dirt and tinsel (2, 452); in which he affirms the conviction that 'in social matters one must set out from an absolute principle of *right*, seek the formation of a new spiritual life *in the people* and let effete modern society go to the devil'.[65] It is true that in the letter to Wilhelm of July 1835 Büchner assures his brother that '*at this moment*' – the emphasis is Büchner's – there could be no hope of a political upheaval in Germany. But to recognize that the time is inopportune is a very different matter from renouncing the revolution in principle. Büchner makes no such renunciation. He merely resolves to wait until circumstances are more favourable: 'Let us trust to time!' (*Hoffen wir auf die Zeit!* – [2, 440]).

We shall find this conclusion confirmed by the two later plays, *Leonce und Lena* and *Woyzeck*. In these plays, especially in *Woyzeck*, we shall find that increasingly intense interest in the people expressed in one of Büchner's last letters to his fiancée:

Lernst Du bis Ostern die *Volkslieder* singen, wenn's Dich nicht angreift? Man hört hier keine Stimme; das *Volk* singt nicht, und Du weißt, wie ich die Frauenzimmer lieb habe, die in einer Soiree oder einem Concerte einige Töne todtschreien oder winseln. Ich komme dem Volk und dem Mittelalter immer näher, jeden Tag wird mir's heller – und gelt, du singst die Lieder? Ich bekomme halb das Heimweh, wenn ich mir eine Melodie summe. (20. Januar 1837, 2, 463)

Büchner's sense of being drawn ever more closely to the people and to the Middle Ages need not be taken as a direct contradiction of the sentences in a letter to Gutzkow written little more than a year earlier:

Sie erhalten hierbei ein Bändchen Gedichte von meinen Freunden Stöber. Die Sagen sind schön, aber ich bin kein Verehrer der Manier à la Schwab und Uhland und der Parthei, die immer rückwärts ins Mittelalter greift, weil sie in der Gegenwart keinen Platz ausfüllen kann. (2, 449)

When Büchner speaks of being drawn to the people and to the Middle Ages he is evidently thinking of the old folk songs and legends which had persisted among the poor peasants and townsfolk of South Germany and Alsace from medieval times down to his own day. He had always loved these things, and his love for them in no way conflicted with his revolutionary determination to secure freedom and justice for the people of his own time. But in the last years and months of his life his interest in folk culture seems to have become even more intense than it had formerly been. *Woyʒeck* is full of folk songs, and we have seen how Büchner, in a late letter to Gutzkow, declares it to be the aim of his revolutionary aspirations 'to seek the formation of a new spiritual life *in the people*'. Here we see the positive side of Büchner's revolutionary activity, and he seems to have been conscious of no conflict between this positive aspect of his political endeavours and their negative or destructive aspect – the attempt to sweep away the remnants of the old feudal order in Germany; though it is perhaps ominous that in Switzerland, where he found his democratic ideals most nearly realized, he also found that the people did not *sing*. Was this merely the expression of a personal prejudice, a homesickness for Alsace where he had left his fiancée and which had always been so dear to him? Or had he a foreboding that the further development of democratic society in the nineteenth century would not produce that 'new spiritual life' which he had hoped to find among the people? But it would be unreasonable to expect Büchner to have foreseen the consequences of the modern technology and industrialization which were then only beginning. These are problems of our time, not of his.

# 3. METAPHYSICAL REVOLT

Büchner's philosophical and religious ideas have been subject to a wide variety of interpretations: some critics have regarded him as an atheist, others as a Christian; some as a fatalist or determinist, others as a believer in spiritual freedom; some as a cynic and nihilist, others as a champion of the dignity of man. The obscurity of the matter and the paucity of the information available to us have left critics largely free to see Büchner, not as he was, but as they would like him to have been; too often their interpretation has been merely an expression of their prejudices. In order to avoid or minimize this fault, it may be useful to follow the example of the political historians and subject our sources of information to a brief critical examination.

All that we know about Büchner's philosophical and religious views is derived from six sources:

1. The three plays and the Novelle *Lenz*.
2. Büchner's correspondence.
3. The reports of friends and acquaintances.
4. Büchner's juvenile writings including the extant essays written during his school days.
5. Büchner's two biological works, the *Mémoire sur le système nerveux du barbeau* and the lecture on cranial nerves (*Über Schädelnerven*).
6. Büchner's notes on the history of philosophy, especially those on Descartes and on Spinoza.

Of these six sources the first is no doubt the most valuable. The finest and most adequate expression of Büchner's Weltanschauung is to be found in his imaginative writings. But these are works of art, and there are obvious dangers and difficulties in trying to restate their import in discursive language. They require to be considered as wholes, and in the later chapters of this book an attempt will be made to consider them so. It is only with the greatest caution that particular sentences may be isolated and regarded as an expression of Büchner's opinion. This is permissible only when Büchner can be shown to have expressed the same thought in his other, non-imaginative, writings; in which case the passage in the play or Novelle may properly be regarded as expanding and deepening the discursive expression of the idea. This is particularly legitimate in the case of passages, such as Payne's discussion with Chaumette and Mercier in *Dantons Tod* or the attack on idealist art in *Lenz*, which are not integral parts of the work of art or which are at least developed more fully than the artistic purpose demands. Here Büchner himself is obviously interested mainly in the theoretical content of the passages, which may therefore quite properly be utilized for the interpretation of his ideas.

The second of our sources, Büchner's letters, also contribute significantly to our understanding of his thought, but their value is subject to two qualifications. There is, firstly, the deplorably negligent and haphazard way in which Büchner's correspondence has been preserved and handed down to us. Many of his letters are completely lost; of others only brief fragments remain; and as some are undated we cannot be sure of their temporal sequence. And, secondly, there is the probability that Büchner to some extent accommodated his letters to their recipients. He certainly did not tell his parents the full story of his political activities, and we must allow for the possibility that in the letters to his parents and to some of his friends his views on controversial philosophical and religious questions are also to some extent veiled or suppressed. It is our misfortune that he had no regular correspondence with any friend of comparable intellectual capacity. The letters to Gutzkow are of more than average interest and weight; but few of them have survived and probably not many were written.[1]

The third source of our information, the reports of friends and acquaintances, must be rated the least reliable of the six. It provides only a second hand account of Büchner's words, and even if we grant the complete honesty of our informants we must still allow for possible lapses or distortions of memory (especially if the report originated many years after the conversation recorded);

and there is again, as in the letters, the possibility that Büchner may to some extent have accommodated his expressions to the understanding and sentiments of the person addressed.

Our fourth source, Büchner's juvenilia including the essays of the secondary schoolboy, are probably of much greater value for our understanding of Büchner's intellectual development than has been generally realized. We have already found these essays useful for the light they shed on his early political attitude; their philosophical significance is even more considerable. Written before Büchner was quite seventeen, they obviously cannot be fully mature productions, yet they already reveal an astonishing independence of thought, and the concentrated reflection embodied in them gives them a value comparable with that of Büchner's letters.

Our fifth and sixth sources, the scientific writings and the notes on Descartes and Spinoza, date from a late period of Büchner's career. As direct discursive expressions of Büchner's considered views unaffected by concern for other people's susceptibilities, they are of the highest value for the elucidation of his philosophical position. In the further course of this chapter we shall have occasion to observe that the importance of the philosophical notes in particular has not always been duly appreciated by the critics and expositors of Büchner.

Finally, in this connexion, it may be permissible to express regret at the loss of what might have been the most valuable of all direct sources of information about Büchner's political and religious views – his diary. Wilhelm and Caroline Schulz, who cared for Büchner during his last illness, both mention this document, and Caroline tells how they and Minna, on the day after Büchner's death, read parts of it and found in it 'rich treasures of genius' (*reiche Geistesschätze*). There is no reason to believe the persistent allegation that Minna was guilty of destroying a complete drama of Büchner's on the subject of Pietro Aretino – the evidence suggests that, though Büchner may well have contemplated such a play, it was probably never written.[2] But it seems impossible to escape the conclusion that, together with other papers of her dead fiancé, Minna must have destroyed his diary, and this offence – prompted by bigotry or prudery? – was serious enough.

## THE EARLY PERIOD

Büchner's childhood was subject to diverse parental influences. His father, in the course of his study and practice of medicine, had developed a thoroughly scientific habit of thought with its accompanying scepticism, while his mother was a person of simple unquestioning piety. As Franzos puts it:

> While Ernst Büchner let his science carry him as far from the realm of faith as it would, Caroline remained a believer – not a fanatical bigot but a pious spirit who was satified with the accustomed forms of worship without worrying her head too much about them.[3]

Caroline's cousin, Eduard Reuss, was professor of theology in Strasbourg, and when Büchner later came as a student to that city he naturally found himself moving in religious circles. His best friends, August and Adolph Stöber, were students of theology and members of an old Protestant family. Another of his friends, Eugen Böckel, was the son of a clergyman, and Minna Jaegle too was the child of a Protestant parson. Thus Büchner must have been continually in the society of convinced practising Christians, he must continually have been confronted with this religion and have had occasion to observe and reflect upon its tenets, ritual and ethos. But equally powerful and directly opposed to this religious influence streaming in upon him from all sides, was the scientific sceptical tendency inherited from his father and re-inforced by his own scientific and philosophical studies.

In his childhood, as was only natural, the religious influence of his mother seems to have predominated. So much appears to emerge from the simple verses which the fifteen-year-old boy offered to his parents as a Christmas gift and which contain such passages as the following:

> Ja heil'ger Gott, du bist der Herr der Welten,
> Du hast den Sonnenball emporgethürmt,

Hast den Planeten ihre Bahn bezeichnet,
Du bist es, der das All mit Allmacht schirmt.

Unendlicher, den keine Räume fassen,
Erhabener, den Keines Geist begreift,
Allgütiger, den alle Welten preisen,
Erbarmender, der Sündern Gnade beut!
Erlöse gnädig uns von allem Übel,
Vergib uns liebend jede Missethat,
Laß wandeln uns auf deines Sohnes Wege,
Und siegen über Tod und über Grab.     ('Die Nacht', 1, 187)

When he wrote these verses Büchner was still a student at the
Darmstadt *Gymnasium*. But the reports which we have of him
in this period suggest that, at least in the later years of his secondary schooling, if not before, he was already beginning to question the dogmas so unreservedly accepted by his mother. A
valuable contemporary document, the leaving certificate signed
by the headmaster of the *Gymnasium*, Carl Dilthey, says of
Büchner: 'He has followed the religious instruction attentively
and on these occasions has given many admirable proofs of
independent thinking.'[4] And a schoolfellow of Büchner's, Friedrich Zimmermann, writing to Franzos some forty-five years later
(13 October 1877), has the following recollection of his friend's
early attitude to religion:

As a fellow-student I had many conversations with Georg Büchner concerning
religion. Of course I have now only a general recollection of them. Relying on
that, I am firmly convinced that he was at that time a bold sceptic but not an
atheist.[5]

This evidence is supported by the testimony of another school
friend, Ludwig Wilhelm Luck, likewise writing to Franzos
(11 September 1878):

Georg Büchner was not a believer in the ecclesiastical sense. But being independent and objective in his thinking, he later became, with increasing maturity,
more prepared to be just to the historical powers of the church as well as to the
faith of individuals whose standpoint was different from his own. In particular,
any sort of proselytizing or propaganda for his own view, all the arts of fabricating
opinions and parties for the direction of the crowd, were foreign to him . . . All
his life long he struggled and searched with a genuine thirst for truth, and for
that reason, I believe, never in his own mind reached a final conclusion . . .[6]

It is possible, indeed, that both Zimmermann and Luck, trusting
to their memory after an interval of more than forty years, may
have underestimated the extent and depth of Büchner's unorthodoxy. This is suggested by the words ascribed to the young
Büchner by another of Franzos's informants:

I am convinced that already in the top class of the *Gymnasium* Büchner was a
radical atheist. He was finished with the church very early. For example, he said
to me once, when both of us were still in our boyhood: 'I don't like Christianity –
it is too gentle for me, it makes us as meek as lambs' [*lammfromm*]. The remark
remained in my memory because I was so shocked by it at the time.[7]

Though their reports are thus in important respects contradictory,
there are at least two points as to which Büchner's friends were
agreed: that even before he left the *Gymnasium* he had developed
a formidable independence of thought on religious matters, and
that he had already at that time ceased to believe in any orthodox
form of Christianity. We find both conclusions amply confirmed
when we turn to his early essays and speeches.

### THE SCHOOL ESSAYS AND SPEECHES

These productions are naturally very strongly coloured by the
classical studies to which Darmstadt's humanistic *Gymnasium*
was dedicated. Other obvious literary influences are Goethe (there
are allusions to *Faust* and *Götz*) and, in a very important instance,
Bürger. While the strongest philosophical influence is probably,
as Lehmann has pointed out, that of Fichte.

Notwithstanding such influences these essays and speeches
show plenty of evidence of that independence of mind which had
so impressed Büchner's friends. No prejudice, however widespread, can sway him; no authority, however pompous, can
overawe him. Though himself still a schoolboy, he can write as
follows about a learned professor who had been guilty of some
unworthy remarks about Cato:

Es fehlt nur wenig, daß der Herr Professor in seinem heiligen Eifer über die
blinden Heiden eine Sektion des Cato vornähme und bewieße, daß derselbe einige
Loth Gehirn zu wenig gehabt hätte. Wahrhaftig, wenn ich ein solches Buch in

die Hände bekomme, möchte ich mit Göthe über unser tintenklecksendes Seculum ausrufen: *Römerpatriotismus! Davor bewahre uns der Himmel, wie vor einer Riesengestalt. Wir würden keinen Stuhl finden darauf zu sitzen und kein Bett drinnen zu liegen.* (2, 21)

In the same article – an extraordinarily acute and mature critique of an essay by an unnamed author on suicide – Büchner shows that intellectual independence was a quality which he consciously valued and no doubt deliberately cultivated. He praises the writer he is discussing for his 'unprejudiced reflections'

die, wenn sie auch nicht alle gleich richtig sind, doch zeigen, daß der Verfasser sich fern gehalten von aller Einseitigkeit, daß er Alles nicht von einem fremden, sondern von einem eignen selbständigen Standpunkte aus betrachtet und beurtheilt und durch eignes Nachdenken schon einen tiefern Blick in die In und Außenwelt des Menschen gethan habe. (2, 23)

The qualities singled out for praise in another writer are the best index to the critic's own aspirations.

Büchner's intellectual self-reliance had already carried him very far from the orthodox piety of the Christmas poem for his parents. There, it will be remembered, he had prayed:

> Laß wandeln uns auf deines Sohnes Wege,
> Und siegen über Tod und über Grab.

Now he absolutely refuses to admit that the life of man on this earth can have any purpose beyond itself:

Die Erde wird nämlich hier ein *Prüfungsland* genannt; dießer Gedanke war mir immer sehr anstößig, denn ihm gemäß wird das Leben nur als *Mittel* betrachtet, ich glaube aber, daß das Leben *selbst Zweck* sey, denn: *Entwicklung* ist der Zweck des Lebens, das *Leben selbst* ist Entwicklung, also ist das Leben selbst *Zweck*. (2, 21)

Büchner's distaste for the idea of the world as a huge examination room will find expression again in *Dantons Tod*:

DANTON. Eine erbauliche Aussicht! Von einem Misthaufen auf den andern! Nicht wahr, die göttliche Klassentheorie? Von prima nach sekunda, von sekunda nach tertia und so weiter? Ich habe die Schulbänke satt, ich habe mir Gesäßschwielen wie ein Affe darauf gesessen. (III. vii. 61)[8]

And the denial of final causes, the conviction that every living creature has its purpose within itself, will recur with full insistence in the late lecture on the cranial nerves. But among the writings of his early period it is the essay entitled 'Heldentod der vier-hundert Pforzheimer' – probably, as Bergemann suggests on grounds of style, intended to be delivered as a speech – in which this idea is most fully elaborated. The essay celebrates the heroism of the four hundred Pforzheimers who, in the year 1622, sacrificed themselves to save their general and the Protestant cause at the battle of Wimpfen. The action of these simple, quiet citizens, unaccustomed to look death in the face (*nicht gewohnt, dem Tod in das Auge zu sehen*), who gave their lives for what they had recognized as true and sacred, is extolled as nobler than anything ever achieved by the disciplined valour of the ancient Romans and Spartans. But what is most remarkable and significant in Büchner's essay is his account of the motives that prompted the Pforzheimers' sacrifice, and of its importance for later generations:

Bekennen wir auch gerne, daß ihr Glaubensbekenntniß nicht das einzige und ausschließliche Mittel war des Himmels jenseits des Grabes theilhaftig zu werden; so ist doch dieß ewig wahr, daß mehr Himmel dießseits des Grabes, ein muthigeres und fröhlicheres Emporblicken von der Erde und eine freiere Regung des Geistes durch ihre Aufopferung in alles Leben der Folgezeit gekommen ist und die Nachkommen ihrer Gegner sowohl, als wir selbst ihre Nachkommen, die Früchte ihrer Mühen bis auf dießen Tag genießen. So also starben sie nicht einmal für ihren eignen Glauben, nicht für sich selbst, sondern sie bluteten für die Nachwelt. Dieß ist der erhabenste Gedanke für den man sich opfern kann, dieß ist Welt-Erlöser-Tod. (2, 13)

No more striking example could be given of Büchner's extreme reluctance to permit or approve the deflection of interest from the present world to the world to come. Though celebrating the heroes of a religious war, he will neither admit that the exclusive pretensions of their religion were well-founded (he expressly denies it) nor ascribe to their sacrifice any specifically religious importance. It is not for opening to us the heaven above that he would thank them; it is for making possible more of heaven on earth. It is for the liberation of the minds and hearts of men, for the 'illumination of Enlightenment' (*das Licht der Aufklärung*). He insists on seeing the sacrificial death of the Pforzheimers, not as a means of saving souls from the corruption of the world, but as a means of saving the world itself – in the phrase which he quotes from Bürger, it is 'world-saviour's death'. Further evidence of the unorthodoxy of Büchner's views is to be found in his speech on Cato of Utica. It is, as Louise Büchner afterwards described it, 'a forthright defence of suicide'.[9] Büchner refers to the Christian condemnation of suicide only to deny its relevance to our judgement of Cato:

Es ist ja doch ein ganz eigner Gedanke, einen alten Römer nach dem Katechismus kritisiren zu wollen! (2, 26)

The underlying thought is developed more fully in the critique already mentioned of an essay on suicide – a critique which evidently provided the theoretical foundation for the more polished periods of the oration. There Büchner boldly adopts the position that it is human insight, not religious doctrine, that must establish ethical principles. Any religious doctrine which contradicts the principles so established must to that extent be wrong:

Nun ist, wie schon gesagt, *Cato* nach allen Gesetzen *menschlicher* Einsicht zu rechtfertigen; widerspricht dießem alsdann wirklich das *Christenthum* so müssen die Lehren desselben in *dießer Hinsicht* unrichtig seyn, denn unsre Religion kann uns nie verbieten, irgendeine *Wahrheit, Größe, Güte* und *Schönheit* anzuerkennen und zu verehren außer ihr und uns *nie* erlauben eine *anerkannt sittliche* Handlung zu mißbilligen, weil sie mit einer ihrer Lehren nicht übereinstimmt. Was sittlich ist, muß von *jedem* Standpunkte, von *jeder* Lehre aus betrachtet *sittlich* bleiben. Ob man aber *wirklich* beweisen könne, daß ein Selbstmord wie der des *Kato* dem Christentum widerstrebe, ist eine *andre* Frage. Denn es wäre doch sonderbar, ja es wäre *unmöglich,* daß eine Religion *welche ganz auf das Princip der Sittlichkeit gegründet ist,* einer *sittlichen* Handlung widerstreben sollte. Es trifft also dießer Vorwurf *keineswegs* das Christenthum selbst, sondern nur diejenigen, welche den Sinn desselben falsch auffassen. (2, 20)

The tone of Büchner's references to Christianity is notably respectful, but it is a respect inspired exclusively by the ethical aspects of Christianity. Like Goethe, he is prepared to bow down before Christ as 'the divine revelation of the highest principle of ethics' (*die göttliche Offenbarung des höchsten Prinzips der Sittlichkeit*),[10] while remaining unmoved and unconvinced by Christian eschatology and supernaturalism.

This conclusion cannot be seriously shaken by the short fragment entitled 'Über den Traum eines Arkadiers', which contains the beginning of an anecdote that would apparently have illustrated the prophetic or telepathic power of dreams. Büchner warns us not to dismiss as mere superstition, as an empty play of imagination, that belief in miracles which cultured Europeans have in common with primitive savages and which he describes as 'a feeling that presses us all to the motherly breast of Nature' (*ein Gefühl, das uns alle an die Mutterbrust der Natur drückt*). But the sentences immediately following show clearly enough that he nevertheless does not himself, in the strict sense, believe in the supernatural, but is only moved by a sense of the infinite mystery and unfathomableness of Nature:

Der rohe Mensch sieht Wunder in den ewigen Phänomenen der Natur, er sieht aber auch Wunder in außergewöhnlichen Fällen des Alltaglebens; für beyde schafft er sich seine Götter. Der Gebildete sieht in den Wundern erstrer Art nur die Wirkungen der unerforschten, unbegriffnen Naturkräfte; aber auch sie sind ihm Wunder, solange das blöde Auge der Sterblichen nicht hinter den Vorhang blicken kann, der das Geistige vom Körperlichen scheidet, auch sie weisen ihn zurück auf ein Urprinzip, einen Inbegriff alles Bestehenden, auf die Natur. (2, 17)

It is evident that if there is any god at all whom Büchner recognizes at this stage of his career, that god is nature itself. True, he does not expressly deify nature; he stops short of deliberate pantheism. But there is surely something approaching religious sentiment in the tone in which he speaks of nature as the mysterious quintessence of all that exists, as the nurturing and protecting Mother of all mankind. Love of nature is one of Büchner's most pronounced and persistent characteristics, though we must expect it to be modified by the darker experiences of his maturer years. One is reminded of the story of a friend who, in the summer of 1831, the year in which Büchner left school, met him returning to Darmstadt looking tired but with shining eyes:

In reply to my question where he had been, he whispered in my ear: 'I will tell you the secret: all day long on the bosom of my beloved!' – 'Impossible!', I cried. – 'It's true,' he laughed, 'from morning till evening in Einsiedel and then in the Fasanerie' [a forest on the outskirts of Darmstadt].[11]

We are also told that this was the reason why Goethe's *Faust* was such a favourite with him – 'because the feeling for nature nowhere finds warmer and deeper expression than here' (*weil sich nirgends das Naturgefühl so innig ausspreche, als hier*).[12]

Büchner's school essays are not yet characterized by the bitter pessimistic tone of his later writing. We find in them intellectual criticism and disapprobation of established religious views but not yet the emotional attitude of 'metaphysical revolt'. Their tone, as we have seen, is on the whole optimistic. There is the conception of the Reformation and of the French Revolution as stages in a grand historical progress which was raising mankind 'to ever freer, ever sublimer thoughts'; there is the grateful assurance that 'more of heaven on *this* side of the grave' has already been achieved; there is the implied belief in the possibility of the salvation of the world (*Welterlösung*).

In the few years immediately after leaving school, during his first stay in Strasbourg, Büchner, as we observed in the preceding chapter, became increasingly aware of the grim realities of political life; but this was still, in the main, a happy time for him. He was in the company of congenial friends, in a fine city enjoying the freer atmosphere of France, within the reach of the magnificent Vosges mountains, and happily in love with the girl who was to be his fiancée. It is not until he is living again in Germany, in the autumn and winter of 1833, that we first notice in his letters that bitter pessimistic or nihilistic tone which recurs so persistently throughout his remaining years.

The change was no doubt largely due to the acute personal suffering which Büchner was then, for the first time in his life, experiencing: the separation from his fiancée, a severe illness, the observation at close quarters of the wretched social and political conditions in Germany. His state of mind is best described in the letter to August Stöber of 9 December 1833 from Darmstadt:

Du magst entscheiden ob die Erinnerung an zwei glückliche Jahre und die Sehnsucht nach All dem, was sie glücklich machte oder ob die widrigen Verhältnisse, unter denen ich hier lebe, mich in die unglückseelige Stimmung setzen. Ich glaube, s'ist beydes. Manchmal fühle ich ein wahres Heimweh nach Euren

Bergen. Hier ist Alles so eng und klein. Natur und Menschen, die kleinlichsten Umgebungen, denen ich auch keinen Augenblick Interesse abgewinnen kann. Zu Ende Oktobers ging ich von hier nach Gießen. Fünf Wochen brachte ich daselbst halb im Dreck und halb im Bett zu. Ich bekam einen Anfall von Hirnhautentzündung; die Krankheit wurde im Entstehen unterdrückt, ich wurde aber gleichwohl gezwungen, nach Darmstadt zurückzukehren, um mich daselbst völlig zu erholen. (2, 421)

And in addition to these personal afflictions there was the deeply disturbing effect of the philosophical and historical studies which he engaged in about this time. In the same letter to August Stöber he writes:

Ich werfe mich mit aller Gewalt in die Philosophie, die Kunstsprache ist abscheulich, ich meine, für menschliche Dinge müßte man auch menschliche Ausdrücke finden; doch das stört mich nicht, ich lache über meine Narrheit und meine es gäbe im Grund genommen doch nichts als taube Nüsse zu knacken. Man muß aber unter der Sonne doch auf irgendeinem Esel reiten, und so sattle ich in Gottes Namen den meinigen.[13]

If we may believe Franzos,[14] it was mainly this study of philosophy, introducing Büchner to a variety of conflicting systems, which broke down the pantheistic or quasi-pantheistic worldview to which he had been inclined in his later school days and in his first Strasbourg period. But still more devastating was his renewed study of the French Revolution, resulting in that famous letter to Minna of March 1834 with its desperate conviction of 'the horrifying fatalism of history', which we noticed in the preceding chapter.

The school essays, it will be remembered, had shown Büchner committed to a thoroughgoing *Diesseitigkeit*, to an absolute determination to seek the value and meaning of human life only within human life itself, not in any supposed life in a supersensible world. And in his later period also Büchner never retreats an inch from this position. But now, in the winter of 1833–4, his historical studies force upon him the terrible insight that the value which he was committed to seeking within human life itself is in fact not to be found there. Remaining uncompromisingly *diesseitig* – now as before aspiring solely to the 'heaven on *this* side of the grave' – he is forced to recognize that on this side of the grave there can be no heaven. Where he had formerly perceived a meaningful historical pattern he can now see only a horrible fatality, an inescapable violence; where he had once dreamed of the salvation of this human world he can now find nothing but the curse of a merciless necessity. And now, his hopes thus shattered, his reaction can indeed be described as 'metaphysical revolt'; he revolts with all the fierce youthful intensity of his spirit against the cruelty and senselessness of the world and against the powers, whatever they may be, that have created and control it. His revolt expresses itself emotionally as blasphemy, philosophically as atheism. In another letter to Minna, probably also written in March 1834, Büchner writes:

ach, wir armen schreienden Musikanten, das Stöhnen auf unsrer Folter, wäre es nur da, damit es durch die Wolkenritzen dringend und weiter, weiter klingend, wie ein melodischer Hauch in himmlischen Ohren stirbt? Wären wir das Opfer im glühenden Bauch des Peryllusstiers, dessen Todesschrei wie das Aufjauchzen des in den Flammen sich aufzehrenden Gottstiers klingt? Ich lästre nicht. Aber die Menschen lästern. Und doch bin ich gestraft, ich fürchte mich vor meiner Stimme und – vor meinem Spiegel. (2, 424)

Büchner's disclaimer of blasphemy looks like a concession to the conventional piety of his fiancée; the blasphemous tendency of the passage can hardly be doubted, and is confirmed by the recurrence of the thought at the desperate and defiant culmination of *Dantons Tod* (IV. v. 71). That is the emotional expression of Büchner's metaphysical revolt. For its philosophical expression we must turn to his notes on Descartes and Spinoza.

THE COMMENTARY ON DESCARTES AND SPINOZA

Büchner's notes on Descartes and Spinoza are the culmination of an interest in philosophy that had extended over many years. In the school essays there are already unmistakable traces of the influence of Fichte; we have noticed his intense preoccupation with philosophy in the winter of 1833–4 (cf. the letter to Stöber of 9 Dec. 1833 quoted above); there are allusions to Spinoza and possibly also to Hegel in *Dantons Tod* and *Leonce und Lena*; and among his extant manuscripts there is an epitome running to

268 pages of the first three volumes of Wilhelm Gottlieb Tennemann's *Geschichte der Philosophie* (cf. 2, 303–409), dealing with the
history of Greek philosophy. It is even asserted by Ludwig
Büchner that his brother would have preferred to lecture on
philosophy during his first semester at Zurich and that it was only
because Professor Bobrik had already announced philosophical
lectures for that semester that Büchner decided to give the
preference to natural science.[15] In view of all these indications of
Büchner's lively interest in philosophy, it is surprising that
Viëtor should dismiss his philosophical papers as having 'so
strongly the character of collections of material that reliable
pronouncements on his own philosophical thinking or on his own
world-view are hardly to be gained from them'.[16] Büchner himself evidently attached considerable importance to these papers,
since they were to be the basis of the lectures which he had quite
spontaneously proposed to offer in Zurich and which, even when
forced to modify his plan, he did not intend to abandon but only
to postpone. There must be something in them which deeply
interested him and which he was convinced was worth communicating to others.

Viëtor may have been influenced by the consideration, already
emphasized by Bergemann,[17] that Büchner's study of philosophy
was not original but dependent on Tennemann's History. But
while this is true enough of his study of Greek philosophy, it is
much less true of his study of Descartes, and scarcely true at all
of his study of Spinoza. Bergemann admits that, in the notes on
Descartes, Büchner 'at times frees himself completely from
Tennemann'.[18] He certainly had a first-hand knowledge of the
principal writings of Descartes, the *De methodo*, the *Meditationes*
and the *Principia philosophiae*. He frequently supplements
Tennemann's account by references to these sources, and deals
much more extensively than Tennemann with any matters that
are of particular interest to him. One example is his examination
of Descartes's 'fantastic cosmogony' (*eine abenteuerliche Kosmo-
gonie*), another is his exposition of Descartes's theory of the
nervous system, a third is his critical discussion of the *Objectiones*

*et Responsiones* which Descartes had appended to the *Meditationes* – publishing his system, as Büchner characteristically expresses it, 'in tatters together with the knives that had hacked it to pieces' (*in seinen Fetzen mit den Messern, die es zerschnitten hatten* – 2, 194). In the section of the notes on Spinoza dealing with the *Ethics* Büchner is obviously referring to, and translating directly from, the original Latin text (his translations are quite different from Tennemann's); and in the section dealing with the *Tractatus de intellectus emendatione* he shows a very exact knowledge of this treatise as well as of the *Tractatus theologico-politicus*.

Thus, notwithstanding his extensive use of Tennemann's work, it must be denied that Büchner's study of philosophy was merely a study at second hand, nor is it possible to agree with Viëtor that from that study reliable pronouncements on Büchner's own philosophical thinking are hardly to be gained.

It is true that Büchner's method is critical rather than constructive. But a philosopher's standpoint may emerge just as clearly from his criticism of other people's opinions as from the direct expression of his own. It is not so much the critical method of Büchner's philosophical writings that we have reason to regret as their very fragmentary condition. It was his declared intention to offer at Zurich 'a course on the development of German philosophy since Descartes' (*einen Kurs über die Entwickelung der deutschen Philosophie seit Cartesius* – 2, 454) or, as he later expresses it, lectures 'on the philosophical systems of the Germans since Cartesius and Spinoza' (*über die philosophischen Systeme der Deutschen seit Cartesius und Spinoza* – 2, 460).[19] It is clearly *German* philosophy that he was to be mainly concerned with, yet his notes contain nothing about any German philosopher. There is only a fairly complete account of Descartes and an incomplete account of Spinoza. Evidently these notes were intended to be merely preliminary to a much more extensive work – a comprehensive critical study of the German philosophical systems from Leibniz to Hegel, and we must suppose that the work was cut short by Büchner's death even before he had quite completed his introduction. That the notes on Spinoza belong to a very late period is confirmed by their apparently close relation to the Zurich lecture *Über Schädelnerven*[20] and by the fact, noted by Bergemann, that they are written on 'the same grey scribbling paper' as the folio manuscript of *Woyzeck*.[21] This, of course, gives them the interest and authority of a fully mature expression of Büchner's views, and *what* they express is the philosophical aspect of his 'metaphysical revolt' – his atheism.

Büchner's Weltanschauung has often been compared with that of Schopenhauer, and, as we shall see, not without reason. But it is typical of Büchner's unromantic, empirical and scientific style that he does not, as Schopenhauer had done, attempt to build a philosophical system of his own. He is content to criticize the philosophical systems already in existence. He does so methodically, fairly and dispassionately, from every point of view; but among the matters which engage his closest attention are Spinoza's proofs of the existence of God.

The discussion is kept on a strictly rational level; there is no appeal to emotion, intuition or mysticism. This uncompromising rationalism is ascribed also to Spinoza, and there is perhaps an undercurrent of admiration in Büchner's recognition of Spinoza's difference from Malebranche in this respect:

Beyde haben nur unter Voraussetzung des Cartesius eine wissenschaftliche Bedeutung, beyde setzen das Fundament des Cartesianismus nur voraus; aber Malebranche wird seinem Lehrer untreu, er wendet sich zur Anschauung, er sieht alle Dinge in Gott, aber unmittelbar ohne Räsonnement, ohne Schluß; Spinoza dagegen bleibt treu, die Demonstration ist ihm das einzige Band zwischen dem Absoluten und der Vernunft . . . der Spinozismus ist der Enthusiasmus der Mathematik. Nur mathematisch gewisse Erkenntniß konnte ihn befriedigen, von intuitiver Erkenntniß kann bey ihm nicht die Rede seyn! Zeigt ihm einen falschen Schluß und er läßt sein ganzes System fallen. (2, 269, 276)

In a discussion conducted on such strictly rational lines the terms used must be capable of exact definition. Büchner understands 'God' as 'the absolutely perfect being' (*das absolut Vollkommne* – 2, 236) or, in another place, as 'the absolutely perfect, moral being of deism' (*das absolut vollkommne, moralische Wesen des*

*Deismus* – 2, 239). For Spinoza God is 'the absolutely infinite and perfect being' *whose essence involves existence.*[22] Büchner concedes that if we accept this definition we must admit the existence of God but argues that, in view of our experience of the world, we are neither obliged to accept it nor justified in accepting it:

Wenn man auf die Definition von Gott eingeht, so muß man auch das Daseyn Gottes zugeben. Was berechtigt uns aber, dieße Definition zu machen? Der *Verstand*? Er kennt das Unvollkommne. Das *Gefühl*? Es kennt den Schmerz. (2, 236)

One may compare the words which Büchner had earlier put into the mouth of Payne in *Dantons Tod*:

Schafft das Unvollkommne weg, dann allein könnt ihr Gott demonstrieren, Spinoza hat es versucht. Man kann das Böse leugnen, aber nicht den Schmerz; nur der Verstand kann Gott beweisen, das Gefühl empört sich dagegen. Merke dir es, Anaxagoras, warum leide ich? Das ist der Fels des Atheismus. Das leiseste Zucken des Schmerzes und rege es sich nur in einem Atom, macht einen Riß in der Schöpfung von oben bis unten. (III. 1. 48)

Büchner is prepared to agree that on Spinoza's premisses one can prove the existence of an infinite eternal substance. But this substance is not God, it is not 'the perfect, moral being of deism'. It is only 'what any atheist, if he is at all consistent, must recognize':[23]

Erst in dem Scholium zum dritten Beweis weist auch Spinoza auf Gott hin. Hier hört der Philosoph auf und er vergöttert willkührlich das, was in sich und worin Alles ist. (2, 240)

As soon as one maintains the existence of a perfect, morally good God, one is confronted with the problem of evil, or, more precisely, the problem of pain; and to this there is no answer. Büchner is tireless and relentless in his denunciation of the feebleness of the answers attempted by the philosophers. He speaks of the 'sophistry' of Descartes's attempt to explain error and evil in relation to God, and describes as 'miserable' (*erbärmlich*) his reply to Gassendi's objections on this point (2, 209). He exposes the inconsistency of which Spinoza is guilty when, notwithstanding his insistence on the perfection of his *deus sive natura*, he allows himself to speak of 'human weakness' and explains evil as due to the limitations of our perceptions (2, 267). In these failures of Descartes and Spinoza Büchner sees so many sad examples of 'the eternal contradiction between that which is in finitude and the eternal to which we try to connect it' (*der ewige Widerspruch zwischen dem, was ist in der Endlichkeit, und dem Ewigen, an das wir dasselbe zu knüpfen suchen* – 2, 268). And he may well have been thinking of such instances of philosophical self-deception and sophistry when he wrote to Gutzkow:

Ich werde ganz dumm in dem Studium der Philosophie; ich lerne die Armseligkeit des menschlichen Geistes wieder von einer neuen Seite kennen. Meinetwegen! Wenn man sich nur einbilden könnte, die Löcher in unsern Hosen seien Pallastfenster, so könnte man schon wie ein König leben. So aber friert man erbärmlich. (2, 450)

Some critics have contended that Büchner's notes on Spinoza cannot fairly be interpreted as a confession of atheism. Viëtor, while granting that they *may* be so interpreted, maintains that it is equally permissible to regard them merely as 'scientific criticism of an unphilosophical argument of Spinoza's'.[24] And Donald Brinkmann, arguing that Büchner is referring only to 'conventional notions, proofs of the existence of God, moral and metaphysical concepts of God', roundly declares that there can be no question of atheism here.[25] This view seems to me untenable. Büchner's criticism is not directed against any merely technical defects in Spinoza's argumentation. His objection is that Spinoza's identification of infinity with perfection is incompatible with our experience of the world. And this objection applies with equal force to any belief in God as an 'absolutely perfect, moral being'. So long as the word 'God' is understood in that sense, Büchner is certainly an atheist.

But may not Büchner have believed in God in some other sense of the word – in some less absolute sense? Benno von Wiese has argued that, though the experience of suffering may have destroyed Büchner's belief in a *perfect* God, it had not destroyed his belief in an *imperfect* God.[26] To this it must be replied that Büchner never, in a philosophical context, countenances the concept of an imperfect God. We have seen how he criticized Spinoza for 'arbitrarily deifying' that which is not absolutely perfect. And the attempt to retain the name of God while abandoning the concept of perfection would no doubt have seemed to him merely an instance of such 'juggling tricks' (*Taschenspielerkünste*) as had provoked his derision in Hegelianism[27] – merely another indulgence in the philosophical pastime of imagining the holes in our trousers to be palace windows. For it is only in relation to the concept of perfection that the question of the existence or non-existence of God can retain its decisive importance for mankind. Once admit that God is not absolutely perfect, not absolutely moral, and there is no longer any *a priori* limit to his possible imperfection, his possible immorality. It is then only experience that can determine how evil the world may be, how grim and irremediable the destiny of mankind. This is surely the meaning of the words in *Dantons Tod*: 'The tiniest twinge of pain, be it perceptible only in an atom' – since it is sufficient to disprove the existence of a *perfect* God – 'makes a crack in creation from top to bottom'.

Büchner's 'metaphysical revolt' directs itself not only against the Christian conception of an omnipotent and benevolent deity, but equally, and with logical consistency, against the Christian view of the nature and destiny of man. Having abandoned the belief in an 'absolutely perfect, moral' God, Büchner can no longer regard mankind as children of God who have a part to play in a divine historical plan. The idea of a providential direction of history, whether in the orthodox form of established Christianity or in the modified form given to it by German idealist philosophy, for example in Hegelianism, is replaced in Büchner's thought, as we have seen, by the idea of a blind and often cruel historical necessity or fatality. And as he can no longer regard the world as created and guided by God the Father, so he can no longer regard the salvation of individual souls as assured by the sacrifice of God the Son:

Wahrlich, der Menschensohn wird in uns Allen gekreuzigt, wir ringen Alle im Gethsemanegarten im blutigen Schweiß, aber es erlöst keiner den Andern mit seinen Wunden. (I. vi. 31)

3-2

These are the words of Robespierre, the 'blood-messiah' (*Blutmessias*) of *Dantons Tod*; but it is significant that the thought also occurs to Lena, the gentle heroine of Büchner's comedy (I. iv. 118).

So much for the *destiny* of man as it appears to Büchner's disillusioned gaze; but the *nature* of man is subjected to an equally profound and disquieting reappraisal. For Büchner man can no longer be the spiritually free and fully responsible individual of the Christian or idealist world-view. Though rejecting Spinoza's conception of God, Büchner seems to be quite at one with Spinoza in his determinism. In a letter to his family of February 1834 he denies the responsibility of human beings for their characters and capabilities:

> *Ich verachte Niemanden*, am wenigsten wegen seines Verstandes oder seiner Bildung, weil es in Niemands Gewalt liegt, kein Dummkopf oder kein Verbrecher zu werden, – weil wir durch gleiche Umstände wohl Alle gleich würden, und weil die Umstände außer uns liegen. (2, 422)

We shall find the denial of moral responsibility reiterated in *Dantons Tod* (I. vi. 27; III. i. 49) and in *Woyzeck* (172).

Büchner's determinism must have been reinforced by his peculiarly modern awareness of the unconscious impulses influencing our conduct: 'What is it within us that lies, murders, steals?' (*Was ist das, was in uns lügt, mordet, stiehlt?* – 2, 426) – a thought that recurs in *Dantons Tod* (II. v. 41). A competent medical authority, W. L. von Brunn,[28] commenting on the characters in Büchner's plays, on the strange yet so fascinating tenseness of their relations, on the ungovernable compulsiveness of their actions, remarks that all this seems unthinkable without knowledge of the modern psychology of the unconscious, and adds that, in fact, in the universities frequented by Büchner there was no instruction whatever in psychiatry. In this respect Büchner seems far ahead of his time. But von Brunn also suggests that Büchner may have been influenced by the physiological textbooks of his time – by the *Coup d'œil sur les révolutions et sur la réforme de la médicine* of Cabanis (1804) and especially by the *Précis élémentaire de physiologie* of Magendie (1816) according to which, as von Brunn writes, 'sensation, memory, judgement, appetence and also the will (!) are all merely modifications of the elementary sensitivity which is connected with the nervous system' – according to which, in short, human beings are merely 'nerve-automata' (*Nervenautomaten*).[29] Büchner must be credited with a very extensive knowledge of the biological and medical literature of his time, and it is not at all improbable that he had read the treatises of Cabanis and Magendie, though they are not mentioned in any of his extant writings. It is at any rate certain that he was very familiar with the thought of human beings as automata. The sovereignty of genius, he had told his fiancée, was a puppet-show. Or as his Danton expresses it:

Puppen sind wir von unbekannten Gewalten am Draht gezogen; nichts, nichts wir selbst! Die Schwerter, mit denen Geister kämpfen, man sieht nur die Hände nicht, – wie im Mährchen. (II. v. 41)

The spiritual freedom and independence of man, so unreservedly accepted and extolled by idealists such as Kant and Schiller, has become so questionable, so tenuous, for Büchner that he is sometimes inclined to deny any essential difference at all between mankind and the other creatures of nature:

Boire sans soif et faire l'amour en tout temps, il n'y a que çe qui nous distingue des autres bêtes.[30]

Büchner's criticism and rejection of the Christian belief in God, his criticism and rejection of the Christian and idealist view of the nature and destiny of man, result in a pessimism deeper and darker than any to be found in the previous history of German thought, with the possible exception of Schopenhauer. In both Büchner and Schopenhauer there is a sense of cosmic horror – a shuddering awareness of the endless pain and distress in the world. Each might have said, with Faust: 'Der Menschheit ganzer Jammer faßt mich an' – and not only 'der Menschheit', the suffering of *all* living creatures. Schopenhauer speaks of 'the limitless universe, full of suffering everywhere, in the infinite past, in the infinite future',[31] and this is the horrifying vision which haunts Büchner also. Indeed, to Büchner it seems even more horrifying, for while Schopenhauer can at least recognize the possibility of a temporary release from the torments of Tantalus in the pure contemplation of art, and even the possibility of complete redemption through the ascetic denial of the will to live, Büchner can recognize neither of these possibilities. This is the darkest and most terrible aspect of Büchner's 'metaphysical revolt'. Notwithstanding the longing for nothingness involved in it, it is better not to call it 'nihilism' owing to the equivocal and misleading connotations of this word. We may be content to regard it as an extreme form of pessimism – not at all, as an English critic has described it, 'a pessimism of a lurid, brutish and sordid kind',[32] but a view of the world that has at least the relative justification which the greatest tragic dramatists from Sophocles to Shakespeare have always conceded to it.

Yet it is psychologically impossible, as we noticed in the context of Büchner's political thought, to remain permanently at such an extreme of desperation; and just as his passionate negation of the political and social institutions of his country had its positive side in the recognition of certain political and social values, so his revolt against the philosophical and religious assumptions of his time clears the way for a cautious and tentative elaboration of a view of nature and man that is not without positive aspects. We have already observed something of this process in Büchner's early essay 'Über den Traum eines Arkadiers', where the denial of miracles in the conventional sense of the word is made to increase our sense of the mystery and marvellousness of nature. The same process is continued at a much higher and more mature level in Büchner's scientific researches.

## BÜCHNER'S SCIENTIFIC WORK

Büchner's contributions to natural science can be adequately discussed only by a professional anatomist, and it is not my intention to try to describe them in detail but merely to call attention to certain aspects of them which are particularly relevant to his *Weltanschauung*. Of his two scientific works, the more narrowly specialized *Mémoire sur le système nerveux du barbeau* and the later trial lecture *Über Schädelnerven*, it is especially the latter which must be of interest to us in this connexion and which we must now briefly consider.

Büchner's scientific writings are closely related to his philosophical studies, not only in respect to the time and circumstances of their composition but also in the deeper sense that, however different they may be in method, they are concerned with similar problems – one might even say: with the same problem. This relation emerges very clearly from the introductory paragraphs of the lecture *Über Schädelnerven*. Büchner begins by rejecting the 'teleological' standpoint in physiology and anatomy preferred in England and France, and by asserting the validity of the rival 'philosophical' standpoint favoured in Germany. The 'teleological' standpoint is that which seeks to explain the phenomena of nature by reference to their supposed purposes or *final causes*. It finds the solution of the riddle of organic life in the useful end which the functioning of each organ serves: it sees the skull as an artificial dome with buttresses designed to protect its occupant, the brain; it thinks of the eyelids and eyelashes as curtains intended to shelter the eye:

ja die Thräne ist nur der Wassertropfen, welcher es feucht erhält. Man sieht, es ist ein weiter Sprung von da bis zu dem Enthusiasmus, mit dem *Lavater* sich glücklich preist, daß er von so was Göttlichem, wie den Lippen, reden dürfe. (2, 291)

The denial of the teleological view of nature had been a striking feature of the philosophy of Spinoza; and Büchner was familiar with Spinoza's bold attack, in the appendix to the first book of the *Ethics*, on the 'prejudices' favouring the belief in final causes. It had required some courage to mount that attack, for among those 'prejudices' was, of course, the view of Hebrew and Christian philosophy that nature had been so ordered by God as to serve the needs of mankind. 'Unchecked', as Matthew Arnold put it, 'this philosophy would gladly maintain that the donkey exists in order that the invalid Christian may have donkey's milk before breakfast.'[33] Spinoza's opposition to teleology had been

THE DRAMA OF REVOLT

energetically continued by Goethe, who, in his contributions to science no less than in his aesthetic principles, had never ceased to insist on a non-teleological conception of nature in spite of the resistance offered by 'the pious way of thinking which wanted to utilize every individual creature directly for the glorification of God' (*Ebensosehr und auf gleiche Weise hinderte die fromme Denkart, da man jedes Einzelne zur Ehre Gottes unmittelbar verbrauchen wollte*).[34] Here Büchner is absolutely faithful to the tradition of Spinoza and Goethe. Like them, he opposes to the 'teleological' view of nature a 'philosophical' view, according to which:

> die Natur handelt nicht nach Zwecken, sie reibt sich nicht in einer unendlichen Reihe von Zwecken auf, von denen der eine den anderen bedingt; sondern sie ist in allen ihren Äußerungen sich unmittelbar *selbst genug*. Alles, was ist, ist um seiner selbst willen da. (2, 292)

It will be recalled that already in his school days, in the review of an essay on suicide, Büchner had insisted that life serves no ulterior end but has its purpose within itself;[35] now, in the fully mature lecture *Über Schädelnerven*, he develops this thought with the utmost deliberation and makes it the cardinal principle of scientific research. Nature being recognized to have no purpose outside of herself but to be absolutely self-sufficient in all her manifestations, it becomes the task of the scientist to discover the fundamental law governing the whole organization of nature:

> und so wird für die philosophische Methode das ganze körperliche Dasein des Individuums nicht zu seiner eigenen Erhaltung aufgebracht, sondern es wird die Manifestation eines Urgesetzes, eines Gesetzes der Schönheit, das nach den einfachsten Rissen und Linien die höchsten und reinsten Formen hervorbringt. (2, 292)

The recognition of that primal 'law of beauty' underlying and organizing the infinite variety of nature, including even its highest and purest forms, had been the culminating insight of Büchner's French dissertation:

> La nature est grande et riche, non parce qu'à chaque instant elle crée arbitrairement des organes nouveaux pour de nouvelles fonctions; mais parce qu'elle produit, d'après le plan le plus simple, les formes les plus élevées et les plus pures. (2, 125)

64

And again one is struck by the affinity with Goethe, who had similarly admired nature above all for the 'adroitness with which, though limited to a few basic maxims, she contrives to produce the utmost variety' (*Unsere Vorfahren bewunderten die Sparsamkeit der Natur . . . Wir bewundern mehr, wenn wir uns auch auf menschliche Weise ausdrücken, ihre Gewandtheit, wodurch sie, obgleich auf wenige Grundmaximen eingeschränkt, das Mannigfaltigste hervorzubringen weiß*).[36]

According to Büchner, the search for the primal law governing the multifarious organization of nature had 'led of itself to the two springs of cognition from which the enthusiasm of absolute knowledge has always intoxicated itself, the intuition of the mystic and the dogmatism of the philosophers of reason' (*führte von selbst zu den zwei Quellen der Erkenntniß, aus denen der Enthusiasmus des absoluten Wissens sich von je berauscht hat, der Anschauung des Mystikers und dem Dogmatismus der Vernunftphilosophen* – 2, 292). Leaving mysticism aside as too foreign to his scientific concern, Büchner proceeds to offer a few remarks on the 'dogmatism' of rationalist philosophy, by which he appears to mean Spinozism[37] and possibly also the nature-philosophy of Schelling, which, though an idealist philosophy, derived much of its inspiration from Spinozism. That this 'philosophy *a priori*' could ever grapple with the living reality of nature was bound to seem highly improbable to Büchner. He himself was too deeply committed to the empirical method of modern science. A thoroughly trained and conscientious observer, extraordinarily skilled in the preparation of anatomical specimens, he was bound to be extremely sceptical of the claims of the speculative philosophers to deduce the laws of nature from the forms of pure reason. Nevertheless, he was prepared to admit that this kind of abstract nature-philosophy, if itself unable to achieve concrete results, had at least given a new inspiration, a new form, to natural science. Influenced by the tendency of nature-philosophy to see all nature as an organic unity, botanists and zoologists such as Goethe and Oken had been able to achieve striking progress in at least some departments of morphology; they had been able to coordinate masses of previously unconnected facts by relating them to a few simple laws, by reducing the variety of forms to the simplest primitive type:

> Hat man auch nichts Ganzes erreicht, so kamen doch zusammenhängende Strecken zum Vorschein und das Auge, das an einer Unzahl von Thatsachen ermüdet, ruht mit Wohlgefallen auf so schönen Stellen wie die Metamorphose der Pflanze aus dem Blatt, die Ableitung des Skeletts aus der Wirbelform; die Metamorphose, ja die Metempsychose des Fötus während des Fruchtlebens; die Repräsentationsidee Okens in der Classification des Thierreichs u.d.gl.m. (2, 293)

Büchner saw his own scientific work as a continuation of these efforts, as a further contribution to the homological researches of Goethe and Oken. 'What Goethe had attempted for the structure of the plant, Büchner undertook for the brain of the vertebrate animal' (Strohl).[38] Setting out from Oken's theory that 'the brain is a vertebral column', Büchner attempted to demonstrate by detailed investigation the truth of the corollaries of that theory: 'the brain is a metamorphosed spinal cord, and the brain nerves are spinal nerves'.[39] More precisely, 'he attempted to prove that there are six pairs of original brain nerves, that six cranial vertebrae correspond to them, and that the development of the cranial masses proceeds in accordance with their origin; from which it follows that the skull and its contents are merely the product of a transformation of the vertebrae and of the medulla' (Helmig).[40] Büchner's immediate predecessors in this field of research, C. G. Carus and Friedrich Arnold, had concentrated their research on the highest forms of vertebrate animals, especially on man; convinced that 'the simplest forms are always the surest guide',[41] Büchner elected to seek the solution of his problem in the study of the *lower* forms of vertebrates, especially the fishes.

There is no question about the skill with which Büchner conducted his researches, and in the nineteenth century his work was highly commended by such competent authorities as the physiologists Johannes Peter Müller and Friedrich Hermann Stannius.[42] In the twentieth century expert opinion appears to be divided as to the validity of Büchner's theories. While Strohl maintains that Oken's and Büchner's view of the relation of the skull to the spine was disproved by the researches of Thomas Huxley, which showed that the inner skeletal part of the cranium is uniform, not segmental like the vertebrae,[43] Helmig on the contrary asserts that Büchner's theory 'agrees in essentials – viz. in the identification of the spinal nerves with the cerebral nerves – with one of the views prevailing today. This achievement must seem particularly creditable when one considers how problematic this field of research remains even in our time'.[44]

For us, in the context of our consideration of Büchner's Weltanschauung, it is not so much his achievements in science that are important as his aims – not so much the validity of his theories as their character and general tendency. It is evident that in these homological researches, these investigations into the comparative anatomy of the lower vertebrates and man, Büchner is again in conflict with the prevailing Christian conceptions of his age. These researches were not only, as we have already remarked, a continuation of the work of Goethe; they had also a certain affinity with the later, epoch-making theories of Charles Darwin; and it will be remembered how so many of Goethe's Christian readers took offence at his discovery of the *os intermaxillare* in man, and what a storm of religious indignation was provoked by *The Origin of Species* and *The Descent of Man*. The effect of all these studies – demonstrating as they did the close physical relation of the lower animals to the highest – was to depose man from the special, privileged position in the universe which Christianity had assigned to him, and they were therefore bound to appear subversive of all established religious doctrine. Thus Büchner's scientific researches tended to reinforce that revolt against the Christian and idealist view of the providential destiny of man which had already been started by his agonizing study of history.[45]

But if to this extent Büchner's scientific studies have something of the revolutionary significance which is characteristic of his work as a whole, they have also – and perhaps more conspicuously and indubitably than his activity in any other sphere – their positive, constructive aspect. If he denies that the world is the creation of a perfect being; if he denies that nature and human life are subservient to purposes outside of themselves, to final causes appointed by God; if he denies that the physical structure of man marks him as essentially different in origin and destiny from all other living creatures – if he denies all this he does so in the interest of the unity of nature, for the sake of the positive recognition of a primal universal law which is also a law of economy and harmony, a 'law of beauty'.[46] It is true that he resists the temptation to deify this law. At least in his scientific writings he consistently retains the careful sobriety of the scientist, eschewing the 'enthusiasm' of the mystic and of the dogmatic philosopher. 'If Büchner at times sees things in Goethe's way, still he never gets involved in pantheistic conceptions' (Strohl).[47] He does not, like Goethe and Schelling, speak of 'the divine and natural principle of things' (*das göttliche und natürliche Prinzip der Dinge*).[48] His admiration for the harmony and beauty of nature cannot seduce him into the unphilosophical position which he criticized in Spinoza, the position of 'arbitrarily deifying' that which is not perfect. But still he *has* this admiration, and it is especially here, in his strictly realistic and scientific recognition of the 'law of beauty', that one can see how Büchner's rejection of a falsely religious glorification of nature as the creation of God could lead to a deepening and intensification of his insight into what is *truly* glorious in nature – how his denial of the wondrousness of nature in a supernatural sense could make possible a finer awareness of the wondrousness of nature in a natural sense. Thus the general tendency of Büchner's scientific work is to serve the function which Strohl declares to be the task of all true scientific research: 'on the one hand to despiritualize nature, to free it from the many-thousand-year-old accretions due to human attitudes – emotional, habitual or indifferent – in order to approach ever closer to its true being; and on the other hand precisely thereby to strengthen the nimbus of that mightiness, that, in a new sense, *wondrous* aspect which is proper to the innermost depths of nature'.[49]

68

## THE SOLIDARITY OF REVOLT

And just as Büchner's rejection of the older religious view of nature clears the way for his more realistic appreciation of nature's true beauty and power, so his destruction of the Christian and idealist conception of the destiny of man makes possible an attitude to mankind which is ever so much less pretentious, which is full of disquiet, but which by no means lacks warmth and sympathy. In the unsparing, unflinching recognition of the weakness and loneliness, the suffering and enslavement of men and women, and in the spontaneous revolt against this cruelty and injustice of the human condition there is found a new solidarity with mankind, a solidarity which expresses itself as pity and love.[50] *Dantons Tod*, *Lenz* and *Woyzeck* are full of 'pitying glances' (*mitleidige Blicke* – 2, 423), and pity, as we have seen, was the very mainspring of Büchner's political activity.[51]

Here again, as in his pessimistic view of the world, Büchner has an affinity with Schopenhauer, who taught that pity was 'the only source of actions having moral value', that pity was 'the foundation of justice and philanthropy, *caritas*'.[52] And this pity and *caritas*, which in Büchner were even stronger and deeper passions than in Schopenhauer – unadulterated by that pride of intellect and misanthropic bitterness to which Schopenhauer was so prone – constituted for both men, in spite of their unbelief, a bond of sympathy with Christianity, which, in its truest form, is so pre-eminently a religion of compassion. Schopenhauer recognized in the Christianity of the New Testament the spirit of Brahmanism and Buddhism which seemed to him so much more profound than the childlike spirit of ancient Greek religion.[53] And Büchner also likes to let his mind dwell on the sentiment and images of the New Testament. In the letter to his parents of February 1834 one may note his use of a Christian concept to express his indignation at aristocratic superciliousness towards the poor and lowly: 'the most shameful contempt for the Holy Ghost in man' (*die schändlichste Verachtung des Heiligen Geistes im Menschen* – 2, 423). And his appreciation of the inestimable value of Christian sentiment in a world so full of suffering may well have been the reason for his disagreement with the attitude of Young Germany towards Christianity. Considered from his pessimistic point of view, Heine's and Gutzkow's advocacy of the 'emancipation of the flesh', their attempt to replace the 'morbid' medieval asceticism of Christianity with a cheerful pagan pantheism, may well have seemed profoundly mistaken. Certainly he wrote to his parents: 'I am far from sharing their opinion about marriage and Christianity' (*Auch theile ich keineswegs ihre Meinung über die Ehe und das Christenthum –* 2, 452).

The 'realistic' view of man which Büchner forms 'in analogy to the Christian view' has been well described by Wolfgang Martens as one 'which includes the perils and abysses, the compulsiveness, the evil in man, and which nevertheless reveals the humanity in the "suffering, oppressed figures", in those who labour and are heavy laden'.[54] But it seems misleading to add, as Martens does, that even in the humblest of these figures Büchner recognizes the dignity of 'a creature of God'. Büchner may use the word 'God' quite freely in non-philosophical contexts, but we must remember that he does not, in a strictly philosophical sense, admit the existence of God. He cannot, therefore, in any strict sense of the expression, regard human beings as creatures of God. And indeed the intensity of his pity springs precisely from the fact that he cannot so regard them. If they were creatures of God there would be hope for them; but they appear to him like lost children, without a father and without hope – and it is precisely this hopelessness that inflames his pity. If Büchner had been more of a Christian in the orthodox sense he would have been less of a Christian in the moral sense. It was precisely the loss of belief in the Christian metaphysic that made the Christian ethic so vital for him. Faith and hope being lost, charity had to do duty for all three.

Similarly, one must not too hastily assume that the pity and *caritas* which are the expression of Büchner's solidarity with suffering humanity imply the transcendence of his philosophical determinism, the achievement and affirmation of the moral freedom of man: 'the sufferers who recognize themselves to be sufferers are no longer puppets' (Müller-Seidel).[55] It is true that men and women can protest and revolt against their common suffering. Their sense of solidarity may give rise to a sense of responsibility for each other, and, if they fail in this responsibility, to a sense of guilt. But may not their pity and love for others be an inevitable consequence of their nature? and may not the consciousness of guilt be as much necessitated by uncontrollable forces as the crimes and sins that occasion it? This at least appears to be Büchner's view. If he maintains that fools and criminals cannot help being foolish and criminal, he is also prepared to draw the logical conclusion that wise men and saints cannot help being wise and saintly. All men act according to their nature, and cannot do otherwise; only some have finer natures than others – 'finer' in the sense that they find their satisfaction in helping and comforting their fellow men, not in injuring or overreaching them. It is these 'finer' natures who have the heaviest sense of responsibility for others, the most insupportable consciousness of guilt if they fail in that responsibility; and the fact that these oppressive feelings may be ultimately irrational does not make them less real. Hence the passage in *Dantons Tod*:

ROBESPIERRE. Du leugnest die Tugend?
DANTON. Und das Laster. Es giebt nur Epicuräer und zwar grobe und feine, Christus war der feinste; das ist der einzige Unterschied, den ich zwischen den Menschen herausbringen kann. Jeder handelt seiner Natur gemäß d.h. er thut, was ihm wohl thut. (I. vi. 27)

It is the infinite gradations and combinations of these feelings of responsibility and compulsiveness, of innocent guilt and guilty innocence, of love and hate, fear and hope, which constitute the richness of human nature and which Büchner, being himself one of the 'finer epicureans', studies with infinite sympathy and patience – not in his philosophical or scientific work but in his imaginative writings, in his dramas and in his Novelle:

Man muß die Menschheit lieben, um in das eigenthümliche Wesen jedes einzudringen, es darf einem keiner zu gering, keiner zu häßlich seyn, erst dann kann man sie verstehen. (*Lenz*, 87)

The increasing intensity of Büchner's interest in men and women otherwise regarded as the meanest of mankind, the sense he expressed of being drawn 'ever nearer to the people and to the Middle Ages',[56] have suggested to some critics that in the closing months of his life he was reverting to a complete acceptance of Christianity; and these critics find support for their view in the changing attitudes represented by the successive versions of *Woyzeck* and in the words which Büchner is reliably reported to have uttered on his deathbed. We must leave the discussion of *Woyzeck* for a later chapter, but we may briefly consider here the sentiments ascribed to the dying Büchner.

In Caroline Schulz's record of Büchner's last days we find the following sentences dated 16 February 1837 (Büchner died on the 19th):

The night was restless; several times the sick man wanted to get away because he imagined he was threatened with imprisonment or was already suffering it and wished to escape. In the afternoon his pulse was absolutely *vibrating* and the heart was beating 160 times to the minute; the doctors gave up hope. Though usually of a pious disposition, I bitterly asked providence – 'Why?' Then Wilhelm came into the room, and when I told him my desperate thought he said: 'Our friend himself gives you the answer; only just now, after a violent storm of fantasies had passed over, he said these words with a calm, elevated, solemn voice: 'We have not too much pain, we have too little, for through pain we enter into God! – We are death, dust, ashes, what right have we to complain?''[57]

No one has questioned, or is likely to question, the truth of Caroline Schulz's report; but the readiness with which the majority of critics have accepted Büchner's words at their face value surely betrays an extraordinary lack of critical sense. According to Wilhelm Schulz Büchner was not delirious when he pronounced those words, but he had just emerged from 'a violent storm' of delirium, and he was only three days removed from death. If in such a situation he had uttered the most shocking blasphemies or obscenities, who would have attached the least importance to them or have held him in the slightest degree responsible for them? But because, superficially considered, his words appear to betoken submission to the Christian faith, they are not only taken very seriously but are actually allowed to outweigh the testimony of all that Büchner had written with the most deliberate care and in the fullest possession of his faculties.

There is nothing surprising in the fact that Büchner, in the extremity of his sickness, should have uttered the words reported by Caroline Schulz. His mind had long been intensely occupied with the problem of suffering, and the fact that his view of the world had been developed in opposition to the prevailing religious conceptions resulted in its being to a considerable extent conditioned by these: he could be attracted by them, critical of them, repelled by them, but he could not be indifferent to them. It is not surprising that thoughts and attitudes which he had often considered but never accepted should have recurred and reasserted themselves under the stress of mortal sickness; but his utterances in such a situation can hardly be regarded as a valid expression of his considered opinions.

In Büchner's imaginative and theoretical writings, the products of a sound state of health, pain is not that by which 'we enter into God'; it is 'the rock of atheism'. And human beings are not 'death, dust, ashes'; they are physically the expression of 'a law of beauty', morally worthy of infinite love: 'One must love mankind . . . none must seem too mean, none too ugly.' Or as Leonce expresses it, 'even the meanest of mankind is much too great for us to be able to love him'. Many critics quote these words with great admiration, and then proceed with equal enthusiasm to assert that in the inspiration of his dying hours Büchner perceived mankind to be death, dust, ashes – too despicable to be entitled to complain of their suffering. Of course one is free to believe, if one wishes, that dying men may have sudden illuminations which outweigh and cancel all the perceptions of their years of health, or, as Viëtor puts it, 'that they may be granted in a few hours insights which in the undisturbed rhythm of life they might have taken years or decades to attain'.[58] But in that case one would expect the new insights to be ever so much finer than those they replace, and who will say that the view of mankind ascribed to the dying Büchner is finer than that expressed in his writings? In the idea that man is so contemptibly constituted that he has no right to complain of his suffering there is an inhumanity and lovelessness which is quite uncharacteristic of Büchner and quite unworthy of him. One may even doubt whether this idea is consistent with the best Christian traditions, according to which man is made in the image of God and stands in the same relation to God as a child to his father. The thought that human beings do not suffer enough because intenser pain would open the way to God, is equally objectionable. A man who feels that he has been improved by suffering may be grateful for the experience and even wish to be exposed to severer ordeals, but there is nothing in the best Christian or humanist tradition that would justify him in wishing that others besides himself – 'we', i.e. mankind in general – should be subjected to an increase of pain. One need only consider the concrete implications of such a wish to appreciate its enormity. At the very moment when the dying Büchner pronounced those words, his friend Weidig was being tormented and tortured to the point of utter desperation in a Darmstadt prison, an agony which was by no means destined to purify and uplift him but only to drive him to suicide. Four days after Büchner's death Weidig slashed his neck and wrists with a fragment of glass and wrote with his blood on the wall of his cell: 'As the enemy denies me any defence, I have freely chosen an ignominious death' (*Da mir der Feind jede Verteidigung versagt, so wähle ich einen schimpflichen Tod von freien Stücken, F. L. W.*). Is it conceivable that, if Büchner had been in his right mind and had known the desperate situation of his friend, he could possibly have said of him: 'He has not suffered enough ... he has no right to complain'?

Büchner, as we have already observed, had a profound sympathy with the true spirit of Christianity; but this sympathy, which was a consequence of his tragic view of the world, had its roots very deep in his nature and was not the result of a late conversion. It was precisely the element of compassion in Christianity that so strongly attracted him, and it is not to be believed that the real Büchner would ever have been inclined to abandon Christian compassion in favour of Christian fanaticism.

# 4. AESTHETIC REVOLT

Büchner's early writings, the essays and speeches of his schooldays and his letters up to the time of his final departure from Germany in 1835, tell us little about his views on literature and art, little about his aesthetic or critical principles. They reveal, of course, traces of his reading; they contain some hints of his tastes and preferences. But the questions which chiefly interest him in this period are not critical or aesthetic; they are political and philosophical. The only account we have of his early attitude to literature is in the reminiscences of Friedrich Zimmermann and Ludwig Wilhelm Luck. Zimmermann writes:

Büchner was especially devoted to Shakespeare, Homer, Goethe, all the folk-poetry we could find, Aeschylus and Sophocles; Jean Paul and the most important of the romantics were read diligently. With all his respect for Schiller, Büchner found much to object to in the rhetorical character of Schiller's poetry. Incidentally, the range of his reading in *belles lettres* was very wide; Calderón too was included. He had no feeling for light reading; his reading had to give him something to think about. His taste was elastic. He devoured *Des Knaben Wunderhorn* and Herder's *Stimmen der Völker*, but he also appreciated French literature... For the antique and for everything that touches the soul in the poetry of modern times he was equally receptive, but was inclined to prefer what had the character of simple humanity.[1]

Büchner's early reservations about Schiller are mentioned only by Zimmermann. But there is no reason to doubt the truth of the report, and since Zimmermann is writing about Büchner's schooldays, we have here another remarkable instance of Büchner's precocious intellectual independence. For Schiller was then at the height of his prestige. Many critics and readers preferred him to Goethe; and Büchner's mother, to whom he was strongly attached and whose tastes might have been expected to influence him, is said to have been especially fond of Schiller and Körner.[2]

That it was above all Shakespeare who had captivated Büchner is confirmed by Luck:

I believe it was at the suggestion of the two brothers already mentioned [Friedrich and Georg Zimmermann], who had infected us with their enthusiasm for

Shakespeare, that we agreed to meet on Sunday afternoons in summer in the fine beech wood near Darmstadt in order to read the dramas of the great Briton which seemed to us the dearest and most stimulating: *The Merchant of Venice, Othello, Romeo and Juliet, Hamlet, King Richard the Third*, etc. We had moments of the truest and most intense rapture and elevation, for example when reading the passage: 'How sweet the moonlight sleeps upon this bank . . .' and 'That man that hath no music in himself . . . Let no such man be trusted'.[3]

After Shakespeare, it was probably Goethe who made the most powerful impression on Büchner. We have already noticed the allusions to Goethe in the school essays and his special preference for *Faust*.[4] We may also assume that – as Zimmermann asserts – Büchner was an avid reader of the romantics. In his later writings there are indubitable traces of the influence of Tieck, Brentano, Jean Paul and Heine, as well as of the French romantics Victor Hugo and Alfred de Musset. It is more difficult to demonstrate a direct influence from Byron, through Ludwig Büchner asserts that, after Shakespeare, it was Byron whom his brother found most congenial.[5]

In attempting to understand Büchner's maturer views on art and literature we are confronted with the difficulty that he has left us no work specifically concerned with aesthetics as *Der Hessische Landbote* is specifically concerned with politics and the notes on Descartes and Spinoza with philosophy. We have to rely on his letters, especially the letters to his family of 28 July 1835, and on two passages in his imaginative writings – the speech of Camille at the beginning of Act II, Scene 3 in *Dantons Tod* and Lenz's disquisition on art in the Novelle – which can safely be accepted as representing Büchner's own opinions. Reliable as these passages no doubt are, so far as they go, there is no reason to regard them as a *comprehensive* expression of Büchner's aesthetic views. They say nothing about lyric poetry, though there is evidence enough in Büchner's plays of a considerable lyrical gift. They say nothing about satire or caricature, though Büchner is a master in these genres. Yet they evidently represent what Büchner had most at heart in aesthetics. They bear witness to an irrepressible concern which insists on expressing itself even at the risk of disturbing the delicate artistic balance of the play or Novelle. Their importance is therefore obvious, and one need make no apology for considering them at some length.

## IDEALIZATION IN CLASSICAL LITERATURE AND ART

Büchner's revolutionary attitude makes itself felt no less immediately in his remarks on aesthetics than in his observations on politics or metaphysics. He writes from a position of radical opposition to the established artistic principles of his age – the principles that were guiding both the taste of the public and the practice of most of the artists in the Germany of his time. Camille's diatribe is as follows:

Ich sage euch, wenn sie nicht Alles in hölzernen Copien bekommen, verzettelt in Theatern, Concerten und Kunstausstellungen, so haben sie weder Augen noch Ohren dafür. Schnitzt Einer eine Marionette, wo man den Strick hereinhängen sieht, an dem sie gezerrt wird und deren Gelenke bey jedem Schritt in fünffüßigen Jamben krachen, welch ein Character, welche Consequenz! Nimmt Einer ein Gefühlchen, eine Sentenz, einen Begriff und zieht ihm Rock und Hosen an, macht ihm Hände und Füße, färbt ihm das Gesicht und läßt das Ding sich drei Acte hindurch herumquälen, bis es sich zuletzt verheirathet oder sich todtschießt – ein Ideal! Fiedelt Einer eine Oper, welche das Schweben und Senken im menschlichen Gemüth widergiebt wie eine Thonpfeife mit Wasser die Nachtigall – ach die Kunst!

Sezt die Leute aus dem Theater auf die Gasse: ach, die erbärmliche Wirklichkeit!

Sie vergessen ihren Herrgott über seinen schlechten Copisten. Von der Schöpfung, die glühend, brausend und leuchtend, um und in ihnen, sich jeden Augenblick neu gebiert, hören und sehen sie nichts. Sie gehen in's Theater, lesen Gedichte und Romane, schneiden den Fratzen darin die Gesichter nach und sagen zu Gottes Geschöpfen: wie gewöhnlich!

Die Griechen wußten, was sie sagten, wenn sie erzählten Pygmalions Statue sey wohl lebendig geworden, habe aber keine Kinder bekommen. (II. iii. 37)

The mention of 'five-foot iambics' is clearly out of place on the lips of a Frenchman. The 'atopism' betrays the fact that Büchner is really thinking of the classical tragedies of his own country, and tends – together with the general consonance of the passage with Büchner's other utterances on the subject – to justify our assumption that Camille is being used here as a mouth-piece for the expression of Büchner's own opinions. What is it, then, that Büchner, through Camille, is attacking? It is evidently various forms of *unrealistic* art as well as the tastelessness and stupidity of a public which prefers the pitiful artificiality of such productions to the power and abundance of reality. Plays where the characters are no more life-like than marionettes, the artifi-ciality of opera, the fantastic creatures of the poet's or novelist's imagination – these are endlessly extolled by everybody, while God's creation, within us and around us, is despised as vulgar and miserable. One may be reminded of the sentence in the letter to Minna Jaegle of 20 January 1837: 'You know how I like the ladies who at soirées or concerts scream to death or whimper a few notes.'[6] We know that Büchner loved folk-songs; but that is the only kind of singing that he seems to have cared for. 'Art'-songs, professional singing of any kind, whether in opera or at concerts, was evidently distasteful to him, appearing to him too artificial, too remote from reality. And it was basically for the same reason, though from a somewhat different point of view, that he rejected the work of the Swabian school of poets, which seemed to him to be 'always reaching back into the Middle Ages' because they were 'unable to occupy a place in the present'.[7] Here too, in this romantic medievalism, he felt that there was an attempt to escape from reality, to evade the actual problems and experience of the nineteenth century.

But there is one kind of unrealistic art which Büchner attacks more relentlessly than all others. It is the deliberately unrealistic art of the classicists, the principle and practice of classical *idealization*. At least since Aristotle the belief in the necessity of idealization, in some sense of the word, had been fundamental to classical aesthetics. For Aristotle it had been a matter of general-ization, of preferring the typical to the individual or the excep-tional; and it was on this poetic power of generalization that he had based his famous proposition that poetry is a more philoso-phical and finer thing than history – 'because poetry tends to express the universal, history the particular'.[8] Similarly, when

Aristotle quotes Sophocles as saying that he represented people as they *ought to be*, Euripides as they *are*,[9] the distinction is intended to be purely aesthetic, not at all ethical. The claim that Sophocles's characters are 'as they ought to be' does not mean that they conform to a moral standard of perfection, but that they conform to a poetic standard of universality. And it was precisely in this sense that Aristotle's doctrine was understood by Lessing and propagated in his *Hamburgische Dramaturgie*.[10] For Winckelmann idealization had meant the refinement and spiritualization of reality in accordance with an ideal, not of universal truth nor or moral excellence, but of beauty:

Bernini expresses a completely unfounded opinion when he declares the story of Zeuxis having selected the most beautiful parts of five beautiful girls in Croton, when he had to paint a picture of Juno there, to be absurd and spurious, because a particular part or limb fits no other body than that to which it belongs. Others have been able to imagine only individual beauties and their doctrine is: the ancient statues are beautiful because they resemble the beauty of nature, and nature will always be beautiful if it resembles the beautiful statues. The former proposition is true, but not separately, only together (*collective*); the latter proposition is false: for it is difficult, indeed almost impossible, to find a product of nature like the Vatican Apollo. – The spirit of rationally thinking beings has an innate tendency and desire to rise above the material into the spiritual sphere, and its true satisfaction is found in the production of new, more refined ideas. The great artists of the Greeks, who had to regard themselves, so to speak, as new creators although they laboured less for the understanding than for the senses, sought to surmount the hard resistance of matter and, if possible, to spiritualize it; and it was this their noble endeavour that gave rise in earlier times to the fable of Pygmalion's statue. For it was by their hands that the objects of sacred veneration were produced which, in order to awaken reverence, had to appear like images taken from superior natures.[11]

The story of Zeuxis selecting the most beautiful parts of five young women in order to piece them together into the image of a Juno would be sure to appeal to Büchner's ribald sense of humour, and it is this or some similar tradition that is parodied in Lacroix's Rabelaisian replique in *Dantons Tod*:

LEGENDRE. Wo ist Danton?
LECROIX. Was weiß ich? Er sucht eben die mediceische Venus stückweise bey allen Grisetten des palais royal zusammen, er macht Mosaik, wie er sagt; der Himmel weiß bey welchem Glied er gerade ist. Es ist ein Jammer, daß die Natur

die Schönheit, wie Medea ihren Bruder, zerstückelt und sie so in Fragmenten in die Körper gesenkt hat. (I. iv. 20)

We shall find Büchner's counter-arguments so apposite to the passage just quoted from Winckelmann's *Geschichte der Kunst des Altertums* that we may be inclined to suspect, though we cannot prove, that he had read that work. It is even more probable that he had read Lessing's *Hamburgische Dramaturgie*, a work which was bound to be of interest to a young writer who regarded drama as his proper field;[12] and, if so, he must have found there, in Lessing's translation, Bishop Hurd's still clearer formulation of the concept of idealization as the transfiguration of reality in conformity with an idea of beauty:

The artist, when he would give a copy of nature, may confine himself too scrupulously to the exhibition of *particulars*, and so fail of representing the *general* idea of the kind. Or . . . in applying himself to give the general idea, he may collect it from an enlarged view of *real* life, whereas it were still better taken from the nobler conception of it subsisting only in the *mind*. This last is the kind of censure we pass upon the *Flemish* school of painting, which takes its model from real nature, and not, as the *Italian*, from the contemplative idea of beauty.[13]

In the expression 'the contemplative idea of beauty' there is probably an echo of Platonism, and there can be no doubt that the Platonic theory of ideas, as well as the Aristotelian theory of essential forms, provided the practice of artistic idealization with what E. H. Gombrich has called 'a slightly specious philosophical halo'.[14] Platonism certainly had a powerful influence on such great masters as Leonardo da Vinci and Michelangelo, and no doubt contributed to that tendency to idealization which made the Italian art of the Renaissance seem so exemplary, not only to Hurd, but to all the classicists of the eighteenth and nineteenth century.

In Büchner's time the theory and practice of idealization in literature and the arts received further support from the philosophy of Kant – still powerfully influential – and the philosophy of Hegel. For Kant the regulative principle in art is 'the ideal of beauty' (*das Ideal des Schönen*),[15] and here the aesthetic ideal also acquires an ethical aspect in so far as beauty is the symbol of what is ethically good (*das Schöne ist das Symbol des Sittlichguten*).[16] For Hegel art proceeds out of the absolute idea and its purpose is 'the sensuous representation of the Absolute' (*die sinnliche Darstellung des Absoluten*).[17] It penetrates to 'the substantiality of nature and spirit' (*das Substantielle der Natur und des Geistes*)[18] and reveals these universal, eternal powers unclouded and undistorted by the fortuitousness, the fragmentariness, the arbitrariness of ordinary experience. Thus for Hegel too art is concerned with a deeper, more general truth than that of empirical reality, and so he is led to endorse, from his own point of view, Aristotle's contention that poetry is a more philosophical and finer thing than history.[19] It is evident that Kant and Hegel, no less than Platonism, endow artistic idealization with a 'philosophical halo', whether or not one chooses to regard this enhancement, with Gombrich, as 'slightly specious'.

German idealist philosophy no doubt had a large share in determining the climate of opinion in Büchner's time, but he hardly ever refers directly to Kant or Hegel. He was evidently much more immediately concerned with the principle and practice of idealization as represented by Schiller. Goethe, too, on emerging from his *Sturm und Drang*, had adhered to the principle of idealization both in the theory and in the practice of art. He paid homage to Winckelmann, whose classicism he in large measure resumed and vindicated.[20] His classical conception of the work of art as representing an *Urphänomen* undeniably involved a form of idealization;[21] and the practical implications are well illustrated by his *Iphigenie in Tauris*, where the characterization of the heroine is controlled by the ideal of a St Agatha of Raphael,[22] and where he feels that the King of Tauris must speak 'as if there were no starving stocking-knitters in Apolda'[23] – a perfect example of what made idealization so suspect to Büchner. But it is Schiller who, in his classical period, is the most eloquent champion of idealization in German literature; and it is accordingly Schiller on whom we shall find Büchner concentrating his attack. Typical of Schiller's attitude is the following passage from his critique of Bürger's poems:

81

One of the first requirements of the poet is idealization, ennoblement, without which he ceases to deserve his name. It behoves him to cleanse away the coarser or at least heterogeneous admixtures from what is admirable in his subject (whether this be form, feeling or action, whether it dwell within him or without); to gather into a single object the rays of perfection scattered among several; to subject features that disturb the symmetry to the harmony of the whole; to elevate the individual and local to the general and universal. All the ideals which he thus forms in particular instances are as it were merely emanations of an inner ideal of perfection which resides in the soul of the poet.[24]

Here we have the doctrine of idealization in all its varieties: as generalization of the individual or local; as refinement, beauty and purity of form in accordance with the poet's inner ideal of perfection; as moral improvement and ennoblement – Schiller's critique is concerned largely with Bürger's alleged moral failings, the crudity of his ethical standards, 'the too sensual, often vulgarly sensual character' of his poetry.[25] In the passage just quoted there is even a suggestion of that selection of a number of beautiful parts to compose one perfect form which we have seen ascribed to Zeuxis in Croton and, parodistically, to Danton in the Palais Royal. Schiller's position remains essentially unaltered in his later writings on aesthetics. In the *Briefe über die ästhetische Erziehung des Menschen* art is regarded as a means to the ennoblement of character; the possibility of the most sublime humanity is considered to be dependent on the enjoyment of beauty or the aesthetic condition of all-embracing unity. Under the influence of Goethe Schiller toyed with the idea of replacing the concept of 'beauty' with that of 'truth' and adopted an attitude of aesthetic indifference to moral criteria in the criticism of art which contrasts strangely with his earlier severity towards Bürger. But in his essay 'On the Use of the Chorus in Tragedy' he makes it very clear that the truth with which he is concerned is metaphysical truth – comparable in this respect with Plato's or Hegel's – not the truth of ordinary experience. Once again, as in Hegel, idealization is held to be the only means of attaining to the *truest* kind of truth; once again it is maintained 'that art only achieves truth by completely forsaking reality and becoming purely ideal'.[26] The essay as a whole is Schiller's most peremptory rejection of any form of realism or illusionism in art. The introduction of metre and lyric verses into drama is commended as an antidote to illusion, and the use of a chorus advocated as a further step in the same direction, as 'an open and honourable declaration of war on naturalism in art'.[27] A chorus in the ancient Greek manner is declared to be the only thing wanting to give Shakespearian tragedy its true significance.[28] It is suggested that a chorus should be the living wall which tragedy draws around itself in order to cut itself off completely from reality and secure its ideal ground, its poetic freedom.[29]

One may sense in such an image that characteristic distrust of reality, that hostility to nature, which Goethe noticed in Schiller with so much wonderment and regret. For Schiller reality is a treacherous adversary whom one must approach with caution and only under the protection of an ideal; he speaks of matter as 'this terrible foe'[30] whom we must war against to ensure that we master it and are not mastered by it. He asserts that Nature by herself, and all merely sensual creatures, can never have the quality of *gracefulness (Anmut)*, though he also asks, with rhetorical inconsistency, 'where do we find more grace than in children, who are nevertheless completely governed by the senses?'[31] Thanks mainly to the example of Goethe, a somewhat friendlier attitude to nature is found in *Über naive und senti-mentalische Dichtung*, though even this treatise is designed to vindicate the modern 'sentimental' poets who are 'not nature' and who, even as they seek nature, retain their ideality. It was inevitable that a poet who had such an inimical, or at least ambivalent attitude to nature, should feel very acutely the need to spiritualize and idealize reality. And if we recall Winckelmann's suggestion that Pygmalion was in ancient times the great mythical prototype of the spiritualizing and idealizing artist, it will hardly surprise us to observe how gladly Schiller's imagination dwells on Pygmalion, how ready he is to see himself in a similar role:

> Glückseliger Pygmalion!
> Es schmilzt? es glüht dein Marmor schon!
> ('Der Triumph der Liebe')

83

Wie einst mit flehendem Verlangen
Pygmalion den Stein umschloß,
Bis in des Marmors kalte Wangen
Empfindung glühend sich ergoß,
So schlang ich mich mit Liebesarmen
Um die Natur, mit Jugendlust,
Bis sie zu atmen, zu erwarmen
Begann an meiner Dichterbrust.

('Die Ideale')

Nature is not credited with her own intrinsic value; value – a
superior, spiritual value – has to be infused into her by the idealizing artist, the modern Pygmalion. Equally to be expected, considering Schiller's whole position, was his agreement with
Winckelmann and Lessing, with Hurd and Goethe on the superiority of the art of ancient Greece and Renaissance Italy to that of
the Netherlands:

In the visual arts the painters of the Netherlands evince a vulgar taste; a grand
and noble taste was shown by the Italians and still more by the Greeks. These
always aspired to the ideal, rejected every vulgar trait and never chose a vulgar
subject.[32]

Bearing in mind the preceding survey of the theory of idealization from Winckelmann and Lessing to Goethe and Schiller, and
remembering the illustrious names that had lent their support to
that theory, we shall better understand the force Büchner had to
exert in order to free himself from its influence. We shall better
understand both the violence of his reaction and the particular
form in which it expressed itself.

## BÜCHNER'S REVOLT AGAINST IDEALIZATION

What is it that Büchner so passionately objects to in idealization?
Why does he think it is so necessary to combat it? He is opposed
to idealization chiefly for two reasons. Firstly, because the attempt
of the idealizing artist to *improve* on nature in some sense – to
ennoble or beautify or transfigure nature, to transform it in
accordance with some perfect ideal – does not and cannot, in his
view, result in something richer or grander or finer than nature

84

but, on the contrary, in something infinitely poorer and weaker and meaner. Instead of transcending nature, he finds that idealizing art falls short of nature; it is simply inadequate to nature. The view of opera expressed by Camille in *Dantons Tod* – that it renders the soaring and sinking of the human soul just about as faithfully as a clay pipe with water renders the nightingale – is the view which in *Lenz* is taken of idealizing art in general:

Die Dichter, von denen man sage, sie geben die Wirklichkeit, hätten auch keine Ahnung davon, doch seyen sie immer noch erträglicher, als die, welche die Wirklichkeit verklären wollten . . . Die Leute können auch keinen Hundsstall zeichnen. (86)

To that favourite principle of classical aesthetics that the artist must not represent human beings as they are but as they ought to be, not the world as it is but the world as it should be, Lenz firmly replies:

Der liebe Gott hat die Welt wohl gemacht wie sie seyn soll, und wir können wohl nicht was Besseres klecksen, unser einziges Bestreben soll seyn, ihm ein wenig nachzuschaffen. (86)

And Büchner himself adopts the same attitude in the letter of 28 July 1835:

Wenn man mir übrigens noch sagen wollte, der Dichter müsse die Welt nicht zeigen wie sie ist, sondern wie sie sein solle, so antworte ich, daß ich es nicht besser machen will als der liebe Gott, der die Welt gewiß gemacht hat, wie sie sein soll. (2, 444)

Büchner's second objection is closely related to the first. It is that – precisely because of the inadequacy of its representation of reality – the art of the idealizers leaves us completely cold; it produces an effect of deadness. Instead of living human beings it offers us puppets or marionettes:

Da wolle man idealistische Gestalten, aber Alles, was ich davon gesehen, sind Holzpuppen. (*Lenz*, 87)

Was noch die sogenannten Idealdichter anbetrifft, so finde ich, daß sie fast nichts als Marionetten mit himmelblauen Nasen und affectirtem Pathos, aber nicht Menschen von Fleisch und Blut gegeben haben, deren Leid und Freude mich mitempfinden macht, und deren Thun und Handeln mir Abscheu oder Bewunderung einflößt. Mit einem Wort, ich halte viel auf Goethe oder Shakespeare, aber sehr wenig auf Schiller. (2, 444)

Büchner's admiration for Goethe may seem at first sight surprising in view of the fact that Goethe, in his classical period, was unquestionably an exponent of idealization in art. But apart from the consideration that Goethe, even in his most classically ideal works, is always much closer to nature than Schiller, we must remember that it is the author of *Werther*, *Götz*, *Faust I* whom Büchner has in mind, not the author of *Iphigenie* or *Tasso*. Büchner never mentions those later works, and it is indeed probable that the sentence with which the discussion of literature begins in *Lenz*:

Über Tisch war Lenz wieder in guter Stimmung, man sprach von Literatur, er war auf seinem Gebiete; die idealistische Periode fing damals an, Kaufmann war ein Anhänger davon, Lenz widersprach heftig . . . (86)

refers precisely to Goethe's early years in Weimar when he was leaving behind him his *Sturm und Drang* and turning to the ideal classical art of his maturity which Büchner could no longer fully approve.

Even when classical art succeeds in achieving an ideal beauty, Büchner remains unimpressed. In the discussion with Lenz Kaufmann adopts Winckelmann's argument that 'it is difficult, indeed almost impossible to find a product of nature like the Vatican Apollo':

Kaufmann warf ihm vor, daß er in der Wirklichkeit doch keine Typen für einen Apoll von Belvedere oder eine Raphaelische Madonna finden würde. (87)

The reply which he puts into Lenz's mouth is Büchner's retort to Winckelmann, Hurd, Schiller and all other idolaters of Greek and Italian art:

Was liegt daran, versetzte er, ich muß gestehen, ich fühle mich dabei sehr todt . . . Die Holländischen Maler sind mir lieber, als die Italiänischen. (88)

Similarly, when aestheticians such as Winckelmann point to Pygmalion's Galatea as the mythical ideal of perfect beauty, Büchner does not deny that beauty but, as we have seen, lets his Camille symbolically expose its sterility: 'The Greeks knew what they were talking about when they said Pygmalion's statue had indeed come alive but had never borne children.'³³ 'The most insignificant face makes a deeper impression than the mere sensation of beauty', says Büchner's Lenz (*das unbedeutendste Gesicht macht einen tiefern Eindruck als die bloße Empfindung des Schönen*). And so it is with *moral* beauty also. Schiller may have seen himself as a modern Pygmalion infusing his youthful creative fire into the coldness of nature, and the children of this poetic union – the Posas and Max Piccolominis and Maids of Orleans – may have been ever so spiritually beautiful. But had they any real life in them, any relation to the men and women who actually inhabit this world? Büchner could see them only as marionettes with sky-blue noses and affected *Pathos*.

The realism which Büchner advocated in opposition to classical idealization was designed to accomplish what he believed classicism had failed to accomplish: to make possible an art which, unlike classicism, would not be hopelessly inadequate in its representation of nature and history but would come as close as possible to the reality of nature and history; and, precisely because of this closeness to reality, would not, like classicism, produce an effect of lifelessness but would achieve the true aim of art as Büchner conceived it – the communication of feeling. Realism is the means; infection with emotion is the end:

Der Dichter und Bildende ist mir der Liebste, der mir die Natur am Wirklichsten giebt, so daß ich über seinem Gebild fühle, Alles Übrige stört mich. (88)

Or, as he expresses it in a passage we have already noticed, the artist must offer us – not puppets or marionettes – but real men and women of flesh and blood *who can infect us with their sorrow and joy and whose actions can excite our horror or admiration*. The essential thing is that art should be instinct with the sense of life, with the possibility of actual existence. Provided this condition is fulfilled, we can forget that concept of 'beauty' with which classical aesthetics was so preoccupied:

Ich verlange in Allem – Leben, Möglichkeit des Daseins, und dann ist's gut; wir haben dann nicht zu fragen, ob es schön, ob es häßlich ist, das Gefühl, daß Was geschaffen sey, Leben habe, stehe über diesen Beiden, und sey das einzige Kriterium in Kunstsachen. Übrigens begegne es uns nur selten, in Shakespeare finden wir es und in den Volksliedern tönt es einem ganz, in Göthe manchmal entgegen. Alles Übrige kann man ins Feuer werfen. (86)

It is thus a 'characteristic' art which Büchner is advocating, not an art of beauty. Art must reflect the true character of nature as faithfully and unpretentiously as a good political constitution reflects the true character of a people; and one can find no better words to describe such 'characteristic' art than those Camille uses in *Dantons Tod* to express his political conception:

Die Staatsform muß ein durchsichtiges Gewand seyn, das sich dicht an den Leib des Volkes schmiegt. Jedes Schwellen der Adern, jedes Spannen der Muskeln, jedes Zucken der Sehnen muß sich darin abdrücken. Die Gestalt mag nun schön oder häßlich seyn, sie hat einmal das Recht zu seyn wie sie ist, wir sind nicht berechtigt ihr ein Röcklein nach Belieben zuzuschneiden. (I. i. 11)

Büchner's demand for 'characteristic' art, an art for which the supreme values would be truth, reality, life, not beauty, had of course been anticipated by the *Sturm und Drang*. The arguments which he directs against Schiller's classicism are very similar to those which Herder, the young Goethe, Lenz, even Schiller himself in his youth, had directed against the principles of an earlier classicism. One may recall the famous sentences of Goethe's *Von deutscher Baukunst* (1772):

They want to persuade you that the fine arts have arisen out of the inclination we are supposed to have to beautify the things around us. That isn't true! ... Art was formative for a long time before it was beautiful, and yet it was just as genuine and great art, indeed often more genuine and greater than beautiful art itself.[34]

Or Lenz's *Anmerkungen übers Theater* (1774):

My feeling impels me to value the characteristic painters, even the caricature painters, ten times higher (hyperbolically speaking) than the ideal artists, for it is ten times harder to represent a figure with the precision and truth with which genius perceives it than to labour for a decade with compass and ruler at an ideal of beauty which after all is only such in the brain of the artist that produced it.[35]

And it was of course this genuine affinity which made it possible for Büchner, without incongruity, to put so many of his own aesthetic principles into the mouth of Lenz in his Novelle. But though Büchner could regard the *Sturm und Drang* as an ally in the struggle against classicism, we must not overlook the differences of opinion and emphasis which separate him from the so-called 'Geniezeit'. The writers of the *Sturm und Drang* were much more subjective than Büchner. Each of them was inclined to regard himself as the vehicle of some divine inspiration, as a prophet or *vates*, as 'the Lord's anointed'.[36] Each of them was, or claimed to be, a genius. But it is impossible to imagine Büchner, whose irony was as unsparing towards himself as towards others, speaking or thinking of himself as a genius. Intense as his feeling is, it is seldom permitted to disturb or distort, though it may guide and refine, his keen, objective observation of nature and mankind. While the *Sturm und Drang* was essentially a poetic movement, relying above all on the force and fire of inspiration, Büchner carries into the sphere of art something of the cool, 'clinical' attitude of the scientist. We may recall Gutzkow's suggestion that Büchner's rare objectivity, his complete freedom from preconceived ideas, his 'autopsy', was probably an effect of his medical training.[37] And Jean Strohl, himself a professional scientist, argued that Büchner's aesthetic principles and his scientific work had a common source in a basic concern for truth:

But this closest possible approximation to the object, never wholly attainable, is also – far removed from literary naturalistic tendencies – one of the chief principles governing the work of the investigator in the field of natural history. In this striving for truthfulness in regard to the objects of nature, undaunted by all the powers of conventionality and custom, the artist and the scientist find themselves at one.[38]

The increasing influence of science, even in the domain of art, is no doubt a general characteristic of the nineteenth century, and may partly explain the fact that some of Büchner's most distinguished contemporaries professed aesthetic principles more or less akin to his. Landau[39] compares the realistic tendencies in Wienbarg's *Ästhetische Feldzüge* (1834), 'the programme of Young Germany'; and it is true that for Wienbarg a great dramatist and every true poet must be 'a mirror in which the age recognizes itself'.[40] It is Wienbarg's conviction no less than Büchner's that life is paramount ('daß das Leben das Höchste

ist');[41] that Shakespeare, precisely because of his abundance of
life and strength, is unsurpassable;[42] that Schiller – whom
Wienbarg nevertheless treats much more respectfully than
Büchner – can no longer be a model for contemporary dramatists.[43] It is possible, though I know of no grounds for assuming
it to be certain, that Büchner had read the *Ästhetische Feldzüge*.
He certainly paid a good deal of attention to Victor Hugo, translating in 1835 the two dramas *Lucrèce Borgia* and *Marie Tudor*,
so we may more confidently assume that he had read the famous
introduction to Hugo's *Cromwell* (1827), where again we find
some ideas which are strikingly similar to Büchner's. Hugo too
rejects the Greek type of beauty ('type d'abord magnifique, mais,
comme il arrive toujours de ce qui est systématique, devenu dans
les derniers temps faux, mesquin et conventionnel');[44] suggests,
like Büchner and Lenz, that it is presumptuous for man to try to
correct God ('la muse moderne . . . se demandera . . . si c'est à
l'homme à rectifier Dieu');[45] insists that the poet must only
consult truth and nature, and the inspiration which is a form of
truth and nature; and expresses admirably, in a form likewise valid
for Büchner, the relation of modern art to beauty ('lorsqu'il lui
adviendrait d'être *beau*, n'étant beau en quelque sorte par hasard,
malgré lui et sans le savoir').[46] But perhaps the contemporary
writer whose view of art was closest to Büchner's was one whom
we must assume he had not read – Stendhal. In Stendhal too we
find a distaste for 'la beauté *connue* de l'ideal'; Clélia Conti is
preferred to the Duchess of Parma precisely because Clélia's
beauty is *not* that of a Greek statue ('elle ne ressemblait en aucune
façon aux têtes de statues grecques'), nor reminiscent, like the
Duchess's, of Leonardo's women.[47] The words of Danton which
serve as a motto for *Le Rouge et le Noir* (1830): 'la vérité, l'âpre
vérité' indicate a harder determination than Hugo's to see the
world as it really is, to represent human beings as they really are.
And Stendhal's famous comparison of the novel to a mirror being
carried along a highway and reflecting the mud of the puddles as
well as the blue of the sky – his consequent disclaimer of all
responsibility for the immorality which his work merely *exposes*[48]

– is strikingly similar in thought and tone to Büchner's defence of
*Dantons Tod*:

Der dramatische Dichter ist in meinen Augen nichts, als ein Geschichtschreiber,
steht aber *über* Letzterem dadurch, daß er uns die Geschichte zum zweiten Mal
erschafft und uns gleich unmittelbar, statt eine trockene Erzählung zu geben, in
das Leben einer Zeit hinein versetzt, uns statt Charakteristiken Charaktere und
statt Beschreibungen Gestalten gibt. Seine höchste Aufgabe ist, der Geschichte,
wie sie sich wirklich begeben, so nahe als möglich zu kommen. Sein Buch darf
weder *sittlicher* noch *unsittlicher* sein als die *Geschichte selbst*; aber die Geschichte
ist vom lieben Herrgott nicht zu einer Lectüre für junge Frauenzimmer geschaffen
worden, und da ist es mir auch nicht übel zu nehmen, wenn mein Drama ebensowenig dazu geeignet ist. Ich kann doch aus einem Danton und den Banditen
der Revolution nicht Tugendhelden machen! Wenn ich ihre Liederlichkeit schildern wollte, so mußte ich sie eben liederlich sein, wenn ich ihre Gottlosigkeit
zeigen wollte, so mußte ich sie eben wie Atheisten sprechen lassen. Wenn einige
unanständige Ausdrücke vorkommen, so denke man an die weltbekannte,
obscöne Sprache der damaligen Zeit, wovon das, was ich meine Leute sagen
lasse, nur ein schwacher Abriß ist. (*An die Familie*, 28. Juli 1835, 2, 443)

And Büchner goes on to argue that moral instruction or edifica-
tion is no concern whatever of the dramatist:

Der Dichter ist kein Lehrer der Moral, er erfindet und schafft Gestalten, er macht
vergangene Zeiten wieder aufleben, und die Leute mögen dann daraus lernen,
so gut, wie aus dem Studium der Geschichte und der Beobachtung dessen, was
im menschlichen Leben um sie herum vorgeht. (2, 444)

Didacticism, whether ethical or political, is rejected by Büchner –
not, as one critic has suggested,[49] because Büchner was too
pessimistic to think it worth while striving for the improvement
of society, but because he did not believe that literature could
effectively serve that purpose. It may be recalled how he derided
the writers of Young Germany for imagining that society could
be revolutionized by means of *belles lettres*. Revolutions, he was
convinced, had to be accomplished by very different methods – the
incomparably tougher methods which he himself had attempted
to use in *Der Hessische Landbote*. And this left literature free,
in Büchner's view, to fulfil its own proper task – not a didactic
or propagandistic task, but the task of studying life objectively,
honestly, without preconceived ideas or ulterior motives, a task
which, as I have already suggested, might almost be regarded as

complementary to the task of science. This objective, empirical view of literature was, as we have noticed, in some respects similar to that of other advanced writers of the time, but none of them were quite so radical, quite so uncompromising in their realism. To Stendhal, in the more classical atmosphere of France, Schiller could appear to be a romantic poet and capable of being associated with Shakespeare.[50] For Büchner Schiller was the very incarnation of academic classicism and at the opposite pole from Shakespeare. Hugo, in the introduction to *Cromwell*, was still prepared to advocate the use of verse in drama. For Büchner verse had become so hopelessly compromised by its use in German classical tragedy that not even the example of Shakespeare could save it from his condemnation. While Hugo is content to call for a style of drama that is frank and forthright, 'osant tout dire sans pruderie', Büchner demands the complete abandonment of the limited, sterilized vocabulary of classicism and advocates a realism of language that will not even stop short of downright obscenity.

So much for the theoretical exposition of Büchner's aesthetics. But Büchner has also offered us some examples which may enable us to appreciate more vividly the kind of art he is advocating, and help us to avoid some possible misunderstandings. After the defiant declaration of his very unclassical preference of the Dutch painters to the Italian, Büchner's *Lenz* goes on to say that the Dutch painters 'are also the only comprehensible ones' (*sind auch die einzigen faßlichen*) and by way of illustration offers a description of two pictures, both Dutch, which he declares to be the only ones that produce on him the effect of the New Testament:

das Eine ist, ich weiß nicht von wem, Christus und die Jünger von Emaus. Wenn man so liest, wie die Jünger hinausgingen, es liegt gleich die ganze Natur in den Paar Worten. Es ist ein trüber, dämmernder Abend, ein einförmiger rother Streifen am Horizont, halbfinster auf der Straße, da kommt ein Unbekannter zu ihnen, sie sprechen, er bricht das Brod, da erkennen sie ihn, in einfachmenschlicher Art, und die göttlich-leidenden Züge reden ihnen deutlich, und sie erschrecken, denn es ist finster geworden, und es tritt sie etwas Unbegreifliches an, aber es ist kein gespenstisches Grauen; es ist wie wenn einem ein geliebter

Todter in der Dämmerung in der alten Art entgegenträte, so ist das Bild, mit dem einförmigen, bräunlichen Ton darüber, dem trüben stillen Abend. (88)

It is now known with certainty that Büchner is referring here to the picture of Christ and the disciples in Emmaus by Carel van Savoy (*ca.* 1621–65), which is still to be seen in the Hessisches Landesmuseum in Darmstadt. Paul Landau rightly remarks that, though not painted by Rembrandt himself but only by one of his pupils, this picture breathes the spirit of Rembrandt.[51] In conception and atmosphere it is not far removed from Rembrandt's picture in the Louvre of Christ at Emmaus. And a spirit and style akin to that of the simpler religious pictures of Rembrandt is evidently what Büchner was aspiring to, not only in the visual arts but in art generally. Carel's picture (see Plate I) is markedly simple and unpretentious. Büchner notices the uniform brown tone. The 'red streak on the horizon' may have been suggested to him by the red in the sky visible through the window. The faces of the disciples are not at all 'idealized' or 'transfigured'. That of the disciple in the foreground is rather coarse – the face of an honest peasant. But with all this realistic plainness, there is deep religious feeling in the picture, feeling that is concentrated in the divinely suffering features of Christ. It is the kind of work of art which Büchner demands: one that renders nature with the utmost reality, so that the viewer *feels* something in contemplating it. A similar simple reality conveying powerful feeling is suggested by Büchner's description of the second of his two pictures, probably, according to Viëtor's suggestion, a work by Nicholas Maes.[52] And this may also help to eludicate Büchner's assertion that the Dutch painters are the only comprehensible ones. They are comprehensible because their work is informed by a single powerful emotion which communicates itself to the viewer so that he can hardly fail to grasp the sense of the picture and is not coldly excluded from it as he may be by the formal perfection of classical art. The unified composition of the baroque artist's work, illuminated by a single source of light, may have contributed to Büchner's sense of 'Faßlichkeit', of comprehensibility.

It would evidently be a misunderstanding if, following the

example of Hans Mayer, we were to describe Büchner's aesthetic as an 'Abspiegelungslehre', a theory of the artistic mirroring or reflection of reality.[53] It is true that Büchner may occasionally express himself as if that were his intention – we shall notice an instance of this presently – but, after all, Rembrandt is not photographic, Shakespeare and Goethe are not naturalistic. It is true that Büchner rejects any attempt to idealize, to beautify or to transfigure nature; it is true that he declares the best art to be that which renders nature 'with most reality' (*am wirklichsten*). But he does not suggest that this 'real' rendering of nature can be achieved by any superficial mechanical process of copying. For the reality that he has in mind is not simply *given* to the artist; it is something which the artist must *discover*, just as – within his own domain and by his own proper methods – the scientist must discover it. And most people never discover it; it remains for ever unknown to them. Even the so-called 'realistic' poets, Büchner suggests, had no inkling of it; and it will be remembered how Camille in *Dantons Tod* asserts that the public sees and hears nothing of the mighty creation which renews itself from moment to moment within and around them. In order to penetrate to significant reality the artist, Büchner declares, must have two things: the gift of vision and the gift of sympathy:

Man muß nur Aug und Ohren dafür haben. Wie ich gestern neben am Thal hinaufging, sah ich auf einem Steine zwei Mädchen sitzen, die eine band ihre Haare auf, die andre half ihr; and das goldne Haar hing herab, und ein ernstes bleiches Gesicht, und doch so jung, und die schwarze Tracht und die andre so sorgsam bemüht. Die schönsten, innigsten Bilder der altdeutschen Schule geben kaum eine Ahnung davon. Man möchte manchmal ein Medusenhaupt seyn, um so eine Gruppe in Stein verwandeln zu können, und den Leuten zurufen. Sie standen auf, die schöne Gruppe war zerstört; aber wie sie so hinabstiegen, zwischen den Felsen war es wieder ein anderes Bild. Die schönsten Bilder, die schwellendsten Töne, gruppiren, lösen sich auf. Nur eins bleibt: eine unendliche Schönheit, die aus einer Form in die andre tritt, ewig aufgeblättert, verändert. (87)

These sentences seem at first sight difficult to reconcile with Büchner's other pronouncements on aesthetics. The wish expressed here that one might have the power of the Medusa's head to *freeze* a scene or situation and hold it fast for ever is one of the passages where Büchner really appears to be propounding an 'Abspiegelungslehre'. Yet the emphasis is clearly on the artist's *vision* ('One only needs to have eyes and ears for it'), and one is free to suppose that it is this vision – the reality as the artist sees it – to which he would wish to give the permanence of marble. But what are we to say about the concept of 'an infinite beauty passing out of one form into another, eternally unfolded, transformed'? How is this to be reconciled with the proposition so emphatically advanced by Büchner that the quality of *life* is the only criterion in matters of art and that we must not ask about beauty or ugliness? Is there not, after all, a suggestion of something metaphysical in that concept? If it is related or analogous to that 'law of beauty' which Büchner postulates in his biological studies we should have to recognize here the influence of the pantheistic nature-philosophy of such thinkers as Goethe and Schelling.[54] The passage is too brief and isolated to permit a confident interpretation, but it seems most probable that Büchner is not thinking of anything metaphysical but merely suggesting that, if the artist approaches nature and mankind with the vision that is born of sympathy he will in fact find an infinite beauty even if it should not be his purpose to seek it. Büchner's insistence on the primacy of life and truth does not involve the denial of beauty. He recognizes both the beauty and the horror of the world. But art is above all a study of life and truth. If it has the qualities of life and truth it will not only do justice to the beautiful aspects of experience, but will acquire a certain beauty even in its representation of the ugly and cruel aspects – like those pictures of the old German school which Büchner describes as 'die schönsten, innigsten'. Thus Büchner seems to be indicating a relation of art to beauty not unlike that indicated by Victor Hugo in the words already quoted: 'lorsqu'il lui adviendrait d'être *beau*, n'étant beau en quelque sorte que par hasard, malgré lui et sans le savoir'.

Sympathy is evidently of the essence of the matter as Büchner understands it, and we must briefly consider here some of the implications of this important part of his theory. Its influence is already perceptible in his criticism of idealization, for, even deeper than his objections to the inadequacy and lifelessness of the idealizing artists is his resentment of what he regards as their arrogance. In their insistence on the necessity of idealization he senses a supercilious disdain for nature and people as they are: 'This idealism is the most shameful contempt for human nature' (*Dieser Idealismus ist die schmählichste Verachtung der menschlichen Natur – Lenz*, 87), and there was nothing that provoked fiercer indignation in Büchner than 'the subtle snobbery of contempt for mankind' (*die feine Aristokratie der Menschenverachtung – Dantons Tod*, III. vi. 56), no matter whether its pretensions were based on birth or on fortune, on moral or on intellectual claims. To this inhumanity and arrogance of the idealizers Büchner opposed his own doctrine of sympathy and humility, his own aspiration to human solidarity: 'One must love mankind in order to penetrate into the peculiar nature of each one; none must seem too mean, none too ugly; only then can one understand them.'[55] The conviction that, for the artist, nobody must seem too mean or ugly had for Büchner the consequence that he could no longer regard any class of society as being outside the pale of art. Even the life of the poorest and most despised people could properly be the subject of poetry and drama. Here also Büchner had been anticipated by the *Sturm und Drang*, and once again he can appropriately express his idea through Lenz:

Man versuche es einmal und senke sich in das Leben des Geringsten und gebe es wieder, in den Zuckungen, den Andeutungen, dem ganzen feinen, kaum bemerkten Mienenspiel; er hätte dergleichen versucht im 'Hofmeister' und den 'Soldaten'. Es sind die prosaischsten Menschen unter der Sonne; aber die Gefühlsader ist in fast allen Menschen gleich, nur ist die Hülle mehr oder weniger dicht, durch die sie brechen muß. (87)

Already in the eighteenth century, when the rising middle classes were striving to wrest some measure of power and prestige from the ruling aristocracy and were consequently demanding a literature in which they and their problems would be adequately reflected, their literary champions and spokesmen had made full use of the argument that 'the vein of feeling is the same in almost all men', that there was therefore no justification for choosing the heroes and heroines of literature exclusively from the ranks of royalty and the nobility.[56] Now, in the third decade of the nineteenth century, Büchner, through Lenz, resorts to the same argument for the purpose of extending the scope of literature, not from the aristocracy to the middle classes, but from the middle classes to the proletariat. And here again classicism stood in the way; it had to be defeated before Büchner's purpose could be achieved. For after Lessing's experiments with middle-class drama; after the more or less revolutionary episode of the *Sturm und Drang*; the courtly classicism of Weimar had reverted to the practice of concentrating attention on the highest strata of society. Even when, in such exceptional works as *Hermann und Dorothea* or *Wilhelm Tell*, it attempted to depict the life of the less exalted classes, these were represented with a degree of idealization that removed them very far from the experience of ordinary men and women. Thus to Büchner the classicism of Weimar must not only have seemed responsible for the artificial restriction of literature to the life of the aristocracy; it must also have seemed guilty of evading or glossing over, by its idealization, the real problems and suffering of the people, the true character of their existence. And from this point of view it becomes apparent that Büchner's struggle against Schiller was not only an aesthetic but also a political struggle. To a comparatively moderate liberal such as Weidig, Schiller could still appear to be the greatest of German poets, much greater than Goethe. To Büchner, hoping as he did for a profound political upheaval, a radical re-ordering of society, poetry such as Schiller's could only appear to be a reactionary influence. Shakespeare and the young Goethe, with their deep truthfulness, their unflinching rendering of the realities of experience, seemed infinitely to be preferred however undemocratic their conscious political attitude may have been. Not many years later we find Marx taking a similar view. In 1859 he advises Lassalle to 'Shakespearize' rather than to 'Schillerize'.[57] Shakespeare he regards as the supreme poet of the modern world; Schiller seems to him aesthetically unsound and counter-revolutionary. As Peter Demetz has pointed out, this view of Schiller, in which Marx concurs with Büchner, contrasts strangely with the official 'Marxist' view of the twentieth century.[58]

Thus Büchner's aesthetic revolt no less than his political and metaphysical revolt had a positive as well as a negative function. Its negative function was to sweep away all the classical clichés and schemata as well as all the metaphysical cobwebs which were shrouding reality and preventing the artist from getting a clear fresh view of it. Its positive function was to enable him to achieve a new intensity in the representation of life, both in its beautiful and in its cruel and terrible aspects. And we have now also seen that in the relation of art to society Büchner's new direction seemed likewise calculated to produce positive results. It would enable the artist to do justice to the great mass of people, the majority of mankind, who were apparently too poor, or too ugly, or too insignificant to be admitted within the fastidious precincts of classical art. It would break down the arrogance of idealism, expose its evasions and insincerities, and compel the artist to turn his attention to the poor and obscure people with whom Büchner believed the best remaining values of society to reside. In the aesthetic as in the political sphere he was trying to rescue the submerged classes of society and bring them into the light. We have already noticed his formulation of his political creed: 'I believe that in social matters one must set out from an absolute principle of right, seek the formation of a new spiritual life in the people, and let the effete modern society go to the devil.'[59] We can now see that this was a programme for art no less than for revolutionary politics.

But Büchner's aesthetic revolt is also closely related to his metaphysical revolt. The increasing empiricism of literature and art in the nineteenth century, the growing intensity of their effort to gain a view of nature and mankind untrammelled by inherited dogmas and prejudices, was no doubt in some measure due to the crumbling of religious faith. This consequence of the abandonment of traditional religion is as obvious, for example, in Keller as in Büchner. Only in Keller it results in a heightened eagerness to enjoy all that is beautiful in this earthly life, now thought to be the only life given to us. In Büchner it induces a more concentrated effort to appreciate both the horror and the beauty of the human condition and to regard mankind with the sympathy, the love and the understanding which have become so important, so indispensable in a world now felt to be irredeemable.

## SOME CRITICAL REMARKS ON BÜCHNER'S AESTHETICS

The revolutionary character of Büchner's aesthetic theory, the fact that it is the product of a radical opposition to the prevailing ideas of his time, must be borne in mind if we are to judge it fairly. It is the theory of a man who is engaged in a fierce struggle, and it inevitably bears the marks of its polemical origin; there are inevitably certain inconsistencies, distortions and exaggerations, if not in the theory itself, then at least in Büchner's formulation of it. We have already noticed how the longing which he ascribed to the artist for the petrifying, perpetuating power of the Medusa's head suggests an aesthetic 'Abspiegelungslehre' which was not really what Büchner was trying to propound. The doctrine that the artist must have a special gift of vision in order to perceive the 'pictures' which nature presents to us implies at least an element of *selection* in the artist's representation of nature, and is not strictly compatible with Büchner's other doctrine that the artist can create nothing finer or more beautiful than the world as it is; for the world as it is includes those elements of reality which the artist, in his selection, prefers to ignore. In the eagerness of his onslaught on idealization Büchner does not stop to consider whether some element of idealization is not inevitable in art. Gutzkow and Strohl may be perfectly right in ascribing to Büchner, as an artist, a degree of objectivity and rigorous truthfulness which we more commonly associate with science. But an eminent scientist has recently pointed out that even science cannot dispense with idealizations.[60] The progress of science does not consist in the replacement of idealizations with objective facts; it consists in the replacement of less adequate idealizations with more adequate ones. And in the last resort this is all that Büchner's 'realism' could be expected to do.

The intensity of the struggle in which he was engaged may also account for the peculiarly narrow limits of Büchner's taste, limits which, as we have seen, excluded opera, concerts, most of the more elaborate and sophicated art-forms and all the strictly classical art of the past, whether it be of ancient Greece or Renaissance Italy or modern Germany. In the severity of these limitations and in the decidedly popular direction which he was striving to give to art, Büchner anticipates another great fighter against the established order of things, Leo Tolstoy. And he resembles Tolstoy also in his completely unhistorical approach to art. In art no less than in politics Büchner sets out from 'an absolute principle of right'; his judgement is governed entirely by what he feels to be the requirements of his own time, and he is little inclined to make allowances for historical circumstances. But the danger of injustice which such an attitude involves is much greater in the aesthetic than in the political sphere. For in politics it is the immediate problems of Hesse and Germany with which Büchner is chiefly concerned. In aesthetics he is called upon to pass judgement on the finest art of periods very remote from his own, and here his unhistorical attitude makes it almost impossible for him not to be unfair. Thus he dwells on the element of idealization in ancient Greek sculpture or in the Italian painting of the Renaissance, but quite fails to do justice to the unparalleled hard-won achievements of Greek sculpture and Italian painting in matching nature with art – the impressive realism of the Greeks in their representation of human anatomy and in the increasingly natural pose of their figures, or of the Italians in their psychological penetration and in their use of perspective. In order to be just to those great periods of art it would have been necessary to consider them from the opposite point of view to Büchner's. Looking back on them from the situation of the nineteenth century, he could only see them as comparatively unrealistic and unnatural; if he could have placed himself in imagination at an early point in their development he would have appreciated the very considerable degree of realism and naturalness which they were gradually to attain. Overreacting against the retrograde demand of neo-classicists such as Winckelmann and the later Schiller for an artificial return to Greek and Italian models, Büchner made the mistake of extending his justifiable criticism of neo-classicism to the great classical artists themselves, failing to see that these too had been inspired by a deep concern for truth and nature and indeed had perhaps had more in common with *him* than with their modern imitators.

But not only Büchner's attitude to Raphael and the Greeks, even his attitude to Schiller has seemed to some critics mistaken and unjust. Thus Benno von Wiese roundly declares that from the very beginning Büchner takes a distorted and false view of Schiller.[61] But the truth of the matter is not quite so simple. The weaknesses and defects which he criticizes in Schiller are not merely figments of Büchner's imagination. They are really in some degree there; and at least for English readers, whose conception of drama has been formed by Shakespeare, it is difficult not to sympathize with Büchner's distaste for Schiller's rhetoric, for the unreality of much of his characterization, for his high-toned but basically conventional representation of nature and history. It may be harsh and excessive to suggest that Schiller's characters are merely 'marionettes with sky-blue noses and affected solemnity'; but even such a sympathetic critic as Emil Staiger sees the characters in *Die Braut von Messina* as 'ideal masks' and the figures in Schiller's ballads as resembling 'departed spirits' dwelling in a region illuminated by artificial light, appearing '*as if* they were alive, but separated from us by a barrier'.[62] It may be harsh and excessive to say that the idealism of such poets as Schiller is 'the most shameful contempt for human nature'. But even Goethe regarded Schiller as decidedly aristocratic,[63] even Carlyle recognized in him a certain 'aristocratic fastidiousness', a certain 'comparatively barren elevation';[64] and in such passages as that where Schiller rebukes Bürger for *mixing* with the people instead of merely *condescending* to them ('Herr Bürger *vermischt sich nicht selten mit dem Volk, zu dem er sich nur herablassen* sollte')[65] it is easy to see the reason for the resentment of such a democratically minded man as Büchner, a man who would have blushed to be thought capable of 'the fatuity of condescension' (*die Lächerlichkeit des Herablassens werdet Ihr mir doch wohl nicht zutrauen* – 2, 423). But if one cannot say that Büchner's view of Schiller is altogether distorted and false, one can fairly say that it is incomplete. It is unjust to Schiller in so far as it nowhere takes account of his positive qualities, the skill and power of his dramatic construction, the breath of greatness in his dramas, his single-minded devotion to his art, his often astonishingly acute insights.

But however unjust Büchner may have been towards the artists of the nearer or remoter past, there can be little doubt that his attitude was right for his own time and country. Just as, in the philosophy and science of the nineteenth century, metaphysics and nature-philosophy had to give way to positivism and empiricism, so also in the literature and art of the period it was necessary to seek a closer and fresher approach to nature. It was also necessary to broaden the scope of art to include the peasantry and the working classes, who were increasingly making their presence felt in Europe. In both respects Büchner was pointing in the right direction, and his aesthetic demands were destined to be largely fulfilled by the great writers and painters of the nineteenth century. It is not surprising that the recognition due to his superior insight should at last have been granted him in the period of naturalism. What is more surprising is that his prestige should have so steadily continued to increase in the twentieth century, when the struggle against classicism has long since been won, when the most progressive art is predominantly unrealistic, and when the realism of the nineteenth century, once so daring and revolutionary, is generally felt to represent conservatism and reaction. But this is a phenomenon which we shall be better able to understand when we have considered Büchner's plays.

# 5. 'DANTONS TOD'

In the letter of 21 February 1835, which Büchner addressed to Gutzkow together with the manuscript of *Dantons Tod*, he remarks that unfortunate circumstances had compelled him to write the play 'in at most five weeks'. As Büchner was desperately in need of the money which he hoped to gain by the publication of the work, in order to finance his flight from Darmstadt, we may be sure that the letter was written immediately after the completion of the play, which we may therefore assume to have been written in the last two weeks of January and the first three weeks of February. The circumstances under which it was composed were indeed in many respects unfavourable, not only because of the necessary haste which Büchner mentions, but also because of the continual fear of being surprised at the work by his disapproving father, or, still worse, of being arrested and imprisoned for his part in the organization of the Society of Human Rights and in the dissemination of *Der Hessische Landbote*. As he later told Gutzkow, in the writing of *Danton* the Darmstadt policemen had been his Muses.[1] Yet, in spite of all these difficulties, *Dantons Tod* is an acknowledged masterpiece. And this is the more astonishing in that Büchner was still only twenty-one and had absolutely no previous experience of play-writing or of any other kind of poetic composition, apart from the few poems of his school-days. In all the history of literature it would be difficult to find another instance of such a brilliant dramatic career beginning so abruptly. *Götz von Berlichingen* and *Die Räuber* were not quite their authors' first essays in drama, and even Shakespeare had to be content to begin with *The Comedy of Errors* and *Titus Andronicus*.

Equally astonishing – astonishing in its boldness – is Büchner's choice of theme: the French Revolution. The great subject which Goethe repeatedly toyed with but could never quite get to grips with, the subject which Hebbel contemplated but felt no one less powerful than Shakespeare would be wise to attempt – it was precisely this great subject which the young Büchner, with an audacity worthy of Danton himself, chose for his first play. But after all, wasn't this choice of subject inevitable for Büchner? Wasn't it inevitable for one who had been so deeply involved in revolutionary action in the political sphere, in revolutionary thought and feeling in the metaphysical and aesthetic spheres? one who was consequently so deeply aware of the problems which such revolutionary attitudes necessarily involve? And doesn't the inevitability of the choice also explain its success? By his brief but intense experiment in revolutionary politics, by the whole direction of his life and thought, Büchner was better prepared for a drama about the French Revolution than any other writer before or since. He could pour into this play the sum of his observation and experience, all the emotions and reflections which his political interests had aroused in him. And we shall consequently find in it, not only many of the ideas familiar to us from Büchner's letters and theoretical writings, but even the very words in which he there expressed them.

For *Dantons Tod*, though written in such a short time, is no doubt the product of a long gestation. Wilhelm Büchner traced its genesis to the early reading of the historical compendium *Unsere Zeit*,[2] and it has been amply demonstrated that Büchner makes extensive use of this work in his drama, frequently copying from it *verbatim*, or with only slight – but usually highly significant – modifications. We know that in the early months of 1834 Büchner was again studying the French Revolution, and that this study prompted that famous letter to his fiancée of March 1834 to which we have already frequently referred. Here, in Büchner's bitter insight into 'the horrifying fatalism of history', we may surely recognize the key-thought of *Dantons Tod*, the seed from which the whole work sprang. But at this stage, in March 1834, there is no indication that Büchner was thinking of writing a play about the French Revolution. Later in that year there *is* such an indication. For the records of the Darmstadt library show that, from 1 October 1834 to 12 January 1835, Büchner borrowed a series of books dealing directly with, or more or less closely

1    *Christ at Emmaus,* by Carel von Savoy (Cf. *Lenz,* 88)

11   Rolf Boysen as Danton, Louise Martini as Marion, Deutsches Schauspielhaus, Hamburg, October 1967

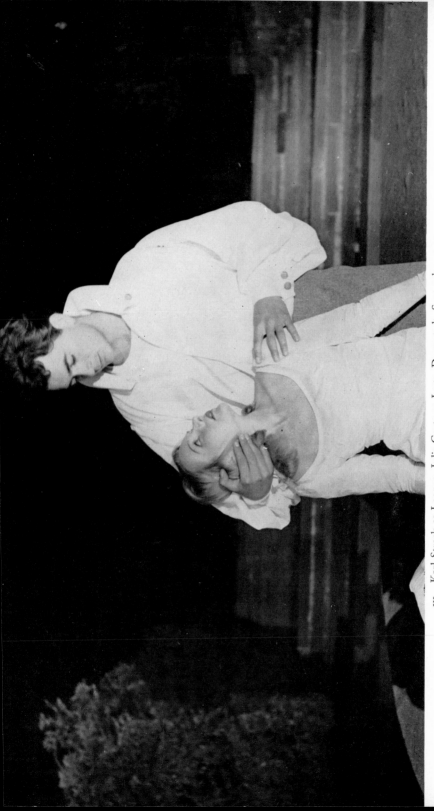

III  Karl Streck as Leonce, Julia Costa as Lena, Darmstadt, September 1951

IV Wolfgang Reinbacher as Woyzeck, Elisabeth Endriss as Marie, 'Die Brucke' 1972

related to, the history of the Revolution – Thiers' *Histoire de la Révolution française*, André Chenier's *Œuvres anciennes*, Mercier's *Tableau de Paris* (1783–9), Rousseau's *Œuvres politiques*, Mercier's *Le Nouveau Paris* (1799), Madame Roland's *Mémoires*[3] – and it looks as if he was now deliberately preparing himself for the writing of his play, which he began, as we have seen, in the middle of January. His preparatory reading was indeed much more extensive than the Darmstadt records indicate – we must note in addition to the works already named Mignet's *Histoire de la Révolution française depuis 1789 jusqu'en 1814*, Riouffe's *Mémoires d'un Détenu* and Vilate's *Mystères*[4] – and impressively evinces the earnestness of his endeavour to immerse himself in the atmosphere of the period he was about to portray. This close attention to the objective reality which was to be re-created in his imaginative writings is typical of Büchner, and we must bear it in mind when trying to grasp the true character of his art. It is perhaps not merely fanciful to recognize here a certain affinity between his artistic work and the objective empiricism of his scientific researches.

But according to Büchner's view of art, as we have learned to know it in the previous chapter, the historical reality which is merely related by the historian must come to life in the hands of the dramatist. The dramatic representation had to satisfy the criterion by which Büchner judged all works of art – it had to have 'life, possibility of being'. And in order to fulfil this requirement it was necessary to develop a new dramatic technique, a technique radically opposed to that of classical historical drama as practised by Schiller and his imitators. If Büchner's artistic theory was revolutionary, so also, naturally, was his artistic practice.

Not that, in developing this novel technique, he had to rely entirely on his own resources. He could learn much from Shakespeare, and the three plays *Hamlet*, *Macbeth* and *Julius Caesar* are no doubt the strongest influence on *Dantons Tod*. Less important, but still considerable, is the influence of Goethe's *Faust* and possibly also of *Egmont*, *Götz* and *Werther*. It has been suggested that Lenz may likewise have contributed something, which is very probable since Büchner was certainly already familiar with Lenz.[5] But the evidence for the view that he was also dependent on Grabbe's *Napoleon* (1831)[6] and Alfred de Musset's *Lorenzaccio* (1834)[7] seems inconclusive. The influence of the Romantics, especially Tieck and Brentano, is noticeable in many details of the dialogue but hardly in the form or structure of the play as a whole.

Yet Büchner remains independent – independent even of Shakespeare notwithstanding his great debt to him. The passages lifted directly from the historical sources have been calculated to amount to about one sixth of the text of *Dantons Tod*,[8] and there are innumerable reminiscences of other writers. Yet Büchner's style and technique remain the adequate expression of his individuality and of his unique situation and experience. They have their roots, not in other literature, but in life itself. It is consequently not merely in a literary sense that they are 'revolutionary', but also in the sense that they reflect Büchner's revolutionary attitude to the world; and they accordingly exhibit those negative and positive aspects which we have found to be characteristic of Büchner's political, metaphysical and aesthetic revolt. The negative aspects are the more prominent, the more immediately apparent. If this is true of Büchner's revolutionary attitude in general, it is naturally also true of the artistic practice which he developed, consciously or unconsciously, in order to express that attitude. And it was no doubt chiefly his determination to do justice to the negative aspects that necessitated his revolt against the artistic practice of the classicists with its initial tendency towards positive stylization. For Büchner the positive aspects can only be evoked out of the most unflinching statement of the negative. Out of the merciless harshness of his representation of reality beauty and goodness seem to emerge almost against the poet's will – but for that reason all the more convincingly! Thus we have a characterization which is at first sight the most unsparing exposure of the weakness, viciousness and impotence of mankind, but which also allows us to feel – and to feel all the more acutely because there can be no suspicion of spurious idealization – the solidarity, the comradeship, the love that can exist under such desperate circumstances. We have a style which shrinks from no crudity or brutality but for which beauty and tenderness – all the more touching for the coarseness of their context – are also possible. And we have a dramatic form which appears to shatter the action into fragments, but which out of these fragments builds up a unity that is all the more impressive for not having been purchased at the price of imprecision or perfunctoriness in detail.

Büchner also imparts to us, directly or indirectly, the thoughts and feelings which his view of the French Revolution – or rather his view of human life as exemplified in the French Revolution – inspired in him. And here too the negative element is the more prominent, perhaps even basically the more powerful.

## CHARACTERIZATION

'The work is based on mood or atmosphere, not on action, not on characters' (*Auf Stimmung beruht das Werk, nicht auf Handlung, nicht auf Charakteren*). These are the words of Friedrich Gundolf who, in his lecture on *Dantons Tod*, was only half-heartedly prepared to concede dramatic reality to the hero, while the other characters in the play seemed to him mere imitations, clichés or contrast-figures.[9] No doubt atmosphere counts for a great deal in the effect of Büchner's plays, yet the more we study *Dantons Tod* the more, I think, we shall be convinced of the injustice of Gundolf's criticism. And it is well for Büchner that it is unjust. We should otherwise have to admit that he had failed in his main objective, which was precisely the creation of living characters, 'human beings of flesh and blood'. We have already noticed his bitter comments on Schiller's failure to satisfy this requirement, and there is exactly the same implication in the remark which Gutzkow reports him to have made about Victor Hugo and Alfred de Musset – that 'Hugo only offered exciting situations' (*aufspannende Situationen*), 'but Musset characters, if only carved out of wood' (*Charaktere, wenn auch ausge-*

*schnitzte*). To satisfy himself, Büchner had to do a good deal better than that. His characters were to be no mere marionettes; he would have been inconsolable if it could have been justly said of them – what Gundolf was to say unjustly – that they only represented 'a standpoint or a profession or a vice or a sorrow'. He was concerned with 'the soaring and sinking of the human soul' and anxious to render it, not as 'a clay pipe with water renders the nightingale', but with some approach to adequacy.

It is in the hero of the play, in the character of Danton, that Büchner offers us the most elaborate study of that 'soaring and sinking of the human soul'. It would be a mistake to look for logical consistency in this character or to blame Büchner for its absence. Its absence is a merit, for Büchner is not concerned with abstract demonstrations but with psychological realities, and his hero has all the complexity and inconsistency that is characteristic of real human beings. He is continually subject to conflicting impulses, oscillating between opposite poles, wavering between irreconcilable convictions. He is as full of contradictions as the historical Danton is said to have been (cf. Mignet: 'Ce puissant démagogue offrait un mélange de vices et de qualités contraires'),[10] as complex as Büchner himself (indeed his problems are largely an objectification of Büchner's problems); and one might almost address to him the words with which Anatole France apostrophized that Shakespearian hero with whom he has in general such a deep affinity: 'Vous êtes prompt et lent, audacieux et timide, bienveillant et cruel, vous croyez et vous doutez, vous êtes sage et par-dessus tout vous êtes fou. En un mot, vous vivez.'[11]

In many respects he is more an anti-hero than a hero. We know that Büchner early renounced the hero-worship of his boyhood in favour of a much more sceptical view of human greatness. We may recall the passage in the letter to his fiancée where he speaks of 'a terrifying uniformity' in human nature, where he vows that he will never 'bow down before the parade horses and corner-men of history'. He imparts this scepticism both to his Danton and to his Camille. Danton can even declare it to be the reason for his antagonism to Robespierre: 'I could never look at such pompous Catos without giving them a kick' (*Ich konnte dergleichen gespreizte Catonen nie ansehn, ohne ihnen einen Tritt zu geben* – I. i. 12); and Camille insists that the differences between people are not so great as is commonly imagined, we are all scoundrels and angels, blockheads and geniuses at one and the same time – tear off the masks and we shall see everywhere 'the same age-old, innumerable, imperishable sheep's head' (*den einen uralten, zahllosen, unverwüstlichen Schaafskopf* – IV. v. 70). Danton, like Camille, is no hero in the conventional sense, and he knows very well that he is not.

Our first glimpse of him, as the play opens, certainly reveals him in anything but a heroic state of mind. We see him listless, bored, dissolute and despairing. An impenetrable loneliness seems to separate him even from the person nearest and dearest to him, his wife Julie; and if he still loves her, it is with a love almost indistinguishable from his longing for the peace of death: 'No, Julie, I love you like the grave' (*Nein Julie, ich liebe dich wie das Grab* – I. i. 9). In the next scene in which he appears he is in the Palais Royal with the beautiful hetaera Marion at his feet. But again his longing for love is unsatisfied: 'Why can't I quite encompass all your beauty, quite enfold it in myself?' (*Warum kann ich deine Schönheit nicht ganz in mich fassen, sie nicht ganz umschließen?* – I. v. 22). And meanwhile, abandoning himself to vain longing and profound despondency, he remains deaf to his friends' most urgent appeals to him for some action to defeat the dangerous machinations of their enemies. Nowhere, in these opening scenes, the slightest stirring of that mighty energy, that boundless audacity, for which the name of Danton was famous.

As the play proceeds we gradually learn the reason for this strange and disconcerting phenomenon. The reasons are complex and not easy to state adequately, but one can discern two principal factors. One is Danton's sense of guilt; the other his sense of moral and political impotence.

It is not that he believes his part in the revolution to have been politically wrong. He never wavers in his claim to have tried to gain freedom for his country. He never admits that it was wrong to have tried to do so. We have already noticed his remark to Payne on being committed to the Luxembourg: 'What *you* have done for the welfare of your country I tried to do for mine. I was less fortunate . . .' In his first speech before the Revolutionary Tribunal he recalls with pride how often his powerful voice had been raised in the cause of the people (*Meine Stimme, die ich so oft für die Sache des Volkes ertönen ließ . . .* – III. iv. 52). He insists that the boldness of his words and demeanour is still dedicated to the welfare of the Republic (*meine Kühnheit, . . . der ich mich hier zum Besten der Republik gegen meine erbärmlichen Ankläger bediene*). He claims that men of his stamp are invaluable in revolutions and that on their brow the genius of liberty hovers (*Männer meines Schlages sind in Revolutionen unschätzbar, auf ihrer Stirne schwebt das Genie der Freiheit*).

Some critics are inclined to discount the importance of this testimony. Wolfgang Martens writes:

Danton in fact capitulates, he strikes his sails, he gives up. His furious resistance before the Tribunal is only a last violent, physical rebellion in which the inborn hue of feeling, rage and indignant pride break through once more. Spiritually, in his inmost being, he is broken, marked by death – from the first scene onwards.[12]

But if it is wounded pride that prompts Danton's passionate defence, the fact remains that the object of this pride is still his part in the revolution, the service he has done to the cause of freedom. And the interpreter is no more entitled to disregard this fact than to ignore what Danton says or does in any of the other scenes of the play. To emphasize Danton's despair, the mortal sickness of his soul, while overlooking his revolutionary pride, is to over-simplify his character and to sacrifice Büchner's conception to the convenience of our interpretation. For there can be no doubt of the sincerity of that pride. Danton is not trying to fool his judges; there is no pretence in his words, no histrionics. The very fact of his despair is sufficient warrant for that; for what has he to gain by lying? He knows that he is doomed, and can end his speech with the words: 'Now you know Danton – only a few hours more and he will fall asleep in the arms of fame' (*Jetzt kennt Ihr Danton; noch wenige Stunden und er wird in den Armen des Ruhmes entschlummern).* In any case, Danton is no Robespierre, no Saint-Just. He is too powerful and magnanimous, even too careless and indifferent, to be capable of the littleness of lying or of any petty stratagem. Who can doubt the depth and genuineness of his indignation as he picks up a copy of the indictment and cries: 'When I glance at this infamous libel I feel my whole being tremble' (*Wenn ich einen Blick auf dieße Schandschrift werfe fühle ich mein ganzes Wesen beben),* or when he exclaims: 'They accuse *me* of having conspired with Mirabeau, with Dumouriez, with Orléans, of having crawled at the feet of wretched despots... You, miserable Saint-Just, will answer to posterity for this calumny!' (*Mich klagt man an, mit Mirabeau, mit Dumouriez, mit Orléans conspirirt, zu den Füßen elender Despoten gekrochen zu haben... Du elender St. Just wirst der Nachwelt für dieße Lästerung verantwortlich seyn!).* And surely it is only because of the complete sincerity of his words that they can so profoundly move his hearers. The icy logic of Saint-Just's speech had also won prolonged applause in the Convention. But Robespierre was obviously in the ascendant then, and it was safe to applaud his henchman. Danton wins greater and more persistent applause at a time when it is highly dangerous to side with him. And what is still more remarkable, and surely deeply significant, is that this effect of Danton's impassioned eloquence extends not only to the people in the play, but also – whenever the work has been adequately performed – to the audiences of the twentieth century. Walter Höllerer – like Martens, playing down the importance of Danton's speeches in his own defence – asserts that the best performances of the play have always been those in which 'the unreal-reality of the smallest action and individual impulse passes judgement on the obviousness of the *heroice dicta*'.[13] How superior a good actor can be to an academic critic, how much greater justice he can do to the complexity of a role, will become evident if one contrasts Höllerer's assertion with Wolfram Viehweg's account of Alexander Moissi's performance of the part of Danton under the direction of Max Reinhardt:

Moissi, one might almost say, was a delicately built Danton, all lightness, with a distant smile. He wore on his head a high, curly rococo wig. His action and speech were soft and restrained until, in the great speech for the defence before the Revolutionary Tribunal, he unleashed the whole force of his temperament. At a guest performance in Basel on 3 June 1917 the audience was so carried away by this scene that it joined with loud shouting and hand-clapping in the stage-crowd's demonstration of sympathy and approval . . . This *Danton* production was an enormous success for Reinhardt. It remained for years on the programme of *Das deutsche Theater*.[14]

A comparable electrifying effect in the Tribunal scene is reported to have been achieved by Gustav Knuth under the direction of Gründgens.[15] Evidently Höllerer's assertion is not in accordance with the facts; we must grant its full significance to Danton's defence of his revolutionary career.

Nor is it strictly faithful to the text to say, as Martens does, that Danton 'strikes his sails, he gives up'. We must look carefully at this statement as it has an important bearing on the often repeated criticism that *Dantons Tod* is deficient in action, that the hero of the play is too passive to be properly dramatic.

Certainly, as we have already observed, in the opening scenes of the play Danton is utterly inert and lethargic. He is almost convinced that his cause is lost, and when his friends urge him to bestir himself he reacts at first not at all and then half-heartedly only. Yet it would not be true to say that he does nothing. He visits Robespierre and taunts him into betraying his state of mind, his probable intentions. Alarmed by the insight thus gained, Danton recognizes the need for immediate action: 'We mustn't lose a moment, we must show ourselves!' (*Wir dürfen keinen Augenblick verlieren, wir müssen uns zeigen!* – I. vi. 27). At the beginning of the second Act we find that he has accordingly consulted the representatives of the 'Sections' of Paris to see how far they might be prepared to support him, but the result has been disappointing: 'they were respectful but like funeral undertakers' (*Ich war bey den Sektionen; sie waren ehrfurchtsvoll, aber wie Leichenbitter* – II. i. 31). Thus he falls back into despondency and lassitude, from which he is only aroused when called upon to defend his honour as a revolutionary in his first speech before the

Tribunal. Yet his weariness and distaste for life make him almost indifferent to the outcome of the trial:

Uebrigens, was liegt mir an euch und eurem Urtheil. Ich hab' es euch schon gesagt: das Nichts wird bald mein Asyl seyn – das Leben ist mir zur Last, man mag mir es entreißen, ich sehne mich danach es abzuschütteln. (III. iv. 53)

It is only when the hideous reality of death draws closer that he fully awakens from his apathy and, in his second speech before the Tribunal, makes his first really serious attempt to save the lives of his friends and of himself. The difference between this second speech and the first has not been sufficiently noticed by the critics. It is only now, in this second and final plea, that Danton utters the name of Robespierre and openly denounces him as a traitor. No longer concerned merely with his personal honour, he moves from defence to attack and fiercely denounces the *policies* of Robespierre and Saint-Just, so that the question whether Danton and his friends can be saved is now seen to be identical with the question whether the Revolution can be saved. Thus if we faithfully follow the text it seems impossible to escape the conclusion that in the course of the play Danton does not become less political but more so – his last public speech is the most political of all. And moreover it nearly succeeds! Saint-Just and his associates are obviously badly rattled. It is only by the most pitiful trickery, by packing the jury and by exploiting the accident of Laflotte's so opportune treachery, that they are able to carry the day and secure the condemnation of the accused. Thus it is not true that there is no dramatic conflict, no element of suspense in the play. Of course we know what the outcome must be if we know the history of the Revolution. But in the action of the play as Büchner presents it to us there is a genuine struggle between Robespierre and Danton, the result of which is not a foregone conclusion but remains long in the balance. And as for the alleged passivity of the hero, one can only say of Danton what one must say of Hamlet: not that he fails to act, but that his action is too long delayed, and that this delay has fatal consequences for others as well as for himself.

Nevertheless, there *is* that delay, and we have still to analyse its causes. Here again a comparison with Hamlet can be helpful, not merely in order to demonstrate – what to most readers is obvious – that Hamlet and Danton are in some sense alike, but because a study of their likeness can throw their differences into relief, and enable us to grasp more precisely the originality and characteristic quality of Büchner's conception. We have already noticed one trait that is common to Hamlet and Danton – their fatal hesitancy, their blunted resolution. And it is not difficult to see that this weakness is also in both cases the effect of a profound melancholy, which seems to deprive life of its purpose and convict energy of futility. The parallel still holds good when we inquire into the cause of this melancholy: in both cases it is due to a strong sense of guilt, a deep disappointment with the quality of human nature. But the guilt which sickens Hamlet and robs him of his faith in mankind is the murderous lust and ambition of his uncle and, more unbearable than all else, the frailty of his mother. The guilt that oppresses Danton is his own.

However proud Danton may be of the service he has rendered to the cause of freedom, he cannot forget that in the course of that service he has been responsible for the most appalling actions, in particular for the massacre of the aristocrats in the prisons in September 1792. He is haunted by the thought of September as Macbeth is haunted by the memory of Duncan and by the ghost of Banquo. Not that he believes the September massacres to have been a needless atrocity. He is convinced that, politically, they were absolutely necessary; and his conviction is shared by Julie:

JULIE. Die Könige waren nur noch vierzig Stunden von Paris . . .
DANTON. Die Festungen gefallen, die Aristocraten in der Stadt . . .
JULIE. Die Republik war verloren.
DANTON. Ja verloren. Wir konnten den Feind nicht im Rücken lassen, wir
    wären Narren gewesen, zwei Feinde auf einem Brett, wir oder sie, der Stärkere
    stößt den Schwächeren hinunter, ist das nicht billig?
JULIE. Ja, ja.
DANTON. Wir schlugen sie, das war kein Mord, das war Krieg nach innen.
JULIE. Du hast das Vaterland gerettet.

DANTON. Ja das hab' ich. Das war Nothwehr, wir mußten. Der Mann am Kreuze
   hat sich's bequem gemacht: es muß ja Aergerniß kommen, doch wehe dem,
   durch welchen Aergerniß kommt. (II. v. 41)

I believe one would completely misinterpret Büchner if one were
to suppose that there is anything either hypocritical or self-
deceptive in Danton's claim to have '*had* to do it'. Danton, I
repeat, is no Robespierre, and to regard as hypocrisy or self-
deception his claim to have been driven by necessity is to reduce
him to the level of Robespierre. It is also to blunt the edge of the
tragedy, to break the force of the dramatic conflict – not the
conflict between Danton and Robespierre, but the still deeper
conflict within Danton's own mind. For the peculiarity of
Büchner's conception is that he sees the sense of guilt arising from
situations that are unavoidable, from actions which, because they
are necessary, can even from a certain point of view be regarded
as glorious and magnificent. The September massacres are actually
mentioned with pride in Danton's first speech before the Tribunal:

Ich habe im September die junge Brut der Revolution mit den zerstückten
Leibern der Aristocraten geäzt. Meine Stimme hat aus dem Golde der Aristocraten
und Reichen dem Volke Waffen geschmiedet. Meine Stimme war der Orkan,
welcher die Satelliten des Despotismus unter Wogen von Bajonetten begrub.
(III. iv. 54)

Yet it is the word 'September' which haunts his dreams, which he
seems to hear at night re-echoing through the silent streets of
Paris, which the very stones seem to prate about. His glorious
deed, the annihilation of the enemies of the Republic, has precisely the same effect upon 'coward conscience' as the vile crimes
of a Macbeth or a Richard III. The necessity of the horror does
not make it less grievous to his feelings. It rather intensifies his
despair. For what kind of a world must it be in which such things
are *necessary*? Danton writhes under the curse of this necessity
(*der Fluch des Muß*), and his whole being revolts against the
divine cruelty or indifference which could pronounce the dreadful
law: 'It must needs be that offences come, but woe to that man
by whom the offence cometh.'
   Here we can see clearly the 'turn of the screw' which Büchner

gave to tragedy, the peculiar insight – related, one must admit, to all modern nihilism – which carried him into darker regions than Shakespeare, except possibly in *King Lear*, ever explored. For in Shakespearian tragedy, as A. C. Bradley remarked, it is never *good* that produces the tragic convulsion but almost invariably evil in the fullest sense, 'plain moral evil'. And since it is only or chiefly evil that disturbs the order of the world, we may infer that 'this order cannot be friendly to evil or indifferent between evil and good, any more than a body which is convulsed by poison is friendly to it or indifferent to the distinction between poison and food'.[16] In other words, the evil is accidental or extrinsic to the order of the world. And that is why, in Shakespeare, when the tragic convulsion has passed over, the State and society can return to their normal healthy condition. (It is true that a recurrence of the disorder is always in principle possible; and it is sometimes so terrible while it lasts that we care infinitely more for the defeated hero, however guilty, than for the normality which his defeat restores.) But in Büchner it can be *good* that produces the tragedy, it can be the best and noblest endeavours of a man – what at least he believes to be the best and noblest in the given situation. In other words, the evil is not accidental or extrinsic but inherent in the order of the world; and the offences which we commit and for which we suffer the torments of remorse are offences which we *must* commit. So that, for Büchner, the tragic convulsion cannot be succeeded by a return to healthy normality. The tragic convulsion is permanent, and *Dantons Tod* concludes with an endless vista of civil strife, dictatorship and war: 'I am leaving everything in a terrible confusion' (*Ich lasse Alles in einer schrecklichen Verwirrung* – IV. v. 69).

The debilitating effect of Danton's sense of guilt is aggravated by his sense of political impotence – by his too clear awareness of the inefficacy of human effort, the deceptiveness of moral freedom. Büchner imparts to his hero his own insight into the unconscious forces that govern our conduct and the uncontrollable laws which determine the course of history. Using almost the same – only slightly stronger – words than those Büchner himself had used in his letter to Minna, Danton asks Julie: 'What is it inside of us that whores, lies, steals and murders?' (*Was ist das, was in uns hurt, lügt, stiehlt und mordet? –* II. v. 41). And, similarly, that awareness of the 'horrifying fatalism of history' which had cast its shadow over Büchner's own political activity is reflected in Danton's symbolical dream:

DANTON. Träumtest? ja ich träumte, doch das war anders, ich will dir es gleich sagen, mein armer Kopf ist schwach, gleich! so jezt hab ich's! Unter mir keuchte die Erdkugel in ihrem Schwung, ich hatte sie wie ein wildes Roß gepackt, mit riesigen Gliedern wühlt' ich in ihrer Mähne und preßt' ich ihre Rippen, das Haupt abwärts gebückt, die Haare flatternd über dem Abgrund. So ward ich geschleift ...

Danton's apocalyptic vision may recall Egmont's demonic image of the bolting 'sun-steeds of time' which leave us no choice but to grasp the reins courageously and try to steer the chariot of our fate clear of rocks and precipices. But Egmont's image at least allows to skill and courage some influence of our fortunes, and the hero can entrust himself with confidence to the power that governs him. In Danton's vision there is neither any such confidence nor any degree of human control over destiny. Danton feels himself dragged along helplessly by the force he has rashly attempted to master, the force of the Revolution. At first the direction of this mighty historical force had concurred with his wishes, and its purposes had been well served by his thunderous voice, by his puissant personality. Dragging him through horror and guilt, the Revolution had raised him to the height of his power: 'We did not make the Revolution, the Revolution made us' (*Wir haben nicht die Revolution, sondern die Revolution hat uns gemacht –* II. i. 32); now it continues uncontrollably on its course and casts him aside like a useless relic. He has lost the support of the Sections, the defeated factions hold him responsible for their defeat, the people envy him his luxurious mode of life, the wealth and leisure that enable him to indulge his vices. He can see only one chance left of overthrowing Robespierre – an appeal to the Convention. But it would involve bloodshed such as had attended the fall of the Girondins: 'It would be another 31st of May, they wouldn't voluntarily yield' (*Es gäbe einen 31. Mai, sie würden nicht gutwillig weichen*). And Danton has no wish to load still further his over-burdened conscience:

Und wenn es gienge – ich will lieber guillotinirt werden, als guillotiniren lassen. Ich hab es satt, wozu sollen wir Menschen miteinander kämpfen? Wir sollten uns nebeneinander setzen und Ruhe haben. Es wurde ein Fehler gemacht, wie wir geschaffen wurden, es fehlt uns etwas, ich habe keinen Namen dafür, wir werden es einander nicht aus den Eingeweiden herauswühlen, was sollen wir uns drum die Leiber aufbrechen? (II. i. 32)

'We should sit down side by side and be at peace.' The word peace – *Ruhe* – is frequently on Danton's lips, and not without reason. It is peace that he longs for above all else. One has the impression that his enormous expenditure of energy in the earlier phases of the Revolution – especially since it appears to have been all in vain – has left him very tired. Indeed he says to Camille, who has accused him of indolence: 'I am not indolent, but tired' (*Ich bin nicht träg, aber müde* – II. iii. 38). It is only in profound peace, in perfect oblivion, that he can see salvation for himself and for mankind in general; but it is a salvation that appears to him for ever unattainable. If nothingness is God, he must confess himself an atheist, for he disbelieves in the possibility of nothingness:

PHILIPPEAU. Was willst du denn?
DANTON. Ruhe.
PHILIPPEAU. Die ist in Gott.
DANTON. Im Nichts. Versenke dich in was Ruhigers, als das Nichts und wenn die höchste Ruhe Gott ist, ist nicht das Nichts Gott? Aber ich bin ein Atheist. Der verfluchte Satz: etwas kann nicht zu nichts werden![17] und ich bin etwas, das ist der Jammer!
    Die Schöpfung hat sich so breit gemacht, da ist nichts leer, Alles voll Gewimmels.
    Das Nichts hat sich ermordet, die Schöpfung ist seine Wunde, wir sind die Blutstropfen, die Welt ist das Grab worin es fault. Das lautet verrückt, es ist aber doch was Wahres daran. (III. vii. 61)

In this 'mad' reversal of values, which makes creation equivalent to a decaying corpse and nothingness equivalent to God, some critics have seen a foreshadowing of existentialism.[18] But in existentialism nothingness is the object of *Angst*, while for Danton it is the object of longing. His attitude is rather comparable with

that of Shakespeare's Timon, whose agony ultimately drives him
to a similar reversal of the values of life and death:

> My long sickness
> Of health, and living, now begins to mend,
> And nothing brings me all things.
> (*Timon of Athens*, V. i)

The work which constitutes the most complete statement of
Schopenhauer's pessimistic philosophy ends with a comparable
apotheosis of nothingness.[19] And R. Majut aptly quotes the remark of Nietzsche:

The hypnotic feeling of nothingness, the peace of the deepest sleep, in short,
*freedom from suffering* – to those who suffer and are most deeply dispirited that
may well appear to be the highest good, the supreme value; they may feel it as
something positive, indeed as that which is essentially positive. (In accordance
with the same logic of feeling all pessimistic religions regard nothingness as
God).[20]

In the light of Danton's political and metaphysical hopelessness
it is not difficult to understand his listlessness, his remissness –
perhaps we may call it his *acedia*.[21] Having no goal within his
reach, no ideal he can aspire to, he has no incentive to action.
Life having lost its purpose, it becomes merely a burden, and
time a yawning expanse which has somehow to be filled up – with
talk and debauchery, with dandyism and narcissism, with the
bustle of activity and all manner of opiates. It is that 'sickness
unto death' of which Kierkegaard speaks – that *ennui* which was
such a prevalent malady in the age of Büchner and Heine, of
Musset and Leopardi.[22] We shall find it one of the principal
themes of *Leonce und Lena*, but it is already prominent enough in
*Dantons Tod*. For Danton there is even an intolerable tedium in
having to dress and undress every day, and he complains about
it in a tone which he has to admit is childish (II. i. 31). It becomes
literally too much trouble to him to raise his voice to save his
life: 'I would have to shout, and it isn't worth while' (*ich müßte
schreien, das ist mir der Mühe zuviel* – II. i. 33). The phrase 'it isn't
worth while' is as frequently on his lips as the word *Notwehr*
in a political context or *Ruhe* in a metaphysical. Nothing seems to

him worth while. When offered an opportunity to escape from Paris and save his life, he cannot convince himself that it is worth while to take it – worth while to preserve his body and his torturing memory and miss the chance of oblivion which the grave – in spite of his philosophical theories – might after all give him (II. iv. 39). True, he also imagines that in any case his enemies won't dare to attack him (*sie werden's nicht wagen*). But that is only an afterthought, it is not the decisive consideration. Danton's attitude to death, as to so much else, is ambivalent. Physically shrinking from it with horror, he is yet powerfully drawn to it, he flirts with it (*ich kokettire mit dem Tod*), he more than half consents to it. *Danton's Death* is the story of Danton's will to die.

Yet in the midst of his despair Danton does not lose his warm and generous humanity, and it moves us all the more deeply for the grimness of the background against which it reveals itself. We have seen how he could rouse himself from his lethargy for a last magnificent release of energy in the speeches in his defence. Notwithstanding his many weaknesses, his occasional posing and affectation, his frequent coarseness and dissoluteness, he deeply loves his wife and is deeply loved by her. If he shrinks from the physical reality of death, he is not cowed by it. He can still mount the scaffold bravely, and in these last moments seems more concerned about his friends than about himself. How touching is his gentleness towards his less robust friend Camille, whose nerves seem in danger of cracking under the vituperation of the rabble: 'Be calm, my boy, you have shouted yourself hoarse' (*Ruhig, mein Junge, du hast dich heiser geschrieen*). And – in the very moment of ultimate defeat – what a triumph of defiant humanity in the words he addresses to the executioner who prevents Hérault from embracing him:

Willst du grausamer seyn als der Tod? Kannst du verhindern, daß unsere Köpfe sich auf dem Boden des Korbes küssen? (IV. vii. 74)

These are his last words of all. Shortly before this, in the last of his soliloquies, his pity and love for his fellow men – that noble

emotion which is characteristic of Büchner himself as well as of
his heroes, and which is worlds removed from the coldness
of consistent nihilism – express themselves in the beautiful
words:

Wie schimmernde Thränen sind die Sterne durch die Nacht gesprengt, es muß
ein großer Jammer in dem Aug seyn, von dem sie abträufelten. (IV. iii. 67)

Not that such loving pity can justify the world whose suffering
so often occasions it. I think we would misunderstand Büchner
if we were to suppose that. He knew too well the limitations of
even the best of human feelings. But as he shows us all things with
the veracity of a true poet, so he shows us these feelings also;
and we find in them – no solution of our problems, no salvation
for mankind – but such consolation as can be given to us:
'comfort in the strength of love', the balm of tears.

Büchner's Danton is certainty a 'human being of flesh and
blood', he certainly has that quality of 'life, possibility of being'
to which Büchner attached such decisive importance. But to what
extent, in drawing this character, has Büchner remained faithful
to his principle that the historical dramatist must 'come as near
as possible to history as it really happened'? To what extent is
his portrait of Danton historically true? It is certainly not true in
every detail. Landau and Bergemann remark that the historical
Danton, though in general given to dissipation, is unlikely to
have consorted with grisettes in the last period of his life when
he was so deeply in love with his young wife Sophie Gély.
Bergemann notes that Danton appeared three times before the
Revolutionary Tribunal, not only twice as in Büchner's play.
Thieberger records words of Danton which Büchner ascribes to
Lacroix, and this is only one of several instances in the play where
Büchner has deviated from the historically authentic allocation of
speeches. But of course there was nothing in Büchner's principles
or convictions that required him to regard all historical facts as of
equal importance. As Thieberger says, Büchner is not at all
concerned about 'l'exactitude du détail historique' but rather
about 'l'atmosphère, la tonalité, le fond'.[23] It is *this* that seems to

him important, and it is to this that he remains faithful. We have already noticed the diligent study of the sources which enabled him to achieve this fidelity. And everywhere, in the play, we find evidence of his deep respect for the historical reality in what appears to him to be its essential aspects. (It is true that it is often precisely in details that the historical reality most vividly manifests itself, and therefore details have a great importance for Büchner – but not because of their factual correctness.) As Viëtor well expresses it:

Büchner is full of reverence – one might say that he has a *piety* – towards reality (*er ist fromm dem Wirklichen gegenüber*). Alterations of the historical material in the free manner which Goethe allows himself in *Egmont* or Schiller in the *Jungfrau von Orleans* must appear to him inadmissible, indeed presumptuous. He wants to present just this precise moment and character in its unadulterated, original reality.[24]

And of course he is least of all concerned with 'ennoblement', with 'transfiguration', with any sort of 'idealization' of his hero.

But there is obviously no *mechanical* way by which Büchner can achieve the truth he is aiming at. He cannot, as the Naturalists are inclined to do, rely on a particular technique to reproduce reality almost automatically. In his technique he is in fact much closer to Shakespeare than to the Naturalists, and he also follows the example of Shakespeare in his manner of dealing with history. Like Shakespeare, he often lifts whole sentences out of the source material, modifying them only slightly or not at all. This has the advantage of helping him to maintain the authentic tone and atmosphere of the period and situation which he is trying to present to us. And it has the further advantage of transfusing into the speeches of his characters something of the original force and passion of their historical prototypes. The stupendous words which Danton addresses to his executioner are, with only the slightest modification, the actual last words of the historical Danton; and the great speeches before the Revolutionary Tribunal owe much of their fire to the passionate sentences with which the real Danton sought to defend himself – sentences which Büchner is content to borrow because he rightly feels that no fictitious eloquence could possibly equal them. But often the historical sources offer only the briefest hint of a scene, which Büchner has then to conjure up before our eyes. The scenes II. iv ('Freies Feld') and II. vi ('Strasse vor Dantons Haus') are based on only a few lines of Mignet and *Unsere Zeit*, and the impressive intervening scene, II. v ('Ein Zimmer. Es ist Nacht') – the vision of the dreadful hallucinations arising from Danton's tormented conscience – is Büchner's work, not the historians'. Indeed, the kind of reality which Büchner is presenting in such passages as the following:

DANTON. Wie ich an's Fenster kam – (*er sieht hinaus*) die Stadt ist ruhig, alle Lichter aus ...
JULIE. Ein Kind schreit in der Nähe.
DANTON. Wie ich an's Fenster kam – durch alle Gassen schrie und zetert' es: September! (II. v. 40)

– this kind of reality is apprehensible only by the poetic imagination, only by that 'gift of vision' which Büchner's aesthetic implicitly demanded. Thanks to this gift, a poet can sometimes offer a truer view of a historical figure than the historians whose works he uses – Shakespeare is said to have achieved this feat in his portraits of Caesar and of Cleopatra.[25] And it is possible that Büchner's Danton also, thanks to the personal experience and imaginative insight devoted to his portrayal, has a deeper as well as a more vivid truth than can be gathered from the pages of Thiers and Mignet.

The character of Robespierre in *Dantons Tod* is an almost equally impressive triumph of 'visionary realism', to use the expression with which Ludwig Marcuse aptly characterizes Büchner's art.[26] This is a briefer, more concentrated portrait than that of Danton – Robespierre appears only in the first two acts of the play – but it is hardly less masterly. Here too we see 'the soaring and sinking' of a human soul; here too we have to do with a psychological rather than a logical consistency. Robespierre also is a character at war with himself, and in some respects his problems are similar to Danton's. He also is tormented by a sense of guilt; he also feels himself to be at the mercy of unconscious, uncontrollable forces. And once again this presentiment is expressed in an astonishingly modern way:

(*Er tritt ans Fenster.*) Die Nacht schnarcht über der Erde und wälzt sich im wüsten Traum. Gedanken, Wünsche kaum geahnt, wirr und gestaltlos, die scheu sich vor des Tages Licht verkrochen, empfangen jezt Form und Gewand und stehlen sich in das stille Haus des Traums . . . Und ist nicht unser Wachen ein hellerer Traum, sind wir nicht Nachtwandler, ist nicht unser Handeln, wie das im Traum, nur deutlicher, bestimmter, durchgeführter? Wer will uns darum schelten? . . . Die Sünde ist im Gedanken. Ob der Gedanke That wird, ob ihn der Körper nachspielt, das ist Zufall. (I. vi. 28 f.)[27]

Thus Robespierre, in one sense the antagonist of Danton, is in another sense akin to him: he is a fainter, distorted reflection of him. His gazing out of the window on Paris at night obviously foreshadows and corresponds to Danton's dreadful nocturnal visions in the second Act, and is a scene of comparable imaginative power.

Yet there is an essential difference between the two men. The strongest driving force in Danton's life has been his love of freedom, his concern for the success of the Revolution; and though this force has now been crossed by his disillusionment and *taedium vitae*, it can still make itself genuinely felt in him. But in Robespierre the strongest force is personal ambition *rationalized* as concern for the Republic, and Robespierre cannot prevent himself from occasionally seeing through his self-deception. When he has the effrontery to ask: 'Who told you that any innocent person has been punished?' (*Wer sagt dir denn, daß ein Unschuldiger getroffen worden sey?* – I. vi. 27), it is not only Danton who is staggered by the enormity of the claim; Robespierre himself, in his inmost soul, knows it to be false. When the thought occurs to him that people will say his attack on Danton was prompted by his jealousy of a greater man, he cannot help wondering – 'And what if they were right?' (*Und wenn sie Recht hätten?* – I. vi. 28). The contemptuous phrases by which Danton suggests to him that his policy is based on a lie, that consistency with his own principles would require him not to confound the innocent with the guilty, keep recurring to his mind like blood seeping through a bandage. And he is at last reduced to the desperate confession: 'I don't know what part of me is deceiving the other' (*Ich weiß nicht, was in mir das Andere belügt*).

He is basically a very uncertain, a very frightened man. But he is all the more dangerous for that! The greater his fear and self-distrust, the more he is forced to seem outwardly firm and incorruptible and the more he must strive to reassure himself. And so he strikes at his enemies with frantic impatience as if he could thereby lay their ghosts, as if by killing them he could stifle the dreadful thoughts they suggest to him: 'Away with them! Quickly! Only the dead never come again! (*Weg mit ihnen! Rasch! nur die Todten kommen nicht wieder*). And again: 'Then quickly, tomorrow. No long death-struggle! I have become squeamish of late. Only be quick about it!' (*Dann rasch, morgen. Keinen langen Todeskampf! Ich bin empfindlich seit einigen Tagen. Nur rasch! – I. vi. 30*).

Robespierre is the type of semi-conscious hypocrite who stylizes himself as a modern Messiah in order to canalize the forces of popular fanaticism. At his very first appearance in the play we hear him addressed in a tone of hysterical religious reverence – in a tone which, as Thieberger observes,[28] is exactly characteristic of a woman fascinated by the figure of a *Führer* or *duce*: 'Hear the Messiah who has been sent to choose and to judge . . .' (*Hört den Messias, der gesandt ist zu wählen und zu richten* – I. ii. 15). Danton describes him as 'the dogma of the Revolution' (*das Dogma der Revolution* – II. i. 32), and Billaud as 'an impotent Mohammed' (*ein impotenter Mahomet* – III. vi. 59). It is probable, as Lehmann argues, that this allusion to Mohammed may be due to the influence of Fichte and ultimately to that of Voltaire, whose drama *Le Fanatisme, ou Mahomet le Prophète* paints an impressive picture of the deliberate exploitation of religious fanaticism for the purposes of political domination;[29] though we should not overlook the fact that Robespierre is described in *Unsere Zeit* as 'a new Mohammed', and Mignet relates that some people identified him with 'the Messiah' whose advent was prophesied by Catherine Théot.[30] What is more important and apparently quite unnoticed by the critics is the possibility that in his characterization of Robespierre Büchner may have been thinking, not only of Mohammed, but also of Cromwell. The similarity of Tieck's remarks about Cromwell in *William Lovell* to the expressions which Büchner puts into the mouth of Robespierre seems unlikely to be merely accidental, especially in view of the obvious influence elsewhere of Tieck's novel on Büchner's play:

> Der Lügner kann auf seine eigenen Erfindungen schwören, ohne einen Meineid zu tun, denn er kann in diesem Augenblicke völlig davon überzeugt sein ... Auf die Art mußte der große Mann (Cromwell) bald zweifelhaft werden, was in ihm wahr, was falsch, was Erdichtung, was Überzeugung sei; er mußte sich in manchen Stunden für nichts als einen gemeinen Betrüger, in andern wieder für ein auserwähltes Rüstzeug des Himmels halten.[31]

Robespierre is not unwilling to think of himself as 'a chosen instrument of Heaven'. When Camille describes him as 'that Messiah anointed with blood ... on a Mount Calvary where he sacrifices and is not sacrificed' (*Dießer Blutmessias Robespierre auf seinem Kalvarienberge ..., auf dem er opfert und nicht geopfert wird* – I. vi. 30), he accepts the expression and proceeds to toy with the madly presumptuous thought that there is more merit in saving mankind by shedding *their* blood (as he has done) than by shedding one's own (as Christ did). Like Danton, he feels that he *had* to kill. But while Danton bitterly resents the necessity of this guilt and can never quite forgive himself for it, Robespierre regards his voluntary acceptance of it as proof of his superior merit:

> Er [Christus] hat sie sündigen gemacht und ich nehme die Sünde auf mich. Er hatte die Wollust des Schmerzes und ich habe die Quaal des Henkers. – Wer hat sich mehr verleugnet, Ich oder er? (I. vi. 30)

And yet he too, in the end, is driven to recognize, as Danton does, that nobody can really save mankind, neither he himself nor any other 'Messiah'; that his pretended superiority is a lie; and that in sacrificing Camille, almost the only person to whom he has ever been greatly attached, he is achieving nothing but the establishment of his own dismal and solitary dominion:

Mein Camille! – Sie gehen Alle von mir – es ist Alles wüst und leer – ich bin allein. (I. vi. 31)

In this moment Robespierre too is human.

On the whole Robespierre is a figure who has become more familiar and intelligible to us in the twentieth century than he could have been in Büchner's own time. He is a remarkable prefiguration of the dictators of our age. Reinhard Roche, in an essay entitled 'stilus demagogicus',[32] has shown in detail how the perfidious rhetoric of Robespierre's covert attack on Danton in the Jacobin club (I. iii. 17 ff.) exactly anticipates the mendacious demagogic style of Hitler and the Nazis. (The bold directness of *Der Hessische Landbote* is far removed from that devious style and is one of the best proofs of the injustice of equating its authors with Robespierre.) Robespierre's physical nervousness – the typical insecurity of a tyrant – which makes him call frantically for lights when he hears some one entering the room in the dark (I. vi. 29) is exactly paralleled by the fearfulness of Stalin in Solzhenitsyn's description:

The more people he destroyed the more he was oppressed by fear for his own life. His brain was constantly at work devising improvements in the arrangements for his security . . .[33]

Robespierre, as Büchner sees him, is the Stalin of the French Revolution.

Whether this is quite fair to the historical Robespierre is disputable. Some historians would deny the element of hypocrisy and egotism in the character of Robespierre, but Büchner's sources insisted on it. Thiers, for example, describes his denunciation of Danton in the Convention as 'le comble de l'hypocrisie et de l'adresse' and Mignet describes him as having 'les dehors du patriotisme', as 'associant toujours la cause de sa vanité à celle de la multitude'.[34] Büchner has evidently tried to represent this character faithfully in accordance with the view of it which his sources conveyed to him; and the result – whether or not it is just to the historical Robespierre – is at any rate a wonderfully truthful delineation of a certain political type. But what is still more admirable, and characteristic of Büchner's boundless human sympathy, is that he is not content to let his Robespierre be merely a type, but also shows him to be a human being; he lets us feel the element of humanity even in this bloodstained monster.

Although, as I have said,[35] it would be a great mistake to regard Robespierre as representing the political position of Büchner, it is nevertheless true that Büchner occasionally allows him to express ideas more or less similar to his own. Thus Robespierre's words: 'The aristocracy is not yet dead, the healthy strength of the people must supplant that surfeited and effete class' (*Die gute Gesellschaft ist noch nicht todt, die gesunde Volkskraft muß sich an die Stelle dießer nach allen Richtungen abgekitzelten Klasse setzen* – I. vi. 26) are very close to Büchner's thought in the later letter to Gutzkow: 'I believe one must . . . seek the formation of a new spiritual life in the *people* and let the effete modern society go to the devil.' And, similarly, insights which he had gained into the character and attitude of the poor peasants of his own time are used by Büchner in his portrayal of the masses of the people in revolutionary Paris. In *Dantons Tod* the people are represented objectively, yet not entirely without sympathy. Büchner recognizes the depth of their suffering, the years of degradation and exploitation which have provoked their fierce desire for vengeance:

JUNGER MENSCH. Erbarmen!
DRITTER BÜRGER. Nur ein Spielen mit einer Hanflocke um den Hals! S'ist nur ein Augenblick, wir sind barmherziger als ihr. Unser Leben ist der Mord durch Arbeit, wir hängen sechzig Jahre lang am Strick und zappeln, aber wir werden uns losschneiden. – An die Laterne.
JUNGER MENSCH. Meinetwegen, ihr werdet deßwegen nicht heller sehen!
DIE UMSTEHENDEN. Bravo, bravo!
EINIGE STIMMEN. Laßt ihn laufen! (*Er entwischt.*) (I. ii. 15)

What a bitterness there is in the incident of the woman with the starving children (IV. vii. 73), who can only divert their attention from their hunger by letting them look on at the executions! The people, as Büchner represents them, are not incapable of generosity, as is shown by their reaction to the young man's brave defiance. But Büchner also shows them to be governed by the two great 'levers' which he recognized in his own political reflections to be the most powerful instruments of revolutionary change: 'material distress and religious fanaticism'.[36] And envy too is a powerful factor; in their misery the people are consumed with jealousy of anyone more fortunate than themselves.

These dominating passions of the people are the great social forces which must determine the outcome of the political struggle between Danton and Robespierre. According to Lukács, in this struggle Robespierre is in the right, Danton in the wrong. Referring to their confrontation at the end of Act I, Lukács writes:

Danton has not a word to say in refutation of Robespierre's *political* view. On the contrary, he avoids a political discussion, he hasn't a single argument against Robespierre's political conception, which in essentials, as we may remember from the letters to Gutzkow last quoted, is the poet's own conception.[37]

This is surely a misinterpretation of the play. The policy of Danton and his friends is, firstly, to stop the Terror, which was justifiable only so long as it was necessary for self-defence, and which becomes no better than murder when the royalist armies have been beaten back and there is no longer a state of emergency:

DANTON. Wo die Nothwehr aufhört fängt der Mord an, ich sehe keinen Grund, der uns länger zum Tödten zwänge. (I. vi. 26)

Secondly, to stabilize the Revolution by bringing it to a halt and consolidating the gains already made:

HÉRAULT. Die Revolution ist in das Stadium der Reorganisation gelangt. – Die Revolution muß aufhören und die Republik muß anfangen. (I. i. 11)

But, according to Büchner's ideas, such a consolidation and stabilization is only possible if the material distress of the people can be remedied. For we know that material distress is always, in Büchner's view, a revolutionary force. So long as it continues, the existing form of society – whatever that form may be – is liable to be overthrown. As soon as it ceases there is also a cessation of the revolutionary situation. The aim of Danton and his friends, therefore, can only be what Hérault proceeds to indicate:

In unsern Staatsgrundsätzen muß das Recht an die Stelle der Pflicht, das Wohlbefinden an die der Tugend und die Nothwehr an die der Strafe treten. (I. i. 11)

Robespierre, on the other hand, declares himself opposed to the halting of the Revolution, arguing that it must continue until the social revolution is complete:

Die sociale Revolution ist noch nicht fertig, wer eine Revolution zur Hälfte vollendet, gräbt sich selbst sein Grab. (I. vi. 26)

But what does Robespierre mean by 'the social revolution'? He can only mean the physical liquidation of the aristocratic and wealthy classes of society, whose political power was already crushed. He cannot mean the socialization of property, since he has just sent the Hébertist faction to the guillotine for 'declaring war on the deity and on property' (*Sie erklärte der Gottheit und dem Eigenthum den Krieg um eine Diversion zu Gunsten der Könige zu machen* – I. iii. 18). Robespierre has in fact no intelligible policy either for the development or for the preservation of the Revolution in its true sense. His real aim is only to maintain his personal power and render it absolute. And for this purpose he relies mainly on the *second* of the two great revolutionary 'levers' – religious or quasi-religious fanaticism. He appeals to the people's need for hero-worship, for an 'infallible' leader. And meanwhile, to prevent his own overthrow, he neutralizes the force of the first 'lever' by diverting the people's attention from their material distress by means of the Terror – by satisfying their lust for blood, their need for a scapegoat, in much the same manner as Hitler was to gratify the baser passions of the Germans at the expense of the Jews. Büchner expresses this in a complex extension of the metaphor of material misery as a 'lever':

LACROIX. Die Hébertisten sind noch nicht todt, das Volk ist materiell elend, das ist ein furchtbarer Hebel. Die Schaale des Blutes darf nicht steigen, wenn sie dem Wohlfahrtsausschuß nicht zur Laterne werden soll, er hat Ballast nöthig, er braucht einen schweren Kopf. (I. v. 25)

Obviously, then, Robespierre cannot afford to bring the Terror to a halt. His policy must be 'the rule of virtue by means of terror' (*die Tugend muß durch den Schrecken herrschen* – I. vi. 26) – 'terror' so that he can rid himself of his rivals, 'virtue' so that the people will be content to tighten their belts in ascetic self-denial and accept the blood of their 'enemies' in lieu of bread. Danton perceives that this policy of Robespierre's can only lead to the defeat of the Revolution. It cannot secure the freedom to which the Revolution was originally and properly dedicated. It can only result in a dictatorship – either the dictatorship of Robespierre or, before very long, that of a more powerful despot. Hence the fierce indictment of Robespierre in Danton's last great speech before the Tribunal:

> Eines Tages wird man die Wahrheit erkennen. Ich sehe großes Unglück über Frankreich hereinbrechen. Das ist die Dictatur, sie hat ihren Schleier zerrissen, sie trägt die Stirne hoch, sie schreitet über unsere Leichen . . . Ich klage Robespierre, St. Just und ihre Henker des Hochverraths an. – Sie wollen die Republik im Blut ersticken. Die Gleisen der Guillotinenkarren sind die Heerstraßen, auf welchen die Fremden in das Herz des Vaterlandes dringen sollen. (III. ix. 63)

Here, surely, is Danton's *political* reply to Robespierre. Here is that refutation of Robespierre's policies which, according to Lukács, Danton does not and cannot attempt. Danton claims – and I see no reason to doubt that Büchner, who is following Thiers and Mignet here,[38] felt the claim to be justified – that it is not he but Robespierre who has betrayed the Revolution. It is Robespierre who has played the reactionary part, both internally, by converting the democracy into a dictatorship, and externally, by so weakening the country with dissension and blood-letting as to facilitate the intervention of the royalist powers. And it is Danton who continues to the last to advocate the policy which, if it could be effected, would be best calculated to save the Revolution both at home and abroad.

Unfortunately, Danton cannot put this policy into effect because, at the decisive moment, he fails to secure the support of the masses. Both the virtues and the defects of his character unfit him for that cunning use of the lever of fanaticism which the situation calls for. He cannot be a hypocrite like Robespierre, he cannot deceive himself to the extent required for the effective deception of others. Nor has he the determined, single-minded, almost pedantic dedication of Robespierre. Worst of all, his indolent self-indulgence excites the ever sensitive envy of the people. And in the end it is this envy that defeats him:

> ZWEITER BÜRGER. Danton hat schöne Kleider, Danton hat ein schönes Haus, Danton hat eine schöne Frau, er badet sich in Burgunder, ißt das Wildpret von silbernen Tellern und schläft bey euren Weibern und Töchtern, wenn er betrunken ist . . . Was hat Robespierre? der tugendhafte Robespierre. Ihr kennt ihn Alle.
> ALLE. Es lebe Robespierre! Nieder mit Danton! Nieder mit dem Verräther!
>
> (III. x. 64)

Each of the two main figures in the dramatic conflict is backed by a less complex supporting figure – Danton by Camille, Robespierre by Saint-Just. Camille has not the power of Danton – he is 'a pistol shot' to Danton's 'thunderbolt' (II. i. 32) – but he is a man of great charm, not only the closest friend of Danton but for a long time even the friend of Robespierre, who, as we have seen, refers to him as 'my Camille' and feels his defection as the seal on his solitude. And for his wife Lucile he is everything in the world; she can hardly conceive how the life of the earth can continue without him (IV. viii. 74). Perhaps it is the intensity with which he returns her love that preserves him from the coarseness of most of the other people in the play. One notices that, unlike Danton and Lacroix, he never indulges in crude witticisms and obscenities. There is something pure and childlike in his nature – Robespierre describes him as 'ein Kind' (I. vi. 29); Danton more than once addresses him as 'mein Junge' – but he has also something of the weakness of a child. He has warm and generous feelings, and the tears that he shed for the Girondists cost him his life:

> ich gehe auf's Schafott, weil mir die Augen über das Loos einiger Unglücklichen naß geworden. (III. i. 50)[39]

His fine and sensitive nature is keenly appreciative of all that is beautiful and pleasing to the senses; he is strongly attracted to the old pagan religion of pleasure, fascinated by the loveliness of ancient Greece. Büchner does not obtrude this trait, but neither does he ever quite lose sight of it. And those critics who are inclined to deny that *Dantons Tod* is a character drama should observe how consistently this aspect of Camille's character is maintained. In the very first words we hear from him there is an allusion to Socrates and Alcibiades, and in the very last he likens the grim scene on the scaffold to a classical symposium at which *blood* is sprinkled as a libation. Hérault beautifully remembers these classical sympathies of his friend in congratulating him on the fineness of the evening which is to be their last on earth:

HÉRAULT (*nimmt Camilles Arm*). Freue dich Camille, wir bekommen eine schöne Nacht. Die Wolken hängen am stillen Abendhimmel wie ein ausglühender Olymp mit verbleichenden, versinkenden Göttergestalten. (IV. v. 72)[40]

But Camille's delicate high-strung nature also has its corresponding weaknesses. His over-excitable imagination pictures the horrors of death and physical decomposition with the morbid vividness of Shakespeare's Claudio[41] or Kleist's Prinz Friedrich von Homburg (III. vii. 60), and there are moments when he seems to have only a precarious hold on sanity. Hence his loss of self-control as he is being carried to the guillotine; hence too his recourse, in his last night in prison, to such a book as Young's *Night Thoughts*. Critics who object that this is inconsistent with Camille's character miss the point.[42] Büchner is suggesting that, as the approach of death increases to breaking point the pressure on Camille's weak nerves, so he is tempted to abandon his classical philosophy and seek refuge in Christianity. The historical Camille also is said to have weakened in the face of death – to have revoked and forsworn much that he had previously professed. He is also said to have died badly – weeping, crying for help and tearing his clothes.[43] Büchner has too much respect for the truth of history to pass these things over unnoticed. But he does not

133

dwell on them. He is content to allude to them cursorily and indirectly – perhaps a little too cursorily and indirectly for complete lucidity. May we surmise that he did not wish these sad failings to be too prominent in our final idea of Camille? – that he wished us rather to think of him as Lucile did, or like the prisoner in the Luxembourg who said of him:

Laßt ihn! Das sind die Lippen, welche das Wort *Erbarmen* gesprochen.
(III. i. 50)

In political matters Camille is free from Danton's misgivings, and pleads with him in vain to take effective action while there is still time. On the side of their enemies, it is Saint-Just who goads Robespierre into action (I. vi. 29). For as Camille is a less complex character than Danton, so Saint-Just is an even worse fanatic than Robespierre, and it is he who is mainly responsible for the slanderous accusations which provoke Danton's indignant and contemptuous cry: 'You miserable Saint-Just . . . !' Saint-Just is prepared to lie, cheat and murder without the slightest compunction for the good of the cause; he is ready to throttle his enemies with his own hands if need be (*Sie müssen weg, um jeden Preis und sollten wir sie mit den eignen Händen erwürgen* – III. vi. 57). Büchner has given him only one long speech, but it is a masterpiece of political characterization, deeply ironical in the objectivity of its portrayal of ideological fanaticism. Though some hints from the historical sources have been utilized, this speech seems to be mainly Büchner's own invention. The expression 'world-spirit' (*Weltgeist*) in the following passage, and more particularly the manner in which that expression is used, suggest the influence of, or an allusion to, Hegelianism;[44] and there could be no more effective exposure of the inhumanity of sacrificing one or more generations of mankind to the supposed requirements of a world historic process such as philosophies of the Hegelian type envisage:

Der Weltgeist bedient sich in der geistigen Sphäre unserer Arme eben so, wie er in der physischen Vulkane oder Wasserfluthen gebraucht. Was liegt daran ob sie an einer Seuche oder an der Revolution sterben? (II. vii. 45)

Danton expresses a rather similar thought, but with a significant difference of tone and expression. Reminding the Revolutionary Tribunal of his great services to the Revolution, he says:

Ich bin nicht stolz darauf. Das Schicksal führt uns den Arm, aber nur gewaltige Naturen sind seine Organe. (III. iv. 53)

Instead of the concept 'world-spirit', with its pretentious and dangerous mysticism, we have here the neutral expression 'Fate', implying no promise whatever of an ultimate millennium; instead of Saint-Just's cold indifference to the fate of millions, we have Danton's sad confession that he is not proud of his great deeds. Saint-Just – a modern and more sinister Moses – is prepared to lead mankind to the Promised Land through a sea of blood:

Gesetzgeber! Wir haben weder das rothe Meer noch die Wüste aber wir haben den Krieg und die Guillotine. (II. vii. 46)

And when he toys with the idea – an idea long familiar to Büchner[45] – that revolutions are 'the locomotive of history', he gives to the thought a laconic twist of blood-chilling cynicism:

Ist es denn nicht einfach, daß zu einer Zeit, wo der Gang der Geschichte rascher ist, auch mehr Menschen außer Athem kommen? (II. vii. 46)

Anticipating Dostoevski's Verhovenski and Shigaliov as well as Flaubert's Sénécal, Büchner's Saint-Just is, as Martens remarks,[46] the first valid representation in literature of 'the type of the fanatical revolutionary, the obsessed ideologist'. He is one of the boldest and most original of Büchner's conceptions.

Equally bold and original is Büchner's characterization of the hetaera Marion. No doubt this figure owes something, as Landsberg and later critics have pointed out, to the influence of the German and French romantics: her name possibly to Victor Hugo's Marion Delorme, certain traits of her character to Friedrich Schlegel's Lucinde and Lisette, to Brentano's Violetta and Annunciata. Yet none of these women, neither the sexually corrupted nor the sexually emancipated, is drawn with quite the boldness of Büchner's Marion, nor do they make such a strong impression on the reader's imagination. It is only Büchner who can let his Marion calmly say of herself and a young man:

Endlich sahen wir nicht ein, warum wir nicht eben so gut zwischen zwei Bettüchern bei einander liegen, als auf zwei Stühlen neben einander sitzen durften. Ich fand dabey mehr Vergnügen, als bey seiner Unterhaltung . . .

(I. v. 21)

Marion is sensual through and through, she is nothing but sensuality. After her first experience of sex she finds herself attracted to all men equally, or rather all men merge for her into one body, and her passion is directed to this masculine body rather than to any individual man (*Es war für mich nur ein Gegensatz da, alle Männer verschmolzen in einen Leib* – I. v. 21). The result is tragedy. The young man who first loved her drowns himself, and she sees his body carried past her window, his forehead pale, his hair wet. But Marion knows as well as Danton that no one can escape his own nature, that one must needs obey it (*Meine Natur war einmal so, wer kann da drüber hinaus?*); and while Danton groans under this necessity, Marion acquiesces in it. The death of the young man makes her weep, she describes it as having been 'the only rupture in her being' (*Das war der einzige Bruch in meinem Wesen*). Otherwise she is always one and the same, always an incessant longing and embracing, a glow, a torrent (*Ein ununterbrochnes Sehnen und Fassen, eine Gluth, ein Strom*). And she cannot understand why people should point their finger at her, why her mother should die of grief because of her, what difference it can make whether one finds one's pleasure in carnality or in crucifixes, in flowers or in children's toys. 'Whoever enjoys the most prays the most' (*wer am Meisten genießt, betet am Meisten*).

Martens argues that this is not to be understood as a Dionysian glorification of sensual enjoyment, that Marion's situation is a tragic one.[47] She is the victim of her sensuality, which has made her responsible for the death of her friend and of her mother and has exposed her to the uncomprehending hostility of the 'respectable' members of society. But one may doubt whether Marion *feels* the tragedy of her situation – where does she ever *appear* to feel it except momentarily at the death of her lover? – and can one say that her fate is tragic if she does not feel it to be so? Marion's sensuality is an elemental force, she compares herself to an ocean that devours everything (*ich wurde wie ein Meer, was Alles verschlang*), to a glowing torrent or a great river. But she has no soul. This is surely what the young man means when he refrains from destroying her beautiful body because 'it was the only thing I had' (*es wäre doch das Einzige, was ich hätte*). But Büchner certainly indicates the calamitous consequences of such elemental passions, and in *Woyzeck* he will return to this theme, showing the effect of such a passion on a heroine who is *not* soulless.

Marion is obviously a very dangerous person, but notwithstanding her complete and fatal amorality, one retains some respect for her. She is no vulgar prostitute. In the other subordinate figures of the play Büchner lets us feel with unsparing intensity the lamentable yet ludicrous misery of the people, the sordidness, craziness, viciousness and barbarity of the life of revolutionary Paris. There is this grotesque kind of pathos, this cruel humour, in the figures of the two grisettes whom Danton insults in the crudest manner and then pities for their failure to earn their supper, and whom we afterwards see soliciting a soldier because they 'have had nothing warm in their bodies since yesterday' (*Wir haben seit gestern nichts Warmes in den Leib gekriegt* – II. ii. 35) – in the prompter Simon, with his drunken sentimentality, his fake heroics and actual degradation, and in his wife who maintains herself and him by prostituting their daughter – in Eugenie and the young gentleman, who pretends to share her mother's delight in the pure joys of nature while whispering salacious gossip into the ear of the daughter – in the gentleman who believes the surface of the earth to be only a thin crust and treads gingerly lest he should fall through – in the atheist Chaumette, who is mortally afraid that God might prove to exist after all, and who relies on Payne to fortify his atheism by means of philosophical arguments – in the treachery of Laflotte and Barrère – in the monstrous inhumanity of Collot and Billaud-

Varennes. What a panorama of vice, folly and distress! It is perhaps in these brief but very vivid sketches of people and incidents that the effect of the play is most bizarre, at times almost surrealistic. Yet there is often a historical basis for them. This is true, for example, of Collot's diabolical reply to the woman who has been in prison for four weeks and who asks to be released from her misery by death: 'Citizeness, you haven't been wishing for death long enough yet' (*Bürgerin, es ist noch nicht lange genug, daß du den Tod wünschest* – III. vi. 57). This, if we may rely on *Unsere Zeit*, is historically authentic, except that these words, 'which should have withered the tongue that spoke them', were in reality Couthon's, not Collot's.[48]

Against the dark background of all this misery and turpitude which Büchner depicts so powerfully, the two pure figures of Julie and Lucile appear in an almost radiant light. Julie is the most quietly but firmly heroic character in the play. Danton seems at first unsure of her, he wonders if he really knows her. But her love for him is absolute and unquestioning. At the end, when she knows that he is lost and cannot bring herself to see him in that state (*sag' ihm ich könne ihn nicht so sehen* – IV. i. 64), she sends him a lock of her hair to assure him that she will accompany him in death, and asks the boy by whom she sends it to return quickly so that she may read in his eyes the reflection of Danton's look. Her devotion to him is as complete as that of Portia to Brutus in *Julius Caesar*, but – unlike Portia's – her death is happy, almost festal:

Man möchte immer so stehn. Die Sonne ist hinunter. Der Erde Züge waren so scharf in ihrem Licht, doch jezt ist ihr Gesicht so still und ernst wie einer Sterbenden. Wie schön das Abendlicht ihr um Stirn und Wangen spielt . . . Ich gehe leise. Ich küsse sie nicht, daß kein Hauch, kein Seufzer sie aus dem Schlummer wecke (IV. vi. 72)

Lucile is no less devoted to Camille than Julie to Danton, but as Camille is weaker, more labile than Danton, so also is Lucile in comparison with Julie. One feels from the beginning the threat of insanity in the morbidity, the hypersensitivity of her imagination, as when Camille leaves her and she feels that he will never be able to turn back but must always go farther and farther away from her, or as when the empty room with the open windows appears to her as if a corpse had been lying in it (II. iii. 39). These are among the moments when Büchner's 'visionary realism' is most effective. His portrayal of the gradual collapse of Lucile's reason under the pressure of fear and grief is as convincing, if less elaborate, than his later study of the insanity of Lenz. No doubt there are some reminiscences of Ophelia here. As Laertes says of Ophelia:

> Thought and affliction, passion, hell itself,
> She turns to favour and to prettiness

– so Camille can say of Lucile:

> Was sie an dem Wahnsinn ein reizendes Kind geboren hat. (IV. v. 70)

And Ophelia's 'We must be patient' is paralleled by Lucile's 'Wir müssen's wohl leiden.' Yet, notwithstanding these common traits, Lucile has a distinctive character, and her part in the play is even more significant than Ophelia's in *Hamlet*. Büchner's play ends with Lucile. In the last scene of all we witness the merciful darkening of her understanding, the saving release of emotion, which enable her to apostrophize the guillotine in the words:

> du stiller Todesengel ... Du liebe Wiege, die du meinen Camille in Schlaf gelullt, ihn unter deinen Rosen erstickt hast. (IV. ix. 75)

And at last she finds the answer to her question: 'My Camille! Where shall I look for you now?' (*Mein Camille! Wo soll ich dich jetzt suchen?*) in the sudden return of lucidity which permits and compels her cry: 'Long live the king!' (*Es lebe der König!*).

Julie and Lucile seem to have a similar importance for Danton and Camille to that which Minna Jaegle had for Büchner. The famous letter to Minna in which Büchner describes the shattering effect which his study of history has had upon him, ends with the words: 'If only I could lay this cold tormented heart on your breast!' (*Könnte ich aber dies kalte und gemarterte Herz an Deine Brust legen!*). Danton seeks the same kind of comfort and relief in Julie. She is almost like a mother to him; he longs for the peace she can give him as one longs to return to the womb of mother earth (I. i. 9). Camille likewise finds solace in Lucile, but it is rather the solace of childlike purity and beauty – an unspoiled refuge from the miseries of life. He calls her 'lieb Kind' – Büchner begins his letter to Minna of 27 January 1837 with the same expression; and how skilfully the conversation about the theatre in II. iii – a conversation whose main function is to state Büchner's aesthetic standpoint – is utilized to bring out this child-like character of Lucile's love! She does not *hear* what Camille says; she loves to *see* him talking (*ich seh dich so gern sprechen*).

It is precisely because Julie and Lucile have this function of providing solace, an escape from the ugliness and brutality of the world, that one might be tempted to suspect Büchner of *idealizing* their characters in a manner inconsistent with his realistic theory. And it is true that, in his representation of Julie, he deviates considerably from the historical records: Danton's young wife did not die at the same time as her husband, but married again and long outlived him. It is also true that the historical Lucile did not become insane, nor did she throw away her life in the manner described by Büchner (though other women are known to have used the cry *vive le roi!* as an indirect but reliable form of suicide).[49] But if the manner of her death was different, still the historical Lucile died no less heroically and devotedly than the Lucile of Büchner's play. There is therefore no essential perversion of the truth here. We must rather conclude that in the character of Lucile, as in certain traits of Danton's character, we have that positive aspect of human nature which Büchner earns the right to express by the radical honesty of his expression of the negative aspect.

## STYLE

Büchner's revolt against classicism makes it impossible for him to adopt the blank verse which had been used for historical drama by Schiller, Kleist and Grillparzer. Nor is it possible for him to indulge in the conventionally poetic language, the exalted diction and resounding rhetoric of his classical and romantic predecessors. Such stylistic characteristics can appear in Büchner's text only in the form of *parody*. Thus we find blank verse and exaggerated rhetoric in the absurd posturing of the prompter Simon:

> So reiß ich von den Schultern dein Gewand,
> Nackt in die Sonne schleudr' ich dann dein Aas. (I. ii. 13)

And the scene 'Eine Promenade' (II. ii. 34 ff.) is a parody of the Easter Sunday scene in *Faust*. The situation is more or less the same: a number of people of various types walking back and forth for their pleasure or profit. But in Büchner everything appears in a much harder, more cynical light. Instead of Goethe's neatly dressed *Bürgermädchen* we have Büchner's two starving prostitutes. Instead of the conventionally gallant strains of Goethe's soldiers:

> Mädchen und Burgen
> Müssen sich geben

we have the lewd equivocations of Büchner's:

> SOLDAT. Du bist sehr spitz.
> ROSALIE. Und du sehr stumpf.
> SOLDAT. So will ich mich an dir wetzen.

Instead of Faust's idealism and ethereal longing, we have Danton's sense of an omnipresent lasciviousness. One might compare the parody of Goethe's garden scene – where Gretchen promenades on the arm of Faust, Frau Marthe with Mephistopheles – in Brecht's parable of the rise of Hitler, *Arturo Ui*. Parody, satire, irony – these are natural forms of expression for Büchner's social and metaphysical revolt. What a satire on Hegelianism is Saint-Just's pretension to be a servant of the *Weltgeist* in its progress towards absolute freedom! There is a similar irony in the claim of the gentleman in II. ii. 36 that 'mankind is hurrying with gigantic strides towards the fulfilment of its lofty destiny' (*Die Menschheit eilt mit Riesenschritten ihrer hohen Bestimmung entgegen*). Spinoza's pantheism, with its implication that God is in all of us, is satirized in Payne's comment that it seems hardly compatible with the dignity of God that in any one of us he can have a toothache or gonorrhoea (III. i. 47). The portentous solemnity of mystical philosophers and theologians is reflected in the ironical remark that God created man 'out of an overflowing need for love, as we so mysteriously whisper in each other's ears' (*aus überschwenglichem Liebesbedürfniß, wie wir uns ganz geheimnißvoll in die Ohren sagen* – III. i. 48).

That overriding concern for 'life, possibility of being' which impels Büchner to make the people in his plays 'real human beings of flesh and blood' also largely determines the characteristics of his style. Everywhere we find him striving for the utmost vigour and vividness of expression. Hence his preference for simple direct sentences rather than elaborate hypotaxis. One might instance Lucile's speech:

Komm, komm, mein Freund! Leise die Treppe herauf, sie schlafen Alle. Der Mond hilft mir schon lange warten. Aber du kannst ja nicht zum Thor herein, das ist eine unleidliche Tracht. Das ist zu arg für den Spaß, mach ein Ende. Du rührst dich auch gar nicht, warum sprichst du nicht? Du machst mir Angst.
(IV. iv. 69)

Here there are nothing but principal sentences, not one subordinate clause. And so it is with Julie's speech in IV. i. 64 and in many other passages in the play.

In his eagerness for forceful and vital expression Büchner is naturally impatient of the literary and bookish locutions, the prolixities and tautologies, which he frequently encountered in the historical sources. He dramatizes the languid sentences of the historians and makes them come to life. The words which Mignet ascribes to Vergniaud:

Citoyens, il est à craindre que la révolution, comme Saturne, ne dévore successivement tous ses enfants

appear on the lips of Danton in the abrupt and energetic form

Ich weiß wohl – die Revolution ist wie Saturn, sie frißt ihre eignen Kinder
(I. v. 25)

The tautological sentence of Robespierre as reported by Thiers:

D'ailleurs le nombre des coupables n'est pas grand; le crime n'a trouvé que peu de partisans parmi nous, et en frappant quelques têtes la patrie sera délivrée.

is abbreviated and amended by Büchner as follows:

142

Die Zahl der Schurken ist nicht groß; wir haben nur wenige Köpfe zu treffen, und das Vaterland ist gerettet. (II. vii. 45)

The weak formulation of *Unsere Zeit*: 'Beherrscht durch den Schrecken die Feinde der Freiheit' is replaced by the forceful 'Zerschmettert durch den Schrecken . . .' (I. iii. 18). Richard Thieberger's edition, with its juxtaposition of the text of the play and the relevant passages from the historians, provides ample material for the study of Büchner's purification and invigoration of his sources.

The unfailing energy and concision of Büchner's style has exposed him to the unjust criticism that the speech of his characters is insufficiently differentiated.[50] His fine command of language certainly makes itself felt throughout, no matter which character is speaking. And an impression of uniformity may also result from his successful reproduction of the characteristic style of revolutionary France – that austere 'republican' style with its grave laconism and its frequent allusions to the ancient heroes of liberty. But these are merits of the play. Nor are they incompatible with a considerable degree of stylistic differentiation in the representation of the characters. Danton's eloquence is different from Robespierre's; the purity of Camille's speech contrasts with the licentiousness of Danton's, Lacroix's and Hérault's; Marion, Julie and Lucile each has her distinctive tone and vocabulary. This realism and objectivity of Büchner's language extends also to the representation of the various classes of society. Not that Büchner uses dialect in the systematic manner of the Naturalists. But neither has he that uniform propriety of expression which is characteristic of classical historical drama – the *Maria Stuart* of Schiller or the *König Ottokar* of Grillparzer. After the cultivated language of Danton and his friends, with its witty innuendoes, its literary allusions and disreputable sophistication, he lets us taste the rude language of the people with its earthiness, its solecisms and its colloquialisms:

da dacht' ich so, der muß sich gut auf der Guillotine ausnehmen, dacht' ich. Das war so ne Ahnung. (IV. viii. 75)

Halt't euren Platz vor! um ein Mädel fährt man nit herum, immer in die Mitt
'nein. (IV. iv. 68)

> Und wann ich hame geh
> Scheint der Mond so scheeh.   (IV. ix. 75)

This last is of course from a folk song, but it is noticeable that
in the folk songs sung by Lucile there is no such broad
dialect.

As might be expected in a writer so hostile to idealization,
Büchner's style always tends to favour the most concrete expressions, to cleave to the hard material realities of the world. Nothing
is glossed over by abstractions or veiled by euphemisms. Both
life and death are experienced in all their inexorable physical
actuality. Death is not, as in *Die Jungfrau von Orleans*, a victory
on the battlefield, a spiritual triumph, an ascension to Paradise on
rainbow-coloured clouds. It is a matter of physical pain, of blood,
of staring eyes which the executioner does not bother to close;
it is the smell of decay, the slow rotting in the grave, a doubtful
oblivion. Nor are the ugly and humiliating aspects of life felt
less acutely. There is the stench of sweat and defecation, the dirt of
untended finger-nails, the putrefaction of syphilis.

To express all this Büchner has to use hundreds of words and
phrases which both the classical and the romantic dramatists would
have felt to be intolerable – even Gottfried Keller, writing late in
the nineteenth century, describes them as 'impossible'.[51] He
frequently has recourse to medical and anatomical terms with
which he had become familiar during his professional training:
*Schädeldecken, Hirnfasern, Sublimatpille, Leibgrimmen, Einge-
weide, Schlagfluß, Rückenmark, das hippokratische Gesicht*; and he
allows himself an absolute freedom – a freedom almost unparalleled in the nineteenth century – in his allusions to sex. There is
not only the frankness of Marion in the story of her elemental
sensuality; there are also many stark obscenities:

Du Judas, hättest du nur ein Paar Hosen hinaufzuziehen, wenn die jungen Herren
die Hosen nicht bey ihr hinunterließen? (I. ii. 13)

Sieh auf dein Zifferblatt; es ist die Zeit, wo die Perpendikel unter den Bettdecken
ausschlagen. (II. vi. 42)

Möchte man nicht drunter springen, sich die Hosen vom Leibe reißen und sich
über den Hintern begatten wie die Hunde auf der Gasse? (II. ii. 35)

These and many similar passages have always been a stumbling
block to editors, producers, critics and interpreters of *Dantons
Tod*. Until quite recently it was customary to omit most of them
in performances of the play, and Max Reinhardt was severely
taken to task by an irate critic for failing to excise *all* of these
'disgusting indecencies' which – 'at least so far as Germany was
concerned where the ruling élite has never descended from its
lofty moral and intellectual level to this low Gallic standpoint' –
were the reverse of realistic.[52] Margaret Jacobs considers that
'the eroticism of the play is of course too exaggerated to be
artistic',[53] and Viëtor seeks to explain though not to excuse it by
ascribing it to a sex-obsession not unnatural in a man of Büchner's
immature age.[54] Gutzkow and Duller, the first editors of the play,
expurgated the most offensive passages, and it was in this more
or less bowdlerized version that *Dantons Tod* first appeared in
book form. But the significant fact is that in the two copies of
the book which are known to have come into his hands Büchner
carefully restored the original expressions which the editors had
considered too improper to be allowed to stand. In Duller's
version the young gentlemen do not let their trousers down when
they are with Simon's daughter; they are only 'nice' to her
(*artig*). Büchner writes three exclamation marks in the margin with
the words *ei! ei!* and *gemein!* – and inscribes his original phrase.
Where Duller has the poetic *buhlen* Büchner insists on his rude
*huren*. Instead of Duller's *es schweift nicht aus* Büchner restores the
original *es geht nicht ins Bordell*. And so on. Evidently Büchner
attached importance to the erotic language of the play and was
not prepared to let it be tampered with. It must have belonged
essentially to his conception of the work, and this hardly squares
with Viëtor's suggestion that it was merely the expression of a
youthful sex-obsession. It is significant that in *Lenz*, which was
written within twelve months of *Dantons Tod*, there is no erotic
language whatever. Evidently Büchner was the master of his
erotic interests and not their slave. He kept them in check where

they would have been inappropriate; he gave them free play where, as in *Dantons Tod*, the artistic and intellectual intention of the work required it. This agrees with his own account of the matter in the letter to his family of 28 July 1835:

Ich kann doch aus einem Danton und den Banditen der Revolution nicht Tugendhelden machen! Wenn ich ihre Liederlichkeit schildern wollte, so mußte ich sie eben liederlich sein, wenn ich ihre Gottlosigkeit zeigen wollte, so mußte ich sie eben wie Atheisten sprechen lassen. Wenn einige unanständige Ausdrücke vorkommen, so denke man an die weltbekannte, obscöne Sprache der damaligen Zeit, wovon das, was ich meine Leute sagen lasse, nur ein schwacher Abriß ist.

(2, 443)

Thus Büchner rests his case on the truth of his representation, and he is fully justified in doing so, for the language of the historical Danton could be very coarse – Thiers mentions his 'expressions obscènes, mais originales'[55] – and Landau reminds us of the corruption of rococo society – 'die im innersten Mark verseuchte und angefaulte Gesellschaft des Rokoko' – as it is so accurately represented, for example, in the writings of de Sade.[56] It is indeed the hideous consequences of illicit sexual indulgence rather than its pleasurable aspects which Büchner emphasizes in *Dantons Tod*. As a student of medicine he must have been only too familiar with the ravages of syphilis, and – far from revelling in sex as Heine and Gutzkow did – he seems rather to have been affected by a kind of 'sex-nausea'. Sexual corruption was another deep shadow in the darkness of his world-view, and it demanded to be represented as faithfully as any other aspect of reality.

But there was also another reason why eroticism had to have a prominent place in *Dantons Tod*: it had an important bearing on the political problem of the play. Büchner understood very clearly and justly that there can be no absolute separation of the domains of private and of public life – that sex can be an important *political* factor. The envy which causes the downfall of Danton is to a great extent sexual envy. The poverty of the people entails not only the want of food, clothing and shelter; it also entails sexual deprivation, and a consequent jealous hostility towards those who are sexually satisfied:

LACROIX. Und außerdem Danton, sind wir lasterhaft, wie Robespierre sagt d.h. wir genießen, und das Volk ist tugendhaft d.h. es genießt nicht, weil ihm die Arbeit die Genußorgane stumpf macht, es besäuft sich nicht, weil es kein Geld hat und es geht nicht ins Bordel, weil es nach Käs und Hering aus dem Hals stinkt und die Mädel davor einen Ekel haben.

DANTON. Es haßt die Genießenden, wie ein Eunuch die Männer. (I. v. 25)

Thus for the impoverished people of revolutionary Paris sexual enjoyment becomes 'the Cain's mark of aristocracy' (*das Cainszeichen des Aristocratismus*); it becomes, as Robespierre puts it, 'not only a moral but a political crime' (*nicht nur ein moralisches sondern auch ein politisches Verbrechen* – I. iii. 19). By his parade of severe republican virtue Robespierre not only avoids becoming the object of this sexual jealousy of the people; he has the demagogic skill to turn the full force of it against Danton, whose fate is exactly expressed in Lacroix's stupendous trope:

Gute Nacht Danton, die Schenkel der Demoiselle guillotiniren dich, der mons Veneris wird dein tarpejischer Fels. (I. v. 26)

If Büchner had not had the audacity to claim absolute freedom of expression in erotic matters, he could not have written such a concise and vivid sentence. Abstractly it means – to adopt Jacobs' paraphrase – that 'Danton's excesses will mean his downfall';[57] but one need only compare it with such an abstract expression of its meaning to appreciate the infinitely greater force and vitality of Büchner's concrete, metaphorical expression. We seem to experience a visionary telescoping of real things – the girl's thighs, the blade and block of the guillotine; we remain on the level of concrete reality, and yet a whole complex of factors and forces are illuminated in a flash (while the allusion to the Tarpeian rock serves to maintain the revolutionary republican flavour of the sentence – what Adolf Beck calls 'the jargon of revolutionary ideology').[58] This concision of expression without abstraction – this telescoping of concrete perceptions – is characteristic of Büchner's use of imagery and is a prime source of the energy of his style. Metaphor becomes a means of probing reality, of establishing the true interrelations of things and people. Camille's 'I go to the scaffold because the fate of some unfortunates *made my eyes wet*' suggests in one simple concrete expression both the humanity which has motivated his ill-fated opposition to Robespierre and the emotional *dimming* of his political vision which has contributed to his fall. Equally impressive, in its fierce brevity, is Danton's question to Robespierre: 'Are you the military policeman of Heaven?' (*Bist du der Policeysoldat des Himmels? –* I. vi. 27); or Robespierre's retort as Danton leaves him:

Geh nur! Er will die Rosse der Revolution am Bordel halten machen, wie ein Kutscher seine dressirten Gäule; sie werden Kraft genug haben, ihn zum Revolutionsplatz zu schleifen. (I. vi. 28)

Occasionally Büchner's probing of reality seems to penetrate into regions which are quite inaccessible to rational thought. Höllerer instances Marion's words: 'Danton, your lips have eyes' (*Danton, deine Lippen haben Augen*), and remarks that this sentence 'runs so athwart the accustomed realities that a hitherto strange and hidden truth becomes visible' – an effect comparable with the alienation of language in Rimbaud and the twentieth century surrealists.[59]

Not, of course, that Büchner's imagery is always equally successful. Saint-Just's metaphor: 'the forgers will provide the hors d'œuvre and the foreigners the dessert. They [the Dantonists] will die of the meal' (*Die Fälscher geben das Ey und die Fremden den Apfel ab. Sie sterben an der Mahlzeit –* I. vi. 30) is somewhat lame. And Camille's comparison of the approach of death to a wedding-night with an old woman: '... when finally the bed-cover is lifted and she slowly creeps in with her cold limbs!' (... *wie dann die Bettdecke gehoben wird und es langsam hereinkriecht mit seinen kalten Gliedern! –* III. vii. 60), though impressive enough in itself, loses something of its value by being too obviously a reminiscence of Tieck's 'Ah, still far more terrible is the lonely sickbed where death little by little creeps in to us, hides itself with us under the same cover and behaves so intimately.'[60] Danton's

Camille! er schläft ... ich will den goldnen Thau des Schlafes ihm nicht von den Augen streifen ... (IV. iii. 66 f.)

suffers similarly by its evident dependence on Brutus's

Boy! Lucius! Fast asleep! It is no matter;
Enjoy the honey-heavy dew of slumber . . .

– though here it is interesting to observe how sensitively Büchner, by avoiding the 'poetic' words *honey-heavy* and *slumber*, adjusts the sentence to the lower key of Danton's speech.

But in spite of occasional infelicities and partial failures Büchner's brilliant use of metaphor is one of the great merits of *Dantons Tod*. Inevitably, in view of the theme of the play, this stylistic brilliance is largely devoted to the portrayal of ugly and cruel realities, and consequently Büchner's language, as we have had ample opportunity to observe in this discussion, often acquires qualities which might themselves seem harsh and repellent. But we should not forget that it is equally effective in its expression of the gentler and finer aspects of experience, and that the hard-won beauty of these passages is heightened by their rarity – by the contrast with the prevailing grimness of tone which serves as a foil to them. We have already noticed some of these lovelier passages in the last monologues of Danton and Julie and in the pure tones with which Lucile, after so many scenes of horror and bestiality, brings the play to a close.

## STRUCTURE

Just as Büchner's striving for life and reality leads him to prefer a paratactic to a hypotactic style, so it leads him to prefer an 'open' to a 'closed' form of dramatic structure.[61] Corresponding to the isolated self-contained statement, we have the isolated self-contained scene. In the classical 'closed' form of drama the individual scene is subordinated to the development of the action as a whole; it is a single link in a causal or motivational chain. But its functional character tends to diminish its vividness and vitality, its openness to precise and uncompromising truth. Büchner prefers, therefore, to break the play up into a series of independent scenes of impressionistic realism, each having its justification primarily in itself, and only secondarily as a component part of the action. There is consequently no exposition in the usual sense of the term; Büchner plunges *in medias res*, the very first lines of the play revealing Danton's deep spiritual depression without any indication of its cause. There is no classical unity of time or place; the action lasts twelve days, and the scene changes freely from place to place as required. It may even change, as in Shakespeare or the young Goethe, for the sake of a scene of only a few lines in length. Two of these short scenes, III. viii and IV. i, are mainly functional; they are necessary steps in the progress of the action. But they are exceptions. In general Büchner's scenes are less concerned with actions or events than with states of being, enduring conditions. Each scene represents one such state or condition with the utmost vividness and intensity, culminating in an epitomizing epigram or in a decision to act. But the culmination is dealt with very summarily; the main body of the scene is static rather than dynamic. Thus the long discussion in I. i expressing the political principles of Camille, Hérault and Philippeau culminates in Danton's dictum:

die Statue der Freiheit ist noch nicht gegossen, der Ofen glüht, wir Alle können uns noch die Finger dabey verbrennen. (I. i. 12)

The vivid picture in I. ii of the starving, vindictive populace culminates in Robespierre's summons to them to follow him to the Jacobin club and be avenged on their enemies.

But though each scene is distinctive and self-subsistent, this does not mean that it has no relation to the scenes before and after it, or that its position in the Act is arbitrary. It *has* a relation to the preceding and following scene, but it is a dramatic rather than a logical relation, a relation of contrast rather than of homogeneity. A scene describing the wealthy epicurean Dantonists is immediately followed by a picture of the hungry, bloodthirsty people. The profoundly tragic expression of Danton's torments of remorse is immediately followed by the brutal ribaldry of the citizens coming to arrest him. Julie's still, tranquil farewell to life is immediately followed by the wild strains of the Carmagnole and the rattling of the tumbrils driving up to the guillotine. The principle underlying these contrasts has been well described by

Viëtor as 'the principle of the antipathetic antithesis'.[62] It is as if Büchner were determined not to let any ethereal fancy carry us too far away from the stark realities of the world. No flight of the imagination is allowed to continue for very long before being brought abruptly back to earth. No warm and generous feeling can escape the derisive counterblast of vulgarity and cynicism. Sometimes Büchner makes the dissonance even more acute by bringing the conflicting elements together in the same scene. In IV. viii Lucile appears together with the guillotine hags, in IV. ix together with the executioners. But here, as Viëtor again well observes, the antipathetic principle is reversed: not the callous jollity of the executioners but Lucile's heroic sacrifice is the note on which the play ends.

Büchner's deeper interest in permanent states of being than in action or intrigue has the consequence that monologue is more important in *Dantons Tod*, dialogue less important, than in most modern dramas. In this respect Büchner's technique differs radically from that of the Naturalists, who rejected monologue as unrealistic. Büchner, unconcerned with verisimilitude in this superficial sense, intent rather on the *inner* reality of his subject, allows himself as free a use of monologue as Shakespeare or Goethe. Not that there is no genuine dialogue in the play. The duologue of Danton and Robespierre in I. vi is a real clash of opinion, and Danton's words certainly make a deep impression on Robespierre. In the same scene the arguments of Saint-Just are decisive in crystallizing Robespierre's resolution. So that it is not quite true to say, as Heyn does, that 'nowhere, in *Danton*, do the opinions expressed spark off the action'.[63] But it is true that the more important characters in the play – Danton, Robespierre, Julie, Lucile – regularly express their deepest thoughts and feelings in monologues. And it is also true that the dialogues occasionally have something of the character of monologues: the speakers are not exchanging opinions or pitting one view against another, but appear, as Scheuer expresses it, 'to be seeking a common support in face of the abyss that threatens them all'.[64] Thus we have 'duets', as in II. v, where Julie and Danton reiter-

ate the same thought, confirming each other in the same conviction; or we have the great antiphonal 'chorus' of IV. v, where
Danton and his friends vie with each other in the symbolical
expression of the same idea.

These are retarding moments in the progress of the play. Yet
in spite of them, and in spite of the predominantly static character
of the individual scenes, the action moves slowly and inexorably
forward. But it is a movement of a peculiar kind. It is rather as if
a huge net had been cast around Danton and his friends and
were being drawn ever closer about them until they are at last
held fast and delivered over to their fate. In this irresistible process
the end of each Act marks the conclusion of a phase. At the end
of Act I we have Robespierre's determination to destroy the
Dantonists. At the end of Act II the Convention's endorsement
of their arrest. At the end of Act III the people's final decision in
favour of Robespierre and against Danton. At the end of Act IV
the executions and Lucile's self-immolation. In so far as each
Act represents and completes a phase of the action, it is clear that
each Act is a dramatic unity notwithstanding the relative independence of its component scenes; and it is clear that the four Acts
together constitute a unified dramatic action. The inexorability of
this action, the futility of Danton's efforts to break free of the
net enclosing him, has seemed to some critics undramatic. But
isn't the action of *Oedipus Rex* – a play never decried as undramatic – no less inexorable? Isn't Oedipus no less foredoomed and
his efforts to save himself no less futile? The form of the action
in Büchner's play is no doubt related to his conception of 'the
horrifying fatalism of history'. But the Greek view of the gods
with their totally arbitrary yet irresistible decrees amounted equally
to the recognition of a dreadful inscrutable fate; and it is understandable, therefore, that *Oedipus Rex*, notwithstanding its
classical structure, should have an action of basically similar form
to that of *Dantons Tod*.

It may be added that the centrifugal tendency of the 'open'
form, the discontinuity of the distinctive, self-contained scenes,
is counterbalanced in Büchner's play not only by the dramatic

unity of each Act and of the action as a whole, but also by certain thoughts and phrases which keep recurring in the same or only slightly varied form: *Notwehr, meine Natur war einmal so, sie werden's nicht wagen, das ist mir der Mühe zuviel*, etc. But it would be strange if Büchner, the realist, the anti-idealist, did not also have a *concrete* symbol integrating and unifying his play. It is the guillotine. In *Dantons Tod* the guillotine has an importance exactly analogous to that of the tilt-wagon in *Mutter Courage*. The guillotine is mentioned in the very first scene of the play, and in every subsequent scene we are oppressively reminded of its existence, we feel it looming ever nearer, until, in the last scenes, it actually dominates the stage in all its hideous reality. Viehweg reports that in Richard Weichert's production of the play in Frankfort in 1928, where a revolving stage was used, the guillotine remained visible in every scene, sometimes as a silhouette, sometimes as a projection on the horizon.[65] And a similar effect was secured by Erwin Piscator in his Marburg production of 1952.[66] Büchner may never have contemplated it, but such an effect, one feels, is not untrue to the spirit of his play.

## POLITICAL AND METAPHYSICAL SIGNIFICANCE

It has been maintained in this chapter that the style and structure of *Dantons Tod* are the adequate expression of Büchner's revolutionary social and philosophical attitude. But the political and metaphysical revolt which underlies and necessitates the revolutionary artistic form of *Dantons Tod* is also expressed *explicitly* in the play. We have noticed in Chapter 2 Lehmann's contention that *Dantons Tod* is, politically, a recantation – a condemnation of Büchner's own earlier activity as a revolutionary agitator and conspirator. Our analysis of the play has not confirmed that view. We have found that Danton, the character with whom Büchner most deeply sympathizes and who indeed has been described as 'son autre moi',[67] nowhere, in a political sense, condemns the Revolution or disowns the part he has played in it. In so far as he deplores the Revolution or his own part in it, he does so for reasons which are not political but ethical or metaphysical. They are reasons which would equally condemn almost any political or military action, even, for example, a just defensive war; and indeed, when Danton describes the September action as 'internal war' (*Krieg nach innen*) he is clearly claiming for it the same justi- fication as that of a defensive war. The fact that, morally and metaphysically, that justification can no longer satisfy him, is not a condemnation of the Revolution as such. It is rather a condem- nation of life in general, a rejection of the necessary conditions of both social and individual existence.

On a strictly political level Danton insists on the necessity of his past policies, and continues to advocate the course which would be most likely to save the Revolution and accomplish its original purpose. His defeat, as we have seen, is due partly to 'the horrifying fatalism of history' – the operation of historical forces beyond human control – and partly to his inability to utilize the two essential 'levers' of revolution, especially the 'lever' of religious or quasi-religious fanaticism which is so much more expertly handled by Robespierre. It is indeed possible that if Büchner intended any political lessons to be learned from *Dantons Tod* it was precisely these two: that revolutions must always depend on the historical constellation, and that the revolutionist must know how to exploit the two great 'levers' of revolution. Is it not perhaps these political lessons that he has in mind when, in the letter to Gutzkow of March 1835 (2, 437), he describes his play as 'a silk cord' and his muse as 'a disguised Samson' (*Mein Danton ist vorläufig ein seidenes Schnürchen und meine Muse ein verkleideter Samson*), thus stressing, not the *anti-* but the *pro*-revolutionary significance of *Dantons Tod*? True, the letter in question is partly jocular, but it is probably by no means wholly so. The hope it expresses for 'a year of crop failures in which only hemp is plentiful' is clearly an allusion to that doctrine of material misery as a 'lever' of revolution which Büchner not long afterwards expounds to Gutzkow with unquestionable seriousness (2, 455).

We know that Büchner himself, in the period after *Dantons*

*Tod*, continued to hope for a successful revolution though not in the immediate future. But in the play Danton is ultimately compelled to abandon that hope; the spirit of political revolt is defeated and the spirit of metaphysical revolt prevails. The latter is expressed in many passages of the play, but most impressively and decisively in that great antiphonal chorus referred to in the previous section. This is, to use Klotz's term, the 'integration point' of the play. The intellectual 'meaning' which is implicit in the diverse scenes of a play in the open form can be integrated and concentrated by its *explicit* expression in a particular passage.[68] So it is here, and the significance of the passage is increased still further by its position: it is the last utterance of Danton and his friends, the summing up of all their experience, before the arrival of the tumbrils that are to carry them to the guillotine:

PHILIPPEAU. Meine Freunde man braucht gerade nicht hoch über der Erde zu stehen um von all dem wirren Schwanken und Flimmern nichts mehr zu sehen und die Augen von einigen großen, göttlichen Linien erfüllt zu haben. Es giebt ein Ohr für welches das Ineinanderschreien und der Zeter, die uns betäuben, ein Strom von Harmonien sind.

DANTON. Aber wir sind die armen Musicanten und unsere Körper die Instrumente. Sind die häßlichen Töne, welche auf ihnen herausgepfuscht werden nur da um höher und höher dringend und endlich leise verhallend wie ein wollüstiger Hauch in himmlischen Ohren zu sterben?

HÉRAULT. Sind wir wie Ferkel, die man für fürstliche Tafeln mit Ruthen todtpeitscht, damit ihr Fleisch schmackhafter werde?

DANTON. Sind wir Kinder, die in den glühenden Molochsarmen dießer Welt gebraten und mit Lichtstrahlen gekitzelt werden, damit die Götter sich über ihr Lachen freuen?

CAMILLE. Ist denn der Aether mit seinen Goldaugen eine Schüssel mit Goldkarpfen, die am Tisch der seeligen Götter steht und die seeligen Götter lachen ewig und die Fische sterben ewig und die Götter erfreuen sich ewig am Farbenspiel des Todeskampfes?

DANTON. Die Welt ist das Chaos. Das Nichts ist der zu gebärende Weltgott.

*Der Schließer tritt ein.*

SCHLIESSER. Meine Herren, Sie können abfahren, die Wagen halten vor der Thür.

(IV. v. 71f.)

Critics who are unwilling to admit the anti-theistic element in Büchner's thought try hard to explain away this passage or to minimize its significance.[69] But Büchner would certainly not have given such elaborate and grandiose expression to those rebellious thoughts, nor would he have placed them at such a climactic point in the dramatic action, if he had not wished to give them the utmost weight and force. This passage is in fact one of the most deliberate and most powerful expressions of metaphysical revolt in all of Büchner's writings. Nor is its Promethean protest against the cruelty of the gods, against the pitiless universe, revoked or mitigated in the concluding scenes of the play. It remains as a constant undertone beneath the accents of friendship and of love which are all that even the best men and women – even a Danton or a Camille, a Lucile or a Julie – have to pit against the merciless-ness of their fate.[70]

We know from Chapter 3 how familiar that mood of meta-physical revolt was to Büchner himself; indeed, in one of the letters to Minna of March 1834 we have seen him expressing that mood in terms almost identical with those that he puts into the mouth of Danton.[71] No doubt that mood was to recur all too often in the later period of Büchner's life, but may we not reason-ably assume that it was precisely because he was able to *express* it in *Dantons Tod* and afterwards in *Lenz* and *Woyzeck* that it could never entirely overwhelm him?[72] It may well be that the writing of these works effected the same catharsis for Büchner as the writing of *Werther* for Goethe. By the expression of the metaphysical revolt which consumes Danton Büchner may to some extent have freed himself from it. The artistic representation of Danton's paralysing despair may have saved Büchner from a like paralysis, and may at least partly explain the paradox that after the writing of such a profoundly pessimistic work as *Dantons Tod* he was still able to go on living and even maintain his hope of political revolution! In his first great play metaphysical revolt had prevailed over political revolt; but it was perhaps precisely because this was so that there remained for Büchner himself the possibility of continuing political interests, of scientific and philosophical research, of life and love in all their potentialities.

# 6. 'LEONCE UND LENA'

*Leonce und Lena* is chronologically the third of Büchner's literary productions, not the second; yet it may be well to consider it immediately after *Dantons Tod* as it is more closely related to that work than to *Lenz* or to *Woyzeck*. Only we must take care that this departure from chronological order does not cause us to forget that Büchner was still working at *Leonce und Lena* when his fatal illness overtook him. The views and attitudes which it represents are still valid for the latest period of his development.

*Leonce und Lena* is exceptional among Büchner's works. Firstly because it is a comedy. Secondly because, more clearly than any of his other productions, it was prompted by an external occasion. On 3 February 1836 the publisher Cotta announced a prize for the best German comedy, and it was this competition that supplied the immediate impulse for the writing of *Leonce und Lena*. The deadline for Cotta's competition was 1 July 1836.[1] Büchner's manuscript arrived too late and was returned to him unopened, whereupon, it appears, he set himself to revise and improve the work. In a letter of September 1836, referring, presumably, to *Leonce und Lena* and *Woyzeck*, he wrote to his parents:

Ich habe meine zwei Dramen noch nicht aus den Händen gegeben, ich bin noch mit Manchem unzufrieden und will nicht, daß es mir geht, wie das erste Mal. Das sind Arbeiten, mit denen man nicht zu einer bestimmten Zeit fertig werden kann, wie der Schneider mit seinem Kleid. (*An die Familie*, 2, 460)

In Zurich, in the last months before his death, Büchner was evidently still engaged in polishing and improving *Leonce und Lena*, for it was stated by Wilhelm Schulz in an obituary published in the *Züricher Zeitung* of 23 February 1837 that 'in the same period [i.e., the last period in Strasbourg] and later in Zurich he completed a comedy which exists in MS, *Leonce und Lena*, a work full of cleverness, wit and saucy humour'.[2] How near it was to being ready for publication is indicated by a sentence in what may have been Büchner's last letter to Minna Jaegle:

⟨Ich werde⟩ in längstens acht Tagen Leonce und Lena mit noch zwei anderen Dramen erscheinen lassen. (2, 464)

After Büchner's death the MS mentioned by Schulz together with that of the fragment *Lenz* came into the possession of Minna Jaegle, who, as a reward for an article on Büchner in the *Frankfurter Telegraf* (June 1837), gave fair copies of these works, written by her own hand, to Karl Gutzkow.[3] *Leonce und Lena* was published by Gutzkow in the *Telegraph für Deutschland* in May 1838, the first Act being given in a fragmentary form together with Gutzkow's summaries of the omitted passages. The first nearly complete publication, based probably on an original MS, was in the *Nachgelassene Schriften* of 1850, edited by Büchner's brother Ludwig. Neither publication can be regarded as reliable. Gutzkow's, as we have noted, is incomplete and based on a copy which may well have been imperfect. Ludwig Büchner can be shown to have mutilated many passages out of 'prudery or negligence'[4] or out of 'political caution, literary incomprehension and pedantic arrogance'.[5] As for the manuscript, only a few scraps of an earlier version are still extant. When criticizing and evaluating *Leonce und Lena* we must remember, not only that it lacked the author's finishing touches, but that it has been handed down to us in a corrupt form.

In his comedy Büchner is not so obviously in revolt against the tendencies of his time as in his serious plays. Whether, and to what extent, the spirit of revolt is present in *Leonce und Lena* also, is a question which must be further considered. But in the field of comedy there was certainly no classicism which could provoke Büchner's direct opposition as it was provoked by the classicism of Schiller in the field of tragedy. In Germany there was the comedy of the romantics, of Tieck and Brentano; in France the comedy of Musset. Büchner did not feel bound to combat either of these forms of comedy but rather, with whatever modifications, to continue and develop them, adopting an attitude comparable with Heine's – a disposition to extend and intensify romanticism to the utmost while infusing into it an element of scepticism, of irony and of parody which offsets and relativizes the romantic elements without completely annulling them. But inasmuch as irony, in all its manifestations, was part of the tradition of German romanticism from the beginning, one must recognize that Büchner no more than Heine completely breaks with that tradition. Not, that is to say, so far as comedy is concerned; his serious works are a different matter.

On the whole, then, there is less of 'aesthetic revolt' in *Leonce und Lena* than in *Dantons Tod*; but, as we shall see, Büchner's modified romantic form still allows a good deal of scope for the expression of his political and metaphysical revolt.

Comparing his method here with that of *Dantons Tod*, *Lenz* and *Woyzeck*, we may note the significant difference that *Leonce und Lena*, unlike those tragic works, is not based on documentary records of real events. The course of the action does not reflect, and is not determined by, the actual experiences of a real historical figure. It is obviously suggested by the action, or by episodes of the action, of other literary works, particularly Brentano's *Ponce de Leon* (1801) and Musset's *Fantasio* (published in the *Revue des deux mondes* in May 1834). Brentano's hero has many traits in common with Leonce; he is described as 'a curious, capricious fellow who amuses everybody and is always bored – witty and shy, cruel and kind, for ever mooning around like a lover, making all the women one after the other fall in love with him and tormenting them with his coldness' (I. x).[6] Like Leonce, Ponce forsakes one of his mistresses (Valeria) and finds a hope of salvation in the arms of another (Isidora). Musset's *Fantasio* is the story of a princess (Elsbeth), who, like Büchner's Lena, is required for reasons of state to marry a prince whom she has never seen and who comes incognito to woo her. The extreme freedom with which Büchner has borrowed from these and other works of Brentano and Musset, as well as from Shakespeare, Tieck, Jean Paul and Heine, has not unnaturally resulted in his comedy being criticized as derivative. Gundolf found that 'the whole thing is a product of the literary imitation of Brentano, Tieck, Shakespeare',[7] and Hans Mayer similarly complained that the people in Büchner's comedy 'have read very many books', that they 'lead a life at second hand'.[8] This criticism has a plausibility which compels consideration and we shall have to return to it presently. Meanwhile it may be observed that, though the degree of *Leonce und Lena*'s dependence on other literary models may suggest a different relation to reality from that which obtains in *Dantons Tod*, it would be a mistake to infer that Büchner's comedy is merely a tissue of literary reminiscences with no basis whatever in real life. The substance of *Leonce und Lena* is in fact basically the same as that of *Dantons Tod*, *Lenz* and *Woyzeck*. It is the fund of experience which Büchner had acquired in his short but very intense life. It is the doubt and despair of his metaphysical speculations and historical reflections; his bitter awareness of the despotism and pettiness of the German principalities and of the agony and brutalization of the people; his sense of frustration, of the pointlessness and absurdity of his own endeavours; his endless boredom. But it is also his love for Minna Jaegle, that love which meant so much to him because he seemed to find in it what his restless tormented spirit most intensely longed for – peace.

All this is expressed in *Leonce und Lena* no less than in *Dantons Tod*, but it has to be expressed now in the tone of comedy. That Büchner should have attempted such an experiment was probably not only due to the external stimulus of Cotta's competition, but also to the fact that the first half of 1836 was a relatively happy period in his life. He had made good his escape from Germany; he was enjoying freedom and the company of his fiancée in his dear city of Strasbourg; his *Dantons Tod* had been enthusiastically acclaimed by Gutzkow; and he was making good progress with his scientific work. Under such circumstances it is understandable that he should have been willing to attempt a work in lighter vein, and in *Leonce und Lena* he certainly achieves a milder tone than in his other plays; in a number of passages there is at least the appearance of cheerfulness and high spirits. Yet the basic experiences underlying the work are, as we have remarked, for the most part grim and gloomy, and from such a source no very joyful laughter can spring. The motto which Büchner chose for Act I –

O that I were a fool.
I am ambitious for a motley coat
(*As You Like It* II. vii)

is already ominous, for these are the words of the melancholy
Jaques whose laughter springs from bitterness and for whom the
freedom of folly is a means 'to cleanse the foul body of th'infected
world.' Büchner himself was prepared to see in folly or madness
a means of escape from intolerable suffering. Thus his Camille can
say of Lucile:

Der Himmel verhelf' ihr zu einer behaglichen fixen Idee. Die allgemeinen fixen
Ideen, welche man die gesunde Vernunft tauft, sind unerträglich langweilig.
Der glücklichste Mensch war der, welcher sich einbilden konnte, daß er Gott
Vater, Sohn und heiliger Geist sey. (*Dantons Tod* IV v. 70)

And Valerio in *Leonce und Lena* is prepared at any time to barter
his unprofitable reason for the flattering visions of megalomania
(see I. i. 107).

In addition to the laughter of madness there are also other
kinds of laughter which Büchner recognizes. There is the
laughter that is prompted by an acute sense of the absurdity of
the world, the futility of human endeavours including one's
own endeavours, the ludicrousness of mankind including one's
own ludicrousness. And there is the laughter that springs from
hatred, the mockery with which Büchner relentlessly pursues
those who, in their 'aristocratic' arrogance, feel entitled to make
a mockery of others:

Man nennt mich einen *Spötter*. Es ist wahr, ich lache oft, aber ich lache nicht
darüber, *wie* Jemand ein Mensch, sondern nur darüber, *daß* er ein Mensch ist,
wofür er ohnehin nichts kann, und lache dabei über mich selbst, der ich sein
Schicksal theile . . . Ich habe freileich noch eine Art von Spott, es ist aber nicht
der der Verachtung, sondern der des Hasses. (*An die Familie*, Februar 1834, 2, 423)

All these varieties of laughter are to be found in *Leonce und Lena* –
the laughter of folly escaping from grief, the laughter of those
who are overwhelmed by the absurdity of the human condition,
the laughter which is Büchner's deadliest weapon in the struggle
against aristocratic superciliousness. But it is obvious that all
three represent, basically, a *negative* reaction to the world; they

arise from suffering, not from joy. And occasionally in *Leonce und Lena*, particularly when Lena speaks, the bright veil of mirth is withdrawn and the dark background frankly revealed. More often the effect is of a kaleidoscope of tones, ranging in a 'chromatic phantasmagoria' from a cheerfulness that is *almost* happiness to a melancholy that is not far removed from despair. No doubt this iridescent effect was deliberately intended by Büchner, and it adds to the charm of the work as much as it challenges and perplexes the interpreter. Small wonder that *Leonce und Lena* has been so diversely understood and evaluated.

Borrowing Hölderlin's terminology, one may say that the *apparent* tone or 'artistic character' (*Kunstcharakter*) of the play is cheerful and comic, but that its *basic* tone (*Grundton*) is melancholy and almost tragic.[9] And one may suspect that it is precisely *because* the basic tone is so profoundly gloomy that the apparent tone has to be so fantastic, so bizarre, in many respects so unrealistic.

This may seem paradoxical in a writer so passionately committed to realism as Büchner professed to be, and at least one critic, Hans Mayer, finds that 'no greater disharmony can be imagined than that between all his other doctrine – the general tendency of his work – and this ironically romantic fantasy of the two royal children'.[10] But we must remember that the artistic principles which Büchner lays down in *Dantons Tod*, in *Lenz* and in his letters, are an incomplete statement of his aesthetic creed – there is no discussion of comedy in his extant writings; and the disharmony of which Mayer complains is after all not so difficult to understand. The truth is that for Büchner reality is essentially tragic. Consequently, in tragedy he can be fully realistic, in comedy not so. A fully realistic representation of life as he sees it would be incompatible with the tone of comedy. If he is to maintain that tone reality must somehow be modified, distorted, reduced, romanticized, burlesqued.[11] Its most intolerable aspects have to be suppressed or subdued and the emphasis placed on those of which the absurdity is not so painful as to forbid laughter. It is this tendency to dwell on the ludicrous and absurd aspects of life, with reduced realism, that has led some critics to see in *Leonce und Lena* a forerunner of the modern 'theatre of the absurd'.

Does this mean that in *Leonce und Lena* Büchner abandons the attitude of revolt? It would certainly mean this if Büchner had carried absurdity to its extreme, since absolute absurdity is incompatible with values, and without values there can be no revolt. When Büchner lets Danton say:

Muthe mir nur nichts Ernsthaftes zu. Ich begreife nicht warum die Leute nicht auf der Gasse stehen bleiben und einander in's Gesicht lachen (*Dantons Tod* II. ii. 36)

we see the sense of absurdity carried to its extreme, and in such a state of mind, obviously, there is no value that can still command respect, no spring of action that is not broken. If Danton had *always* been of this mind he could never have been a revolutionary. And this is no doubt the reason why revolutionary and 'engaged' writers such as Brecht, Frisch, the later Adamov have been so critical of the absurd theatre or directly opposed to it. But Büchner does not carry absurdity to its extreme, not even in *Leonce und Lena*. Familiar as he was with that derisive mood which he ascribes to Danton, he never completely loses his sense of values. Even in *Leonce und Lena* there is still a feeling for political justice and political reason; there is still a feeling for the beauty of nature, and a suggestion, however hesitant, of the redemptive power of love. And so *Leonce und Lena* cannot be claimed for the absurd theatre. But in so far as its comic tone involves an evasion or distortion of reality it represents a movement in the direction of the absurd and consequently a weakening of the attitude of revolt. As we found the tone of the work wavering between the tragic and the comic, so we shall find the sense of it wavering between revolt and absurdity, the technique between realism and romanticism, the tendency between materialism and idealism. It is particularly the last of these antitheses that is suggested by the apocryphal utterances ascribed to Alfieri and Gozzi in the freakish 'preface' to the comedy:

Alfieri: 'E la fama?'
Gozzi: 'E la fame?'

## CHARACTERIZATION

That modification or reduction of reality which for Büchner is necessitated by the comic tone manifests itself in the sphere of characterization in a diminution of the humanity of his figures. While his Danton and Woyzeck are perfectly comparable for complexity and vividness of characterization with the heroes of Shakespeare's tragedies, his comic characters have little of the plasticity, the many-sided humanity of Falstaff, Benedick, Beatrice or Rosalind. And the difference is no doubt due to the fact that Shakespeare's comedy, at least in its earlier and happier period, is not a comedy of revolt nor, basically, a comedy of evasion but a comedy of delight in nature and in the rich variety of human character. Shakespeare can let his eye rest long and lovingly on his Violas and Portias and portray them with full psychological realism because his comedy is a comedy of happiness:

DON PEDRO. Your silence most offends me, and to be merry best becomes you; for out of question, you were born in a merry hour.
BEATRICE. No sure my lord, my mother cried, but then there was a star danced, and under that was I born. Cousins, God give you joy. (*Much Ado About Nothing* II. 1)

That is a comic tone which was not given to Büchner, nor indeed to anybody in the Germany of his time. 'Life, the possibility of being' – that could be his artistic ideal in his serious works, but in comedy it was precisely what he had to avoid or tone down. His comic characters could not be, in the full sense, 'human beings of flesh and blood' but had to have the comparative lifelessness and unreality of puppets or automata, a quality which Büchner otherwise abhorred. Or they could have the conventional unreality of the stock characters of *commedia dell'arte*. Valerio is clearly a kind of Harlequin, King Peter a kind of Pantaloon; and the Governess and courtiers are of a similar type. By the grotesqueness of these types Büchner achieves an effect of comic alienation (*Verfremdung*) which both serves as a relief from the tension of reality and lends itself admirably to the purposes of caricature and satire. Only Leonce und Lena themselves (as Viëtor observes),[12] and to some extent Valerio, partially emerge from this 'alienation' and acquire, at least temporarily, something of the character of real human beings. But even Leonce, in I. i. 106, describes himself as 'a poor puppet', and in III. iii. 131 Valerio introduces Leonce and Lena as 'the two world-famous automata' (*die zwei weltberühmten Automaten*).

Leonce has much in common with Danton, and no doubt with Büchner himself. Like Danton he is not, and is not intended to be, a rationally consistent character; but he is an infinitely less complex figure. Büchner limits the portrait to those characteristics which best accord with the tone of comedy, the more tragic aspects being mentioned comparatively lightly and briefly. There is nothing of Danton's torment of remorse, his fear of physical pain, his loathing of the noisomeness of life and of death, his helpless subjection to the blind fate which destroys everything dear to him. But, like Danton, Leonce is very tired, very idle, and, even more intensely than Danton, he suffers from boredom, from an overwhelming sense of the pointlessness and tedium of existence; and a considerable part of the dialogue and of the action is taken up with his half desperate, half comic writhing under this incubus:

Mein Leben gähnt mich an, wie ein großer weißer Bogen Papier, den ich voll-schreiben soll, aber ich bringe keinen Buchstaben heraus. Mein Kopf ist ein leerer Tanzsaal, einige verwelkte Rosen und zerknitterte Bänder auf dem Boden, geborstene Violinen in der Ecke, die letzten Tänzer haben die Masken abgenom-men und sehen mit todmüden Augen einander an. Ich stülpe mich jeden Tag vier und zwanzigmal herum, wie einen Handschuh. O ich kenne mich, ich weiß was ich in einer Viertelstunde, was ich in acht Tagen, was ich in einem Jahr denken und träumen werde. Gott, was habe ich denn verbrochen, daß du mich, wie einen Schulbuben, meine Lection so oft hersagen läßt? (I. iii. 112)

While still young in years, he is already old in spirit, and Lena immediately senses his irremediable misery:

Er war so alt unter seinen blonden Locken. Den Frühling auf den Wangen, und den Winter im Herzen. Das ist traurig. Der müde Leib findet ein Schlafkissen überall, doch wenn der Geist müd' ist, wo soll er ruhen? Es kommt mir ein entsetzlicher Gedanke, ich glaube es gibt Menschen, die unglücklich sind, un-heilbar, blos weil sie *sind*. (II. iii. 123)

If the source of one's unhappiness is not the untoward conditions of life but, fundamentally, life itself, the mere fact of existence, what remedy can there possibly be? It is again a moment when one feels the proximity of Büchner to Schopenhauer.

Büchner depicts Leonce's *taedium vitae* powerfully and with an insight born of personal experience; but it was, as we have already observed in connexion with Danton, a very general malady in Büchner's time and he could enhance his representation with many traits borrowed from Brentano, from Musset, from Hugo and probably also from Gautier. Lena's words would seem to suggest that Leonce's unhappiness is a reaction to the eternal nature of things. But why should the ennui of which he complains have been so widely prevalent in the early nineteenth century? Was it a consequence of the decline of religious faith? Or did the political conditions of the time, the defeat of the Revolution and the oppressive reaction of the age of Metternich, at least contribute to it? Büchner himself suggests a political explanation when he recognizes boredom to be characteristic of the effete ruling class of the period:

Das ganze Leben derselben besteht nur in Versuchen, sich die entsetzlichste Langeweile zu vertreiben. Sie mag aussterben, das ist das einzig Neue, was sie noch erleben kann. (*An Gutzkow*, Straßburg 1836, 2, 455)

Critics are divided as to whether Büchner expects us to recognize a development in Leonce's character in the course of the play. A development of some kind is certainly suggested. But of what kind? And how far does it go?

At the beginning of the play we see Leonce inert, indolent and feckless, labouring to pass the time by spitting on a stone or tossing sand in the air and catching it on the back of his hand. The tedium of his empty life has given him a touch of hardness and cruelty. He recognizes the meanness of his behaviour towards the President of the Council who comes to inform him of the impending arrival of his fiancée and who, in his extreme nervousness and obsequiousness, cannot refrain from snapping his fingers; but Leonce still finds pleasure in that meanness (*Es steckt nun aber doch einmal ein gewisser Genuß in einer gewissen Gemein-heit* – I. iii. 116). And it is with an even more sadistic pleasure that he watches the death-throes of the love which had once bound him to Rosetta and which now merely bores him. Like Gautier's d'Albert, he can understand very well a Caligula or a Nero; he has enough in common with them.[13]

But in Act II there is the meeting with Lena, and Büchner clearly intends us to understand that this experience has a profound effect on Leonce. So much is already indicated by the motto of this Act, the modified quotation from Chamisso:

> Wie ist mir eine Stimme doch erklungen
> Im tiefsten Innern,
> Und hat mit Einemmale mir verschlungen
> All mein Erinnern.

And that this meeting marks a new beginning for Leonce, that quite a new spirit is awakened in him by that voice, is confirmed by his words:

> O diese Stimme: Ist denn der Weg so lang? Es reden viele Stimmen über die Erde und man meint sie sprächen von andern Dingen, aber ich hab' sie verstanden. Sie ruht auf mir wie der Geist, da er über den Wassern schwebte, eh' das Licht ward. Welch Gähren in der Tiefe, welch Werden in mir, wie sich die Stimme durch den Raum gießt. (II. iii. 123)

The extent of the change he has undergone is further indicated by his new attitude to marriage. In I. iii. 116 marriage had seemed to him like trying to drink a well dry; it had been associated in his mind with the monthly clock-winding ceremony by which Tristram Shandy's father had been accustomed to remind himself that it was time once again to make love to his wife. But now he is immediately willing to marry Lena. And when Valerio expresses some surprise at his master's willingness to bind himself for all eternity, he replies with those remarkable sentences which come naturally enough to Lenz but which sound strange on the lips of Leonce:

> Weißt du auch, Valerio, daß selbst der Geringste unter den Menschen so groß ist, daß das Leben noch viel zu kurz ist, um ihn lieben zu können? Und dann kann ich doch einer gewissen Art von Leuten, die sich einbilden, daß nichts so schön

und heilig sei, daß sie es nicht noch schöner und heiliger machen müßten, die Freude lassen. (III. i. 126)

Admirable sentiments! But are they quite in place here? Lena is by no means one of 'the meanest of mankind'. We must assume that Leonce is enraptured with her, and the thought of the infinite patience and love which even the lowliest of the earth deserve is hardly the reflection that might most naturally and aptly occur to a passionate lover at such a moment. Moreover, the allusion to people who cannot refrain from trying to gild the lily is clearly an echo of Büchner's aesthetic creed, which one is astonished to hear in the kingdom of Popo. This is one of the passages of the play where one feels the need for retouching, for the final revision which Büchner did not live to carry out.[14]

Appropriate or not, the passage would seem to indicate a profound change in Leonce's attitude. What a contrast between the infinite charity advocated here and his earlier supercilious rudeness to the President of the Council! Leonce's language now acquires almost a religious tone. Note the word 'holy' in the last quotation, the Biblical allusion in the last but one, and compare his remark to Lena in III. iii. 133: 'Why, Lena, I think that was the flight into Paradise' (*Ei Lena, ich glaube das war die Flucht in das Paradies*). We may recall the similar use of religious language – whimsical on the surface but with an undertone of deepest seriousness – in the letter in which Büchner announces to his fiancée his return to Strasbourg:

Sie sagen, ich sei verrückt, weil ich gesagt habe, in sechs Wochen würde ich auferstehen, zuerst aber Himmelfahrt halten, in der Diligence nämlich. Lebe wohl, liebe Seele, und verlaß mich nicht. (Gießen, Februar 1834, 2, 423)

Are we to assume, then, that Leonce's melancholy, which Lena had felt to be incurable, is in fact cured by her love? that, as some critics maintain, Leonce is converted from a sceptic into a believer, his chaos transformed into a cosmos? It is almost as if Büchner *wished* to portray such a development – and simply could not.

It is already disquieting that, precisely in his moment of highest bliss, with Lena's kiss still on his lips, Leonce feels irresistibly drawn towards suicide and has to be saved by Valerio. After that one divine moment the world, it seems, has nothing more to offer him and death alone remains. Hardly the attitude of one who has become truly reconciled to life. We may presume that, thanks to Lena's love, life has acquired a new value for Leonce, but it is a value which can find no adequate expression. At the end of the play the situation – politically, psychologically, meta-physically – is still essentially the same as at the beginning. There has been no political revolution. There is still the absurdity of court ceremonial contrasting with the brutalization of the starving peasants. Leonce, in his very last speech, runs through the list of possible occupations and pastimes almost as helplessly and with as little relish as in Act I. And the conclusion is substantially the same now as then: to seek refuge in Italy, or at least in the thought of Italy; to escape to the *dolce far niente* of the south:

Aber ich weiß besser was du willst, wir lassen alle Uhren zerschlagen, alle Kalender verbieten und zählen Stunden und Monden nur nach der Blumenuhr, nur nach Blüthe und Frucht. Und dann umstellen wir das Ländchen mit Brenn-spiegeln, daß es keinen Winter mehr gibt und wir uns in Sommer bis Ischia und Capri hinaufdestilliren, und wir das ganze Jahr zwischen Rosen und Veilchen, zwischen Orangen und Lorbeern stecken. (III. iii. 134)

This is hardly the 'Mozartian opera-finale' that Viëtor took it to be.[15] The truth is, there was nothing in Büchner's experience that could provide an adequate basis for a happy ending and he was too sincere a writer to disavow entirely his continuing perplexity. As in his tragedy so also in his comedy: there can be no return to healthy normality because for him normality – the normal human condition in general, the normal political situation in particular – is essentially sick, absurd, unjust. The difference is that in tragedy the gloomy reality can be frankly acknowledged; in comedy, if there is to be anything like a happy ending, it has to be somehow disguised or neutralized. And this is no doubt the reason why the irony which is almost continuously perceptible throughout the play has to be redoubled in the closing scenes – why Leonce und Lena, elsewhere the most lifelike characters in the play, become so puppet-like in the final Act. Here one may see very clearly how the need to maintain the comic tone involves the intensification of the ironical, the fantastic, the absurd and grotesque elements in the work.

As Leonce is related to Danton and to Hamlet – in II. ii. 123 he actually quotes Hamlet – so Lena is related to Lucile and to Ophelia. Bradley remarked of Ophelia that 'to the persons in the play, as to the readers of it, she brings the thought of flowers'.[16] And the same is true of Lena. In a fragment of an earlier version Leonce says of her:

Sie ist so Blume, daß sie kaum getauft seyn kann, eine geschlossne Knospe, noch ganz geschlossen vom Morgenthau und dem Traum der Nachtzeder. (142)

In the final version we are told how she can hardly bear to live within doors; she 'needs dew and night-air like the flowers' (*Ich brauche Thau und Nachtluft wie die Blumen* – II. iii. 124). And as she shrinks from the shame of having to marry a man whom she does not love she sees herself as a flower that has been violated: 'Tomorrow all the fragrance and radiance will be stripped from me' (*Morgen ist aller Duft und Glanz von mir gestreift* – I. iv. 118). It is perhaps a little disturbing that Lena should say this *about herself*. Simplicity and innocence, as Faust laments, 'never recognizes itself and its sacred worth'.[17] Büchner seems to falter for a moment here, ascribing to Lena his own thoughts about her rather than those that might naturally occur to her. But, if so, it is the only blemish in the brief but so effective portrayal of his heroine. If she owes something to Ophelia and to Musset's Elsbeth, Lena nevertheless remains vividly in our memory as an independent and original character. She has a closeness to nature which Büchner may have felt to be typically feminine and in which Leonce can find peace as Büchner himself found it in the love of Minna Jaegle; it has been truly remarked that at the end of the play Leonce is quite prepared to give himself up to that life in nature which is Lena's proper sphere.[18] Yet that flower-like, elemental quality which makes her respond so sensitively to atmospheric conditions and to which she owes her admirable freshness and soundness of spirit is still not the whole of her character. Notwithstanding her natural healthiness and stability, she feels very acutely the loneliness of life and would gladly escape from it through love. But it must be a pure, not a desecrated love. And when she is threatened with such desecration, when she knows that the purity of her love is to be sacrificed to the interests of the State, she is capable of reflections as tragic as any to be found in *Dantons Tod*:

Mein Gott, mein Gott, ist es denn wahr, daß wir uns selbst erlösen müssen mit unserm Schmerz? Ist es denn wahr, die Welt sei ein gekreuzigter Heiland, die Sonne seine Dornenkrone und die Sterne die Nägel und Speere in seinen Füßen und Lenden? (I. iv. 118)

One may compare Robespierre's 'Truly, the Son of Man is crucified in all of us, we all writhe in bloody sweat in the Garden of Gethsemane, but no one redeems the other with his wounds.' Christ, in this view, is not the redeemer of mankind. There is no redeemer. Schröder's argument that Lena's words 'we must redeem ourselves with our pain' imply that we *can* so redeem ourselves surely overstrains the interpretation.[19] Her final sentence leaves us only with the grand surrealistic vision of a whole world suffering crucifixion with no promise anywhere of redemption. Büchner, like 'les révoltés' of Camus, 'annexes Christ' to his camp, making of him, not our saviour, but only our fellow-sufferer of the agony and injustice of the world.[20]

It is her experience of such tragic reflections that enables Lena, notwithstanding her flower-like innocence, to understand Leonce so well, to recognize so clearly the weariness of spirit under his apparent youthfulness. But together with these darker insights she also has a frank and healthy sense of the richness and beauty of the world:

O sie ist schön und so weit, so unendlich weit. Ich möchte immer so fort gehen Tag und Nacht. (II. i. 120)

It is this simple, unsentimental responsiveness to beauty and goodness – one of the most purely 'positive' traits in any of

Büchner's characters – that enables Lena to 'save' Leonce, so far as he can be saved. She makes possible for him a new kind of love, incomparably deeper and truer than he has ever before experienced. Yet even for Lena, no less than for Leonce, the most intense experience of love is akin to the longing for death. And the dialogue in which that experience is expressed already breathes the spirit of the *Liebestod* of Wagner's *Tristan und Isolde*:

LENA. Der Mond ist wie ein schlafendes Kind, die goldnen Locken sind ihm im Schlaf über das liebe Gesicht heruntergefallen. – O sein Schlaf ist Tod. Wie der todte Engel auf seinem dunkeln Kissen ruht und die Sterne gleich Kerzen um ihn brennen . . .

LEONCE. Steh auf in deinem weißen Kleide und wandle hinter der Leiche durch die Nacht und singe ihr das Todtenlied.

LENA. Wer spricht da?

LEONCE. Ein Traum.

LENA. Träume sind selig.

LEONCE. So träume dich selig und laß mich dein seliger Traum sein.

LENA. Der Tod ist der seligste Traum.

LEONCE. So laß mich dein Todesengel sein. Laß meine Lippen sich gleich seinen Schwingen auf deine Augen senken. (*Er küßt sie.*) Schöne Leiche, du ruhst so lieblich auf dem schwarzen Bahrtuch der Nacht, daß die Natur das Leben haßt und sich in den Tod verliebt. (II. iv. 124)

But the 'happy' end of the comedy cannot, like Wagner's tragic denouement, allow the lovers to sink blissfully into the arms of death; it confronts them with the task of continuing to live. And since, as we have already remarked, Büchner's experience was not such as to enable him to portray a life of happy activity, and since the simplicity and directness of Lena's nature does not permit her, like Leonce, to take refuge in irony and persiflage, she is reduced in the final Act to almost complete silence. In the whole of Act III, the most bizarre and fantastic of all the Acts, she utters just seven words; and in response to Leonce's whimsical list of possible pastimes she can only lean against him and shake her head. Her part ends with that head-shake. It is as if she senses that the love she has given to Leonce is doomed to find no worthy fulfilment. He will never be able to propose to her the kind of life to which she could say *yes*.

As in *Dantons Tod*, Büchner provides his principal characters with companions and confidants who are useful *ficelles* in the dramatic action: Leonce with Valerio, Lena with the Governess, and it is on these two subordinate characters that the comic element in the play is mainly concentrated. Well acted, these roles can be very effective and contribute much to the success of the play on the stage.

Valerio is a comfortable, lazy epicurean, who thoroughly enjoys the inactivity which for Leonce is the most intolerable boredom, and whose main interest in life is in eating and drinking. When we first see him he is 'half drunk' (I. i. 106), and we have to imagine him fat and red-nosed in contrast to the paleness and leanness of his master, his solid, good-natured materialism and vulgarity effectively balancing Leonce's nervous fastidiousness and feverish fancies. His highest hope is for a commodious religion (III. iii. 134), his rule of life *'ergo bibamus'* (II. ii. 121), his feeling for nature a satire on the romantic feelings of Werther:

Ich werde mich indessen in das Gras legen und meine Nase oben zwischen den Halmen herausblühen lassen und romantische Empfindungen beziehen, wenn die Bienen und Schmetterlinge sich darauf wiegen, wie auf einer Rose. (I. i. 106)[21]

It is to Valerio that Büchner entrusts some of his smartest gibes at kings and princes (I. iii. 113, 116) and even at the metaphysical perplexities of the philosophers and theologians:

VALERIO. Es war vor Erschaffung der Welt –
HOFPREDIGER. Daß –
VALERIO. Gott lange Weile hatte – (III. iii. 132)[22]

As the character of Valerio contrasts with and complements that of Leonce, so the grotesque figure of the Governess with her enormous nose – 'as the tower of Lebanon which looketh toward Damascus' (II. ii. 122) – and her sentimental longing for an errant prince is a foil to the tender beauty and naturalness of Lena. The comic effect produced by the Governess can be so powerful, if not carefully controlled, as to jeopardize the balance of the play. Armin Renker tells of a performance of *Leonce und Lena* in Berlin in 1914 where the part of the Governess as played by Ilka Grüning was so exquisitely comic that the delicate lines of Lena were drowned in the laughter of the audience.²³ Yet neither the Governess nor Valerio is an original creation of Büchner's. As has often been remarked, Valerio owes a good deal to Falstaff, perhaps also to Sancho Panza; and the Governess has an obvious resemblance to Elsbeth's governess in Musset's *Fantasio* with the addition of a few traits borrowed from Dame Pluche in *On ne badine pas avec l'amour*. Büchner has taken what he needed from other writers, and no one will blame him for that; but one cannot allow him to have had much of the gift of Shakespeare, Molière or even Musset for the creation of original comic figures direct from life.

Perhaps he comes nearest to such a triumph in his portrayal of King Peter. Here too, no doubt, there is some indebtedness to other writers, most of all to Tieck (King Gottfried in *Der gestiefelte Kater*, King Gottlieb in *Prinz Zerbino*) and perhaps a little to Lenz whose Captain Pirzel in *Die Soldaten* anticipates King Peter's obsession with the need to *think* and his habit of laying his finger on his nose in his moments of profoundest meditation. Yet the characterization of King Peter achieves, on the whole, an original effect, and the reason is not far to seek. It is that the comedy here is of a different kind – for Büchner a more congenial kind – than in the portrayal of Valerio and the Governess. It is no longer the comedy of pure laughter or of *Galgenhumor* or of the escape into absurdity. It is satirical comedy, the comedy in which Büchner aims to wound if not to kill, and in this genre he is a master. Here we have *the comic expression of Büchner's political revolt*, and it is something quite new in German drama. There is no political element in *Ponce de Leon* and only the slightest in *Fantasio*; there had been political satire of a mild kind in Tieck's *Zerbino*, but nothing comparable with the vigour and verve with which Büchner satirizes German absolutism in *Leonce und Lena*. His portrait of King Peter and his courtiers may verge on caricature, but its simplifications and exaggerations do not serve to veil or evade reality but only to underline more firmly the truth as Büchner sees it, or at least certain aspects of the truth.

In that sense there is a certain realism in these passages,[24] contrasting admirably with the dreamlike atmosphere of the romantic scenes. But Büchner, with a tact and skill which – one must agree with Viëtor[25] – is remarkable in such a young dramatist, takes care that his allusions to the very real political evils of his time are not so bitter or so frequent as to envenom the whole tone of the play; he contrives to keep the satire within the bounds of comedy. How does he achieve this? Partly, no doubt, by means of the play of language which prevents any too prolonged seriousness; partly by emphasizing the ludicrous rather than the cruel and tyrannous aspects of German autocracy. Even the very names of the two kingdoms involved, *Popo* and *Pipi*, are a derisive comment on the pettiness of the German principalities. And what a monument to the absurdity of absolute rulers Büchner has created in the character of King Peter!

Peter is not a vicious person. It is part of Büchner's comic strategy to keep the king free from the meanness and corruption which so disgusted him in many of the actual rulers of Germany and Europe. He even endows Peter with some rather lovable characteristics: he has the will to serve his subjects by *thinking* for them; he is touched by the 'wisdom' of his councillors; he is prepared to surrender his throne to his son in order to devote himself to meditation. Yet how effectively Büchner, through this not unprepossessing character, satirizes the institution of monarchy, and, incidentally, the idealistic philosophy of Hegel which was helping to bolster up that institution in the thirties of the last century! King Peter presents the ludicrous spectacle of boundless stupidity striving for philosophical profundity and logical stringency. He is willing to sacrifice the happiness of his son for some absurd reason of state which is never properly explained, and he is so woolly-minded that he ties a knot in his handkerchief to remind himself of his people – a superbly satirical touch! Yet all his subjects are required to 'share his feelings', his grotesque joy and still more grotesque melancholy, 'so far as it is possible and seemly for subjects to do so' (*so weit es für Unterthanen möglich und schicklich ist* – III. iii. 129), and when he perspires his courtiers too must wipe their faces. Obsessed with the need for order, he lives in a perpetual muddle, maniacally insisting that his courtiers should 'walk symmetrically', for ever 'confused' by their 'complicated' replies, and reduced to desperation when the clothes he is being dressed in cannot be made to tally with the articles of his philosophical system and 'the free will in front gapes shamelessly open' (*pfui! der freie Wille steht davorn ganz offen* – I. ii. 108). In this splendid burlesque the philosophical terminology appears to be partly derived from Spinoza, partly from Fichte; but the satire is perhaps also directed against Hegel. We may recall Büchner's contempt for the 'juggling tricks' of Hegelianism, for 'the dogmatism of philosophies of reason' which seek to deduce the laws of nature from the laws of thought:

Die Philosophie a priori sitzt noch in einer trostlosen Wüste; sie hat einen weiten Weg zwischen sich und dem frischen grünen Leben, und es ist eine große Frage, ob sie ihn je zurücklegen wird. (*Über Schädelnerven*, 2, 293)

And we may note that King Peter is described by Leonce as a practitioner of the *a priori* method (I. iii. 116). In the sentence 'Substance is that which is "in itself" – that's me' (*Die Substanz ist das 'an sich', das bin ich* – I. ii. 108), the word *substance* is probably to be understood in the Spinozistic sense, in which case King Peter must be claiming virtual identity with God! But in general one can accept Viëtor's suggestion that King Peter is 'a living satire' on the Hegelian doctrine that 'the prince is the apex of the State'.[26] In one of the most bitter strokes in the play we are reminded how the kings and princes of Germany had cheated their subjects with unfulfilled promises of free institutions:

PETER. Aber mein Wort, mein königliches Wort!
PRÄSIDENT. Tröste Eure Majestät sich mit andern Majestäten. Ein königliches Wort ist ein Ding, – ein Ding, – ein Ding, das nichts ist. (III. iii. 130)

And in the preparations for the wedding of Leonce and Lena there is actually a dramatic enactment of the fierce passage in *Der Hessische Landbote*[27] where the peasants are urged to go to Darmstadt when a crown prince and princess are being married, to see the table cloth through the open doors of the palace, and to smell the lamps illuminated with the fat of the peasants:

SCHULMEISTER. Seid standhaft! Kratzt euch nicht hinter den Ohren und schneuzt euch die Nasen nicht mit den Fingern, so lang das hohe Paar vorbeifährt und zeigt die gehörige Rührung, oder es werden rührende Mittel gebraucht werden. Erkennt was man für euch thut, man hat euch grade so gestellt, daß der Wind von der Küche über euch geht und ihr auch einmal in eurem Leben einen Braten riecht. (III. ii. 127)

It is the same insistence on the brute fact of hunger as during the period of Büchner's most intense revolutionary activity. This comedy of 1836 is no less an indictment of the selfishness and injustice of autocratic régimes than *Der Hessische Landbote* of 1834. So much for Lehmann's contention that Büchner had recognized the attitude of the *Landbote* to have been wrong. In 1836 Büchner's attitude remained the same, and he declined to conceal the fact even in a work which he was submitting for a prize and which, as he must have known, was likely to be disqualified by such a strong infusion of political satire. Even some fourteen years later, as Lehmann himself remarks,[28] Büchner's more cautious brother Ludwig, in the edition of *Leonce und Lena* in the *Nachgelassene Schriften*, found it advisable to suppress some of the sharper political innuendoes. The fact that Büchner was determined to include them in a work which he was still preparing to publish when his fatal illness began may fairly be taken as evidence that at heart he remained to the end the political revolutionary he had always been.

## STYLE AND STRUCTURE

The element of revolt which is still present in *Leonce und Lena* expresses itself stylistically in the form of parody and burlesque. Büchner parodies the learned language of the philosophers, the musty phrases of officialdom, the ecstatic nature-rhapsodies of the romantics. Leonce's flights of fancy are balanced by the earthiness of Valerio's expressions, the mincing compliments of the President of the Council by the schoolmaster's rough address to the peasants. This rudely realistic element, contrasting with passages of ethereal poetry and with the character of the action which is almost like that of a fairy-tale, considerably enhances the effect of the comedy. It gives it a degree of solidity which is a great improvement on the insubstantiality of the comedies of Tieck and Brentano. But it is of course only in comparison with the romantics that *Leonce und Lena* can be felt to be more realistic. In comparison with *Dantons Tod* the diction of the comedy is much more selective, much more inclined to compromise, much less determined to represent the whole unvarnished truth of things. There is still the cynical or derisive use of medical expressions:

VALERIO. Man darf Kinder nicht während des Pissens unterbrechen, sie bekommen sonst eine Verhaltung.

LEONCE. Mann, fassen Sie sich. Bedenken Sie Ihre Familie und den Staat. Sie riskiren einen Schlagfluß, wenn Ihnen Ihre Rede zurücktritt. (I. iii. 114)

And there is still some erotic suggestiveness which the prudery of Ludwig Büchner felt bound to bowdlerize. But it is very mild in comparison with the unflinching frankness, the blunt obscenities of *Dantons Tod*. In general there is less striving for the vital, concrete expression than in the earlier play. In the monologues and dialogues of *Leonce und Lena* there is even a certain prolixity which contrasts with the fierce laconicism of the tragedy.

The underlying melancholy of *Leonce und Lena* is reflected in its style no less than in its characterization. There are moments, indeed, when Büchner seems to achieve a genuine cheerfulness, moments when one can laugh heartily and happily at Valerio, at the Governess, at King Peter. But much of the fun, it must be admitted, has the character of *Galgenhumor* rather than of true humour. It is laughter won from despair. A good example is Leonce's sardonic reflections on boredom:

Was die Leute nicht Alles aus Langeweile treiben! Sie studiren aus Langeweile, sie beten aus Langeweile, sie verlieben, verheirathen und vermehren sich aus Langeweile und sterben endlich an der Langeweile und – und das ist der Humor davon – Alles mit den wichtigsten Gesichtern, ohne zu merken warum, und meinen Gott weiß was dabei. (I. i. 106)

A very similar passage occurs in *Lenȝ* (96) without seeming out of place in that grimly serious work. Or one might instance Valerio's virtuoso performances as punster and equivocator:

O Himmel, man kömmt leichter zu seiner Erzeugung, als zu seiner Erziehung. Es ist traurig, in welche Umstände Einen andere Umstände versetzen können! Was für Wochen hab' ich erlebt, seit meine Mutter in die Wochen kam! Wieviel Gutes hab' ich empfangen, das ich meiner Empfängniß zu danken hätte?

(I. iii. 113)

If one can laugh at this it is with a laughter tinged with pain. And just as the conflict between the underlying sadness of the work and its apparent cheerfulness drives the characterization in the direction of grotesquerie and abstraction, so it also tends to divorce the language of the play from reality, robbing the words of their content, emphasizing their sound at the cost of their significance. This is surely the effect of all the punning and quibbling in which Valerio particularly so often indulges and which prompts the exasperated Leonce to say to him:

Mensch, du bist nichts als ein schlechtes Wortspiel. Du hast weder Vater noch Mutter, sondern die fünf Vokale haben dich miteinander erzeugt. (I. iii. 115)

The play of language becomes an end in itself, veiling the reality to which it is ostensibly related. It is not only by the equivocations that Büchner produces this effect, but also, as J. Schröder has pointed out, by an extensive array of rhetorical figures: 'simple repetition, variation, accumulation of expressions, parallelism, double, treble, quadruple and quintuple articulation, anaphora, chiasmus, oxymoron etc'.[29] One may agree with Schröder that in Leonce's question:

Aber Edelster, dein Handwerk, deine Profession, dein Gewerbe, dein Stand, deine Kunst? (I. i. 107)

the sense of the question has become merely a pretext for a display of verbal juggling.

The proliferation of puns in *Leonce und Lena* was no doubt encouraged by the example of Shakespeare, both directly and indirectly, the example having already been followed and reinforced by Brentano. But this is an aspect of Shakespeare's work which even his most devout admirers are unable to regard with much enthusiasm. There are probably not many readers who would be inclined to dispute the remark of Sir Arthur Quiller-Couch that Shakespeare's '"wit" – the chop-logic of his fools, the sort of stuff that passes for court-conversation and repartee – is usually cheap, not seldom exasperating'.[30] And many of the verbal witticisms in Büchner's comedy are equally feeble. He seldom achieves the imaginative freshness of Nestroy's humorous coinages – his *philobestialisch* (III. i. 126) is an admirable exception. The excessive frequency of his puns makes them seem merely mechanical and can produce an effect of aridity:

LEONCE. Was deine Empfänglichkeit betrifft, so könnte sie es nicht besser treffen, um getroffen zu werden. Drück dich besser aus, oder du sollst den unangenehmsten Eindruck von meinem Nachdruck haben. (I. iii. 113)

LEONCE. Sagen Sie einem höchsten Willen, daß ich Alles thun werde, das ausgenommen, was ich werde bleiben lassen, was aber jedenfalls nicht so viel sein wird, als wenn es noch einmal so viel wäre . . . Valerio gieb den Herren das Geleite.

VALERIO. Das Geläute? Soll ich dem Herrn Präsidenten eine Schelle anhängen?

(I. iii. 115)

Modern audiences are more likely to be embarrassed by such 'wit' than amused by it.

The limited fertility of Büchner's comic imagination is perhaps also indicated, as Gundolf and Hans Mayer thought, by the heavy dependence of *Leonce und Lena* on the work of other writers. Already in *Dantons Tod* Büchner had availed himself very freely of the right of the poet to borrow from his predecessors, but he exercises that right even more extensively in *Leonce und Lena* and not always to such good advantage. Lehmann speaks of 'quotation montage' (*Zitatmontage*) in this connexion, suggesting that the dramatist may achieve special and valuable effects by means of it.[31] One may grant that when Büchner lets Leonce quote Hamlet or Valerio allude to Falstaff (III. i. 126) he establishes a relation between his hero and clown and the corresponding figures of Shakespeare, thus widening the scope and resonance of his play. But how much is really gained by the reference to *Tristram Shandy* already mentioned?[32] To readers unfamiliar with Sterne it is simply unintelligible; to those who have read the novel it can only seem a rather clumsy adaptation of a thought that was much more appropriate and amusing in its original context. On other occasions a quotation may be justified by its satirical or parodistic effect in its new setting. But again the effect is lost on readers unable to recognize the quotation, and some of Büchner's are recognizable only to scholars and specialists. Better frankly admit that many of the quips and jests which Büchner copies from Tieck, Brentano, Heine and Musset serve no special purpose whatever, but are merely borrowed plumes with which Büchner decks out those passages of the comedy which his own flagging wit is unable to adorn.

Apart from the splendidly comic representation of King Peter, it is in fact not in the comic scenes that Büchner's style is at its best but in the serious or semi-serious passages devoted to Lena and Rosetta. It is to Rosetta that Büchner's most beautiful lyric, comparable with the best of Theodor Storm's, is entrusted; and in the words of Lena there is a pure music of incomparable sweetness and melancholy. Even more than by her beauty Leonce is enchanted by her voice. The part of Lena appeals above all to the ear.

Considering the work as a whole, one must admire the variety of tones with which Büchner has succeeded in enlivening it. Brentano, as Renker remarked, had only one colour on his palette;[33] or as Landau put it, in *Ponce de Leon* 'all the characters speak the same precious witty language'.[34] In *Leonce und Lena* every character has a language of his own – the puns, for example, are almost exclusively the property of Valerio – and the consequent diversity of style adds considerably to the dramatic impact of the play.

The air of unreality which we have noticed in the characterization and in the style of the comedy adheres equally to its structure and action. Here too we may observe that flight from reality which the comic mood, except in satire, seems to necessitate for Büchner. Just as most of the characters have the abstract simplicity of puppets, so the structure of the play has the abstract symmetry of a fairy-tale. The kingdom of Popo is exactly balanced by the kingdom of Pipi, Leonce by Lena, Valerio by the Governess. The fantastic absurdity of the beginning and of the end form a perfect circle enclosing the love scenes in the middle. Such a pattern makes light of verisimilitude, and this humorous disrespect for reality – an attitude strongly reminiscent of romantic irony – betrays itself equally in the farcical improbabilities of the details of the action. People appear out of nowhere just when the exigencies of the slender plot require them (II. ii. 122; III. iii. 130); a prince and a princess, fleeing from the compulsion to marry each other, meet by chance in a distant country, fall in love and are eventually married, their identity still unknown to each other; the whole of the third act is a fantastic though not unpleasant travesty.

The play is after all a comedy whatever its underlying tone may be, and Büchner has a right to expect that his readers will accept it in the spirit in which he offers it: not as a work of tragic seriousness but as a kind of holiday from reason and reality in which the farcical elements are to be gaily enjoyed, not soberly dissected. But there are grounds for suspecting that the refusal to be quite serious has been carried so far as to impair the quality of the workmanship. One has the impression of a certain negligence or awkwardness in the construction of the play. The Rosetta scene, for example, is impressively beautiful in itself, but it is scarcely integrated into the structure of the comedy; Rosetta simply disappears after this scene and has no further influence on the action. Much the greater part of the first Act is occupied solely with dialogue, the action making no progress whatever (in I. ii King Peter *almost* succeeds in making a decisive announcement but at the vital moment forgets it!). The motives of the two rulers for wishing to compel their children to marry is nowhere so satisfactorily explained as in Musset's *Fantasio*, where the heroine is clearly being sacrificed to prevent a war. The third Act is rather sketchy and perfunctory, having neither the poetry of the second not the wit of the first.

This brings us to the difficult but inescapable question: how is *Leonce und Lena* to be judged as a whole? what would be a fair critical assessment of it?

Considerable allowances must certainly be made for the un-polished and mutilated condition in which the work has been handed down to us. If Büchner had been able to finish it properly and supervise its publication many passages which now seem unsatisfactory might well have produced quite a different impres-sion. But this consideration seems hardly adequate to dispose of the critical problem, for in fact all of Büchner's works have been more or less disfigured by incompetent or impertinent editors, and *Lenz* and *Woyzeck* are also unfinished, yet the reputation of these works is now fully established while that of *Leonce und Lena* remains controversial. Gundolf and Hans Mayer, as we have noted, were severely critical of it, and the judgement of Henri Plard is equally unfavourable. Lehmann, on the other hand, quotes the remark of Arthur Adamov: 'Il n'y a rien entre Shakespeare et le Don Juan de Molière jusqu'à Brecht que Büchner', and adds that this enthusiasm for Büchner on the part of a prominent exponent of the modern absurd theatre is in no way surprising because 'Büchner has written the first drama of the absurd theatre of high artistic rank: *Leonce und Lena*, the tragi-comedy of human meaninglessness, the absurd comedy of boredom.'[35] Even the warmest admirers of Büchner may well feel that Adamov's praise is exaggerated, implying as it does that Büchner is superior to Goethe and to Kleist and that even *Faust* is negligible in com-parison with *Dantons Tod* and *Woyzeck*! Büchner himself, clear-sighted as he was and treasuring *Faust* above everything, would have protested against such a judgement. But what of the asser-tion that *Leonce und Lena* is 'the first drama of the absurd theatre of high artistic rank'? One may observe, first of all, that it is a dangerous and dubious way of praising a writer of the past to say that he has anticipated contemporary movements in literature. Büchner has been claimed as a forerunner by both Naturalists and Expressionists, but whether they were thereby doing him much honour must be considered questionable in view of the fact that the bulk of their work has perished while his remains vigorously alive. It is still too soon to say how much of the absurd theatre will prove durable. Adamov himself, in his last period, totally rejected that theatre, including his own experiments in it; and if it were true that *Leonce und Lena* belonged to the absurd theatre he would have been bound to condemn it also.

In fact, as the preceding analysis has shown, *Leonce und Lena* is essentially not a comedy of absurdity but a comedy of revolt – in its tragic passages a comedy of metaphysical revolt, in its satirical passages a comedy of political revolt. It is only in some of its aspects that it tends to the absurd, and in these aspects it is neither particularly original nor of the highest aesthetic merit. Perhaps the greatest weakness of the play is the characterization of Leonce, in which there is a lack of complete consistency or at least of complete lucidity. But in the portrayal of the other characters also we have found less originality and vividness than is usual with Büchner, and in the style and structure of the work there has occasionally appeared to be a certain awkwardness, derivativeness and infelicity.

Our analysis has suggested that the basic reason for these weaknesses is that Büchner's attitude to reality is in the main an attitude of revolt, not an attitude of acceptance. Reality, for him, is associated with tragedy, comedy with unreality; so that, if he wishes to write comedy, it cannot be comedy of a positive kind (in which reality is directly and happily contemplated), but only of a negative kind (in which reality is ironically distorted, burlesqued, travestied). But in this negative attitude Büchner is not at his best, he is unable to deploy the full force of his genius. He is strongest when directly confronting reality, revealing its inmost nature with visionary truth, exhibiting it in the tragic or grimly grotesque light in which it naturally appears to him, without compromises or concessions. He can then show something of the imaginative power of Shakespeare or the young Goethe, and there is no absurdity in comparing him with these great masters even if one must refrain from putting him on an equality with them. But his negative comedy is not comparable with the positive comedy of Shakespeare or Molière; it is simply an inferior kind of comedy, having little of the substantiality, the richness and vitality of the great comic dramatists. As a tragic dramatist Büchner is akin to the greatest; as a comedian he is not quite of the highest order.

But it is only in comparison with the comedies of Shakespeare and Molière, of Lessing and Kleist, or in comparison with Büchner's own work in other genres, that *Leonce und Lena* can be considered inferior. Judged by any standard less than the highest, it must be regarded as a work of great value and merit. Its superiority to the comedies of Brentano and Tieck is evident, especially in the passages of political satire and in the memorably beautiful scenes with Rosetta and Lena, but also in the skilful variation and contrast of tones in the play. It is a measure of its worth that, almost alone of Romantic comedies, *Leonce und Lena* is regularly performed in Germany and can still delight the audiences of our time.

# 7. 'LENZ'

The predominant influence on *Dantons Tod* and *Leonce und Lena* is clearly Shakespeare. In *Lenz* and *Woyzeck* the Shakespearian influence, though still latently present, is much less obvious and direct and Büchner's style becomes more individual and mature. This is one of the reasons and justifications for closely associating *Lenz* with *Woyzeck*, notwithstanding the fact that they are chronologically separated by *Leonce und Lena*. They are also alike in that they are primarily concerned with the life of poor and humble people, not, like *Dantons Tod* and *Leonce und Lena*, with that of kings and princes and famous historical figures. This development is consistent with Büchner's aesthetic principle that the artist must be prepared to immerse himself in the life of the lowliest of mankind, and with his political conviction that it was necessary to seek the formation of a new spiritual life among the *people*. If it had been given to him to live longer it is presumably in this direction – the direction initiated in *Lenz* and continued in *Woyzeck* – that his poetic and dramatic production would have proceeded.

It is not known with certainty when Büchner first conceived the idea of writing about Lenz. The collected works of this gifted and unfortunate poet appeared for the first time in 1828, edited by Tieck; and this edition may have come to the notice of Büchner even before his first visit to Strasbourg. In Strasbourg his circumstances were certainly calculated to nourish an interest in Lenz. Only a few years before, in 1826, J. J. Jaegle, the father of Büchner's fiancée, had delivered the funeral sermon on Jean-Frédéric Oberlin, the man who had once been Lenz's generous host and friend. In 1831 D. E. Stöber, the father of Büchner's friends August and Adolf Stöber, had published a biography of Oberlin in which Lenz's visit to Waldersbach was related. In the same year August Stöber had published in the Stuttgart *Morgenblatt* Lenz's letters to Salzmann and an account of his stay at Waldersbach based on a record by Oberlin which was to become

the principal source of Büchner's Novelle. Evidence of continued
interest in Lenz during Büchner's period in Giessen is to be found
in the letter to Minna of March 1834 (2, 428), which contains a
quotation from Lenz's poem about Friederike Brion, 'Die Liebe auf
dem Lande':

> War nicht umsonst so still und schwach,
> Verlass'ne Liebe trug sie nach.
> In ihrer kleinen Kammer hoch
> Sie stets an der Erinnrung sog;
> An ihrem Brodschrank an der Wand
> Er immer, immer vor ihr stand,
> Und wenn ein Schlaf sie übernahm,
> Er immer, immer wieder kam . . .
> Denn immer, immer, immer doch
> Schwebt ihr das Bild an Wänden noch
> Von einem Menschen, welcher kam
> Und ihr als Kind das Herze nahm.
> Fast ausgelöscht ist sein Gesicht,
> Doch seiner Worte Kraft noch nicht,
> Und jener Stunden Seligkeit,
> Ach jener Träume Wirklichkeit,
> Die, angeboren jedermann,
> Kein Mensch sich wirklich machen kann.

The depth and persistence of Friederike's love for her faithless
lover Goethe, so admirably expressed in these lines, explain the
jealousy which Büchner ascribes to Lenz in the Novelle and which
is such an important motif in it.

Although he had so long been interested in Lenz, it is not until
May 1835 that we find the first indication of Büchner's intention
to write a Novelle about him. On the 12th of that month Gutzkow
writes to him:

I presume your Novelle *Lenz* will be about the shipwrecked poet, since Strasbourg
suggests this subject.[1]

Then, on 28 September 1835, Gutzkow, eager for material for his
projected journal *Deutsche Revue*, suggests that Büchner might
be able to deal with Lenz more easily and quickly in the form of
an essay:

Give us, if nothing more for the beginning, *Recollections of Lenz*: you seem to
have facts there which it would be easy to write up.[2]

And Büchner appears at first to fall in with this proposal, for he writes to his family in October 1835:

Ich habe mir hier allerhand interessante Notizen über einen Freund Goethes, einen unglücklichen Poeten namens Lenz, verschafft, der sich gleichzeitig mit Goethe hier aufhielt und halb verrückt wurde. Ich denke darüber einen Aufsatz in der Deutschen Revue erscheinen zu lassen. (2, 448)

The material on which Büchner proposed to base his work was obtained largely, if not wholly, from August Stöber, and it included the manuscript of Oberlin's record of Lenz's visit. This record was published by Stöber for the first time in 1839 in the journal *Erwinia*, and a second time in Stöber's monograph *Der Dichter Lenz und Friederike von Sesenheim*, Basel, 1842, which contains the following footnote on Oberlin's report:

On this essay is based the Novelle *Lenz* of my deceased friend Georg Büchner, which unfortunately remains a fragment. For a long time in Strasbourg he entertained the idea of making Lenz the hero of a Novelle, and I gave him as material all the manuscripts I possessed.[3]

To Gutzkow's inquiry of 6 February 1836: 'You were proposing once to write a Novelle *Lenz*' (*Eine Novelle Lenz war einmal beabsichtigt*) no reply has been preserved, and indeed Büchner makes no further mention of *Lenz* in any of the letters that have come down to us – unless we suppose that *Lenz* was one of the two 'dramas' referred to in Büchner's last letter to Minna which were to be published together with *Leonce und Lena*. It is impossible to say precisely when the Novelle, in the form in which we have it, was written. It was evidently later than October 1835, since at that time Büchner was still proposing to deal with the subject in the form of an essay. And it was probably earlier than 1 January 1836, since *Lenz* was presumably one of the 'articles' which, as he remarks in his letter of that date, he was thinking of publishing in the *Phönix*.

As we have already seen, Gutzkow's valedictory article of June 1837 brought him as a reward from the hand of Minna Jaegle a fair copy of the manuscript of *Lenz* together with the copy of *Leonce und Lena*. Gutzkow published the Novelle in the *Telegraph für Deutschland* in 1839 under the title *Lenz*. *Eine*

*Reliquie von Georg Büchner*. The next publication was by Ludwig Büchner in the *Nachgelassene Schriften* of 1850 under the title *Lenz. Ein Novellenfragment*. The original manuscript and Minna Jaegle's copy have been lost, but some of the numerous errors and misprints in the first two publications can be corrected by reference to the record of Oberlin on which the Novelle is largely based.

It will have been observed that both August Stöber and Ludwig Büchner refer to the Novelle as a fragment; but it is now generally considered to be virtually complete. The conclusion, describing the condition of hopeless apathy and emptiness in which Lenz is sent away from Waldersbach and arrives in Strasbourg and in which he is doomed to go on living indefinitely (*So lebte er hin*), corresponds to the conclusion of Oberlin's record and is the logical end of Büchner's narrative. It is true that there is a lacuna in Büchner's text at the point where Oberlin describes his secret preparations for removing Lenz from Waldersbach, but Büchner has used the most interesting part of that description elsewhere (cf. 471, 37–40 and 478, 9–15) and in the remainder there is little that could have seemed worthy to be incorporated in his Novelle. Yet it must be recognized that *Lenz* no less than *Leonce und Lena* lacks the author's final revision. There are some slight inconsistencies in the text and an occasional harshness in the grammatical constructions which Büchner might eventually have eliminated. Further difficulties are caused by the loss of the manuscript and the careless and incompetent editing already mentioned.[4]

The subject with which Büchner deals in *Lenz* could hardly be more serious. It is the story of the attempt of a young man of genius to escape the insanity that is overtaking him and of the failure of this attempt, the story of the gradual disintegration and destruction of his mind and soul. And Büchner deals with this subject in a tone as earnest as his theme. There is no ironical or whimsical diversion, as in *Leonce und Lena*. There are not even the touches of grim humour which occasionally relieve the tension in *Dantons Tod* and *Woyzeck*. The tragic reality is confronted simply and directly and rendered as it is, without distortion or mitigation. If in the remarks on literature and art which he puts into the mouth of Lenz we have the most perfect theoretical expression of Büchner's revolt against classicism and idealism, in the Novelle as a whole we have an admirable illustration of the consequences of that revolt for his literary and poetic practice. In this Novelle Büchner both preaches realism and practises it. He strives to render nature with the deepest truth, to seize and communicate that reality, that life, of which, as he lets his Lenz say, even the so-called realists had no conception and which was even more wretchedly travestied by the idealizers. He brings to the task the objectivity of a scientist as well as the imagination of a poet, and in his attitude of detached and uncompromising realism there is no doubt something of that implicit protest against Romantic illusions and chimeras, against Idealist dreams of perfection, which Hugo Friedrich has declared to be characteristic of nineteenth century realism in general.[5] But, as has already been observed in our discussion of Büchner's aesthetic revolt, one must be careful that one knows what one means when applying the equivocal word 'realism' to Büchner. Höllerer is no doubt right in his contention that Büchner's vivid compressed images often seem to anticipate the surrealists rather than the realists. But when he infers that 'Büchner, one of the fathers of realism, is at the same time one of the ancestors of so-called surrealism'; when he suggests that in some passages Büchner 'is nearer to surrealism and supranaturalism than to realism'; he appears to be introducing a dichotomy into Büchner's work which Büchner himself would have disclaimed.[6] It seems to be implied that Büchner is at one time a realist, at another time a surrealist or supranaturalist. But in truth Büchner is always a realist in the only sense that matters for him – in the sense that all his work is devoted to the one great aim of 'giving us nature with the utmost reality', of communicating his vision of reality with the utmost exactness, whether it be a vision of the external world or a vision of the human soul. He is not restricted in his choice of means; he can use exact descriptions or bold imaginative images:

Auf dem kleinen Kirchhof war der Schnee weg, dunkles Moos unter den schwarzen Kreuzen, ein verspäteter Rosenstrauch lehnte an der Kirchhofmauer,
verspätete Blumen dazu unter dem Moos hervor, manchmal Sonne, dann wieder
dunkel. (84)

[wenn] die Wolken wie wilde wiehernde Rosse heransprengten, und der
Sonnenschein dazwischen durchging und kam und sein blitzendes Schwert an
den Schneeflächen zog, so daß ein helles, blendendes Licht über die Gipfel in die
Thäler schnitt. (79)

But one sees that the descriptions and the images serve the same
purpose: the exact communication of the impression received,
and the latter are no less necessary to this end than the former.
This intentness on the precise impression seems to me to dis-
tinguish Büchner after all from the modern expressionists and
surrealists, and to place him with Stendhal and Flaubert and
Chekhov rather than with Barlach or Klee or Kafka. Camus's
comparison of Melville and Kafka still holds good when Büchner's
name is substituted for Melville's:

Like the greatest artists, Melville has constructed his symbols out of concrete
experiences, not out of the stuff of dreams. The creator of myths has a claim to
genius only in so far as he inscribes them in the density of reality and not in the
fleeting clouds of the imagination. In Kafka it is the symbol that gives rise to the
reality described, the incident springs from the image; in Melville the symbol
emerges from the reality, the image is born of the perception. That is why Melville
always remains in contact with the flesh and with nature, which are obscured in
Kafka's work.[7]

It is not his dreams that Büchner is trying to convey, nor any
abstraction; it is no 'Wesensschau' or 'Tiefenschau'; it is the
phenomena of life as he has experienced and observed them. And
that is why, unlike the surrealists and expressionists, he is by no
means averse to precise localization in space and time: the events
of his Novelle occur to well known people at specific dates in a
particular valley of the Vosges mountains. Present fashions should
not tempt us to deny or minimize this strong realistic tendency
which Büchner himself plainly and proudly recognized in his
work.

It is this tendency which impels him once more, as in *Dantons
Tod* and later in *Woyzeck*, to base his work on a careful study of
historical documents. We have already noticed the relation of the

Novelle to Oberlin's record of Lenz's visit. But that record is by no means the only source of Büchner's information. He has also taken many details from D. E. Stöber's biography of Oberlin, a work which he must have read attentively. In the Novelle as in the biography we are told how Oberlin was saved by an invisible hand from falling to his death from a bridge; how Oberlin counselled and comforted his parishioners and advised them on practical matters such as the construction of roads; how he heard mysterious voices and was interested in clairvoyance; how, in his childlike faith in God, he trustingly allowed his conduct to be determined by drawing lots.[8] And one may compare Büchner's sentence:

Ein andermal zeigte ihm Oberlin Farbentäfelchen, er setzte ihm auseinander, in welcher Beziehung jede Farbe mit dem Menschen stände, er brachte zwölf Apostel heraus, deren jeder durch eine Farbe repräsentirt würde . . . (86)

with the following from Stöber:

Le rouge signifie la foi; le jaune, l'amour; le bleu, la science . . . Chacun des douze apôtres de notre Seigneur et Sauveur Jésus-Christ a sa couleur, qui le distingue particulièrement.[9]

One may agree with Voss that by means of such details Büchner is able to give more plasticity to his portrait of Oberlin and at the same time communicate something of the religious, mystical and superstitious atmosphere of the Steintal.[10]

Goethe's *Werther* and Tieck's *Der Aufruhr in den Cevennen* (1826) are the fictional works which have most strongly influenced *Lenz*. Ludwig Büchner relates that when Minna Jaeglé visited Büchner in Darmstadt in the autumn of 1834, he and she read Tieck's Novelle with great interest and pleasure;[11] and there are some striking parallels between particular passages in *Der Aufruhr in den Cevennen* and in *Lenz*. Büchner's account of the religious enthusiasm of the people of the Steintal may also have been influenced generally by Tieck's description of the religious fanaticism of the *Camisards*.

But more important than all these external sources are the personal experience and observation which Büchner has embodied in his Novelle. According to Ludwig Büchner, his brother 'found in Lenz's life and character spiritual conditions akin to his own, and the fragment is more or less a self-portrait of the writer'.[12] Without wishing to press this last assertion, one must agree that Büchner really had much in common with Lenz and that the extraordinary power and authority of his Novelle is largely due to this natural affinity. He had himself experienced the pantheistic raptures and sudden despairs which he ascribes to his hero, and he shared Lenz's passion for drama, his aesthetic principles, his sympathy for poor and oppressed people. Moreover, during the sickness and acute distress which he had suffered in Giessen in the winter of 1833–4 Büchner had experienced and had described in his letters states of mind which, as Landau remarks,[13] were not far removed from madness and not unlike those ascribed to the insane Lenz of the Novelle:

Der erste helle Augenblick seit acht Tagen. Unaufhörliches Kopfweh und Fieber, die Nacht kaum einige Stunden dürftiger Ruhe. Vor zwei Uhr komme ich in kein Bett, und dann ein beständiges Auffahren aus dem Schlaf und ein Meer von Gedanken, in denen mir die Sinne vergehen ... Meine geistigen Kräfte sind gänzlich zerrüttet. Arbeiten ist mir unmöglich, ein dumpfes Brüten hat sich meiner bemeistert, in dem mir kaum ein Gedanke noch hell wird. (*An die Braut*, März 1834, 2, 424 f.)

But Büchner's happier experiences also have found expression in *Lenz*. When, in the letter just referred to, he tells Minna that her image continually stands before him, that he sees her in every dream, we are reminded of Lenz's visions of Friederike Brion in the Novelle (*Er rettete sich in eine Gestalt, die ihm immer vor Augen schwebte* – 89). And the Vosges mountains, which Büchner wandered over on foot in the summer of 1833 and described with so much enthusiasm in his letter of 8 July of that year – later he tells Gutzkow that he loves the Vosges like a mother and knows every peak and valley of them (2, 449) – provided him with the perfect and inevitable setting for the varying moods of his hero, the momentarily peaceful moods and the wildly tragic ones.

Considering the breadth and depth of the personal experiences of Büchner embodied in the Novelle, one is astonished at the degree of self-effacement which he nevertheless achieves in it. Everything is objectivized, converted into life and action, and the author all but vanishes behind his creation. *Lenz* is typically the Novelle of a dramatist; it is pre-eminently a dramatic Novelle.[14]

## STRUCTURE AND STYLE

When Büchner decided against writing an essay on Lenz and chose instead to write a Novelle about him, he set himself a similar task to that which he had already attempted in *Dantons Tod* and was again to attempt in *Woyzeck* – the task of the dramatist who, as Büchner expresses it in the letter of 28 July 1835, is superior to the historian in that 'he creates history for a second time and, instead of giving us a dry narrative, transports us directly into the life of an epoch, giving us, not characterizations but characters, not descriptions but real figures'. In *Lenz* too Büchner is concerned to give us characters rather than characterizations, real figures rather than mere descriptions. And since his aim in the Novelle is essentially the same as in his serious dramas, since he is as much intent here as there on the realization of the most intense life, the most penetrating sense of reality, it is not surprising that the technique of *Lenz*, its style and structure, should be in so many respects akin to that of *Dantons Tod* and *Woyzeck*. Emil Staiger, in a celebrated essay, has shown how the Novellen of Heinrich von Kleist are characteristically dramatic in style and form; but they are the Novellen of a master of the classical 'closed' form of drama, and their technique is analogous to that of the closed dramatic form. *Lenz* is characteristically the Novelle of a master of the revolutionary 'open' form of drama, and its technique is analogous to that of the open dramatic form.

It begins as abruptly as *Dantons Tod* or *Woyzeck*: 'On the 20th of January Lenz went over the mountains' (*Den 20. Januar ging Lenz durch's Gebirg* – 79), and in the opening pages there is hardly a trace of anything that could be called an exposition. As in the dramas we have a series of vivid self-contained scenes which are barely connected with each other. As a rule only their temporal relation is briefly indicated by such phrases as 'on the following morning' (85), 'about this time' (86), 'towards evening' (92), 'meanwhile' (92), 'some days later' (94) etc. Logical connexions and other transitions are reduced to a minimum. Baumann's phrase, 'a drama of parataxis',[15] applies as much to Büchner's Novelle as to his plays, and as much to the relation of the scenes as to the relation of the sentences. Every scene must have its full individual value undistorted by any regard for what goes before or comes after. Büchner is as anxious as ever to avoid everything unessential, everything merely functional. He declines to make the slightest concession to conventional requirements and refuses to *impose* any form on the vigorous life of his conception. As Voss well expresses it: 'In contradistinction to classicism, which seeks to derive life from the form, this "baroque" art derives the form from life.'[16]

The scenes retain something of the 'static' character which we noticed in connexion with *Dantons Tod*: they are concerned with portraying states of mind, conditions of the soul – sometimes, it is true, extremely restless and violent conditions – rather than the phases of a connected action. And the monological tendency in *Danton* has its counterpart here in those suggestions of *monologue intérieur* to which Höllerer first called attention:

Er sprach, er sang, er recitierte Stellen aus Shakespeare, er griff nach Allem, was sein Blut sonst hatte rascher fließen machen, er versuchte Alles, *aber kalt, kalt.* (82)

Dieser Glaube, dieser ewige Himmel im Leben, dies Seyn in Gott; jetzt erst ging ihm die heilige Schrift auf. *Wie den Leuten die Natur so nah trat, alles in himmlischen Mysterien; aber nicht gewaltsam majestätisch, sondern noch vertraut!*
(83)

As Höllerer remarks,[17] the words here italicized do not belong merely to the narrator's report; they are Lenz's words, Lenz's thoughts; one may think of them as being in inverted commas. They are as much an expression of Lenz's vision as the soliloquies of Danton or Robespierre.

The Novelle differs from the dramas, however, in the greater uniformity of its point of view. Not that absolutely everything is presented as it appears to Lenz. Occasionally the reader's attention is drawn to aspects of the situation of which Lenz is unconscious; and, partly because these occasions are so exceptional, a peculiar and most impressive effect may be thereby achieved:

Endlich dämmerte es in ihm, er empfand ein leises tiefes Mitleid mit sich selbst, er weinte über sich, sein Haupt sank auf die Brust, er schlief ein, der Vollmond stand am Himmel, die Locken fielen ihm über die Schläfe und das Gesicht, die Thränen hingen ihm an den Wimpern und trockneten auf den Wangen, so lag er nun da allein, und Alles war ruhig und still und kalt, und der Mond schien die ganze Nacht und stand über den Bergen. (85)

But, unlike the heroes of the plays, Lenz is present in every scene, and, notwithstanding the exceptions, it is his point of view that overwhelmingly predominates. There is consequently no possibility of the sharp contrasts of mood, the 'antipathetic antitheses', which characterize *Dantons Tod* and *Leonce und Lena*. The mood of *Lenz* is one of unrelieved seriousness.

The scenes of the Novelle are sometimes freely invented by Büchner, sometimes suggested by a remark in Oberlin's record, like those scenes of *Dantons Tod* which were suggested by a sentence of Thiers or Mignet. Thus Oberlin briefly reports that on 3 February Lenz 'had tried to waken to life a child called Friederike who had just died in Fouday, but the attempt had failed'. Büchner imagines the whole scene of the attempted resurrection and paints it in detail:

Lenz schauderte, wie er die kalten Glieder berührte und die halbgeöffneten gläsernen Augen sah. Das Kind kam ihm so verlassen vor, und er sich so allein und einsam; er warf sich über die Leiche nieder; der Tod erschreckte ihn, ein heftiger Schmerz faßte ihn an, diese Züge, dieses stille Gesicht sollte verwesen, er warf sich nieder, er betete mit allem Jammer der Verzweiflung, wie er schwach und unglücklich sey, daß Gott ein Zeichen an ihm thue, und das Kind beleben möge; dann sank er ganz in sich und wühlte all seinen Willen auf einen Punkt, so saß er lange starr. Dann erhob er sich und faßte die Hände des Kindes und sprach laut und fest: 'Stehe auf und wandle!' Aber die Wände hallten ihm nüchtern den Ton nach, daß es zu spotten schien, und die Leiche blieb kalt. (93)

Büchner's description of Lenz's preaching (84 f.) is another example of a complete scene springing from a bare statement of Oberlin's.

Though invariably serious, there is still a considerable variety of tone and mood in the episodes of the Novelle. They range from gravely idyllic scenes, as in the picture of the people assembling at the church (84), to the awesome beauty of the descriptions of the mountains. Büchner's visions often have something of the tender piety of those Dutch pictures which his hero admires so much (88); and he also offers us striking momentary impressions comparable with Lenz's description of the two girls sitting on the stone, one binding up her hair, the other helping her (87).

It was that 'beautiful group', it will be remembered, that led Lenz to speak of 'an infinite beauty, passing out of one form into another, eternally unfolded, transformed'.[18] Yet, notwithstanding the view there ascribed to his hero, if one considers Büchner's practice in the Novelle as a whole one will find it impossible to say that he is consistently concerned with the pursuit of such 'an infinite beauty'. True to his aesthetic principles, he is concerned above all with truth and reality; and not less frequent than his fine impressionistic evocations of the light and atmosphere of the Steintal with their idyllic beauty are his grim representations of gloom and horror and agony. Indeed, as the story progresses, it is the dark and dreadful visions that increasingly prevail until the desperate conclusion is reached. So that, notwithstanding the episodic structure of the Novelle, an overall pattern emerges. The self-contained episodes are found to have an atmospheric relation which shapes and integrates them – a relation characterized, though with minor fluctuations, by an increasing intensity of sombreness. This atmospheric pattern, which is reinforced, as we shall see, by stylistic elements, corresponds to the curve of Lenz's fortunes during his stay with Oberlin. A similar technique may be observed in Goethe's *Werther*, where each of the letters which constitute the novel describes a particular episode having its own distinctive mood and atmosphere, while all the letters together reflect the growing desperation of the hero. As the young Goethe too was a master of the open form of drama – one may instance *Götz* and *Urfaust* – it is not surprising that his novelistic technique should have been in some respects akin to Büchner's. But the tone of Büchner's work is in general harder and harsher than Goethe's. It has little of Werther's lyrical effusiveness, nothing of Werther's occasional sentimentality.

*Lenz* has the character of 'paratactic drama' not only by virtue of its episodic structure but also by virtue of its style in the narrower sense of the word. Apart from one extraordinarily long and complex sentence (79 f.), possibly influenced by Goethe's nature descriptions, and a few less remarkable exceptions, Büchner's style in *Lenz* carries parataxis to an extreme. Even the longer periods are composed almost entirely of simple direct statements placed side by side with few or no conjunctions:

Eines Morgens ging er hinaus, die Nacht war Schnee gefallen, im Thal lag heller Sonnenschein, aber weiterhin die Landschaft halb im Nebel. Er kam bald vom Weg ab, und eine sanfte Höhe hinauf, keine Spur von Fußtritten mehr, neben einem Tannenwald hin, die Sonne schnitt Krystalle, der Schnee war leicht und flockig, hie und da Spur von Wild leicht auf dem Schnee, die sich ins Gebirg hinzog. (83)

It may be observed how the concentration on the experience to be conveyed, together with the determination to avoid everything unessential, results not only in the elimination of conjunctions but even, very often, in the suppression of verbs: 'the landscape half in mist', 'no longer any trace of footsteps'; so that the effect is occasionally almost that of a telegram style. The tendency to paratactic co-ordination may even appear in the isolation of individual words, which thereby acquire a special weight and significance:

Er ging hinauf, es war kalt oben, eine weite Stube, leer, ein hohes Bett im Hintergrund. (81)

Er verzweifelte an sich selbst, dann warf er sich nieder, er rang die Hände, er rührte Alles in sich auf; aber todt! todt! (93)

der Himmel war ein dummes blaues Aug, und der Mond stand ganz lächerlich darin, einfältig. (94)

The words which are thus isolated and emphasized are mostly words of special importance, key-words, in the Novelle.

Comparison with Oberlin's record reveals the same process of stylistic purification and invigoration that characterized Büchner's treatment of his sources in *Dantons Tod*: awkward and antiquated expressions, prolixities and irrelevancies are eliminated; description is replaced by action, indirect speech by direct speech. Many of Oberlin's sentences, especially in the latter part of the narrative (cf. 1, 466 f.) are adopted almost without modification, having a pathetic or tragic force which even Büchner could not improve upon; but where necessary he retouches 'with unerring stylistic tact' (Herrmann).[19] Comparison with Oberlin also reveals another characteristic which is common to *Lenz* and to *Danton*, in both cases evidently a consequence of Büchner's realistic approach: just as, in *Danton*, he strives to reproduce the authentic style of his hero and of the period in which he lived, so, in the Novelle, he tries to reproduce the style of the historical Lenz and of the *Sturm und Drang*. If it is true, as Höllerer remarks, that Büchner occasionally achieves insights and visions 'which are anything but *mimesis*',[20] we must not forget that there is nevertheless a great deal of *mimesis* in his work, and here we have another example of it. He copies the 'broken, often hardly intelligible phrases' which Oberlin ascribes to Lenz (1, 462); and it has been convincingly suggested by Hasubek that in the 'verbal dynamics' of the Novelle – for in contrast to the sentences which omit the verb there are others which contain verbal expressions of extraordinary energy: *springen, sich schütteln, werfen, streichen, drängen*, etc. – Büchner is deliberately imitating 'not only the poet Lenz but, even more strongly, the style of the literary epoch to which Lenz's work belonged'.[21] Hasubek also suggests that the frequent use of *so* in the Novelle: 'so träg, so plump', 'so klein, so nahe, so naß' etc., may similarly reflect a peculiarity of Lenz's prose-style; but it may equally be due, once again, to the influence of Goethe's *Werther* where we find many such phrases: 'daß ich sie so ganz allein, so innig, so voll liebe', 'so kindlich ihr Gefühl, ihre Dichtung!', 'alles so unverdorben, so ganz!' etc.

To an even greater degree than in *Dantons Tod*, indeed to a greater degree than any work of Büchner's except *Woyzeck*, the style of *Lenz* is characterized by the use of key-words, some of which we have already noticed. The most frequent are *ruhig* and *Ruhe*, which together occur no less than thirty-five times, *Gott* (fifteen times), *allein* (fourteen times) and *kalt* (eleven times).[22] Other important key-words which, though occurring less frequently, acquire emphasis and significance from their position and context, are *ewig*, *starr*, *entsetzlich*, *leer* and *Leere*, *retten* and *Rettung*, *Trost* and *trostlos*, *heimlich* and *unheimlich*, *tot* and *Tod*, *Licht*, *dunkel* and *finster*, *drängen* and *treiben*. As in the plays, the regular occurrence of such key-words serves to counteract the disintegrating tendency of the parataxis; but they also contribute to that 'atmospheric pattern' which we noticed in connexion with the structure of the Novelle. For their distribution in the text is not arbitrary, but is regulated, consciously or unconsciously, by a principle: as the narrative proceeds the negative terms become dominant: instead of *ruhig* and *Ruhe* we find, increasingly, *unruhig* and *Unruhe*, while *ruhig* and *Ruhe* undergo a sinister change of meaning; instead of *heimlich* we find *unheimlich*. But the significance of the key-words can only be fully understood in relation to Büchner's conception of Lenz's tragic fate, and this we must now consider.

## LENZ AND OBERLIN

If Büchner's Danton is as much an anti-hero as a hero, the Lenz of his Novelle is a no less unconventional protagonist. Though madness had often enough been treated in literature before Büchner, it had never been studied with this cool clinical precision, this tenacious and unflinching objectivity. 'We cannot but be astonished', Gutzkow commented, 'at such an anatomy of vital and mental disturbance.'[23] It still seems astonishing to the psychiatrists of to-day. Walter Schulte refers to *Lenz* as 'that classical study of schizophrenia',[24] and regards it as proof that poetic utterances can anticipate scientific advances by decades. Gerhard Irle admires the boldness with which Büchner attempts a subject which could hardly have been regarded as 'aesthetic' in his time and deals with it in such a truly scientific spirit:

> Büchner's Novelle is written in a detached, cool, 'scientific' manner, which, like a chronicle, allows only the actual events to emerge. The phenomena of mental illness are represented without any obtrusive emotionalism. Among the first sentences, describing Lenz on his way over the mountains, there is the nonchalant remark: 'He felt no tiredness, but sometimes it seemed to him unpleasant that he could not walk on his head.' Or, a little later: 'Everything seemed to him so small, so near, so wet; he would have liked to put the earth behind the stove.' The enormity of a psychic illness is represented as soberly and factually as any normal phenomenon – a shower of rain, for example.[25]

And it is worth noting that the validity and penetration of Büchner's study of a schizophrene – qualities which even now, in the opinion of Schulte and Irle, make it well worth the attention of professional psychiatrists – are due to that intentness on the phenomena of the subject which we have found to be of the essence of Büchner's realism. According to Irle, the Novelle *Lenz* brilliantly confirms the observation of the psychiatrist H. C. Rümke that 'authors who are able to reproduce the surface in all its form and variants' can convey a deeper understanding of human existence than 'those who try to give us an insight into the hidden depths'.[26] Realism in Büchner's sense, Höllerer has told us, 'is not representation [*Abschilderung*], but is imbued with the strongest symbolical power'.[27] We may readily grant this 'strongest symbolical power', and we must certainly not forget the symbolical significance of the insanity described in *Lenz*. But the testimony of the psychiatrists indicates that Büchner's realism is also, in a sublime sense, representation, and that this precisely is its virtue. Certainly not a representation that could be divorced from insight, imagination, feeling, experience – it presupposes all these and is bound up with them – but still representation. Büchner is a realist in the sense that, whatever the symbolical power of his work, he sets out from the phenomenon and never loses sight of it.

*Lenz* is evidently a work of considerable scientific interest, but it is still a work of art, and for Büchner the great aim of art is the communication of feeling. The truth of the representation

(Büchner's 'realism') finds its justification in the communication of feeling which it makes possible. Notwithstanding the detached scientific attitude of the narrator, the Novelle is instinct with feeling; it appeals to our emotions, our fears and our sympathies as powerfully as any drama; and indeed in its delineation of the fate of the hero no less than in its style and structure *Lenz* is essentially dramatic. It is a drama that is played out within the soul of Lenz himself, but it also involves tensions and conflicts with other persons and powers – especially with Oberlin, but also with the simple people of the Steintal, with the memories of Lenz's mother and of Friederike Brion, and with the all-pervading influence of nature in the country of the Vosges.

As the story opens we see Lenz crossing the mountains in the direction of the Steintal. We are not immediately told where he is coming from nor where he is going; nor do we know the reason for his journey. But we are shown his state of mind (both *Dantons Tod* and *Woyzeck* begin similarly), and it is a state of imminent madness. In the tenth sentence, which in its enormous complex structure seems to be striving to gather the whole landscape into one impression, Lenz still appears capable of an ecstatic pantheistic adoration of nature akin to Werther's. But only momentarily; the threat to his sanity soon reasserts itself with redoubled force. Many of the characteristics of Lenz's disease are already indicated in these opening pages; later they will only become more pronounced, more dreadful in their manifestations. They are the characteristics expressed by the key-words *drängen*, *entsetzlich*, *Angst*, *einsam*, *leer*, *finster*, which are opposed by the positive values implied in *Licht*, *ruhig*, *retten*. Lenz's madness has not yet fully overtaken him, but he feels it approaching as a physical presence, as something that human beings cannot bear to look upon:

es faßte ihn eine namenlose Angst in diesem Nichts, er war im Leeren, er riß sich auf und flog den Abhang hinunter. Es war finster geworden, Himmel und Erde verschmolzen in Eins. Es war als ginge ihm was nach, und als müsse ihn was Entsetzliches erreichen, etwas das Menschen nicht ertragen können, als jage der Wahnsinn auf Rossen hinter ihm. (80)

It is evident from this and many other passages that Lenz's suffering – a suffering so intense that it shakes his whole body and covers his face with cold sweat (99) – consists above all in fear itself, the 'nameless fear' that is here so powerfully described. We may think of it, according to Viëtor's suggestions, as 'the primal fear of the abyss of life',[28] the dread of the infinite ever-present possibility and actuality of suffering in the world. But for Lenz this infinite horror takes the shape of madness, and madness itself appears in a particular form. It appears as *emptiness*, the loss of substance, the loss of contact with the world, the loss of the sense of reality and of one's own identity. In its most extreme manifestation it can be a mere living death, a 'torpid rest bordering on non-existence' (*der dumpfen an's Nichtseyn gränzenden Ruhe* – 100), the apathy which is a classical symptom of schizophrenia. Büchner once (84) uses the term *Starrkrampf* to describe it – spiritual numbness, paralysis – and it is significant that in the letter to his fiancée of March 1834 he uses that word to describe his own condition – a clear instance of his drawing on his own experience in his portrayal of Lenz. Like Lenz, Büchner had often longed to be capable of feeling and of the expression of feeling, to be released from 'the sense of being dead' (*das Gefühl des Gestorbenseins* – 2, 424), the sense of being a soulless automaton.

At least in the earlier stages of the development described in the Novelle Lenz's condition is aggravated by darkness and solitude. Under such circumstances his contact with reality becomes even more attenuated. He feels utterly *alone*; indeed he is not sure that the whole world is not only a dream, that he himself is not only a dream. Everything seems arbitrary; he has an impulse to do whatever occurs to him, to stand on his head, to turn people and houses upside down; and the unreality of his experience is accentuated by the hallucinations of schizophrenia, auditory and haptic hallucinations. The bending of his foot, the silence of the horizon, resound in his ears like thunder. He feels a pain in the arm with which he once embraced Friederike. And his agony is intensified by the memory of his former dreams, his former fullness of life.

But against all this there is the inextinguishable urge to *save* himself, a powerful instinct of self-preservation (*ein mächtiger Erhaltungstrieb*) which drives him independently of his will to resist the force that is impelling him towards the abyss:

es war als sey er doppelt und der eine Theil suchte den andern zu retten, und rief sich selbst zu. (99)

Paradoxically, it is this instinct of self-preservation that drives him to bathe at night in the icy water of the well, to knock his head against the wall, to throw himself from the window, to make repeated half-hearted attempts at suicide. It is not that he wishes to die. Like Danton, Lenz does not expect peace in the grave, does not believe in the possibility of annihilation. But he hopes by means of the self-infliction of severe physical pain to re-establish contact with reality and rescue his foundering sanity.

It is this longing to be saved that brings him to Oberlin and to the Steintal, and here he appears at first to find what he is seeking – release both from his appalling sense of emptiness and from the incessant restless urge to fill up this void. Here, for a while, he finds *peace* in the true sense of the word. Everything in the Steintal is peaceful; the quiet valley of Waldersbach; the people, who are quiet and serious 'as if not daring to disturb the tranquillity of their valley' (*als wagten sie die Ruhe ihres Thales nicht zu stören*); and above all Oberlin himself, who is the very incarnation of *peace* (*Ruhe*) – Büchner cannot reiterate the word sufficiently when describing him:

Es wirkte alles wohlthätig und beruhigend auf ihn, er mußte Oberlin oft in die Augen sehen, und die mächtige Ruhe, die uns über der ruhenden Natur, im tiefen Wald, in mondhellen schmelzenden Sommernächten überfällt, schien ihm noch näher, in diesem ruhigen Auge, diesem ehrwürdigen ernsten Gesicht. (82)

Gradually Lenz feels more at home. He thinks of his mother and her tranquil love, and it is a hallowed moment when he sees how 'a rainbow of rays' envelops his shadow. The very spirit of nature seems to touch his forehead and to speak to him (83).

Lenz is a trained theologian, and in his new confidence offers to preach in place of Oberlin. We are told how he speaks simply to the simple villagers, how he feels that they are all suffering together with him, and how it is a comfort to him if he can turn their thoughts away from their material distress, their obscure grief, towards Heaven. The words they sing, which are now known to be quoted by Büchner from a pietistic source,[29] are an affirmation of suffering as devotion to God:

> Laß in mir die heil'gen Schmerzen,
> Tiefe Bronnen ganz aufbrechen;
> Leiden sey all mein Gewinnst,
> Leiden sey mein Gottesdienst.

But Lenz himself seems to find little comfort in these words. We are told that the whole universe seems to him wounded, lacerated, and that he feels indescribable pain because of this (*Das All war für ihn in Wunden; er fühlte tiefen unnennbaren Schmerz davon*). And the following lines, describing the 'divine twitching lips' which bend down over him and press themselves to his, suggest Lena's apocalyptic vision of a crucified world in which Christ cannot save the victims but only share their suffering. Yet, painful as it is, this is one of Lenz's happiest moments, for his soul is fully alive, he is at least free from his spiritual paralysis.

A still higher degree of spiritual liberation is achieved by Lenz in his disquisition on literature and art, which follows soon after the description of his preaching. Assuming the views he expresses to be substantially those of Büchner, we have already analysed them in Chapter 4. But we have now to consider their significance in the artistic economy of the Novelle. So considered, they must be rated higher than the corresponding passage in *Dantons Tod* where Camille expresses comparable opinions; they betoken a notable advance in Büchner's artistic skill and maturity. The views on literature and art which Camille expresses are not particularly appropriate in his mouth. For Camille is a journalist, not an artist; and moreover there is an inconsistency between the basically anti-classical aesthetics which he champions and the enthusiasm for the world of ancient Greece which he displays elsewhere in the play. In the Novelle there is no such inconsistency. Nothing could be more appropriate than Lenz's speech attacking idealization in art and demanding truth to nature and sympathy for humble people. For Lenz is not only a theologian; he is also a poet. It is natural that he should be interested in poetic and artistic problems. And indeed what better way could Büchner have found to illustrate this essential aspect of his hero's nature than by letting him discuss poetry and art, and discuss them in this particular manner, in this particular sense? It is only a poet that could express himself as Lenz does in his description of the two Dutch pictures, in his examples of the 'infinite beauty, passing out of one form into another, eternally unfolded, transformed'. And everything he says is not only true to the historical Lenz but perfectly consistent with the attitude ascribed to him throughout the Novelle – perfectly consistent with the deep interest he shows in the simple country people, in the spirit of the New Testament, in nature as he observes it around him. It is significant that Lenz's speech on art and literature is not disfigured by the broken sentences and mental blockages which characterize his more distracted utterances. The sentences flow easily and eloquently, revealing the full power and distinction of a noble mind that is not yet overthrown. In this moment Lenz is free from the furies that pursue him, and can afford to forget his personal cares in his eager contemplation of wider issues:

In der Art sprach er weiter, man horchte auf, es traf Vieles, er war roth geworden über dem Reden, und bald lächelnd, bald ernst, schüttelte er die blonden Locken. Er hatte sich ganz vergessen. (88)

But now we reach the turning point in Lenz's fate, the peripeteia of his drama. The demon of insanity which he has momentarily held at bay returns to the attack with renewed force, and the peace he has temporarily won is shattered by a series of blows each more severe than the last. The first of these setbacks is Kaufmann's suggestion that he should obey his father and return home. The agitation into which he is thrown by Kaufmann's officiousness, his dismay at the thought of having to leave the tranquillity of the Steintal which he has found so salutary, is evident in the abrupt, ejaculatory manner of his reply:

Es ist mir jetzt erträglich, und da will ich bleiben; warum? warum? Eben weil
es mir wohl ist; was will mein Vater? Kann er mehr geben? Unmöglich! Laßt
mich in Ruhe. (89)

Kaufmann persuades Oberlin to visit Switzerland in his company,
and Lenz finds the empty house uncanny (*unheimlich*). Whereas
formerly the Steintal was becoming homely and familiar to him,
the expression *unheimlich* occurs now with increasing frequency.
But the stillness of the mountains enables him, once more, to
recover his peace of mind, and he has the impression of lying by
an infinite sea softly billowing up and down (90).

More serious are the consequences of his second ordeal, his
eerie experience at night in the mountain hut with the sick girl
whose expression is sometimes one of 'indescribable suffering',
and with the forbidding fanatic who has the reputation of being
a saint and a seer. The experience of this night makes a powerful
and sinister impression on Lenz: he feels himself being driven
by 'an inexorable force' (*eine unerbittliche Gewalt*) towards an
abyss. Like all of Büchner's heroes, Lenz has virtually no voli-
tional freedom, he is under the curse of necessity, he is driven by
forces beyond his control and beyond his understanding (hence
the frequency in the Novelle of expressions like *es trieb ihn, es
drängte ihn*). They are no puppets, these heroes of Büchner –
Danton, Lenz, Woyzeck; they are 'human beings of flesh and
blood'. But it is their tragedy that natural or historical necessity
treats them like puppets. With a living soul in their breast, they
are treated like dead things.[30] And nowhere is the revolting
injustice of their fate more evident than in the sense of guilt that
torments them even when they are guiltless, even when their
'crime' has been inevitable. This was so with Danton and it is
equally so with Lenz. It is especially in relation to Friederike Brion
that he feels guilty. In his conversation with Madame Oberlin Lenz
paints a charming picture of Friederike as he had once known her:

wenn sie so durch's Zimmer ging, und so halb für sich allein sang, und jeder Tritt
war eine Musik, es war so eine Glückseligkeit in ihr, und das strömte in mich
über, ich war immer ruhig, wenn ich sie ansah, oder sie so den Kopf an mich
lehnte . . . (92)

And in the Steintal too, during the earlier and happier part of his stay, Lenz could still find refuge in the recollection of Friederike as well as in the present strength of Oberlin (89). But when he is accidentally reminded of her after his dreadful night in the mountain cottage, when his mental stability has again been so severely strained and his hold on sanity so much weakened, his memory of her becomes associated with an agony of remorse. Her fate weighs on his heart with the pressure of hundredweights (*centnerschwer*). As he later tells Oberlin, Friederike had loved him, but she had also loved another (Goethe), and in his accursed jealousy he had sacrificed her; he had murdered both her and her mother. Oberlin's record had suggested that Lenz's relation to women – and Friederike is expressly mentioned as his 'Geliebte'[31] – as well as his disobedience to his father and other failings had been the cause of his insanity. Büchner, with a deeper insight which has won the praise of modern psychiatrists,[32] represents Lenz's sense of guilt as the effect, not the cause, of his insanity. As the Oberlin of the Novelle assures him, there was no reason to believe that he had injured Friederike and her mother; for all that was known of them, they might still be well and happy. But the irrationality of his contrition does not make it less painful. When the intensity of his madness reaches its extreme, he runs at midnight through the courtyard crying the name 'Friederike' 'with the utmost speed, confusion and despair' (*mit äußerster Schnelle, Verwirrung und Verzweiflung*); and it is especially on this night that the maids hear a sound from his room like that of a shepherd's pipe which, it is suggested, may have been his whimpering 'with hollow, fearful, desperate voice' (*mit hohler, fürchterlicher, verzweifelnder Stimme*).

After Kaufmann's so unwelcome suggestion, after the so disquieting night in the mountain hut, Lenz suffers his decisive defeat in his attempt to awaken the dead child in Fouday. That the child is called Friederike suggests that he may have been trying, in an obscure, confused manner, to repair the wrong he felt he had done to Friederike Brion. But the attempt is also, and pre-eminently, part of what Büchner describes as Lenz's 'religious torments' (*religiöse Quälereien*). Remembering the former intensity of his reactions and feeling himself now so *empty*, so *dead*, he appeals to God to rekindle the glow within him by performing a miracle upon him. He asks God for a sign; and when, shortly afterwards, he hears of the dead child in Fouday he assumes that God is about to grant his prayer: he would succeed in awakening the child to life again, and this would be the miracle that would restore the fervour of his faith and fill the spiritual void within him. When the attempt fails, the experience that was to be the proof of God's care for his creatures becomes the proof of the contrary: evidently God cared nothing for this poor solitary child whose gentle features were now doomed to decay. What follows is the mightiest and fiercest outburst of metaphysical revolt in all of Büchner's writings. Amidst the gloom and mist of a sinister landscape Lenz, elsewhere so humble, so contrite, is moved to the ultimate blasphemy:

Er rannte auf und ab. In seiner Brust war ein Triumph-Gesang der Hölle. Der Wind klang wie ein Titanenlied, es war ihm, als könnte er eine ungeheure Faust hinauf in den Himmel ballen und Gott herbei reißen und zwischen seinen Wolken schleifen; als könnte er die Welt mit den Zähnen zermalmen und sie dem Schöpfer in's Gesicht speien. (93)

It may be true, as Bergemann suggests, that in the 'Titan's song' there is a reminiscence of Goethe's *Prometheus*; but even in that passionate hymn of the young Goethe there is hardly such a force of rebellious anger and hatred as we have here. Such indignation, however, is possible only so long as one can believe in the existence of a creator who has deliberately calculated and planned the evil in the world. As Lenz wanders higher up the mountains the world no longer looks to him like the creation of a cunning and malignant genius. It appears rather like a tragic farce, infinitely painful, but adventitious, pointless, grotesque:

So kam er auf die Höhe des Gebirges, und das ungewisse Licht dehnte sich hinunter, wo die weißen Steinmassen lagen, und der Himmel war ein dummes blaues Aug, und der Mond stand ganz lächerlich drin, einfältig. Lenz mußte laut lachen, und mit dem Lachen griff der Atheismus in ihn und faßte ihn ganz sicher und ruhig und fest. (94)

With the realization of the absurdity of the world, its undesigned and senseless misery – a realization marked by Lenz's loud and painful laughter – blasphemy gives way to atheism, and the depth and certainty of this atheism are underlined by the polysyndeton *ganz sicher und ruhig und fest*, in which the three adverbs are virtually synonyms and, with the repeated *und,* have the steady rhythm of unshakeable conviction.

Büchner has undoubtedly been influenced by Tieck here. Compare the following sentences from Tieck's *Der Aufruhr in den Cevennen*, where the young hero, Edmund, is relating his adventures to his father:

Bald ruhend, bald wandelnd kam ich mit der Dämmerung der Frühe in die Gegend von Sauve hinüber, im innern Gebirge. Sie kennen, mein Vater, die hohe Lage der dortigen traurigen Landschaft, kein Baum, kein Strauch weit umher, kaum einzelne Grashalme auf dem dürren weißen Kalkboden . . . Sonderbar, wie sich hier mein Gemüt verwirrte. Ich kann es in keinen menschlichen Worten wiedergeben, wie mir plötzlich hier jedes glaubende Gefühl, jeder edle Gedanke untersank, wie mir die Schöpfung, die Natur, und das seltsamste Rätsel, der Mensch, mit seinen wunderbaren Kräften und seiner gemeinen Abhängigkeit vom Element, wie toll, widersinnig und lächerlich mir alles dies erschien. Ich konnte mich nicht zähmen, ich mußte unaufhaltsam dem Triebe folgen, und mich durch lautes Lachen erleichtern. Da war kein Gott, kein Geist mehr, da war nur Albernheit, Wahnwitz und Fratze in allem, das kreucht, schwimmt und fliegt, am meisten in dieser Kugel, die denkt, sinnt und weint, und unterhalbe frißt und käut . . . Ich war ganz zerstört, und schwer ward mir der Rückweg zum Leben, aber ich fand ihn endlich mit Hülfe des Erbarmenden.' (Tieck's *Schriften*, Berlin, 1853, vol. 26, p. 170)

Notwithstanding Tieck's more diffuse style, there is an obvious likeness here, both in thought and situation, to the passage from *Lenz*. But Tieck, though he implies atheism, avoids using this ugly word, and the strange aberration of the hero is very brief, his return to God very speedy. Büchner not only does not shrink from using the word atheism, he strongly emphasizes it; and there is no suggestion that Lenz's lapse is only temporary, no promise of the saving intervention of God's mercy. This passage is in fact the climax of Lenz's tragedy. The experiment which he had hoped would renew his faith in God has actually destroyed it. His whole attempt to find peace and healing in the religious life of Oberlin and the Steintal is seen to have miscarried.

It is true that on the following day Lenz is horrified at the blasphemy he has been guilty of. We still hear of his praying 'almost all night long' (97); and he still feels that the way to God is to be found in Oberlin and only in him (94). But after the experience on the mountain top it appears that his faith in God, though it returns to him in some measure, is never again as complete and confident as it had once been. If he does not now deny the existence of God, he can no longer believe that God can save him. He thinks of himself as an apostate, as damned in all eternity like the Wandering Jew. And when Oberlin urges him to seek Christ's grace which would surely not be withheld from him, he can only wring his hands and exclaim: 'Ah! ah! divine consolation . . .' (*Ach! ach! göttlicher Trost* . . .). He cannot, as in Oberlin's record, go on to say: 'ah – divine, oh – I pray – I worship!', adding that he recognized and revered God's dispensation which had so soon brought Oberlin back to comfort him. It is significant that Büchner, though he is otherwise following Oberlin's record here, omits that latter part of the sentence. The effect, as Voss remarks,[33] is to alter the implication of Lenz's apostrophe to 'divine consolation'. It is no longer, as in Oberlin's record, an expression of trust in God and of submission to his will, but has rather a wistful tone of doubt and questioning.

And indeed it becomes only too clear in the remaining pages of the Novelle that whether or not Lenz prays to God, whether or not he implores Christ's grace, no consolation or comfort is to be granted to him. It is expressly stated that his condition becomes more and more comfortless:

Sein Zustand war indessen immer trostloser geworden, alles was er an Ruhe aus der Nähe Oberlins und aus der Stille des Thals geschöpft hatte, war weg; die Welt, die er hatte nutzen wollen, hatte einen ungeheuern Riß, er hatte keinen Haß, keine Liebe, keine Hoffnung, eine schreckliche Leere und doch eine folternde Unruhe, sie auszufüllen. Er hatte *Nichts*. (97)

Thus the condition he had feared most – that state of utter apathy and emptiness, that living death – proves after all to be his ultimate fate. The inexorable force which he had so desperately struggled to resist sweeps him finally into the abyss, 'the abyss of irredeemable madness, a madness through all eternity' (*die Kluft unrettbaren Wahnsinns, eines Wahnsinns durch die Ewigkeit* – 99).

In the concluding pages of the Novelle, Büchner, following Oberlin's record more closely now but still including many insights of his own, gives a detailed account of the latest and most agonizing stages of Lenz's malady, an account which need not be recapitulated here. Suffice it to say that it is a picture of unimaginable suffering, ending in the sad description of Lenz's departure from the Steintal 'with cold resignation'. Ironically, the Vosges mountains appear at their most beautiful during this journey – Büchner offers a final glimpse of them in a few lines of incomparable splendour – but it is a beauty that can no longer mean anything to Lenz. 'He was completely indifferent... calmly Lenz stared out, no inkling, no impulse' (*er war vollkommen gleichgültig . . . Lenz starrte ruhig hinaus, keine Ahnung, kein Drang*). And when he arrives in Strasbourg it is 'in dull rainy weather' (*bei trübem regnerischem Wetter*), on a morning as bleak as his condition.

The 'infinite suffering' which Büchner describes with such acute insight, with such power and vividness, is presented to the reader with unfailing objectivity, more objectively indeed than in Oberlin's record. But whereas Oberlin leaves us in no doubt as to his conviction that it is a consequence of Lenz's erring ways, in Büchner's account the fault is not Lenz's and there is a latent yet persistent protest against the injustice of a world in which so much agony can be inflicted on an innocent person. Büchner's dramatic method does not permit him to express that protest directly in the naive manner in which Oberlin expresses his censure of Lenz; like a true dramatist, Büchner prefers simply to present the facts and let them speak for themselves. Yet there is one passage where Büchner does after all allow the implicit protest to become explicit. It is the passage near the end of the Novelle describing Lenz's reaction to Oberlin's last appeal to him to trust in God:

Oberlin sprach ihm von Gott. Lenz wand sich ruhig los und sah ihn mit einem Ausdruck unendlichen Leidens an, und sagte endlich: 'aber ich, wär' ich allmächtig, sehen Sie, wenn ich so wäre, ich könnte das Leiden nicht ertragen, ich würde retten, retten, ich will ja nichts als Ruhe, Ruhe, nur ein wenig Ruhe und schlafen können'. Oberlin sagte, dies sey eine Profanation. Lenz schüttelte trostlos mit dem Kopfe. (99)

This is Lenz's last allusion to religion, the theme which, in one form or another, has pervaded the Novelle from the beginning; and its occurrence in this final position gives the passage a special weight and significance, which is increased still further by the deliberate and coherent form in which Lenz expresses himself here in contrast to the inarticulate phrases of his other utterances during this extreme stage of his illness. In the 'open' dramatic structure of the Novelle this passage has, in fact, the effect of the 'integration point' which is characteristic of the 'open' structure of Büchner's tragic dramas. In *Lenz* as in *Dantons Tod* and *Woyzeck* there is a pause for thought immediately before the catastrophe, and in that moment the philosophical significance which underlies and integrates the whole work and which in each of the other scenes is expressed in dramatic terms finds expression for once in intellectual terms – symbolically, mythically or discursively.

The thought ascribed to Lenz in this passage is certainly Büchner's. There is no suggestion of it in Oberlin's record and it does not, so far as I can see, occur anywhere in Lenz's plays or poems; though we may note that Schlosser at a slightly later period than that dealt with in the Novelle describes Lenz as 'unbelieving towards God and man',[34] so that the ascription of the thought to Lenz is not necessarily unhistorical. But if the thought is hardly characteristic of Lenz, it is certainly characteristic of Büchner, and has been recognized to be so by most of the critics. It is the thought of Büchner's philosophical writings that the suffering of mankind and of other living creatures is inconsistent with the alleged perfection of God; it is the thought of Payne in *Dantons Tod* that 'the slightest twinge of pain, be it perceptible only in an atom, makes a crack in creation from top to bottom'. (It is perhaps significant that Lenz's world also is said to have an 'enormous crack' in it – the word *Riß* occurs only in these two passages in all Büchner's imaginative writings.) It is indeed not far removed from the thought of Danton and his friends when, at the integration point of that play, they wonder whether the suffering of mankind may not serve only for the diversion and delectation of the gods. Büchner, it is true, does not let Lenz expressly draw his own conclusion that no perfect being – therefore no 'God' in the strict sense of the word – can exist. But he does let Lenz point to the discrepancy between the experience of mankind and the alleged omnipotence of God, leaving it to the reader to draw the obvious inference. Büchner's metaphysical revolt finds expression not only in Lenz's furious blasphemy on the mountain but equally in the deliberate 'profanation', the virtual atheism, of his final response to Oberlin's religious appeal.

Not that *Lenz* is a *pièce à thèse*. As a dramatist and imaginative writer Büchner is not a didacticist nor propagandist. Very often, I think one must admit, he does let us feel where his sympathies lie, he does somehow indicate what appears to him to be true and what absurd. But it must be the overriding concern of every great dramatist to do justice to reality, even at the cost of apparent contradictions and philosophical inconsistencies; and for Büchner too that is the overriding concern. In *Lenz*, consequently, the treatment of religion is not subordinated to his philosophical views, and there is no general anti-religious tendency. Oberlin, the religious leader of the Steintal community, is regularly mentioned with the greatest respect. Only in the final stages of Lenz's mental disintegration, when the loss of hope and faith has plunged him into infinite vacuity and tedium and when all activity seems to him to have no other purpose than to beguile boredom, only then is he tempted once, in a passage reminiscent of *Leonce und Lena*, to describe Oberlin's practical and charitable activity as 'a comfortable pastime' (*einen behaglichen Zeitvertreib* – 96). It is perhaps in the account of Lenz's sermon (84) that Büchner appears to be most sympathetic towards Christianity, to appreciate most deeply its power to comfort poor and unhappy people. But though Büchner does justice to this aspect of Christianity,

Lenz's later revolt against the Christian conception of God is not thereby invalidated. The hymn-strophe which the congregation sings immediately after Lenz's sermon – part of it reappears in *Woyzeck* – has been related by critics to the words spoken by Büchner on his deathbed and recorded by Caroline Schulz; it has been taken as evidence of an increasingly religious tendency in Büchner's later thinking, and as proof that the words reported by Caroline really represent his considered views. The alleged relation certainly exists, though there are important nuances of meaning differentiating the hymn strophe from the words of the dying Büchner. The thought of the positive value of suffering and of the impulse voluntarily to embrace it was evidently often present to his mind, and it is understandable that it should have found expression in some form in his last hours. But that thought is not the dominant thought in *Lenz*. As we have already noticed, Lenz seems much more acutely aware of the 'wounds' of the world than of the profit or redemption which they are alleged to make possible. And indeed for him at least, as the further course of the narrative reveals, there is no profit or redemption to be gained thereby. At least for Lenz the words of the dying Büchner: 'it is by pain that we enter in to God', are not true. The violent pain which Lenz undergoes or deliberately inflicts on himself, his 'infinite suffering', does not bring him closer to God but draws him farther away from him. In the end it destroys his faith and reduces him to complete indifference. Shortly after the religious enthusiasm of the divine service with its fervent hymn the curve of Lenz's fate begins its downward course and continues downward to its termination in a prospect of unrelieved misery. Even *Dantons Tod* hardly ends so tragically, for there, even to the last moment, there is still the comradeship of Danton and his friends, there is still the love of Julie and Lucile challenging and prevailing over death. But in the end Lenz has neither love nor friendship because he has become insensible to them; he has, as Büchner says, *nothing*.

There is only one work in German literature that is both akin to

*Lenz* and of comparable value: *Die Leiden des jungen Werther*. It is a measure of the extraordinary value of Büchner's Novelle that it can so well bear comparison with Goethe's inspired novel. More than a few traits in Büchner's portrait of Lenz are borrowed from Goethe's hero, but the Novelle as a whole has its own distinctive tone and style – much less lyrical, more relentless and incisive than that of *Werther*. In his command of language, in the brilliance and originality of his descriptions of nature, Büchner is not inferior to Goethe, and in his psychological insights he ventures into stranger and more dreadful regions of the mind than had ever before been explored in German literature.

Of the later German writers only Gerhart Hauptmann appears to have been directly influenced by *Lenz*. There are traces of its influence in *Bahnwärter Thiel* (1887);[35] and *Der Apostel* (1890) has clearly been modelled on it without, however, achieving anything like the solidity, the power, or the many-sided interest of Büchner's work.

# 8. 'WOYZECK'

*Woyzeck* is the culmination of Büchner's dramatic career. In the last year before his death he had become surer of his aims than at the time of *Dantons Tod*; his greater maturity and fuller command of his dramatic resources gave him the confidence to attempt something even more daring, even more original than his first great tragedy. *Woyzeck* is Büchner's boldest and most successful attempt to apply the artistic principles set forth in the Novelle *Lenz*. In doing so he was continuing a distinctively German tradition, the tradition initiated by Reinhold Lenz himself. But in continuing that tradition Büchner also radicalized it. The plays of Lenz which were in some degree his models, *Der Hofmeister* and *Die Soldaten*, were still, after all, middle-class dramas. The hero of the former was a man of education, the hero of the latter a merchant. Büchner dared to choose as his hero a proletarian outcast, and so became the first dramatist of Europe to write a working-class tragedy.

Unfortunately – it is indeed one of the greatest misfortunes in the history of modern literature – this play which was Büchner's greatest and most original achievement, is incomplete. It is a fragment in a different and graver sense than *Lenz* or *Leonce und Lena*. Much as we may regret the imperfect condition in which these two works have been handed down to us, we can at least be confident that they are substantially complete. Not so with *Woyzeck*. All that we possess is a number of sketches or drafts, each of which is obviously fragmentary and no possible combination of which can be accepted as fully representing Büchner's intention. The play which is known to theatregoers by the name of 'Woyzeck' can only with many reservations be said to be Büchner's work; to a considerable degree it is the concoction of editors or producers. Only a pedant or a purist would object to such attempts, sadly imperfect as they must be, to make the play viable on the stage. But for anybody who seriously wishes to study *Büchner's Woyzeck* the fragmentary condition of the work has certain ineluctable consequences. We cannot proceed as if we had a complete text at our disposal, since no such text exists. We cannot assume that we know how Büchner intended the play to end, since that is a matter of dispute. The only sound procedure is to accept the fragmentary drafts as they are given in the extant manuscripts; to study them, so far as possible, in chronological order; and, since we cannot know the goal which Büchner had set himself, to ascertain at least the direction in which he was moving. Such a *genetic* method of study is rather laborious, but it is a labour which must not be shirked, for it provides the only reasonably firm foundation for the interpretation and criticism of the play. In particular, it is the only way in which we can hope to answer the frequently mooted question: to what extent did Büchner's intention change in the course of his work on *Woyzeck*? to what extent did he himself change? Even so, we cannot expect certainty; there are problems in the textual criticism and interpretation of *Woyzeck* which will never be fully solved. We must be content with probable solutions and the elimination of the impossible.

### SOURCES AND GENESIS

Like *Dantons Tod* and *Lenz*, *Woyzeck* had its origin in experiences which occurred to Büchner long before he thought of embodying them in a work of imaginative literature, especially in the experiences of that desperate Giessen period which has been aptly described as Büchner's 'inferno'.[1] It is possible, indeed, that his interest in condemned murderers may have been excited at a still earlier stage – perhaps as early as 1824, when Johann Christian Woyzeck was executed in Leipzig for the murder of Johanna Christiana Woost and when Dr Clarus, medical officer of the city of Leipzig, published his second report on the sanity of the condemned man. The case excited great interest at the time and may well have been discussed in the Büchner household, Büchner's father being professionally interested in such matters. The Clarus report was republished the following year in the *Zeitschrift für die Staatsarzneikunde*, a journal to which Ernst Büchner was both a subscriber and a contributor. A few years later there was the somewhat similar case of Johann Diess, who, on 15 August 1830, stabbed to death his mistress Elisabeth Reuter. The crime was committed near Darmstadt, where Büchner, then nearly seventeen years of age, was still attending the *Gymnasium*. Diess was condemned to imprisonment for life, but died on 23 May 1834, whereupon his body was consigned for dissection to the anatomical theatre in Giessen, precisely at the time when Büchner was studying anatomy there. It is highly probable, as Egon Krause remarks,[2] that Büchner assisted at the dissection of the corpse. Still another case which was to have an influence on Büchner's play – a more important influence than the Diess case and almost as important as the Woyzeck case – was that of Daniel Schmolling, who, on 25 September 1817, stabbed to death his mistress Henriette Lehne. There is conclusive evidence that, at some time prior to the writing of the first sketch of *Woyzeck*, Büchner must have read Dr Horn's account of Schmolling's crime in the *Archiv für medizinische Erfahrung* (Berlin, March–April, 1820). The reports of Horn and Clarus have the same importance for *Woyzeck* as the writings of Thiers and Mignet for *Dantons Tod* and Oberlin's record for *Lenz*. As Winkler well observes:

Büchner had a sense of responsibility towards the world: he wanted to represent the given world outside of him, not some imaginary world within him ... So the Clarus source and the other sources are for him a piece of nature and history; he tries to see this piece truly, to interpret it rightly, and then to embody it in a work.[3]

With the deep sympathetic vision of which he had spoken in *Lenz* – 'One must love mankind in order to penetrate into the peculiar nature of each one' – Büchner sought to enter into the mind of a murderer such as Schmolling or Woyzeck, to appreciate truly his character and his fate, and to reproduce what he had grasped with imaginative accuracy. It was probably a harder task than he had accomplished in any of his other works, for no doubt he himself had much more in common with Danton or Lenz than with Woyzeck or Schmolling; but, as he had also insisted in the Novelle, 'the vein of feeling is the same in almost all men', and he was triumphantly to prove this community of feeling in the deep truth of his final masterpiece.

In addition to the reports of Horn and Clarus, Büchner evidently drew extensively on his own observations of the ordinary people of Giessen and Darmstadt – the artisans, the soldiers and the women as they were to be seen in the streets and in the taverns, at fairs and at dances. Karl Vogt, in his memoirs, mentions a large inn in Giessen, the *Gasthaus zum Hirsch*, probably well known to Büchner, which was frequented by coachmen and where one of the songs was sung which reappear in *Woyzeck* ('Ach Tochter! Liebe Tochter! Was hast du gedenkt, / Daß du dich an die Landkutscher und die Fuhrleut' hast gehenkt?').[4] And we also owe to Vogt some illuminating information about that egregious Professor Wilbrand who was evidently the primary though probably not the only model for the doctor in Büchner's play. In particular we are told how Wilbrand required his own son to perform the feat which Büchner's doctor compels Woyzeck to perform:

The highlight of this anatomical lecture was the demonstration of the ear muscles. The professor's son, who was brilliant at moving his ears, was then required to appear, and they say the following scene would occur. After describing the ear muscles the professor would say: 'These muscles are obsolete in humans. Humans cannot move their ears, only monkeys can do that. Jolios, show how it's done!' The unfortunate Jolios would then have to stand up and wag his ears. (Cf. *Woyzeck*, H3, 1)[5]

But Büchner's portraits of the doctor and the captain in *Woyzeck* are based not only on his experience of one or two individuals such as Wilbrand, but on his observation of a whole class of people, that 'educated and well-to-do minority' (*die gebildete und wohlhabende Minorität* – 2, 455) which considered itself superior to the common people and entitled to look down on them. And if his attitude to the poor and unfortunate was characterized by a profound though by no means sentimental sympathy, his attitude to that 'superior' minority was marked by implacable hatred. In his letter to his family of February 1834 he had declared that hatred was as permissible as love, and that he cherished it in the fullest measure against those *who despise others* (*Der Haß ist so gut erlaubt als die Liebe, und ich hege ihn im vollsten Maße gegen die, welche verachten* – 2, 423). In *Woyzeck* he has given powerful expression to both feelings – the most compassionate love and the most savage indignation.

Though the origins of *Woyzeck* are thus to be found in a comparatively early period of Büchner's career, the evidence suggests that it was probably not until the spring of 1836 that he began writing the play. There is no hint that he was occupied with such a work in the letters of 1835 nor in those of the first few months of 1836, unless one can see an allusion to *Woyzeck* in the words of his letter of 1 January: 'I go my own way and remain in the field of drama' (*Ich gehe meinen Weg für mich und bleibe auf dem Felde des Dramas* – 2, 452). But that may have been merely a statement of intention, and we must remember that during the winter of 1835–6 he was intensely occupied with his zoological dissertation. The first extant reference to 'Woyzeck' – the title had better be put in inverted commas here, since at this early stage Büchner had not yet decided to use this name for his hero – appears to be Gutzkow's remark in his letter to Büchner of 10 June 1836: 'From your "piglet dramas" I expect something more than piggishness' (*Von Ihren 'Ferkeldramen' erwarte ich mehr als Ferkelhaftes* – 2, 491), which I take to be an allusion to *Woyzeck* and *Leonce und Lena*. Probably we can assume that the first sketch of the play (H1) was already completed by that date. The sentence in Büchner's letter of 2 September 1836 to his brother Wilhelm: 'At the same time I am just about to let some people kill or marry each other on paper' (*Dabei bin ich gerade daran, sich einige Menschen auf dem Papier todschlagen oder verheirathen zu lassen* – 2, 460) alludes in all probability to the marriage and the murder with which *Leonce und Lena* and *Woyzeck* are respectively concerned. And doubtless it is again these two plays that he has in mind when he speaks of 'my two dramas' in the letter to his family of the same month, and declares himself to be still in many respects dissatisfied with them. We may assume that at this time Büchner was working at the second and third draft of *Woyzeck* (H3 and H2), and that these are contemporaneous with the notes on Spinoza, who is mentioned in the letter to Wilhelm of 2 September.[6] As the fourth and last draft of *Woyzeck* (H4) is incomplete we must suppose it to belong to the latest period of Büchner's life and to have been cut short by his fatal illness.[7] *Woyzeck* was no doubt one of the three dramas which, according to Büchner's last letter to Minna Jaegle, were to be published 'within at most a week'. The optimism of that expectation is hard to understand in view of the fact that even the latest draft of the play is obviously not ready for the press. It breaks off after the 17th scene; there are lacunae still to be filled (notably H4, 3 and probably H4, 9); and the handwriting of the MS, with its numerous abbreviations and other imperfections, would have been impossible copy for a compositor. Must we assume, then, that a later and better MS existed which has been lost? It has been suggested that a fair copy of *Woyzeck* could have been lost in the same way as Büchner's diary, the MSS of *Leonce und Lena* and *Lenz* and the putative sketches for *Pietro Aretino*.[8] But when Büchner died, his diary, the *Woyzeck* fragments and the MSS of *Lenz* and *Leonce und Lena* were certainly available to Minna Jaegle and to Wilhelm and Caroline Schulz, whereas an immediate and repeated search of his room failed to discover any complete version of *Woyzeck* or any MS of *Pietro Aretino*.[9] The most natural and reasonable inference is that neither the one nor the other existed.

Ludwig Büchner considered the *Woyzeck* fragments to be too illegible and defective to be worth inclusion in his edition of 1850. The first publication of the work was in Franzos's edition of 1879, where it appeared under the title *Wozzeck*. Franzos applied chemicals to the MS in order to make it temporarily more legible, and has been accused of permanently damaging it by that procedure. He was also responsible for numerous alterations, omissions and additions which gravely prejudiced the interpretation of the play. A notorious example is the stage-direction 'drowns' (*ertrinkt*), inserted without authority at the end of the scene by the pond where the hero wades into the water to wash away the blood on his hands and arms (H1, 20). Franzos's edition – in spite of its great faults a meritorious achievement – remained the basis of Büchner scholarship and theatre performances until 1920, and had the distinction of providing the text for Alban Berg's opera *Wozzeck*. A considerable advance in the textual criticism of the play was achieved in the editions of Georg Witkowski (1920) and Fritz Bergemann (1922), the latter being thenceforth regarded as the standard edition of Büchner's works until the publication of the first volume of the historical-critical edition by Werner Lehmann in 1967. It is regrettable that during that period of more than forty years the popular reprints of the Bergemann edition continued to mislead students of Büchner by their contamination of the various versions of the play and by their unwarranted rearrangement of the scenes. Lehmann's edition, a model of expert and meticulous scholarship, has corrected those faults, offering a sound basis for further research as well as a respectable attempt – it does not claim to be more than that – to provide a playable version for the theatre. While recognizing the value of these services, a few critical observations on Lehmann's edition are nevertheless necessary, since they have a bearing on the interpretation of the play. (1) One may regret that Lehmann has included in the first volume of his edition the Clarus reports on Woyzeck but not, either in full or in part, the Horn report on Schmolling. This must suggest to users of the edition that only the Woyzeck case is relevant to Büchner's play. In fact, the Schmolling case is also very relevant, especially for the first draft (H1), and therefore also for the final draft (H4) in so far as this is dependent on the first. The documentation in Egon Krause's edition is in this respect more satisfactory. (2) It is doubtful whether Lehmann is justified in letting the stage version of the play conclude with the scene H3, 2, where Woyzeck returns from the pond and finds that his own child shrinks from him. This ending is not authorized by the MSS, and, for reasons which will emerge later, may be considered to falsify Büchner's intention. (3) It is impossible to accept Lehmann's view that the draft or fragment which he refers to as H3 is later than that which he

223

designates H2. One must rather agree with Winkler that H3 is the earlier of the two fragments. (In that case, of course, the symbols should properly be reversed, but to avoid confusion I shall adhere to Lehmann's use of them.) H3 is a separate sheet of manuscript containing only two scenes, the first being that in which the professor or doctor compels Woyzeck to demonstrate the wiggling of the ears; the second the scene just referred to where Woyzeck is repulsed by his child. Winkler maintains that the professor or doctor of H3, 1 is only a preliminary study for the doctor of H2, and offers the following arguments in support of this view:[10] (a) that in H3, 1 Büchner wavers between the titles 'professor' and 'doctor' for his unspeakable scientist, whereas in H2, as in H4, the title 'doctor' is used consistently throughout – which suggests that H2 and H4 are chronologically nearer to each other than H3 and H4; (b) that in the later phases of the work, as we can see in H4, Büchner tended towards a greater generalization in his portraits of the doctor and the captain, and that the particular idiosyncrasies copied in H3 from Professor Wilbrand are the mark of a comparatively early phase. Lehmann has not yet fully replied to Winkler's arguments – he may be expected to do so in the third volume of his edition; but I doubt if any quite convincing reply is possible,[11] and quite apart from Winkler's arguments, there is another consideration which seems to tell strongly against Lehmann's view. If Lehmann is right in thinking that H3 is later than H2, then the ear-wiggling scene (H3, 1) must have been written at a later date than the scene (H2, 6) in which the doctor blames Woyzeck for urinating on the street and in which he recognizes with delight the supposed symptoms of insanity in Woyzeck, promising him a bonus on that account. And moreover, on Lehmann's hypothesis, H3, 1 must occur at a later point in the action of the play than H2, 6; for in the final version (H4), where the scenes are in their definitive order, H2, 6 is included in a modified form, while H3, 1 is not represented at all. Evidently, if H3, 1 was to be included in this final version, it could only find a place in the later part of the play which has not yet been reached at the point where H4 breaks off.

And that is in fact the position in which Lehmann places it in his stage version. But this is impossible. For in H3, 1 Woyzeck is being presented to the students for the first time as an instructive specimen. All the features of his case that could be of interest to the students are enumerated: his irregular pulse and fixed gaze, the fact that he has eaten nothing but peas for the last three months, his ability to control his ear muscles. But not a word is said about his 'delightful *alienatio mentis*'. If at this stage the doctor had already diagnosed in Woyzeck the insanity which seemed to him so exciting and 'beautiful', he would surely have mentioned it to the students. Evidently H3, 1 does not, as Lehmann supposes,[12] follow and 'radicalize' H2, 6; but, on the contrary, H2, 6 follows and radicalizes H3, 1. In H3, 1 we hear of an experiment with a diet of peas; in H2, 6 that experiment is combined with an experiment on urination. In H3, 1 the doctor is delighted merely on account of Woyzeck's *trembling*; in H2, 6 his enthusiasm is excited by Woyzeck's supposed *madness* – clearly a stronger and more bitter satirical touch.

One can sympathize with the reluctance of a producer to forego the very effective ear-wagging scene, but I am afraid the evidence indicates that Büchner had decided to discard it in favour of H2, 6 in its modified form, and it must obviously be dangerous to ignore the intentions of a dramatist such as Büchner. Producers who cannot bring themselves to omit the scene should at least place it early in the play, preferably just after the first scene with the captain (H4, 5).[13] Its late position in Lehmann's stage version produces an anticlimax and a most undramatic interruption and retardation of the action at a point where it is moving swiftly towards the catastrophe. It is hardly conceivable that, at a time when Woyzeck has become fully convinced of his mistress's infidelity and has actually bought the knife with which he is about to kill her, when he has been physically beaten by his rival and has bequeathed all his wordly possessions to his friend – it is hardly conceivable that at such a time he should continue to lend himself to the doctor's absurd experiments and actually wag his ears for him! The meagre remuneration which he has been earning from the doctor has now become superfluous, and his continuing to serve him could only place him in an impossibly mean and servile light.

It has seemed necessary to dwell a little on this question because Lehmann's stage version is likely to remain the basis for performances of the play in Germany and elsewhere for many years to come. And the determination of the right chronological sequence of the four fragments is also important for our attempt to study the play genetically. Having decided that the right sequence is H1, H3, H2 and H4, we must proceed to consider them in that order.

### THE FIRST FRAGMENT (H1)

The first fragmentary draft of the play, H1, consists of twenty-one scenes, varying in length from a single line to some four or five hundred words. The name of the principal character is Louis, not yet Woyzeck. Büchner, at this early stage, is drawing his material from various sources and has not yet made up his mind about the names of his hero and heroine. For the present he makes do with 'Louis' and 'Margreth'.

In these twenty-one scenes Büchner outlines the whole action of the play from the first meeting of the heroine with the junior officer who seduces her to the official examination of her dead body preparatory to the indictment of the hero on a charge of murder. But some important links in the action are missing. The scene of the seduction and that in which Louis comes into possession of the fatal knife are only vaguely indicated. And there are also some repetitions and false starts, bearing witness to the extremely tentative and rudimentary character of this draft. Only a few of the scenes are worked out fully – the actual scene of the murder and the scenes immediately before and after it. Evidently it was the events to be represented here that first fired Büchner's imagination, and it is really only here, in the first version, that he deploys the full power of his dramatic genius. It is fortunate that he did, for the later drafts break off before this phase of the action is reached, and it is necessary to fall back on the first draft for the representation of the catastrophe. Unfortunately, that dramatic and poetic power is not maintained to the end. The first draft tails off in a number of tentative, fragmentary scenes which provide no really effective conclusion to the play and leave us in considerable doubt as to how Büchner envisaged the conclusion.

Though outlining the whole extent of the action, H1 is for the most part merely a sketch, and in such a sketch there is no room for the full development of character. The hero, Louis, is hardly recognizable as a person. He remains a shadowy figure consisting of nothing but unfathomable, ungovernable passion: the fever of jealousy, the compulsion to kill, the fear of detection and retribution. Like Danton, Louis too, within his narrower sphere, is subject to an inexorable necessity, a horrifying fatality, and, if he were of a more reflective disposition, might echo Danton's words: 'What is it inside of us that whores, lies, steals and murders?' To his friend Andres he is incomprehensible, seeming either insane or drunk (H1, 7; H1, 8). But, little as we are told about him, we can at least recognize that he is free from any mean or contemptible trait, approximating less to the historical proto-type Woyzeck, who had some very brutal characteristics, than to Schmolling, who was described in Horn's report as affable, peaceable and industrious.[14] The short scene 'Freies Feld' (H1, 12):

LOUIS. (*Er legt das Messer in eine Höhle.*) Du sollst nicht tödten. Lieg da! Fort! (*Er entfernt sich eilig.*)

may have been suggested by the remark in Horn's report that Schmolling claimed to have been always well aware of the fifth commandment.[15] But Schmolling's crime was not motivated by jealousy, and the scenes of jealousy in H1 are clearly based on the Woyzeck documents. Incidentally, this duality of the sources may account for Büchner's apparent wavering in this draft between alternative possibilities of developing the action. In H1, 7 Louis seems about to *buy* his weapon as the historical Woyzeck had done; in H1, 11 he seems to *find* it, as Schmolling had done.

It is strange that so many critics have been inclined to identify Louis with the barber of scenes H1, 10 and H1, 21, and that even after Wolfgang Martens' vigorous refutation this view is still occasionally held.[16] It owes such plausibility as it has to the fact that the historical Woyzeck was a barber, as is the hero of Büchner's final version of the play. But, as has already been repeatedly remarked, the hero of the first draft is modelled as much on Schmolling as on Woyzeck, and Schmolling was not a barber. And why should Büchner, who elsewhere consistently refers to his hero as 'Louis', refer to him as the 'barber' in scenes ten and twenty-one? But the decisive argument against the identification of the barber with Louis is that the barber is obviously a quite different and much less estimable character. He has many of the absurd views and odious traits which Büchner in the later versions of the play assigns to the captain, the doctor and the *Handwerksburschen*; his tasteless and vulgar loquacity is in direct contrast to Louis's deep seriousness and brevity of expression; and he is described as a 'dogmatic atheist', as 'cowardly' and 'contemptible' (*Dogmatischer Atheist . . . feig, schlecht* – H1, 21), qualities which it is impossible to ascribe to Büchner's hero and which, if they *could* be ascribed to him, would destroy the play.

The character of the heroine in H1 is even farther from being a complete representation than that of the hero. Margreth, in the brief part assigned to her, shows no love for Louis. The non-commissioned officer immediately feels that she is of an extremely sensual disposition: 'That is a wench that would look through seven pairs of leather breeches' (*Das ist ein Weibsbild guckt siebe Paar lederne Hose durch* – H1, 2), and there is nothing to indicate that his idea of her is mistaken. She immediately accepts his flirtatious approaches, evidently conscious of the impression she has made on him; she recognizes, apparently with satisfaction, that his superior rank gives him the power to command Louis; and she delights in his imposing male physique: 'Ah! a man more than another' (*Ha! Ein Mann vor einem Andern* – H1, 3). In the next two scenes she is already dancing with him and encouraging his erotic attentions, and Andres can only wonder why Louis concerns himself 'about such a whore' (*wegen des Menschs*). But Louis's concern is overpowering, his love inextinguishable; and it is only this love, not anything she herself says or does, which makes us feel that Margreth is not just a common slut. When he can have no further doubt that she is lost to him and he is irreversibly determined to kill her, he can still say of her: 'But, Andres, she was a pearl of a girl' (*Aber Andres, sie war doch ein einzig Mädel* – H1, 8). One cannot but regret that these simple words, to which no translation can do justice, have not been preserved in the later and more authoritative versions of the play. Though entirely original and distinctive, they correspond closely to the words of Othello in a like situation: 'But yet the pity of it, Iago; Oh Iago, the pity of it.' And as Othello kills Desdemona in love, not in hatred, so Louis, even as he is about to stab Margreth to death, can still say to her:

Friert's dich Margreth, und doch bist du warm. Was du heiße Lippen hast! (heiß, heiß Hurenathem) und doch möcht' ich den Himmel geben sie noch eimal zu küssen. (H1, 15)[17]

It is evident that at this comparatively early stage in the composition of the play Büchner is not yet primarily concerned with the portrayal of character but rather with the imaginative realization of certain experiences of Schmolling and Woyzeck which he had found recorded in his sources. It is these experiences which he re-creates so powerfully and vividly in the scenes of the hero's jealousy, in the murder scene, and in the scenes of fear and horror after the murder. The process is essentially the same as that which we have already observed in *Dantons Tod* and in *Lenz*. Here as there, Büchner sets out from the recorded facts and makes them live for us. Once again he performs what he considered to be the proper task of the dramatic poet, not 'giving us a dry narrative', but 'transporting us directly into the life of an epoch' – only in this case the epoch is not that of the French Revolution nor of the German *Sturm und Drang* but Büchner's own lifetime. Thus the Clarus report offers us 'the dry narrative':

At the time when the fair was at Gohlis he had laid in bed in the evening and had thought of Frau Woost. He had thought that she might well be dancing there with another man. And then it had come over him so strangely – as if he could hear the dance music, the violins and the basses mixed together, and, keeping time with them, the words: *Go on, go on !*[18]

But Büchner transports us into the living reality of that dancing and music making:

LOUIS (*lauscht am Fenster*). Er – Sie! Teufel! (*Er setzt sich zitternd nieder. Er späht, tritt an's Fenster.*) Wie das geht! Ja wälzt euch übernander! Und Sie: immer, zu – immer zu;

and lets us directly witness how the rhythm of the pipes and violins transmutes itself in Louis's soul into the inner command to kill his mistress:

(*Freies Feld*)

LOUIS. Immer! zu! – Immer zu! – Hisch! hasch, so gehn die Geigen und die Pfeifen. – Immer zu! immer zu! Was spricht da? Da unten aus dem Boden hervor, – ganz leise, was, was? (*Er bückt sich nieder.*) Stich! Stich! Stich die Woyzecke todt! Stich! stich die Woyzecke todt! Immer Woyzecke! das zischt und rumort und donnert. (H1, 6)

Similarly, the details of Schmolling's confession as recorded in Horn's report – how his mistress had had to go home to prepare the evening meal, how he had invited her to accompany him part of the way to the town, how he had asked her to sit down because he thought he could kill her more easily so than if she were standing, how he had kissed and embraced her before stabbing her[19] – provide the initial impulse for Büchner's recreation of the scene:

MARGRETH. Also dort hinaus ist die Stadt. S' ist finster.
LOUIS. Du sollst noch bleiben. Komm setz dich.
MARGRETH. Aber ich muß fort . . . das Nachtessen richten. (H1, 15)

And from this beginning the whole scene rises before our eyes in its terrifying reality, its deadly atmosphere – the darkness, the stillness, the night-dew, the moon rising 'wie ein blutig Eisen',[20] the short desperate duologue, and finally the knife thrusts, wildly repeated again and again.

This concern for vivid reality results, as in *Dantons Tod* and

*Lenz*, in a concentration on the most vital moments of the action, subordinate or transitional elements being omitted or reduced to a minimum. So once again we have a very pronounced example of the 'open' form of drama, and once again Büchner has to counteract the danger of disintegration incidental to that form by his use of key-words. How consciously and deliberately he used them, even in the first draft of the play, is indicated, as Lehmann remarks,[21] by his willingness, on occasion, to sacrifice the dialectal colouring of the language, important as this is for the atmosphere of the play, to the maintenance of the pattern of key-words. Thus in H1, 17 the dialect expression *als*, which Büchner had originally written, is deleted and replaced in the MS by *immer* to permit the recurrence of the key-expression *immer zu*, varied in the murder scene to *immer noch*. Other words which have this special importance in the thematic material of the play are: *Mensch*, *Welt*, *Natur*; *heiß*, *kalt*; *rot*, *Blut*; *Messer*, *stechen*, *tot*. By the reiteration and contrast of these expressions in their various connotations and nuances Büchner binds together his individual impressionistic scenes, so that, as Klotz expresses it, 'texture performs the functions of structure'.[22] And, like the key-words in *Lenz*, these unifying expressions largely determine the atmosphere of the work – an atmosphere of fatality, of violent passion, of doubt and despair as to the destiny and worth of man and nature.

This effect is reinforced by the scraps of folksongs which are liberally interspersed even in the first version of the play. We may remember how, in the discussion about art in *Lenz*, the sense of 'life, possibility of being', for Büchner the highest of artistic values, was said to be more abundantly present in folksongs than in any other poetry. And so it is hardly surprising that in Büchner's last and most characteristic play folksongs should be so largely represented. It was in and through these songs that Büchner felt he could come closest to the real life of the people; and therefore the folksongs he favours are not the idyllic or nostalgic songs beloved of the romantics but those which he himself had heard on the lips of carters, soldiers and servant girls – songs redolent of the rough cynicism and humour of the people but also, very often, with an underlying sense of tragedy. As Landau remarked, the interspersed folksongs imbue the play with something of the grim simplicity of folk poetry, the eerie mood of an old ballad.[23] And it is no doubt the folksongs as well as the episodic structure of the play that have prompted some critics to describe *Woyzeck* as 'a dramatic ballad' or 'balladesque drama'.[24]

In such a brief sketch as the first draft of *Woyzeck* – a sketch, moreover, in which the only people who appear are members of the least educated class of society – there can be little room for philosophical reflection. Such reflections as it contains are for the most part parodistic and satirical, and it has been too often overlooked or forgotten that not all of them are to be accepted as Büchner's opinions. On the contrary, Büchner frequently uses the device of indicating his dissent from an opinion by letting it be expressed by an absurd or contemptible character. Thus it is the muddleheaded *Marktschreier* who argues that clothes make the man (H1, 1), and it is the despicable barber who says:

Was ist der Mensch? Knochen! Staub, Sand, Dreck. Was ist die Natur? Staub, Sand, Dreck. (H1, 10)[25]

The only really serious and deep reflection in the first version of the play is not expressed in the confused discursive manner of the barber or the showman, but in the form that is most consistent with the popular tone and subject-matter – the form of the fairy-tale. Most critics have felt that the grandmother's tale in H1, 14 is the 'integration point' of the play, the passage which conveys its innermost meaning. And this view is confirmed by the critical position which the grandmother's tale occupies in the dramatic action: like the 'integration point' in *Dantons Tod* and in *Lenz*, it is placed immediately before the catastrophe. The grandmother has no sooner finished speaking than Louis enters to lead Margreth to her death.

And what is the innermost meaning that emerges at this climactic moment? Undeniably, a most pessimistic, not to say

nihilistic meaning,[26] and the desperate import of the thought
seems all the more sinister by its contrast to the childlike form –
the traditional fairytale form – in which it is expressed; so that the
term *Antimärchen*, or 'anti-fairytale', seems not inappropriate.
As Winkler pointed out,[27] Büchner has in fact borrowed some
motifs from Grimms' tale of the seven ravens, which also tells
of a child who visits the sun, the moon and the stars. But at least
the stars are friendly to the little girl, and the story ends happily
with her reunion with her seven brothers. Büchner's story is one
of infinite disillusionment ending in the gloom of complete
solitude:

Es war eimal ein arm Kind und hat kei Vater und kei Mutter war Alles todt und
war Niemand mehr auf der Welt. Alles todt, und es ist hingangen und hat greint
Tag und Nacht. Und weil auf der Erd Niemand mehr war, wollt's in Himmel
gehn, und der Mond guckt es so freundlich an und wie's endlich zum Mond kam,
war's ein Stück faul Holz und da ist es zur Sonn gangen und wie's zur Sonn kam,
war's ein verreckt Sonneblum und wie's zu den Sterne kam, warens klei golde
Mück, die waren angesteckt wie der Neuntödter sie auf die Schlehe steckt und
wie's wieder auf die Erd wollt, war die Erd ein umgestürzter Hafen und war
ganz allein und da hat sich's hingesetzt und geweint und da sitzt es noch und ist
ganz allein. (H1, 14)

In the context of Büchner's play we naturally relate the grandmother's tale to the fate of the hero and heroine, themselves poor
children doomed to suffer and die in solitude; and their story
gains thereby a wider dimension, becoming a symbol for the
fate of all mankind in a world without God, a world that is basically dead. Before Büchner, Jean Paul had painted a similar picture
in his 'Rede des toten Christus vom Weltgebäude herab, daß
kein Gott sei'.[28] There it is Christ who visits the sun and the
stars in a fruitless quest for God; there Christ as well as the children are 'without a father',[29] and 'each one is so alone in the broad
charnel-house of the world' (*Wie ist jeder so allein in der weiten
Leichengruft des All!*). The similarities are so striking that one
may wonder if Büchner was not perhaps thinking of Jean Paul
when he wrote his *Antimärchen*. But there is an essential difference.
The dreadful vision which Jean Paul describes is only a dream
from which one may and must awaken to a renewed faith in God.

For Büchner there is no awakening. And if our love and compassion for the solitary child must be all the more intense for that fact, our revulsion from the pitiless universe must be all the more passionate. Thus in *Woyzeck* as in *Dantons Tod* and *Lenz* the 'integration point' proves to be an expression of profound metaphysical revolt.

Büchner's deepest and most immediate concern in the first draft of the play is evidently the suffering of his hero and its metaphysical implications. He is much less concerned to show us the circumstances of Louis's life, the social pressures to which he is subjected, though there are already some hints of these. We learn that Louis is the batman of an officer for whom he fetches wine (H1, 8); we notice how impressed Margreth is by the mere fact that the non-commissioned officer possesses a watch (H1, 2). And above all, in the short scene with which H1 ends, we see how the process of 'justice' begins which will lead to the condemnation of Louis for having killed the being that was dearest to him in the world. It was with this vista, evidently, that Büchner intended H1 to conclude. Both Schmolling and Woyzeck had been brought to trial and condemned to death – Schmolling's sentence was afterwards commuted to life imprisonment – and it was not Büchner's practice, nor consistent with his artistic principles to deviate *radically* from the historical facts. The scene in which the court-attendant, the barber, the doctor and the judge are assembled – presumably for the post-mortem examination of the corpse – and in which the court-attendant, anticipating the callousness of the doctor in the later versions, expresses his delight at 'the beautiful murder', is the last scene in the MS of this draft (H1, 21), and the only conclusion to the play that can be regarded as having any sanction from the manuscript. The fact that Louis is not mentioned at the beginning of this fragmentary scene is no proof that Büchner did not intend him to appear in the course of it, either giving himself up or being led in under arrest;[30] for it was Büchner's invariable practice to list at the beginning of a scene only those persons who are actually on stage when the scene opens, not those who enter later. One may compare the concluding scene of *Dantons Tod*, where the most important person appearing in the scene, Lucile, is not mentioned at the beginning of it.

Wolfgang Martens, having rightly concluded that the barber in this scene is not to be identified with Louis, proceeds to argue that we are 'compelled' (*genötigt*) by this fact to assume that Büchner did not intend his hero to be brought to trial and condemned, that the social protest implicit in such a development was not part of his purpose, and that the death of Louis by drowning is the only probable and appropriate conclusion to the play.[31] But Martens, like the majority of German critics, is too idealistic in his interpretation of Büchner and consequently too inclined to play down the element of social protest in his dramas. To say that the fact of Louis and the barber not being identical 'compels' us to infer that Büchner did not envisage the trial and condemnation of his hero, is a palpable *non sequitur*. And there is no justification in the text for the assumption that Louis dies by drowning. An event of such decisive importance would have been indicated by Büchner in the stage directions, which are already quite numerous and detailed in H1; but in fact, as we have previously remarked, it is Franzos, not Büchner, who is responsible for the stage direction 'drowns' in the scene by the pond. It is not in order to seek death that Louis wades into the water. On the contrary, it is to remove the incriminating evidence of the knife and the blood stains. He is evidently intent on preserving his life and liberty, and his mind appears to be functioning quite clearly to that end. His condition is therefore not, as some critics suppose, like that of Lady Macbeth, who seeks to wash away blood stains which exist only in her diseased imagination and which are therefore indelible. The blood which Louis washes away is real blood, the blood of Margreth, the blood which the people in the inn have suspiciously noticed. Thus there can be no question of suicide, and there is no indication of any baleful hallucination luring him to his death. If Louis drowns it can only be by accident, surely a rather feeble ending to such a great tragedy.[32]

It is no doubt very convenient for society when its victims

remove themselves by accident or suicide; it is spared the invid-
ious necessity of having to dispose of them itself. Dürrenmatt's
*Der Besuch der alten Dame* is particularly instructive in this
respect. But it was not Büchner's business to provide alibis, and
nothing could have been farther from his thoughts than the desire
to relieve society of the responsibility for its actions.

All in all, the first draft of *Woyzeck* can be regarded as con-
stituting a framework for the great proletarian tragedy which
Büchner envisaged; but, apart from a few magnificently realized
scenes, it is hardly more than a framework. The characterization,
as we have seen, is still very sketchy and there is little more than
a suggestion of the social background; so that the motivation
of the hero's actions, in so far as these depend on character and
social circumstances, is also very imperfect. In the later drafts
of the play Büchner addresses himself to the task of remedying
these deficiencies.

## THE SECOND AND THIRD FRAGMENTS (H3 AND H2)

To equip himself for that task Büchner appears to have reread
Clarus's second report on Woyzeck. The numerous details
borrowed from this report in the two scenes of H3 and the nine
scenes of H2 suggest that it must have been fresh in his memory,
while there is no similar evidence of a renewed study of the
Schmolling documents. Evidently Büchner felt that the Woyzeck
case could provide him with the best material for his purpose,
and we accordingly find that, from H3 onwards, he regularly
uses the name 'Woyzeck' for his hero, or the Christian name
'Franz'; so that we can now with more justification regard
*Woyzeck* as the proper title of the play (there is no official title
authorized by Büchner). The heroine, who does not appear in
H3, is called Louise or Louisel in H2.

H3, 1 ('Der Hof des Professors') is not only the first scene
in which the name 'Woyzeck' is regularly used, but also the first
in which Büchner attempts to expand his representation of the
social situation of his hero. Woyzeck is shown acting as the

guinea-pig of the professor in the manner already mentioned in our discussion of the sources and chronology of the play. Thus a function ascribed to the barber in the first fragment: 'I am a living skeleton, an object of study for all humanity' (*Ich bin ein lebendes Skelett. Die ganze Menschheit studiert an mir* – H1, 10) is transferred to Woyzeck in the succeeding drafts, and it is not difficult to understand why. In this play Büchner is not only concerned with the fate of his hero and heroine but also with the representation of the class-structure of society. But this involved the danger that his play would fall apart into the scenes dealing with the upper class and those dealing with the lower. To avoid this danger, Büchner had to bring his representatives of the two classes into regular contact with each other, and Woyzeck's function as guinea-pig of the doctor and – in H2 and H4 – as barber and servant of the captain serves that purpose admirably. This and other far-reaching changes in the economy of the play which emerge from the comparison of H1 with H3 and H2 indicate that Lehmann's designation of H1 and H2 as two groups of scenes belonging to the same version (*Erste Fassung: Szenengruppe 1 und Szenengruppe 2*) is unsound. H1 and H2 are based on substantially different conceptions of the play, and cannot be regarded as parts of one and the same version.

The doctor's experiments have evidently made Woyzeck very weak and sick. He suffers from the trembling, the irregular pulse, the darkening of vision which had afflicted the historical Woyzeck;[33] and when he is treated as if he were on exactly the same level as the cat and the louse which are likewise the object of the doctor's researches, he can only protest against the public humiliation with a faint 'Ach Herr Doctor!'

In the next draft, H2, we have Büchner's first serious attempt to offer a rounded portrait of Woyzeck's character. We see his superstitious fear of the freemasons – another trait borrowed from the historical Woyzeck – his apocalyptic sense of approaching calamity; we see his faithful care for his mistress and child, and at the same time his obsessive sense of something indescribably terrible in the world:

Sieh um dich! Alles starr, fest, finster, was regt sich dahinter. Etwas, was wir nicht fasse. Geht still, was uns von Sinnen bringt, aber ich hab's aus. (H2, 2)

In this draft Büchner also begins, though still with restraint, to stress the *poverty* of Woyzeck. We learn that he submits to the doctor's experiments for the sake of 'three farthings and board' (his diet of peas) per day (*Geb' ich Ihm dafür alle Tag 3 Groschen und Kost?* – H2, 6), and he has to *save* the money with which he takes Louise to the fair (H2, 2). The word *arm*, which had occurred only once in H1, begins to be used, though still sparingly, as a key-word in H2, and no longer in its figurative but in its literal meaning.

Thus the hero of H2 presents a picture of material distress, of physical and psychical sickness, of degradation and humiliation at the hands of a society which systematically refuses to recognize him as a human being. And his relation to Louise is largely conditioned by these circumstances. It is not only because of her beauty that he loves her (*Louisel du bist schön!* – H2, 8), but because she is the only lovable thing he possesses in a world of merciless exploitation and inveterate hostility. His love for her is an expression of his reaction to that world, of his longing for escape from it, of his trust in her as his only refuge from it. So it is with the love of all of Büchner's heroes, because it was so with his own love.[34] We have noticed in an earlier chapter of this book how Danton turns to Julie as Büchner himself had turned to Minna to find rest and solace for his 'cold and tormented heart'. So Woyzeck turns to Louise. Against the background of his bitter world his dependence on her has become absolute. And Louise, alone of Büchner's heroines, proves faithless.

That this is the centre of the tragedy emerges most clearly from the scene where the captain, with stupid and brutal joviality, suggests to Woyzeck that Louise may be betraying him with the drum major, and Woyzeck replies:

Herr Hauptmann, ich bin ein arm Teufel, – und hab sonst nichts auf der welt Herr Hauptmann, wenn Sie Spaß machen – (H2, 7)

In this cardinal passage we have surely the answer to the question which has worried so many critics and interpreters of the play – the question whether *Woyzeck* is a drama of social protest or of universal human passion. Here we see clearly that it is both, and that these two aspects of the play are not arbitrarily but integrally combined in it. It is not, as some critics suggest, that the human passion is the main matter and that the social criticism is added, as it were, for good measure. The tragedy arises from a particular unique situation in which human passion and social injustice are equally essential factors. Thus even in this passage of most intense emotion the key-word *arm*, with all its social implications, conspicuously and necessarily occurs.

But how is it possible that Louise – unlike Julie, Lucile and Lena but with some resemblance to Marion – can prove so false to the man who loves her so much? Büchner's portrayal of her has to serve the dual purpose of making both the love and the betrayal intelligible. The Louise of H2 is not a mere wanton like the Margreth of H1; she is a fine woman, high-spirited, defiant, proudly conscious of her beauty and of the force of her character. She is not to be cowed, either by her neighbour's venomous allusions to her status as *Frau Jungfer* ('Mrs Maiden') or by Woyzeck's threats of violence (H2, 8). But she has the natural sensuality of a healthy female animal, the natural physical attraction to such a splendid specimen of the opposite sex as the drum major, whose tall figure is 'like a tree' (*wie e Baum*) and whose gallant greeting makes her eyes gleam. Whereas Woyzeck's unhealthy spirituality, his persistent sense of mysterious terrors, frightens and repels her as it frightens and repels his friend Andres:

Der Mann schnappt noch über, et hat mir Angst gemacht. Wie unheimlich, ich mag wenn es finster wird gar nicht bleiben, ich glaub' ich bin blind, er steckt ein an. Sonst scheint doch als die Latern herein. Ach wir armen Leut. (H2, 2)

Louise too, one observes, has the oppressive awareness of poverty that afflicts Woyzeck; but this is not yet fully developed in H2. And there is only the merest hint of another aspect of her character – her inclination to seek consolation in religion.[35] The characterization of the heroine is still very imperfect in H2; it is only in the final draft, H4, that it approaches completion. But the sympathetic though unsparing truthfulness with which Büchner studies his principal characters is already evident.

As I have already suggested, however, the tragedy of Woyzeck and Louise is not only a tragedy of character but also a tragedy of social injustice, of class oppression; so that Büchner has not only to show us his impoverished hero and heroine but also the representatives of that 'educated and well-to-do minority' which, as he had written in his last letter to Gutzkow, 'will never abandon its inimical attitude to the mass of the people' (*die gebildete und wohlhabende Minorität . . . wird nie ihr spitzes Verhältniß zur großen Klasse aufgeben wollen* – 2, 455). And it is not with love and sympathy that Büchner depicts these representatives of the privileged classes; it is with a restrained but intense hatred – the hatred which, as he had declared in his letter to his family of February 1834, was as legitimate as love. Winkler truly remarks that this letter to his family together with the letter to Gutzkow is 'almost the programme for the captain and the doctor'[36] in Büchner's play. He had told Gutzkow that Young Germany 'would never get over the gulf between the educated and the uneducated classes of society'.[37] In the relation of his hero and heroine to the captain and doctor Büchner incisively demonstrates that gulf.

It is significant that, unlike Woyzeck and Louise, the captain and the doctor are given no proper names; they are called only by the names of their profession. Evidently they are important to Büchner as types rather than as individuals, and that is also the reason why his representation of them, though no doubt based originally on the observation of particular persons, becomes progressively less idiosyncratic and more generalized in the successive phases of the composition – in H2 as compared with H3, in H4 as compared with H2. And what types they are! Büchner's picture of them is perhaps the most powerful piece of satirical portraiture that German literature has produced in the last two centuries. Already in *Leonce und Lena* he had pitted 'arrogance against arrogance, mockery against mockery'; but the ridicule which he had heaped on King Peter and his court was comparatively mild and good-natured; his characterization of the captain and the doctor has the concentrated virulence, the deadly penetration of Pope or Swift. Heine's satire, with all its wit and cleverness, seems light in comparison.

The doctor is one of the many scientists and scholars who, 'in possession of a ridiculous veneer called culture or dead lumber called learning, sacrifice the great mass of their brothers to their supercilious egotism' (*Es gibt deren eine große Zahl, die im Besitze einer lächerlichen Äußerlichkeit, die man Bildung, oder eines todten Krams, den man Gelehrsamkeit heißt, die große Masse ihrer Brüder ihrem verachtenden Egoismus opfern* – 2, 423). So Woyzeck is sacrificed to the supercilious egotism of the doctor, who hopes by means of his absurd experiments to revolutionize science and achieve immortality (*Ich sprenge sie in die Luft, alle miteinander . . . ich werde unsterblich* – H2, 6). Obsessed with the delusion of his superiority, he rates Woyzeck somewhat lower than the rarer species of animals, and thinks nothing of exposing him to public contempt. We are reminded of Danton's bitter allusion to the painter David, who was said to have regarded the unfortunate victims of the Terror as mere occasions for the exercise of his art, thus divorcing art from humanity. In the doctor we see the divorce of science from humanity. Woyzeck's sickness and distress, even his supposed insanity, are for the doctor merely phenomena to be studied with 'scientific' objectivity for the gratification of vanity. This scientific callousness reaches its extreme in the scene where Woyzeck utters those anguished words 'Sir, I am a poor devil – and have nothing else in the world . . .' In this moment of most intense human suffering the doctor can only think of Woyzeck's pulse: 'Your pulse, Woyzeck, your pulse, slight, hard, skipping, irregular' (*Den Puls Woyzeck, den Puls, klein, hart, hüpfend, unregelmäßig* – H2, 7). Truly a modern situation, a species of inhumanity unknown to the tragedy of earlier ages, but all too familiar in the twentieth century. In his representation of the doctor Büchner anticipates one of the

most appalling phenomena of the modern world, the dehuman-
ization of science.

The portrait of the doctor is balanced by the portrait of the
captain, equally a representative of the 'educated and well-to-do
minority'. His character is not complete in H2, where he appears
in only one scene; but we can already see that he, no less than the
doctor, is guilty of that *Aristokratismus* which in Büchner's view
amounted to 'the most shameful contempt for the Holy Ghost in
man' (*die schändlichste Verachtung des heiligen Geistes im Menschen* – 2, 423). He has the cowardice of the barber of H1, the
intellectual and spiritual vacuity of the doctor; yet he also shares
the doctor's sense of superiority, the conviction that he is justified
in despising his subordinates. Knight describes him as 'a good-
natured fool',[38] and there are indeed not a few critics who take
a surprisingly favourable view of him. Nadler even went so far
as to say that 'the captain and medical officer treat him [Woyzeck]
well, with a kind of benevolent familiarity'![39] It is true that the
captain claims to be well disposed towards Woyzeck (*ich mein's
gut mit Ihm* – H2, 7); it is true that he describes both Woyzeck
and himself, maudlinly, as 'ein guter Mensch'. But how much his
'good-nature' and benevolence are worth is shown only too
clearly by the pleasure he takes in the torturing doubts which he
instils into Woyzeck's mind and by the brutal threats with which
he beats down Woyzeck's faint, despairing protest. The truth is,
both the captain and the doctor, like the class of society which
they represent, are basically unwilling to recognize any bond of
common humanity in their relation to Woyzeck. They see him
as belonging to quite a different and immeasurably lower grade
in the scale of living creatures. And under these circumstances
'good-nature' and 'benevolence' can only be empty words;
they must reveal their hollowness at the first serious trial.

Thus there can be no understanding, no communication,
between Woyzeck and his masters. One is reminded of the remark
in *Der Hessische Landbote* that the rich 'speak a language of their
own' (*reden eine eigene Sprache* – 2, 34). It is literally true that the
captain and the doctor speak a different language from that of

Woyzeck and Louise. These express themselves in the simplest terms, not in the consistent Hessian dialect of Niebergall's plays, but in words and forms coloured by that dialect and with an expressiveness which cares nothing for academic correctness:

LOUISEL. Und was ne Wesp hat dich gestoche? du siehst so verrückt aus wie n'e Kuh, die die Hornisse jagt.
FRANZ. Mensch! (*Geht auf sie los.*)
LOUISEL. Rühr mich an Franz! Ich hätt lieber ein Messer in de Leib, als dei Hand auf meine. Mei Vater hat mich nicht angreifen gewagt, wie ich 10 Jahr alt war, wenn ich ihn ansah. (H2, 8)

In contrast to this passionate plainness, the language of the doctor is for the most part free of dialect, grammatically correct, and loaded with pretentious pseudo-scientific expressions calculated to distract attention from its illogical form and absurd content:

Meine Herrn wir sind an der wichtigen Frage über das Verhältniß des Subjects zum Object. Wenn wir nur eins von den Dingen nehmen, worin sich die organische Selbstaffirmation des Göttlichen, auf einem so hohen Standpunkte manifestirt und ihr Verhältniß zum Raum, zur Erde, zum Planetarischen untersuchen, meine Herrn, wenn ich dieße Katze zum Fenster hinauswerfe, wie wird dieße Wesenheit sich zum centrum gravitationis und dem eigenen Instinct verhalten? (H3, 1)

This is a passage from the doctor's grotesque lecture to the students, but his habitual style is more or less similar, and its effect is to intensify Woyzeck's isolation, never for a moment allowing him to forget the 'gulf' which separates him from the 'educated and well-to-do minority'.

With the introduction of the doctor and the captain, each in his way representing that privileged minority, it becomes possible for Büchner in H3 and H2 to have a larger admixture of philosophical reflection than the narrower scope of H1 had permitted. But as it is the reflection of a social class which Büchner condemns, it still appears, like the reflective passages in the first fragment, for the most part in a satirical or parodistic form. Thus we have the pomposity of the doctor's affirmation of the Kantian doctrine of spiritual freedom – and its immediate deflation in the prosaic ending of the same sentence:

Woyzeck der Mensch ist frei, im Menschen verklärt sich die Individualität zur Freiheit – seinen Harn nicht halten können! (H2, 6)

And we have the parody of the pretentious obscurity of idealist philosophy – Schelling's or Hegel's – in the passage already quoted from the lecture to the students. In the speech of the *Handwerksbursch* in H2, 4, which to some extent corresponds to the grotesque harangue of the barber in H1, 10, Büchner interpolates a burlesque of that teleological view of nature which he had always disliked and which he was about to denounce again in his Zurich lecture on cranial nerves:

Warum hat Gott den Mensche das Gefühl der Schamhaftigkeit eingeflößt? Damit der Schneider lebe kann. Ja! Ja! Also! – Darum! Auf daß! damit!

And in the speech of the showman in H2, 3 (corresponding to H1, 1) Büchner returns to the satirical attack on Hegelian ideas of progress:

Sehn Sie die Fortschritte der Civilisation. Alles schreitet fort, ein Pferd, ein Aff, ein Canaillevogel! Der Aff ist schon ein Soldat, s'ist noch nit viel, unterst Stuf von menschliche Geschlecht!

The song of the old man as the child dances:

Auf der Welt ist kein Bestand,
Wir müssen alle sterben,
Das ist uns wohlbekannt! (H2, 3)

is one of the few reflective passages in H2 which need not be regarded as satirical. It is an expression of the melancholy view of the world which is basic to Büchner's play.

All in all, the two scenes of H3 and the nine scenes of H2 are an impressive poetic achievement. They are on the whole considerably less sketchy than most of the scenes in H1. Büchner is no longer merely outlining the situations of his play; he is envisaging them with the liveliest poetic imagination and fully, though economically, presenting them. Yet H3 and H2 offer even less of a connected action than H1. They fill some of the gaps in the action, but by no means all. There is still no dialogue between the drum major and Louise, and H2 breaks off when the play is only half finished. Nevertheless, having now written three

fragmentary drafts, Büchner evidently felt that he had enough
material at his disposal and a sufficiently clear conception of the
whole to attempt a definitive presentation of the play. The result
is the fourth and final fragment, H4.

## THE LAST FRAGMENT (H4)

The last draft of *Woyzeck* consists of seventeen scenes, one of
which (H4, 3) is represented only by the stage direction 'Buden.
Lichter. Volk.' One-and-a-half pages of MS are empty here,
which Büchner probably intended to fill with material taken from
H1, 1, H1, 2 and H2, 3, but was still unsure as to how this was
to be done. There is a similar though briefer space in the MS after
H4, 9 ('Hauptmann. Doctor'), which Büchner may well have
intended to fill with the modified material of H2, 7.[40] With these
two exceptions, the final draft of *Woyzeck*, so far as it goes,
presents the incidents of the action without omissions and in the
proper order; so that it now becomes possible, for the first time,
to discern more or less clearly the structure which Büchner
intended the finished composition to have. In order to achieve
this important advance towards the completion of the work, it
was necessary for Büchner to write a number of quite new
scenes – actually there are five such scenes in H4, or six if one
regards H4, 16 as quite new – to fill the lacunae in the earlier
drafts. And he had also to take over, in a modified and improved
form, those scenes of H1 and H2 which seemed to him worthy of
a place in the definitive version of the play. The scenes thus
transferred to the last version are regularly scored off in the
earlier MSS, and the fact that H1, 1, H1, 2, H2, 3 and H2, 7 are
not thus scored off is one of the reasons why it has been thought
that Büchner was not finished with these scenes but was still
meditating their possible transference to the final version.

Pursuing our purpose of trying to ascertain the *direction* in
which Büchner was working, we must look carefully at the
modifications which the scenes of the earlier MSS undergo as they
are transferred to the last version, and then consider the character

of the new scenes, the structure of the play as it begins to emerge in H4, and the intellectual implications of the work in this final form.

The first two scenes of H4 are taken over from H2, and when we compare the earlier and later form of these scenes we are struck by Büchner's striving for ever greater economy and vigour of expression. Everything inessential is omitted in the last version – the repetition of *Sieh nicht hinter dich*, the unnecessary question *Hast du Stecken geschnitten für den Major?*, even the pronoun in *Ich kann nit*; and whole sentences are compressed into a few syllables: *Der Mann schnappt noch über, er hat mir Angst gemacht* becomes *Der Mann! So vergeistert.* Throughout H4 we find this intensified insistence on concision and force of expression. Explanation is replaced by action, speech by mimicry, the movements and expression of the characters being carefully noted in the stage directions.[41] Compare, for example, the scene 'Freies Feld' in its original form (quoted above p. 230) with the same scene as it appears in H4:

*(Freies Feld)*

WOYZECK. Immer zu! immer zu! Still Musik! (*Reckt sich gegen den Boden.*) Ha was, was sagt ihr? Lauter, lauter, – stich, stich die Zickwolfin todt? stich stich die Zickwolfin todt. Soll ich? Muß ich? Hör ich's da auch, sagt's der Wind auch? Hör ich's immer, immer zu, stich todt, todt.

Woyzeck does not *describe* the music as the Louis of H1 had done; he frantically appeals to it. He does not ask himself what voices are speaking from under the earth, but throws himself to the ground and directly challenges them.[42] Similarly, instead of the *statement* of H2, 1: 'the earth is swaying under our feet!' (*die Erde schwankt unter unsern Sohlen*) we have the *action* of H4, 1:

WOYZECK (*stampft auf den Boden*) Hohl, hörts du? Alles hohl da unten.

It is an exclamatory rather than discursive style, associative rather than logical in its transitions, the weightier words being isolated in the manner we have already noticed in *Lenz*. It is a style that has all the force and expressiveness but also, on occasion, all the coarseness of popular speech; and this popular tone is enhanced by the interspersed folksongs which are even more numerous in H4 than in the earlier drafts. Thus in *Woyzeck*, to a greater degree than ever before, Büchner achieves that vigour of expression and closeness to reality, that sense of 'life, possibility of being', which was his highest artistic ambition. Or as Adamov expressed it: 'Il a trouvé la phrase rapide, simple, poétique, qui allait de pair avec la première accession du prolétaire à la scène.'[43]

Not only the scenes adapted from the earlier drafts but also those that appear for the first time in H4 are characterized by this power and concentration. And the effect of brevity and rapidity is increased still further by the elimination of the redundancies of the earlier drafts. Thus the two scenes H1, 7 ('Ein Zimmer') and H1, 13 ('Nacht. Mondschein') are compressed into one in H4, 13 ('Nacht').

No doubt all this emphasis on speed and economy presents a problem for the producer of the play. Where the scenes are so short there is a danger that the intervals between them will seem too numerous and that the audience will become restive. Adamov, who admired so much this 'déroulement rapide, parfois presque incohérent, des situations',[44] also admitted that of the five productions of the play which he had seen not one had been satisfactory. Yet the difficulty is not insuperable. A critic of the *Wiener Arbeiterzeitung* tells how Eugen Klöpfer, by his skilful use of spot lights and by the speed of his scene changes on a darkened but open stage, solved the problem to such a degree that the audience were hardly conscious of the fragmentary character of the work.[45]

The new scenes in H4 have the function, not only of bridging the gaps in the action which had been left by the earlier drafts, but also of completing the portrayal of the main characters. The scene in which Woyzeck shaves the captain (H4, 5) contributes so effectively to the characterization of both that some critics and editors, in defiance of Büchner's clearly indicated intention, have been tempted to let the play begin with this scene. This is certainly unjustifiable. But the scene nevertheless occurs at an early point in the action, and therefore Büchner presents Woyzeck's situation here with a certain restraint to permit the possibility of dramatic intensification, the possibility of *Steigerung*, in the later scenes of the play. As Lehmann remarks, 'the captain shows himself at his best, a comfortable, jovial fat-belly'.[46] But to closer inspection that 'best' already reveals itself as decidedly sinister. The captain's complete disregard for the feelings of his subordinates betrays itself in the insolence with which he tells Woyzeck to his face that he is 'quite abominably stupid' (*ganz abscheulich dumm*)[47] and lectures him for having 'no morality'. His own sanctimonious claim to be 'a virtuous man, a good man' (*ich sag mir immer: Du bist ein tugendhafter Mensch*, [*gerührt*] *ein guter Mensch*) recalls the self-righteousness with which Dr Clarus, after having virtually signed the death-warrant of the historical Woyzeck, felt entitled to admonish the younger generation that 'at the sight of the bleeding victim' they should 'impress on themselves the truth that laziness, gambling, drunkenness, unlawful gratification of the sexual urge and bad company can gradually and insidiously lead to crime and to the gallows'.[48] The boredom which arises from the captain's utter emptiness and uselessness, his dismay at the prospect of having ten more minutes to kill (*Was soll ich dann mit den zehn Minuten anfangen, die Er heut zu früh fertig wird?*), mark him as a worthy representative of that 'effete' class of society of which Büchner in his last letter to Gutzkow had said: 'Its whole life consists only of attempts to dispel the most dreadful boredom. Let it die, that's the only novelty that is left for it to experience.'

The conversation between the captain and Woyzeck has a distant yet unmistakable affinity with that between Robespierre and Danton. Like Robespierre, the captain upholds an abstract principle of 'virtue' and claims thereby to rise superior to the demands of nature. He is at one with the doctor in his bumptious pretension to spiritual freedom. Woyzeck, on the contrary, like Danton, feels himself entirely subject to natural impulses: 'nature just comes over one' (*es kommt einem nur so die Natur*). But Woyzeck, though more reflective here than elsewhere in the play, lacks the intellectual experience and scepticism that prompt Danton to inpugn the veracity of those who pretend to moral freedom. Woyzeck does not question the reality of the captain's 'virtue', but – with unconscious and profound irony – regards it as one of the blessings incidental to a good income, like a gold watch, an elegant hat and coat, or a cultivated manner of speaking. Already in the period of his association with the 'Society of Human Rights' Büchner had maintained that 'it is no great feat to be an honest man when one has soup, vegetables and meat to eat every day' (*Es ist keine Kunst, ein ehrlicher Mann zu sein, wenn man täglich Suppe, Gemüse und Fleisch zu essen hat*).[49] Already in *Der Hessische Landbote* he had anticipated the Marxist principle that the State is only the instrument by which the ruling class maintains its oppressive dominion. Now, through the mouth of the man whom the captain regards as 'abominably stupid', he foreshadows the Marxist doctrine that morality too is only part of the ideological 'superstructure' which is ultimately based on economic relations and class distinctions. For the poor there is no morality, no virtue. There is only endless toil:

Wie der Bub schläft ... Die hellen Tropfen steh'n ihm auf der Stirn; Alles Arbeit unter der Sonn, sogar Schweiß im Schlaf. Wir arme Leut! (H4, 4)

Christ said 'Suffer little children to come unto me.' But for Woyzeck and his child there is no salvation on either side of the grave:

Unseins ist doch einmal unseelig in der und der andern Welt, ich glaub' wenn wir in Himmel kämen so müßten wir donnern helfen.

The new scenes of H4 likewise contribute decisively to the characterization of the heroine. She is no longer called Margreth or Louise in the final version, but Marie – possibly, as Holger Hamann has suggested,[50] because Büchner wishes to stress her affinity with the sinful but penitent Mary Magdalene, but perhaps merely as a hint of the fact that in the portrayal of his heroine he owed something to the Marie of Lenz's *Die Soldaten*.[51]

In H4 Büchner develops the characterization of his heroine in two directions: on the one hand, he deliberately intensifies our impression of her sensuality; on the other hand he now depicts fully what had previously been barely suggested – the contrition which follows upon her yielding to her sensual nature. In H2 the drum major had appeared to her, in his splendid stature, 'like a tree'; in H4 she feels above all his puissant animality and is as fascinated by it as he is by hers:

> MARIE (*ihn ansehend, mit Ausdruck*). Geh' einmal vor dich hin. – Über die Brust wie ein Rind und ein Bart wie ein Löw – So ist keiner – Ich bin stolz vor allen Weibern . . .
> TAMBOUR-MAJOR. Und du bist auch ein Weibsbild. Sapperment, wir wollen eine Zucht von Tambour-Majors anlegen. He? (*Er umfaßt sie.*) (H4, 6)

And whereas in H1, 5 it is not perfectly clear that Marie actually pronounces the erotic incitement 'go on – go on', there is no doubt about it in H4, 11:

> MARIE (*im Vorbeytanzen*). Immer zu, immer zu.

It is significant that, notwithstanding Büchner's increasing concern for brevity, this scene is actually longer in the later version than in the earlier: Büchner needed a greater space for his more elaborate evocation of the atmosphere of eroticism surrounding, and exuded by, his heroine.

But if Marie resembles Danton's Marion in her sensuality, she by no means shares Marion's hedonistic conviction that it is all one 'whether one finds one's pleasure in carnality or in crucifixes, in flowers or in children's toys'. On the contrary, even as she defies Woyzeck to call her a whore she feels in her heart that she *is* a whore and that she could kill herself for it (*Ich bin doch ein schlecht Mensch. Ich könnt' mich erstechen* – H4, 4). In the last scene but one of this version (H4, 16) we see her longing for the forgiveness that had been granted to the woman taken in adultery, longing for the true repentance of Mary Magdalene yet unable to *feel* such repentance, feeling only that within her everything is dead (*Alles todt!*).

Evidently the Marie of H4 is a considerably more complex figure than the heroine of the earlier drafts; the conflicts within her make her a truly tragic character and the play now becomes the tragedy of Marie as well as of Woyzeck. It is not only her sensuality that decides her fate, not only her shrinking from Woyzeck's morbid fancies, not only that longing for escape and adventure suggested in her song of the gypsy boy:

> Mädel mach's Ladel zu,
> S' kommt e Zigeunerbu,
> Führt dich an deiner Hand
> Fort in's Zigeunerland. (H4, 4)

More fatal than all her passions and longings is that peculiar hopelessness or defeatism which seems to afflict her in the most critical situations and paralyse her resistance to evil:

> Ach! Was Welt? Geht doch Alles zum Teufel, Mann und Weib. (H4, 4)
>
> Meintwegen. Es ist Alles eins. (H4, 6)

It is in this mood of apathy and demoralization that she yields to her seducer, and we shall probably not be mistaken in tracing its source to that perpetual poverty and misery which Marie experiences no less painfully than Woyzeck. There is a significant difference in tone between the scene in which Marie, bedecked with ill-omened jewels, looks at herself in a mirror and the scene of Goethe's Gretchen tragedy which Büchner must have *intended* it to recall. Gretchen recognizes the fate of the poor with wistful resignation:

> Was hilft euch Schönheit, junges Blut?
> Das ist wohl alles schön und gut,
> Allein man läßt's auch alles sein;
> Man lobt euch halb aus Erbarmen . . .
> Ach, wir Armen!

But in Marie's words, in her pointed comparison between the beauty which she sees in her own little fragment of mirror and the beauty (perhaps less exquisite) which great ladies contemplate in mirrors as tall as themselves, there is an unmistakable accent of revolt, a resentful sense of wrong.[52]

This insistence on the poverty of the hero and heroine is a remarkable feature of the last version of *Woyzeck* and one which has not been sufficiently recognized by the critics. It is precisely in the new scenes of H4 that it is most evident, but it pervades the whole fragment. We have seen Marie, in H4, 4, resuming more bitterly Gretchen's meditations on poverty; we have seen Woyzeck, in H4, 5, expatiating almost in the spirit of Karl Marx on the decisive importance of financial circumstances. And it is significant that the word *arm* ('poor'), which occurs only once in H1 and only three times in H2, occurs six times in H4. The word *Geld* ('money'), which does not occur at all in the earlier drafts, occurs no less than eight times in the final version. No doubt Büchner had always thought of his hero and heroine as very poor people; but it is evident that the longer he worked at the play the more he emphasized that factor in their situation, the more he insisted on their material disabilities. Some critics are reluctant to admit this increasingly 'materialistic' tendency in *Woyzeck*, but the chronological study of the fragments shows it to be an undeniable fact. It confirms the view I have already suggested: that *Woyzeck* is not, as the majority of critics maintain, a tragedy of primitive passion or metaphysical suffering in which social circumstances are more or less irrelevant. It is a tragedy of human feeling in a world of social oppression, and the humanity and the oppression are alike integral to it.[53]

We arrive at the same conclusion if we consider the structure of the play, which was still indeterminable in the earlier versions but which becomes apparent in H4. It becomes evident here that the arrangement of the scenes is intended to conform to a pattern in which the scenes concerned primarily with Woyzeck's relation to Marie regularly alternate with those concerned primarily with his relation to society – two groups of scenes which are nevertheless closely and systematically connected. Once again we may suspect the influence of Lenz. The technique of contrasting groups of scenes is anticipated in *Die Soldaten*, where we have the scenes showing the development of the hero and heroine and those illustrating the life of the army officers. But we must also notice the characteristic difference between Lenz and Büchner. Lenz's didactic intention, his desire to reform or at least neutralize the moral corruption of the soldiers leads him to dwell unduly – unduly, that is, from a strictly dramatic point of view – on his portrayal of army life, and there are a number of scenes in which neither the hero nor the heroine appears. In Büchner's play the two sides of the duality are much more closely integrated. Everything – the moralizing of the captain, the doctor's experiments, the behaviour of the drum major, of the *Handwerksburschen*, of the people at the fair – is shown in direct relation to the hero or heroine and only in so far as it affects them. So that – with one exception – there is no scene in which either Woyzeck or Marie does not appear. The one exception is H4, 9 ('Hauptmann. Doctor'), where only the captain and the doctor are present; and the fact that this scene is, in this respect, anomalous is another reason, in addition to the space in the manuscript mentioned above, why one may doubt whether it is really complete, whether Woyzeck was not after all intended to appear in it.

After the introductory scene ('Freies Feld. Die Stadt in der Ferne'), with its sinister atmosphere of hidden terror and impending doom, the alternation of the scenes showing the course of Woyzeck's relation to Marie and those showing his treatment at the hands of society is characterized by a continual increase of dramatic tension, a gradual intensification of emotional stress.[54] In proportion as Marie drifts farther away from Woyzeck – in proportion as the pain he suffers on her account becomes more acute – so the persecution and humiliation inflicted on him by society become more agonizing. There is first the comparatively mild ill-usage to which he is subjected by the captain; then the harsher inhumanity of the doctor, followed, possibly, by a scene corresponding to the unmitigated cruelty of H2, 7; then the alien world of the tavern with its coarse and stupid revelry; and, finally, the physical defeat, the brutal castigation of Woyzeck by his rival. Thus in proportion as Woyzeck's need for Marie becomes more urgent, the more he is abandoned by her; or, conversely, the more her infidelity reduces him to desperation, the more his misery is mocked, his distress exacerbated by society. The two strands of the action are thus interwoven, each exciting and enflaming the other to the point where Woyzeck's resolution to kill Marie becomes inevitable.

But also proportionate to Woyzeck's ever increasing agony is the growing sense of injustice with which we, the audience, observe this process. From the moment when the captain describes Woyzeck – incomparably more intelligent than himself – as 'abominably stupid', we know that we are in a topsy-turvy world, 'eine verkehrte Welt', as Elema calls it,[55] in which it is the better man who goes down and the worse who triumphs. And the succeeding scenes intensify this impression until the injustice of Woyzeck's fate reaches its culmination.

It has occasionally been suggested that the action of the play is circular, that the end is implicit in the beginning.[56] This is evidently not so. The action has rather the form of a spiral ascending to an acme of tragic suffering. It is still legitimate, I think, to regard this as an 'open' form of drama in so far as each scene has its centre of interest within itself – in so far as Büchner presents only the high points of the action without the close continuity of classical drama. But there is nevertheless an architectonic principle shaping the work as a whole. It was so in *Dantons Tod* and in *Lenz*, and it is equally or even more so in *Woyzeck*. Within the wider category of the 'open' form each work has its own individual form, and the features differentiating it from the 'closed' form are in each work more or less pronounced. *Woyzeck* is basically a drama in the 'open' form, but on that basis it might have achieved, if completed, an architectonic grandeur comparable with that of the greatest examples of the 'closed' form of drama.[57]

The scenes illustrating Woyzeck's social situation are not only necessary for our understanding of his fate; they also enlarge the scope of the play, suggesting the wider implications of the individual tragedy. And this effect is enhanced by the folksongs which are so extraordinarily numerous in H4. Fink has shown that these folksongs have the function of a chorus – not the anti-illusionistic function of Schiller's chorus, but rather a 'realistic' function consonant with Büchner's conception of art. They constitute a 'realistic' chorus in the sense that they reflect in a wider sphere the real experience of Woyzeck, showing it to correspond more or less to the experience of poor people everywhere, and commenting on it with the illusionless wisdom of the people. Thanks to them, and in spite of the extreme economy and concentration of Büchner's style, the play achieves, as Fink puts it, 'a certain stereometric, in the last resort universal human profundity'.[58] The play which, in H1, began as little more than a sketch of a story of individual passion and desperate action, becomes in its final form the representation of a whole society, the picture of a tragic world.

## REVOLT IN 'WOYZECK'

H4, the last and most authoritative of the *Woyzeck* fragments, ends with the seventeenth scene ('Caserne'), at a point in the action prior to the murder of the heroine; and there is no agreement among the critics as to how Büchner envisaged its continuation, or even as to whether he intended to continue it at all. The question demands our attention as it has a vital bearing on the interpretation of the play as a whole. Was it Büchner's intention – an intention which only sickness and death prevented him from carrying out – to let H4 continue more or less along the lines indicated in the later scenes of H1, Marie being stabbed to death by Woyzeck? Or did Büchner now propose to let the play proceed according to a quite different plan? Or, finally, had he decided to let it remain a fragment in the manner of the Romantics? The last suggestion, made by Egon Krause,[59] need not detain us long. Büchner is not a Romantic, even if he owes a good deal to the Romantics, and in his other works shows no inclination towards fragmentary composition. Even *Lenz*, as we have seen, is substantially complete. Nor is there much force in the arguments by which Krause seeks to persuade us that Büchner had abandoned the idea of letting Woyzeck kill Marie. In that case the scene 'Freies Feld' (H4, 12), where Woyzeck hears the fatal voices urging him to 'stab the she-wolf dead', would be pointless; and equally so the scene in which Woyzeck buys the knife from the Jew (H4, 15). Not surprisingly, Krause is unable to make satisfactory sense of these scenes and is forced to ask whether they do not produce 'inconsistencies' (*Unstimmigkeiten*) in H4.[60] He fails to consider that the contradictions and obscurities which he finds in Büchner's text[61] may be due merely to his own unsound approach to it. It speaks ill for an interpretation if it can only be true on the assumption that the dramatist is a bungler, and Krause's interpretation makes Büchner out to be a bungler on more than one count: not only because, on Krause's showing, Büchner introduces scenes which forebode with fatal necessity a murder that is never to take place, but also because – still on Krause's showing – he gratuitously chooses for his hero, who is to remain innocent of murder, the name of a notorious murderer. The case of the historical Woyzeck was still quite recent and very well known in Büchner's time; thousands of people had seen the condemned man executed in the Leipzig market-place, and the matter had been widely publicized. If it was Büchner's intention to tell quite a different story, his choice of the name 'Woyzeck' was not only pointless but inept. We must agree with Lehmann[62] that by his choice of that name Büchner provocatively asserted the historical authenticity of his play and committed himself to reproducing – not every detail but – the essential facts of the historical case, including the murder.

Thus we can only conclude that, if his fatal sickness had not prevented him, Büchner would have continued to transfer to H4 the murder scenes of H1. In doing so he would no doubt have considerably modified these scenes, as he modified every scene taken over from the earlier MSS. And very probably, also, he would have supplemented them with quite new scenes in accordance with his usual practice in H4. But everything indicates that H4, if it had been completed, would have continued on substantially the same lines as the latter part of H1. The essential harmony of the two fragments is proved by the fact that when the scenes of H4 are followed in the theatre, as they always are, by the murder scenes of H1, the audience is not conscious of any break or discrepancy; the transition is imperceptible and the end is felt to be perfectly adapted to the beginning. The evidence of the key-words likewise indicates that Büchner did not intend to abandon the later scenes of H1 but would have incorporated them in some form in the definitive version of the play. Thus the new scenes of H4 are deliberately linked to the murder scenes of H1 by means of the key-words *rot*, *Blut*, *immer ʒu*, and by the *motif* of the knife. And that Büchner still intended to include the grandmother's tale in the final version is indicated by the recurrence of its key-phrase *Alles todt* ('all dead') in the scene of Marie's abortive attempt to pray (H4, 16), as well as by the fact that the sentence of H2, 1: 'Still, quite still, like death' (*Still, ganʒ still, wie der Tod*) is altered in H4, 1 to make it foreshadow, or at least to bring it into closer harmony with the grandmother's tale: 'Still, everything still, as if the world were dead' (*Still, Alles still, als wär die Welt todt*).[63] It has been plausibly suggested by Margaret Jacobs[64] that Woyzeck's mother, mentioned in H4, 17, is to be identified with the grandmother of H1.

Assuming for these reasons that the murder scenes would have been included in the definitive version of the play, we must also assume that that version would have ended with a scene corresponding to H1, 21, where we witness the beginning of the official procedure – the post-mortem examination of Marie's body – which must lead to the trial and execution of Woyzeck. This is one of the scenes dealing with the *social* aspect of the tragedy; and if even H1, which is less concerned with that aspect, ends with such a scene, then *a fortiori* H4, where the emphasis on the social aspect is so much greater, must end similarly. Evidently that rhythmical alternation of scenes of social oppression and private agony which characterizes this last fragment would have continued to the end of the play in an ascending scale of suffering and injustice culminating in the supreme irony: the condemnation of the lowliest and best human being by those who are socially his superiors but in every other respect immeasurably his inferiors. It would have been a situation which, as Elema remarks,[65] Büchner was familiar with from his own experience and observation – a situation like that of Weidig and many other generous men and women who had been judged, condemned and ultimately driven to their death by infamous creatures such as Georgi. Such a paradox may have struck Büchner in his reading of Clarus's report on Woyzeck, and may well have been one of the deepest sources of his interest in the subject.

It is at any rate clear that performances of *Woyzeck* in the theatre and attempts to edit it for the general public should properly end with the autopsy scene from H1, not only for the reasons already given in our discussion of the first fragment (see above, pp. 226 ff.), but also because such an ending best accords with the rhythmical structure of the play and with Büchner's deepest intentions. The scene H3, 2 ('Der Idiot. Das Kind. Woyzeck') which Lehmann places at the end of his 'reading and stage version' is less appropriate in this position, because, though deeply pathetic, it does not provide a properly *dramatic* ending to the play (contrast the ending of *Dantons Tod*), and still more because it misplaces the emphasis at the critical moment of the play's conclusion. Büchner was concerned not only with the personal fate of Woyzeck, however pathetic, but also with his relation to society; and as the story of the historical Woyzeck merges into the story of society's reaction to his crime, so Büchner's play most properly ends, not with the full representation, but with the prospect, the anticipation of that reaction.[66]

It has been suggested that *Woyzeck*, and particularly the fragment H4, bears witness to a profound change in Büchner's Weltanschauung. Thus Wilfried Buch writes:

It has been recognized for some time now that Büchner turned away 'from materialistic cynicism, from radical nihilism', but this development did not take place, as hitherto supposed, between *Dantons Tod* and *Woyzeck* but within the *Woyzeck* drafts.[67]

Krause argues that Büchner's own spiritual progress between *Dantons Tod* and *Woyzeck* is reflected in the evolution of his hero from the 'Louis' of H1 to the 'Woyzeck' of H4, the latter tending ever more strongly towards the 'surmounting of suffering'.[68] And a similar view is expressed by Mautner:

We find the most marked change of a moral-philosophical or metaphysical tendency in H [i.e. H4], in the interpolation of Woyzeck's farewell from Andres, which indicated, in comparison with the earlier drafts, a positive attitude to the suffering of the world . . . This attitude is religious and close to the Christian attitude.[69]

How much truth is there in these suggestions of Buch, Krause and Mautner? It is true, I think, that Büchner had a deep sympathy with the Christian *spirit*, with the moral attitude of Christianity in its finest expressions. But I see no reason to believe that it was only in the latest period of his life that he felt that sympathy; it appears rather to have been a natural consequence of that tragic view of life which he had accepted ever since attaining maturity in the Giessen period of 1833–4. One naturally finds traces of this sympathy in *Woyzeck* as in Büchner's other works, for example in Marie's longing for Christ's forgiveness or in Woyzeck's repetition of the words 'Suffer little children to come unto me'. But I see nothing in H4 to justify the view that Woyzeck succeeds in surmounting suffering or that there had been any considerable change in Büchner's attitude to religion since *Dantons Tod*. As we have seen, all the evidence indicates that Büchner still intended the murder to take place in H4. Shortly before the end of the fragment we have seen Woyzeck purchasing the fatal weapon from the Jew, and we must expect the play to continue as in the first fragment: there will be the grandmother's tale, and then Woyzeck will lead Marie away to kill her. How is it possible, in view of such events, to speak of a 'surmounting of suffering'? Marie's fate may in some respects recall Gretchen's, especially as Büchner himself, in H4, 4, appears deliberately to suggest such a relationship; but what a contrast between Gretchen's appeal to the heavenly powers with the answering 'voice from above': 'She is saved!' and the last desperate cry of Büchner's heroine – a cry which remains *unanswered*: 'For Heaven's sake, help – help!' (*Um des Himmels willen, Hü – Hülfe!*)! Mautner asserts that in Woyzeck's speeches in H4 there is 'not a single word of accusation against God or of despair at the government of the world'.[70] But is there really no despair, no implied complaint against Providence, in those words of Woyzeck already quoted to the effect that the children of the poor have to work even in their sleep, that they are debarred by poverty from any aspiration

towards virtue and morality, that they are once and for all
unblest in this and in the other world? According to Mautner,[71]
evidence of a more positive and more Christian attitude towards
suffering is to be found in the words which Woyzeck has come
upon in his mother's Bible:

> Leiden sey all mein Gewinst,
> Leiden sey mein Gottesdienst.
> Herr wie dein Leib war roth und wund,
> So laß mein Herz seyn aller Stund. (H4, 17)

But this is not a new thought for Büchner. He had already quoted
the first two of these lines in *Lenz*,[72] but had nevertheless proceeded to describe the unrelieved tragedy of Lenz's fate and the
gradual crumbling of his faith in God. And long after the date
of his Novelle Büchner was still capable of writing, in his notes
on Spinoza, his destructive criticism of the belief in God as a
perfect being and, in the first draft of *Woyzeck*, the deeply pessimistic or nihilistic grandmother's tale. Evidently the expression
of that thought in *Lenz* had *not* signified a profound revision of
Büchner's attitude to religion – had *not* signified his acceptance
of the Christian view of the world. So why should the expression
of the same thought in *Woyzeck* have that significance?

On the contrary, considering that the final version of the play
must still proceed to its desperate ending and that, as the key-
words indicate, the grandmother's tale would probably have been
included in it, we can hardly escape the conclusion that, in its
definitive form no less than in its first draft – and perhaps even
more than in its first draft – *Woyzeck* would have been a powerful
expression of metaphysical revolt.

But also of political revolt. It has become almost a cliché of
Büchner interpretation to say that in his later period Büchner
'turned away from politics',[73] that *Woyzeck* is concerned with
a vision of suffering 'to which all political and even social considerations become increasingly irrelevant'.[74] But this is the
reverse of the truth. Our analysis has shown, on the contrary,
that the relevance of social considerations, barely discernible in
the first draft of the play, becomes increasingly evident in every

subsequent draft; and we must not forget that for Büchner those social considerations have very clear political implications. It was precisely the 'gulf between the educated and the uneducated classes of society', so vividly illustrated in the relation of Woyzeck to his social superiors, that determined Büchner's revolutionary strategy in his 'Society of Human Rights', and its decisive political importance is still explicitly recognized in his last letter to Gutzkow. Woyzeck's relation to his superiors is a particularly striking example of that relation of the poor to the rich which for Büchner was 'the only revolutionary element in the world'. Thus one cannot say with reference to *Woyzeck* what I have ventured to say with reference to *Dantons Tod* that 'the spirit of political revolt is defeated and the spirit of metaphysical revolt prevails'.[75] *Woyzeck*, the most powerful expression of Büchner's metaphysical revolt, is also the most powerful expression of his social and political revolt. It is in fact the most distinctive achievement of Büchner's dramatic genius that in this play neither of these elements is sacrificed to the other, that at last a balance of the two is established.

How is this possible? It is possible because Büchner allows us to see more clearly in *Woyzeck* than in any of his other works that the evil and suffering in the world are not independent of the character and behaviour of human beings but manifest themselves largely *through* character and behaviour. The suffering of Woyzeck and Marie, the loneliness of the child in the grandmother's tale, are – not wholly but largely – caused by social injustice and by the brutality and selfishness of particular people. One may say that the captain and the doctor cannot be otherwise than they are, that their character has been formed by influences beyond their control, just as the social order has been formed by historical necessity. This is true, and it is this *necessity* of evil that justifies the metaphysical protest of the play. But one also sees that those who *feel* the evil of that necessity are not prevented from hating and combating it, just as they are not prevented from loving and pitying the victims of it (once again: 'hatred is as permissible as love'). And this hatred of injustice, this love and pity for its victims, may have their enormously valuable effectiveness even if they cannot undo the suffering that has already existed in the world and that will continue to exist, in some degree, to all eternity. Büchner, in his play, can only show us these facts. It is not his business, as an objective dramatist, to point a moral. He is never, in a narrow or direct sense, a didacticist. His play is not a *pièce à thèse*. But, as he remarked in the letter to his family of 28 July 1835, though the dramatist is concerned solely with truth, one can learn from the truth of art just as one can learn from the observation of history and of the reality surrounding one.[76] And what one can learn from *Woyzeck* is not only the eternal suffering of the world but also the extent to which that suffering is actualized through the lovelessness of individuals and the injustice of an inequitable social order. Without indulging in utopian hopes or closing one's eyes to the unalterable tragedy of the world, one can still – with limited but by no means negligible effect – combat that selfishness and injustice and learn to regard one's suffering fellow men with pity and love. We may agree with Fink that in *Woyzeck* there is an implicit longing for something other than the play actually shows, a longing 'for a true community which concedes its place to love'.[77] But there is also, for the reflective reader and spectator, a clear indication of the means by which that 'other' may be partially – never more than partially – achieved. Thus in *Woyzeck* we have the rare synthesis of a pessimistic world-view and a progressive social and political activism. It is a peculiarly modern attitude, perhaps the only attitude that can still seem valid in the twentieth century. It is the attitude of Camus's *La Peste*, the attitude suggested by Ernst Toller:

Only the weak give up when they find themselves incapable of the full realization of the longed-for dream. The strong lose nothing of their passionate will when their eyes are opened. What we need to-day is not people who are blinded by their intense emotion; we need those who have will – although also awareness.[78]

It can be asserted without hesitation or qualification that *Woyzeck* has had more influence on modern German drama than any other play of the nineteenth century. It has fascinated dramatists of the most diverse schools and styles – Naturalism, Impressionism, Expressionism, Epic Drama – and traces of its influence are to be found in Hauptmann (*Die Weber*), Wedekind (*Frühlingserwachen*), Toller (*Hinckemann*), Horváth (*Kasimir und Karoline*), Walser (*Eiche und Angora*), Frisch (*Andorra*) and Brecht (*Baal, Puntila*).[79] Adamov reports that Brecht, only a few months before his death, told him that he regarded *Woyzeck* as the beginning of modern theatre. And Adamov fully endorses that comment on Büchner's masterpiece – 'this play which moves me so profoundly'.[80]

No doubt the intense interest which *Woyzeck* has excited in our time is partly due to the problems with which it is concerned – the problems of social oppression and metaphysical despair in a 'post-Christian' society convulsed by political and social unrest. But the problems in themselves would hardly have attracted so much attention to the work if it had not been such a powerful and impressive drama. In evolving this new dramatic form Büchner owed something, as we have seen, to Lenz. But the form of *Woyzeck* is nevertheless very different from that of *Die Soldaten* and *Der Hofmeister*. It is free from the moralizing, the prolixity of Lenz's work; it is spare, concentrated, economical; in its powerful directness extraordinarily modern. It seems to achieve all that later revolutionary dramatists have been aiming at, and to achieve it more convincingly than their partial and distorted attempts.

In *Woyzeck* Büchner has been uniquely successful in combining and integrating heterogeneous artistic elements – realism and satire, tragedy and grotesquerie, vulgarity and pathos; so that later dramatists of the most diverse character have all been able to find in this play the realization of *some* of their ideals. But it is important to remember that *Woyzeck* is nevertheless different in style from the work of all its imitators or continuators. It is not naturalistic, not expressionistic, not Brechtian; and attempts to perform it in any of these later styles do violence to it and falsify it. Its realism is not the mechanical imitation, the circumstantial heaviness of the naturalists; it does not, like the work of the expressionists, tend to abstraction and to direct symbolism; it is free from the aridity of *Andorra*; it has a more intense poetry than Horváth's plays (though in other respects Horváth has perhaps more affinity with Büchner than any other twentieth century dramatist); and though it shares with most of Brecht's plays the 'open' dramatic form, it is nevertheless nearer on the whole to the drama of empathy than to the drama of alienation. Certainly, in the scenes portraying the captain and the doctor there is enough to stimulate the critical reflection of the audience (and it is precisely these scenes which have influenced Brecht's *Puntila*). But Büchner, though avoiding the didacticism of the author of the *Lehrstücke*, confronts the reality of his time much more directly – beneath the surface of his dramatic objectivity much more passionately than Brecht, and achieves a tragic power hardly equalled in more recent literature. So that, even in the fragmentary form in which it has come down to us, the first proletarian tragedy remains the best.

# 9. CONCLUSION

As we look back on our study of the phenomenon of revolt in Büchner's life and work, the question suggests itself: to what extent has this approach to Büchner proved fruitful? is it possible in this way to do justice to his achievement? The answer must be, I think, that our method of study has shown itself to be in some respects helpful and illuminating but that it is not comprehensive, not exhaustive. It requires to be supplemented by other methods.

For evidently not all of the values expressed in Büchner's work are values of revolt. It is not from any kind of revolt that, for example, the love of nature springs which appears to have been such a strong passion with Büchner even in his boyhood, but which is also evident in his scientific researches and occasionally in his imaginative writings (perhaps most of all in *Leonce und Lena*) – though our inquiry has suggested that Büchner's revolt against the obsolete, dogmatic views of nature accepted in his time made possible for him a fresh positive insight into the value of nature, into the 'law of beauty' prevailing in it. Nor is the love of women in Büchner's writings directly an expression of revolt, but rather of a longing for solace and escape. And still another value unrelated to revolt which must have been of the greatest psychological importance for Büchner is the sheer delight of the artist in perfect expression which even a pessimist or a nihilist cannot help feeling if he is such a great writer as Büchner was.

All this must be admitted, and yet it may still be claimed that it has proved possible, from our chosen point of view, to consider without strain or distortion an extraordinarily large number of aspects of Büchner's work. And this has been possible, evidently, because the attitude of revolt is in fact Büchner's characteristic attitude, the spirit of revolt is the prevailing spirit in his life and work. It is significant that in all three of his completely serious works – *Dantons Tod*, *Lenz* and *Woyzeck* – the 'integration point'

265

has been found to be an expression of intense metaphysical revolt. And we have also found that, contrary to the received opinion, the element of social and political revolt remains equally persistent throughout Büchner's career, and increases rather than decreases in intensity. *Woyzeck*, the last of his plays, is also in every respect – socially and politically as well as aesthetically and metaphysically – 'the most revolutionary'.[1] Critics have mistaken Büchner's merely strategic withdrawal from active politics for a complete change of heart. They forget that revolutionary action is only possible in a revolutionary situation – a fact which was as clear to the realist Büchner as it ever was to Marx or Lenin – and that, as his experiment with the 'Society for Human Rights' had amply demonstrated, a revolutionary situation was not given in Büchner's time.[2]

But if the recognition and analysis of the various expressions of revolt in his life and work can be accepted as a contribution to the *characterization* of Büchner, how much does it contribute to the *criticism* of Büchner? Nothing directly, I would say; for an attitude of revolt is compatible with almost every degree of poetic merit or demerit. But perhaps something indirectly; for, given the indefinable and inexplicable quality of genius, the tendency to revolt may to some extent determine the direction in which the main force of that genius is exerted and consequently the degree of success achieved in the various fields of its activity. What does Büchner, as a thinker and as an artist, gain or lose by his attitude to revolt? in what respects does it strengthen him, in what respects weaken him?

One can perhaps say that, thanks to his revolt, Büchner achieves a drastic but fruitful *simplification* in certain spheres of thought – in politics, in art, in philosophy. And it should be noted that to describe his achievement as a 'simplification' is not necessarily disparaging, since there is often no more urgent task in the world of art or science or politics than to find the *right* simplification, or at least the best possible under the circumstances.

Revolting violently against the dogmas and prejudices of his time, Büchner sees with dazzling clarity certain truths which remain completely dark to the great majority of his contemporaries.

In politics he is one of the first to recognize the importance of the economic element, the insufficiency of the merely liberal, the merely constitutional approach to the problems of his time. Already perceiving that true democracy is impossible without the solution of the social problem and the solution of the social problem impossible without true democracy, he becomes, in the most exact sense of the word, one of the first of Germany's *social-democrats*.

In aesthetics he recognizes the need for a new art that will do justice to the new reality of the nineteenth century, the new awareness of the oppressed classes of society.

In philosophy he sees the untenability of the prevailing religious and idealistic attitudes and clearly perceives the unalterably tragic element in human life.

But it may be argued that in each of these domains – politics, art, philosophy – he pays a certain price for his new insight; that in order to establish his idea in opposition to the prevailing view he is forced into a certain excessiveness or one-sidedness, at least in the expression if not in the substance of his reflections.

This emerged most clearly from our study of his aesthetic principles, where his acute and most fruitful sense of the new direction demanded by the age appeared to be purchased at the price of some injustice to classicism and the abandonment of any attempt at a *historical* understanding of art.

It might similarly be contended that there is a certain one-sidedness in his view of 'the horrifying fatalism' of history. No doubt there is a great deal of truth in this view, and in the twentieth century especially it has been impossible not to recognize it. (How helpless we have been in face of the immense calamities of our time – famine, genocide, the great economic depression, the two world wars which everybody could see approaching and nobody could prevent!) It is at least a truer view than those to which Büchner was opposing it – the Christian idea of a beneficent Providence guiding the course of history, or the romantic idea of perpetual progress as propounded by such thinkers as Fichte, Hegel and Marx. But even as one grants this, one may still feel that there is another side to the question to which Büchner, in theory if not in practice, does not do justice. For even if we can never fully comprehend and never fully control the laws of history, is it not going too far to suggest that human beings are merely 'foam on the wave', merely 'puppets pulled on a string by unknown powers'? Is it not nevertheless true that human effort, even in the domain of politics, may have a certain efficacy, however limited? Can it plausibly be maintained that the efforts of the Greeks to resist Persian domination, the struggle of the western democracies and of the Soviet Union against Nazi Germany, were entirely useless? In theory Büchner fails to recognize this. In his practice as a social-democratic revolutionary and in his imaginative writings, especially *Woyzeck*, his attitude is more constructive and implies a criticism and correction of his theory.

Finally, in this connexion, one might ask whether Büchner's pessimistic view of life is not also rather partial – an aspect of the truth rather than the whole truth. Here again, it seems to me, his view has at least more validity than the rival philosophies of his time, more validity than the optimism of Fichte and Hegel and afterwards of Marx. The profound and eternal tragedy of the world must be recognized. And yet one can perhaps object to Büchner as Feuerbach objected to Schopenhauer (in some ways so akin to Büchner) that human beings nevertheless have an innate drive towards happiness, that they are, as it were, 'made for happiness',[3] and that, as Spinoza so convincingly argued, it is only in happiness and joy that they are really strong.[4] This too is an aspect of the truth – one which does not cancel the aspect so justly perceived by Büchner and Schopenhauer, but which also has a claim to recognition; and in Büchner's writings no adequate recognition is accorded it. Bertrand Russell used to say that it is only after the fullest acknowledgement of the dreadfulness of life that one can begin to be happy. Büchner acquits himself amply of the acknowledgement, but has little to say about the happiness that is supposed to follow it.

Turning our attention from Büchner the thinker to Büchner the dramatist, we find that the same criticism applies. Here too the strength which he derives from his rebellious spirit is in some degree offset by certain correlative weaknesses. Schiller once suggested that Prometheus, the hero of one of the grandest of ancient tragedies, can be regarded as a symbol of tragedy in general.[5] If so, it need not surprise us that a writer who had so much of the Promethean spirit as Büchner should have been so eminently successful as a tragic dramatist. But we have found him not quite so convincing in comedy. Those positive values unrelated to revolt which, as we noticed at the beginning of this chapter, were also present in his nature, are insufficiently represented in his work. He has given us a modern *Hamlet* and *Othello*, but no *Twelfth Night* nor *Winter's Tale*. He has given us an *Inferno*, but no *Paradiso*.

This is a limitation of Büchner's *œuvre*, but not necessarily of his potentialities. He simply did not live long enough, nor under sufficiently favourable circumstances, to unfold the full richness of his nature. If fortune had been kinder to him, if he had been granted anything like a normal life-span, he might conceivably have achieved a greater degree of serenity – that degree of serenity which Shakespeare achieved after *his* tragic period.

Yet it seems not only ungrateful but unsound to say of him, in those sentimental words of Herwegh which disfigure his tombstone:

Ein unvollendet Lied, sinkt er ins Grab,
Der Verse schönsten nimmt er mit hinab.

It is both ungracious and absurd to extol the potential achievement of a poet at the expense of his actual achievement, and particularly so when the actual achievement is as magnificent as Büchner's. All such criticisms, and they are unfortunately not infrequent, which tend to discredit Büchner's work by insisting on his youth, must be firmly rejected.[6] The insights of youth are different from those of age, but not necessarily less valid. The older poet is not necessarily the better poet. And whatever Büchner might have achieved in a longer lifetime, it would not have invalidated and one can hardly conceive that it would have overshadowed the power and truth of *Dantons Tod* and *Woyzeck*.

# NOTES

## 1. INTRODUCTION

1  Cf. Margaret Jacobs, p. xxvi: 'He was a revolutionary not only in the political, but also in the literary field . . . In ideas and technique he made a definite break with the past'; and Heyn, p. 11: 'Büchner war ein "Protestant" im eigentlichen ernsten Wortsinn . . . als Politiker . . . als Ästhetiker . . . als Dichter . . .' [For the full titles of works referred to in these Notes see the Bibliography.]

2  Hölderlin, 'Die Prinzessin Auguste von Homburg', v. 26 f.

3  Cf. Camus, *Essais*, Bibliothèque de la Pléiade, 1965, p. 1703: 'Pour moi, je ne disposais que d'une révolte sûre d'elle-même, mais encore inconsciente de ses raisons'; and p. 1714: 'J'attendrai seulement que ceux, d'où qu'ils viennent, qui sont partis comme moi d'une négation, en soient enfin sortis et nous en fassent sortir sans escamoter nos contradictions.' For a comparison of some aspects of Büchner's thought and Camus's see Martens, 'Ideologie und Verzweiflung: religiöse Motive in Büchners Revolutionsdrama' (Martens, 1965, p. 423 and pp. 432 f.).

## 2. POLITICAL REVOLT

1  'Sie scheinen die Arzeneykunst verlassen zu wollen, womit Sie, wie ich höre, Ihrem Vater keine Freude machen. Seyen Sie nicht ungerecht gegen dies Studium; denn diesem scheinen Sie mir Ihre hauptsächliche force zu verdanken, ich meine, Ihre seltene Unbefangenheit, fast möcht' ich sagen, Ihre Autopsie, die aus allem spricht, was Sie schreiben. Wenn Sie mit dieser Ungenirtheit unter die deutschen Philosophen treten, muß es einen neuen Effekt geben' – Gutzkow to Büchner, 10 June 1836, 2, 490.

2  'Mein Vater . . . hatte die größte Sympathie für die Bewegung der Geister, und gehörte zu seiner liebsten Lektüre, die erlebten Ereignisse in der später erscheinenden Zeitschrift "Unsere Zeit" zu repetieren und zu ergänzen. Vielfach wurden diese abends vorgelesen, und nahmen wir alle den lebhaftesten Anteil daran. Wohl möglich, daß bei dem ohnehin freien Geist der Familie die Wirkung dieser Lektüre von besonderm Einfluß insbesondere auf Georg war, und ist wohl diese Lektüre der Entstehungsmoment von "Dantons Tod"' – Wilhelm Büchner an Franzos, 9 September 1878, Bergemann, 286.

3  Fichte, *Reden an die deutsche Nation*, VII (Hamburg, 1955, p. 121): 'Und so trete denn endlich in seiner vollendeten Klarheit heraus, was wir in unsrer bisherigen Schilderung unter Deutschen verstanden haben. Der eigentliche Unterscheidungsgrund liegt darin, ob man an ein absolut Erstes und Ursprüngliches im Menschen selber, an Freiheit, an unendliche Verbesserlichkeit, an ewiges Fortschreiten unsres Geschlechts glaubt, oder ob man an alles dieses nicht glaube.'

4   'Er spricht in der Sitzung vom 24. Mai 1832 "in etwas zu grellen Farben von der Verderbtheit der deutschen Regierungen und der Roheit der Studenten auf vielen Universitäten, namentlich in Gießen und auch in Heidelberg"'—Mitteilung Marie-Joseph Bopps aus den Protokollen der 'Eugenia'. Bergemann, 269.

5   See Viëtor, 1939, p. 36.

6   'Mäßigung wird ja doch nur für Schwäche angesehen, die zum Übermute, und Rechtlichkeit für Dummheit, die zum Betruge auffordert . . . Schwert gegen Schwert . . . Die Gewalt muß entscheiden. Besiegen könnt ihr uns, aber täuschen nicht mehr'—Börne, *Briefe aus Paris*, 13. Oktober 1831 (*Sämtliche Schriften*, III, Düsseldorf, 1964, 302 f.).

7   'Ihr wollt nichts wissen von der sozialen Reform, so beugt Euch denn unter die soziale Revolution'—Quoted by Viëtor, 1939, p. 79.

8   Hegel, *Grundlinien der Philosophie des Rechts*, § 258, Zusatz: 'Der Staat an und für sich ist das sittliche Ganze, die Verwirklichung der Freiheit . . . es ist der Gang Gottes in der Welt, daß der Staat ist: sein Grund ist die Gewalt der sich als Wille verwirklichenden Vernunft.'

9   Nöllner, p. 421.

10  Nöllner, p. 421: 'So ist es gekommen, daß man bei aller parteiischen Vorliebe für sie doch sagen muß, daß sie eine ziemlich *niederträchtige Gesinnung* angenommen haben, und daß sie, es ist traurig genug, fast an keiner Seite mehr zugänglich sind als gerade am *Geldsack*.'

11  Nöllner, p. 422: 'Der materielle Druck, unter welchem ein großer Teil Deutschlands liege, sei eben so traurig und schimpflich, als der geistige; und es sei in seinen Augen bei weitem nicht so betrübt, daß dieser oder jener Liberale seine Gedanken nicht drucken lassen dürfe, als daß viele tausend Familien nicht im Stand wären, ihre Kartoffeln zu schmälzen.'

12  Nöllner, pp. 421 f.: 'Seht die Östreicher, sie sind wohlgenährt und zufrieden! Fürst Metternich, der geschickteste unter allen, hat allen revolutionären Geist, der jemals unter ihnen aufkommen könnte, für immer in ihrem eigenen *Fett* erstickt.'

13  Marx, *Thesen über Feuerbach*, § 11: 'Die Philosophen haben die Welt nur verschieden *interpretiert*; es kommt aber darauf an, sie zu *verändern*.'

14  Cf. Dieter Kerner, 'In memoriam Georg Büchners', *Deutsches medizinisches Journal*, Berlin, 14 (1963), 658, where Büchner's *Hessischer Landbote* is described as 'das Produkt eines Egozentrikers, eines Fanatikers, eines Geltungshungrigen' and where A. Bartels is quoted as follows: 'Büchner war ohne Zweifel eine jener frühreifen, herrschsüchtigen Naturen, die da glauben, mit den Menschen spielen zu dürfen und höchst gewissenlos handeln können, wenn es um ihr Prestige geht.' Büchner must have known that if the secret of the conspiracy was kept few people would know about his revolutionary activity, and that if it was betrayed he would be in disgrace even with his own family.

15  Cf. Büchner's letter to his family, 19 March 1834 (2, 426). Also Golo Mann, *Deutsche Geschichte des neunzehnten und zwanzigsten Jahrhunderts*, Frankfurt a. M., 1958, pp. 134 f.: 'Eine neue Welle von Verfolgungen beginnt [after the Hambach demonstration of 1832], bösartiger als die von 1819;

in Preußen, in Hessen, selbst im gemütlichen Bayern. Hunderte von Todesurteilen werden gefällt, zwar nicht vollstreckt, aber die Verurteilten in Zuchthäusern und Festungen in ihrem Lebensmut gebrochen.' Karl Vogt in his memoirs (*Aus meinem Leben*, Stuttgart, 1896, p. 134) describes the savage punishments regularly meted out in Hesse – in the case of his cousin Gladbach it was a matter of eight years in solitary confinement – for the mere *suspicion* of political dissent. In view of this evidence it is impossible to accept the suggestion of Knight (p. 39) that Büchner exaggerated the evil.

16  Wilhelm Büchner to Franzos, 9 September 1878, Bergemann, p. 285.

17  See above, pp. 16 f. – According to Becker (Nöllner, p. 425), Büchner had intended to distribute pamphlets like *Der Hessische Landbote* in other German states.

18  Cf. Ricarda Huch, *Alte und neue Götter. Die Revolution des neunzehnten Jahrhunderts in Deutschland*, Berlin/Zürich, 1930, p. 99 – For a modern account of economic conditions in Germany in Büchner's time see J. Kulischer, *Allgemeine Wirtschaftsgeschichte des Mittelalters und der Neuzeit*, 2. Aufl. München, 1958. Viëtor lists the relevant contemporary literature (1939, pp. 128 f.). See especially the comments of Fr. List (1844), *Gesammelte Schriften*, Stuttgart/Tübingen, vol. II, pp. 288 f.: 'Man wußte bei uns nicht, was man in England unter den "notwendigsten Lebensbedürfnissen" verstand. In vielen Gegenden Deutschlands versteht man darunter Kartoffeln ohne Salz, eine Suppe mit Schwarzbrot zur höchsten Notdurft geschmälzt, Haferbrei, hie und da schwarze Klöße. Die, welche sich schon besser stehen, sehen kaum in der Woche einmal ein bescheidenes Stück frisches oder geräuchertes Fleisch auf ihrem Tisch, und Braten kennen die meisten nur vom Hörensagen.'

19  Börne, *Briefe aus Paris*, ed. cit., III, p. 442: 'Tausende wandern jährlich nach Amerika aus, . . . um in einem fremden Weltteile ihren Hunger zu stillen'; p. 441: 'der arme Häusler im Spessart, der sich glücklich schätzt, wenn ihm nur drei Tage in der Woche die Kartoffeln mangeln'; p. 444: 'wenn es kalt ist in Hannover, aber recht kalt, so daß die Tränen der Unglücklichen zu Eis werden, dann – wird in der Nacht Stroh gestreut auf dem Steinboden des Marstalles, quer über die durchlaufende trübe Gosse gelegt, und die armen Leute, die kein Holz haben und kein Bett und keine Suppe haben, ihre erfrornen Glieder zu wärmen, dürfen dahin kommen und dort schlafen zwischen den königlichen Pferden bis der Tag graut.'

20  'In Ober- und Rheinhessen vereinten sich Elementar-Ereignisse (Hunger-jahre, Überschwemmungen) mit unerträglichem Steuerdruck, um eine so jähe und allgemeine Verarmung herbeizuführen, daß Tausende nach Amerika zogen, die Anderen aber, welche nicht auswandern konnten oder mochten, in dumpfer, trotziger Verzweiflung die Hände in den Schoß legten. Der Staat, selbst an ewiger Finanznot leidend, konnte nicht helfen und suchte den Schrei der Not dadurch zu ersticken, daß er die Kammern nach Kräften mundtot mache' – Franzos, p. lxxviii.

21  Viëtor, 1939, p. 91.

22  Nöllner, p. 249: 'Die Grundlage seines Patriotismus war wirklich das reinste Mitleid und ein edler Sinn für alles Schöne und Große.'

23 Nöllner, p. 425: 'Mit der von ihm geschriebenen Flugschrift wollte er vorderhand nur die Stimmung des Volks und der deutschen Revolutionäre erforschen. Als er später hörte, daß die Bauern die meisten gefundenen Flugschriften auf die Polizei abgeliefert hätten, als er vernahm, daß sich auch die Patrioten gegen seine Flugschrift ausgesprochen, gab er alle seine politischen Hoffnungen in bezug auf ein Anderswerden auf.'

24 Nöllner, p. 423: 'Überhaupt war Weidig in allem der Gegensatz zu Büchner; er [Weidig] hatte den Grundsatz, daß man auch den kleinsten revolutionären Funken sammeln müsse, wenn es dereinst brennen solle: er war unter den Republikanern republikanisch und unter den Konstitutionellen konstitutionell.'

25 Enzensberger, p. 53: 'Es steckte in ihm, aller Schwärmerei fürs gute Alte ungeachtet, ein Realist, der von der Zukunft der Bourgeoisie mehr als Büchner begriff, nämlich fast soviel wie Engels.'

26 See above, pp. 18 f. – Büchner's disbelief in the possibility of an alliance between the wealthy bourgeoisie and the impoverished masses was to be fully vindicated in the abortive revolution of 1848, when, as Marx and Engels were forced to recognize, the bourgeoisie elected to join forces with the reactionary kings and princes as soon as it felt its interests threatened by the rising proletariat.

27 Nöllner, p. 423: 'Sie [Weidig's version] unterscheidet sich vom Originale namentlich dadurch, daß an die Stelle der Reichen die Vornehmen gesetzt sind, und daß das, was gegen die sogennante liberale Partei gesagt war, weggelassen und mit anderem, was sich bloß auf die Wirksamkeit der konstitutionellen Verfassung bezieht, ersetzt worden ist . . . Die biblischen Stellen, sowie überhaupt der Schluß, sind von Weidig.'

28 Nöllner, p. 422, p. 424.

29 Nöllner, pp. 223 f.

30 For Koch's evidence and for a discussion of the version of the declaration of human rights probably used by Büchner see Viëtor, 1939, pp. 42 ff.

31 Nöllner, pp. 425 f.: 'Büchner meinte, in einer gerechten Republik, wie in den meisten nordamerikanischen Staaten, müsse jeder ohne Rücksicht auf Vermögensverhältnisse eine Stimme haben, und behauptete, daß Weidig, welcher glaubte, daß dann eine Pöbelherrschaft, wie in Frankreich, entstehen werde, die Verhältnisse des deutschen Volks und unserer Zeit verkenne. Büchner äußerte sich einst in Gegenwart des Zeuner sehr heftig über diesen Aristokratismus des Weidig, wie er es nannte, und Zeuner beging dann später die Indiscretion, es dem Weidig wieder zu sagen. Hierdurch entstand ein Streit zwischen Weidig und Büchner, welchen ich beizulegen mich bemühte und welcher die Ursache ist, daß ich diese Einzelheiten behalten habe.'

32 De Tocqueville, *Democracy in America*, Part I, Chapter IX. Translated by Henry Reeve, London, 1965, p. 110.

33 Cf. S. E. Morison, *The Oxford History of the United States*, vol. II, London, 1927, p. 25: 'State constitutional changes between 1830 and 1850 tended

NOTES TO PP. 20–30

towards government of, for, and by the people. Religious tests and property qualifications for office were generally swept away, and manhood suffrage adopted.'

34  Nöllner, p. 425: 'Von den Konstitutionellen sagte er oft: Sollte es diesen Leuten gelingen, die deutschen Regierungen zu stürzen und eine allgemeine Monarchie oder auch Republik einzuführen, so bekommen wir hier einen Geldaristokratismus wie in Frankreich, und lieber soll es bleiben, wie es jetzt ist.'

35  Cf. *The Cambridge Modern History*, vol. XI, 1934, pp. 240 f.: 'The new Cantonal Constitutions, framed in 1830–1 . . . made representative government the prevailing government in Switzerland . . . Property qualifications for the franchise disappeared almost everywhere.'

36  The sentence in the concluding section of *Der Hessische Landbote*: 'Deutschland ist jetzt ein Leichenfeld, bald wird es ein Paradies seyn' (2, 58) could be regarded as chiliastic, and Bergemann (p. 183) ascribes it to Büchner. But it obviously refers back to Weidig's quotation from Ezekiel 37: 'Der Herr führte mich auf ein weites Feld, das voller Gebeine lag, und siehe, sie waren sehr verdorrt' (2, 56). It should be remembered that, according to Becker, 'die biblischen Stellen sowie überhaupt der Schluß sind von Weidig'. It seems most probable, therefore, that the chiliastic sentence quoted above is also by Weidig, especially as he has already insisted on the power of the Almighty to transform 'ein Land des Jammers und des Elends wieder in ein Paradies' (2, 54). Lehmann (1969, pp. 16 f.), on the basis of the allusion to Ezekiel, accuses Büchner of indulging in 'einer geschichtsphilosophischen Utopie'. He does not consider that he may be blaming Büchner for the words of Weidig.

37  Heinrich von Treitschke, *Deutsche Geschichte im neunzehnten Jahrhundert*, 4. Teil, Leipzig, 1928, p. 304; 'ein Meisterstück gewissenloser demagogischer Beredsamkeit'.

38  Viëtor, 1939, p. 92: 'Solche demagogischen Kapriolen.'

39  See above, note 14.

40  Lehmann, 1969, p. 13.

41  Treitschke, op. cit., 4, pp. 294 f.

42  Ibid., 4, p. 415: 'sinnlose demagogische Kraftworte'.

43  Ibid., 4, p. 416: 'Geister oder Gesellen . . . , die auf der Hochschule des Demagogentums an der Seine ihre Grundsätze eingesogen hatten.'

44  Ibid., 4, p. 413: 'Er besaß was die Juden mit den Franzosen gemein haben, die Anmut des Lasters, die auch das Niederträchtige und Ekelhafte auf einen Augenblick verlockend erscheinen läßt.'

45  Börne, *Menzel der Franzosenfresser*, ed. cit., III, p. 966: 'wenn ich ihn *einen Prokurator der deutschen Bundesversammlung* genannt . . .'

46  Treitschke, op. cit., 4, p. 427: 'das vaterlandslose Judentum zersetze und zerstöre alle unsere Begriffe von Scham und Sittlichkeit, und wenn der Pöbelwahn des Mittelalters die Juden fälschlich der Brunnenvergiftung beschuldigt hätte, so müsse die alte Anklage jetzt mit vollem Rechte auf dem Gebiete der Literatur erneuert werden.'

47  Börne, *Menzel der Franzosenfresser*, ed. cit., III, p. 906: 'Ich liebe Deutsch-

land mehr als Frankreich, weil es unglücklich ist und Frankreich nicht; im
überigen bin ich soviel Franzose als Deutscher.' Treitschke, op. cit., IV,
p. 414, quotes only the last six words. Cf. also Treitschke's assertion about
Börne (ibid., p. 414): 'Er schmähte nur auf alles, was in Deutschland
bestand' with Börne's own words in that polemic against Menzel which
Treitschke cites and must therefore have read: 'Aus dem deutschen Boden
sind alle jene große Ideen hervorgegangen, die von geschicktern, unter-
nehmendern oder glücklichern Völkern ins Werk gesetzt und benützt worden
sind. Deutschland ist die Quelle aller europäischen Revolutionen, die Mutter
jener Entdeckungen, welche die Gestalt der Welt geändert haben. Das
Schießpulver, die Buchdruckerei, die religiöse Reform sind aus ihrem
Schoße hervorgegangen – undankbare und vermaledeite Töchter, die
Prinzen geheiratet und ihre plebejische Mutter verhöhnt haben' (*Menzel
der Franzosenfresser*, III, p. 914).

48   Treitschke, 'Unsere Ansichten', reprinted in *Der Berliner Antisemitis-
musstreit*, ed. by W. Boehlich, Frankfurt a. M., 1965, p. 12.

49   'In den einfachen Bildern und Wendungen des Neuen Testaments müsse
man die heiligen Rechte der Menschen erklären.' Büchner as reported by
Koch. Cf. Viëtor, 1939, p. 43 and pp. 125 f.

50   Cf. Voltaire, *Le Fanatisme, ou Mahomet le Prophète* II. v:

> Oui; je connais ton peuple, il a besoin d'erreur;
> Ou véritable ou faux, mon culte est nécessaire . . .
> Ma loi fait des héros.

And Fichte, *Reden an die deutsche Nation*, VIII (ed. cit., p. 138): 'Denken
Sie sich z.B. einen Mohamet – nicht den wirklichen der Geschichte, über
welchen ich kein Urteil zu haben bekenne, sondern den eines bekannten
französischen Dichters – , der sich einmal in den Kopf gesetzt habe, er sei
eine der ungemeinen Naturen, die da berufen sind, das dunkle, das gemeine
Erdenvolk zu leiten . . . der nun . . . nicht ruhen kann, bis er alles, das nicht
ebenso groß von ihm denken will, denn er selbst, zertreten hat, und bis aus
der ganzen Mitwelt sein eigner Glaube an seine göttliche Sendung ihm
zurückstrahle: ich will nicht sagen, wie es ihm ergehen würde, falls wirklich
ein geistiges Gesicht, das da wahr ist und klar in sich selbst, gegen ihn in
die Kampfbahn träte, aber jenen beschränkten Glücksspielern gewinnt er
es sich ab, denn er setzt alles gegen sie, die nicht alles setzen; sie treibt kein
Geist, ihn aber treibt allerdings ein schwärmerischer Geist, – der seines
gewaltigen und kräftigen Eigendünkels.' The importance of Fichte's
influence on Büchner was first recognized by Lehmann.

51   Cf. Büchner's letter to his family, 1 January 1836 (2, 451): 'Der König von
Bayern läßt unsittliche Bücher verbieten! da darf er seine Biographie nicht
erscheinen lassen, denn die wäre das Schmutzigste, was je geschrieben
worden!' In the *Landbote* Ludwig I of Bavaria is described (probably by
Weidig) as 'das Schwein, das sich in allen Lasterpfützen von Italien wälzte'
(2, 54), and Bergemann remarks (p. 392) that he appears here 'in kaum
übertriebener Despotennatur'. Regarding the Electorate of Hesse-Cassel,
Börne writes (*Briefe aus Paris*, ed. cit., III, p. 323): 'In Kassel liegen die

Beamten und Offiziere der Neuen Mätresse zu Füßen, und bald wird auch die Konstitution da liegen.'

52 Lehmann, 1969, p. 14: 'Er will verhindern, daß Für und Wider gegeneinander abgewogen werden. Er will nur das Wider, das Gegen, das Kontra.'

53 Ibid., p. 14: 'Der Agitator Büchner balanciert wie ein Tänzer auf dem Seil, das zwischen Lüge und Wahrheit gespannt ist. Er macht bewußt eine Teilwahrheit zur ganzen Wahrheit und degradiert sie damit zur ideologischen Lüge.'

54 Cf. Franzos, pp. cviii f.: 'Büchner wußte, daß der Ertrag von Domänen keine "Steuer" ist, daß auf dem hessischen Richterstande nicht *wegen*, sondern *trotz* seiner überaus schlechten Besoldung kein Makel der Bestechlichkeit hafte, daß endlich Versorgung alter Staatsdiener eine *Pflicht* sei, der sich kein Staatswesen, also auch nicht die Republik, entziehen könne! ... aber ebenso entschieden müssen wir betonen, daß Büchner dem Staate von 1834 im Ganzen und Großen kein Unrecht getan hat! Was er z. B. mit Ausnahme jener einzigen unbegründeten Anschuldigung über die hessische Justiz sagt, ist Alles wahr und unbestreitbar. Verwaltung und Gerichtspflege unter *ein* Ministerium gestellt, Polizei und Justiz in *einer* Hand – schon dies war ein unleidlicher Zustand und naturgemäß die Quelle größter Mißbräuche. Dazu die Rechtspflege teuer, langsam und schwerfällig, die Gerichtstaxen fast unerschwinglich ... diese Justiz urteilte in politischen Prozessen mit unerhörter, wahrhaft barbarischer Strenge, weil sie jedem Wink von Oben willig gehorchte, gehorchen mußte! Und vollends berechtigt werden uns die meisten Anklagen der Flugschrift erscheinen, wenn wir uns auf jenen Standpunkt versetzen, von dem sie geschrieben ist, den Standpunkt des armen, bedrückten, rechtlosen Bauers und Arbeiters.'

55 Enzensberger, p. 52: 'Sein Irrtum, ein bald erkannter Irrtum, war es, daß er auf die Bauern gezählt und sie für eine Klasse gehalten hat, die fähig gewesen wäre, die gesellschaftlichen Verhältnisse umzustürzen.'

56 Honigmann, p. 14: 'die uns heute absurd anmutende Idee, auf den konservative gesinnten Bauer die Revolution zu stellen.'

57 Lenin, 18 December 1910, *Collected Works*, 1963, vol. XVI, p. 353.

58 Enzensberger, p. 167: 'Engels hat recht gehabt gegen ihn, aber unrecht behalten ... Die chinesische, die algerische, die cubanische, die Revolution in Vietnam, das heißt, alle siegreichen Revolutionen in der Mitte des zwanzigsten Jahrhunderts sind Bauernrevolutionen gewesen.'

59 Lukács, 'Der faschistisch verfälschte und der wirkliche Georg Büchner', Martens, 1965, p. 205.

60 Mayer, 1972, p. 365: 'Hier rächt sich die Unkenntnis von Hegels Dialektik – und die Unreife der gesellschaftlichen Umstände. Vom Fels des Atheismus aus erblickt Marx ein Gelobtes Land, Büchner dagegen nur das Grau in Grau hoffnungslosen Elends.'

61 Marx, 'Zur Kritik der Hegelschen Rechtsphilosophie', 1843–44, *Marx – Engels Werke*, vol. I, p. 379: 'Die Aufhebung der Religion als des *illusorischen* Glücks des Volkes ist die Forderung seines *wirklichen* Glücks. Die Forderung, die Illusionen über seinen Zustand aufzugeben, ist die Forderung, *einen Zustand aufzugeben, die der Illusionen bedarf.* Die Kritik

der Religion ist also im Keim die Kritik des Jammertales, dessen Heiligen-schein die Religion ist.'

62   See above, p. 31.

63   Lehmann, 1969, pp. 21 f.: 'In diesen und ähnlichen Passagen [from Saint Just's speech in *Dantons Tod* II. vii] . . . taucht ein Vokabular auf, das trotz seiner Verfremdung ins Radikale auf Rousseau und Fichte, vor allem aber auf den *Hessischen Landboten* und die Frühschriften zurückweist. Alle Attribute des absoluten göttlichen Wissens, alle Attribute der Unfehlbarkeit werden den Oligarchen des Terrors, durch welche der Herr die Völker aus der Dienstbarkeit zur Freiheit führt, beigelegt. Sie sind durchdrungen von dem doktrinären Fanatismus ihres Auserwähltseins, sie haben das Rätsel der Geschichte, des Menschen und der Natur durchschaut und setzen, wie Robespierre, ihre Mission in engste Beziehung zur Heilsmission Christi. – Alle diese Motive . . . liegen auf einer Linie mit der agitatorischen Welt- und Geschichtsdeutung, die uns aus den Frühschriften und dem *Hessischen Landboten* her bekannt ist. Was uns von daher freilich nicht bekannt sein kann, ist die Tatsache, daß sich Büchner in den wenigen Monaten, die zwischen dem *Landboten* und der Abfassung des *Danton* liegen, von dieser Linie bereits entschieden zurückgezogen hat. Er steht seiner agitatorischen, vernunftidealistischen und pseudotheologischen Welt-, Geschichts- und Menschendeutung nicht mehr affirmativ, sondern kritisch und feindlich gegenüber.'

64   Ibid., p. 26: 'In diesem Brief, der thematisch auf die Frühschriften zurück-weist und der ein dreiviertel Jahr später in seinen wesentlichsten Passagen im *Danton* wörtlich wieder aufgenommen wird, vollzieht sich ein ent-scheidender Wandel im Denken Georg Büchners. Eine tiefe Enttäuschung, eine nicht mehr zu steigernde Verdüsterung und Ratlosigkeit spricht aus diesen Zeilen, in denen eine Bewußtseinswelt zusammenstürzt.'

65   See above, pp. 38, 26, 13.

### 3. METAPHYSICAL REVOLT

1   For the *Überlieferung* of Büchner's letters see Bergemann, 1922, pp. 753 ff.

2   Franzos, 'Über Georg Büchner', *Vossische Zeitung*, 4 January 1901, asserts that Minna Jaegle had been in possession of the MS of Büchner's *Aretino* but had declined to publish it, and that it was no longer to be found after her death. The suggestion that Minna had destroyed it is repeated by Bergemann, 1922, pp. 664 f. and by Knight, p. 16. The arguments against this view are presented by Meinerts, pp. 486 ff. and by Benn, 1963, p. xii. See also Chapter 8 of the present work, p. 222.

3   Franzos, p. xvi: '. . . während sich Ernst Büchner von seiner Wissenschaft so weit aus dem Reiche des Glaubens hinwegführen ließ, als sie ihn eben leiten wollte, blieb Caroline gläubig, keine fanatische Frömmlerin, aber ein frommes Gemüt, welches sich auch gerne für seine Verehrung die gewohnten Formen gefallen ließ, ohne viel darüber zu grübeln.' Anton Büchner (p. 22) says of Franzos: 'Ihm standen noch mündliche und schriftliche Mitteilungen der nächsten Angehörigen zur Verfügung, und die Porträts, die er entwirft,

werden im wesentlichen als richtig anzusehen sein, wenn er auch seine wortreichen Darstellungen der Dichtereltern zweifellos im Hinblick auf Goethes Eltern etwas stilisiert hat.'

4 'Den Religionsstunden hat er mit Aufmerksamkeit beigewohnt und in denselben manche treffliche Beweise von selbständigem Nachdenken gegeben.'

5 'Als Mitschüler hatte ich mit Georg Büchner viele Unterredungen, welche die Religion betrafen. Davon habe ich natürlich nur allgemeine Erinnerung. Ihr folgend, bin ich fest überzeugt, daß er damals zwar ein kühner Skeptiker, aber nicht Atheist war.'

6 'Ein Gläubiger im kirchlichen Sinn ist Georg Büchner nicht gewesen. Aber selbständig und objektiv in seinem Denken, ist er später, als Reiferer, auch gerechter gegen die geschichtlichen Mächte der Kirche geworden sowie gegen den Glauben des einzelnen, der auf einem andern Standpunkt stand als er. Namentlich war er von aller Aufdringlichkeit und Propaganda seiner Anschauung, von Ansicht- und Parteifabrikationskünsten für die zu dirigierende Menge weit entfernt . . . Er hat lebenslang aus wirklichem Durst nach Wahrheit gesucht und gerungen und deshalb, wie ich glaube, nie mit sich abgeschlossen.'

7 Franzos, p. xxxi: '"Ich bin überzeugt", schreibt der eine, "daß Büchner bereits in der Prima des Gymnasiums ein radikaler Atheist war. Mit der Kirche war er schon früh fertig. So sagte er mir einmal, noch in unserer Knabenzeit: 'Das Christentum gefällt mir nicht – es ist mir zu sanft, es macht lammfromm.' Die Äußerung ist mir in Erinnerung geblieben, weil ich mich damals so sehr darüber entsetzte."'

8 Jacobs, p. 132, following Bergemann, 1949, p. 390, suggests that the expression 'die göttliche Klassentheorie' is 'probably an allusion to Linnaeus' or Oken's artificial classification of plants'. But it is difficult to see how that could be relevant here; for Philippeau, in the speech to which Danton is replying, has said nothing about a metamorphosis of plants from one variety into another; he has referred to the transplantation of the *same* plants from one position to another ('Blumen, die versetzt werden . . .'), or as Danton rudely expresses it: 'Von einem Misthaufen auf den andern!' It seems more probable that 'die göttliche Klassentheorie' means the theory according to which the universe is, as it were, a divinely appointed system of *school classes* in which souls who prove their worth are promoted (*versetzt*) from one class to the next higher one – from the earth to purgatory, from purgatory to paradise. In that case the 'first class' must be taken to mean, as in England, the lowest class, not, as usually in Germany, the highest class. The mention of *Schulbänke* in the last sentence of Danton's speech makes it certain that, whatever else he may be thinking about, he is *also* thinking of school classes.

9 Cf. Louise Büchner's novelistic fragment *Ein Dichter*, where the hero, Ludwig Brandeis, represents Louise's recollections of her brother Georg and where the oration on Cato is referred to as 'diese unumwundene Verteidigung des Selbstmords'. Louise Büchner, *Nachgelassene Schriften*, vol. I, Frankfurt a. M., 1878, p. 212.

10 Eckermann, *Gespräche mit Goethe*, den 11. März 1832.
11 Franzos, p. xxxv: 'Im Sommer 1831 begegnete ich Georg Büchner einmal in der Dämmerung am Jägertor. Er sah sehr ermüdet aus, aber seine Augen glänzten. Auf meine Frage, wo er gewesen, flüsterte er mir in's Ohr: "Ich will's dir verraten: den ganzen Tag am Herzen der Geliebten!" "Unmöglich!" rief ich. "Doch", lachte er, "vom Morgen bis zum Abend in Einsiedel und dann in der Fasanerie!"
12 Ibid., p. xxxvi.
13 The last sentence of this passage suggests that Büchner may already have conceived the plan expressly mentioned in later letters (to Gutzkow, 1836, 2, 454; to Wilhelm Büchner, 2 September 1836, 2, 460) to prepare himself to be a university lecturer in philosophy.
14 Franzos, p. lxiv.
15 Ludwig Büchner, pp. 37 f.
16 Viëtor, 1949, p. 249: 'Büchners philosophische Papiere haben so stark den Charakter von Materialsammlungen, daß ihnen kaum verläßliche Aussagen über sein eigenes philosophisches Denken oder seine Weltansicht abzugewinnen sind.'
17 Bergemann, 1922, pp. 742 f.
18 Ibid., p. 743: 'Auch macht sich Büchner zeitweise vollkommen frei von Tennemann.'
19 See the letters mentioned in note 13 above.
20 The sentence in the lecture *Über Schädelnerven*: 'Die Frage nach einem solchen Gesetze [einem Urgesetz, einem Gesetz der Schönheit] führte von selbst zu den zwei Quellen der Erkenntniß, aus denen der Enthusiasmus des absoluten Wissens sich von je berauscht hat, der Anschauung des Mystikers und dem Dogmatismus der Vernunftphilosophen' (2, 292) clearly belongs to the same sphere of thought and expression as the comments on Spinoza: 'Der Spinozismus ist der Enthusiasmus der Mathematik' (2, 276); 'Aber jetzt kommt die eigenthümliche Wendung des Spinozismus: diese Erkenntniß soll nicht das absolute Anschauen des Mystikers, es soll eine intellektuale Erkenntniß seyn' (2, 269); 'Cartesius war so gut als Spinoza Identitätsphilosoph, wie es überhaupt jeder dogmatische Philosoph seyn muß' (2, 277). One may fairly infer that the words of the lecture 'Dogmatismus der Vernunftphilosophen' refer specifically to Spinoza, just as the phrase 'Anschauung des Mystikers' may refer to Malebranche (cf. 2, 269).
21 Bergemann, 1922, p. 745: 'Die Bogen bestehen aus demselben grauen Konzeptpapier wie die Foliobogen der Woyzeck-Entwürfe.' The reference is not to the whole of the Spinoza MS but to the 'Lagen XV (d. i. 16) bis XIX (20)' (Lehmann, 2, 266–86). Comparison with the MSS confirms the correctness of Bergemann's observation.
22 Spinoza, *Ethik*, I, vii: 'Dasein gehört zum Wesen der Substanz ... d.h. ihr Wesen involvirt nothwendig das Daseyn'; I. xi. 3. Beweis (Scholium): '... so daß wir der Existenz keines Dinges gewisser seyn können, als der des absolut unendlichen oder vollkommnen Wesens d.h. Gottes. Denn insofern sein Wesen jede Unvollkommenheit ausschließt, und eine absolute Voll-

kommenheit involvirt, so hebt es von selbst jede Ursache zum Zweifel an seinem Daseyn auf und giebt darüber die höchste Gewißheit' (Büchner's translation, 2, 231; 2, 239).

23 'Sie [die aus unendlichen Attributen bestehende Substanz] ist für ihn die Welturenche, worin Alles ist; sie ist ewig und unendlich, – aber sie ist nicht Gott, sie ist nicht das absolut vollkommne, moralische Wesen des Deismus, – sie ist nichts anders, als was jeder Atheist selbst, wenn er einigermaßen consequent verfahren will, anerkennen muß' (2, 239 f.).

24 Viëtor, 1949, p. 249: 'Wenn man will, kann man diese Stelle als ein Bekenntnis zum Atheismus nehmen . . . Aber es ist ebenso erlaubt, die Sätze nur als wissenschaftliche Kritik an einer unphilosophischen Wendung des Spinoza aufzufassen.'

25 Brinkmann, p. 36: 'Diese Problemstellung führt zwanglos über Welt- und Menschenbild zur dritten Urfrage alles Philosophierens, zur Frage nach Gott. Wie wir schon gezeigt haben, überwiegen bei Georg Büchner hier die kritischen Äußerungen. Sie beziehen sich aber stets auf konventionelle Vorstellungen, Gottesbeweise, moralische und metaphysische Gottesbegriffe. Von einem Atheismus kann keine Rede sein, solang man sich nur dieser dialogischen Auseinandersetzung ständig bewußt bleibt.'

26 Benno – v. Wiese, 1963, p. 128 – v. Wiese's assumption that Büchner recognized the possibility of 'an imperfect God' leads to the ascription to Büchner of a kind of Gnostic mysticism which is quite foreign to him. v. Wiese bases his assumption partly on the words of Büchner's Danton (III. vii. 61): 'Das Nichts hat sich ermordet, die Schöpfung ist seine Wunde, wir sind seine Blutstropfen, die Welt ist das Grab worin es fault.' According to v. Wiese, this means 'daß Gott durch die Schöpfung der Welt sich selbst gleichsam "ermordete" und damit ins Nichts verkehrte'. But Danton does not say that God has murdered himself; he says *nothingness* has murdered itself (by becoming the creation). Danton does not say that God 'thereby converted himself into nothingness', but on the contrary that nothingness, by destroying itself, converted itself into *something*, viz. the creation, which is, as it were, the decaying corpse of nothingness. It is true that Danton, in the intensity of his longing for extinction, bitterly identifies nothingness with God; but the fact remains that he does not see the world as God converted into nothingness, but as nothingness tragically converted into being. Baumann, p. 56, following v. Wiese, offers an interpretation equally at variance with the text: 'Die Welt als das Leiden Gottes an sich selbst, Gott, der sich in der Schöpfung nicht offenbart, sondern verleugnet; das Leiden aber gewährt dem Menschen Teilnahme am Göttlichen.' Where does Danton say anything remotely like that?

27 Cf. the reminiscences of Ludwig Wilhelm Luck: 'Das Bewußtsein des erworbenen geistigen Fonds drängte ihn fortwährend zu einer unerbittlichen Kritik dessen, was in der menschlichen Gesellschaft oder Philosophie und Kunst Alleinberechtigung beanspruchte oder erlistete. – Daher sein vernichtender, manchmal übermütiger Hohn über Taschenspielerkünste Hegelischer Dialektik und Begriffsformulationen, z.B.: "Alles, was wirklich, ist auch vernünftig, und was vernünftig, auch wirklich." Aufs tiefste

'verachtete er, die sich und andere mit wesenlosen Formeln abspeisten, anstatt für sich selbst das Lebensbrot der Wahrheit zu erwerben und es andern zu geben' – Bergemann, p. 277.

28 v. Brunn, p. 1356.
29 Ibid., p. 1359.
30 Quoted by Büchner from Beaumarchais's *Le Mariage de Figaro* II. xxi, Bergemann, 1922, p. 765, note 1. Cf. my article 'Büchner and Gautier', *Seminar*, 1973.
31 Schopenhauer, *Die Welt als Wille und Vorstellung*, I. Teil, 4. Buch, Insel-Verlag, p. 465: 'die unbegrenzte Welt, voll Leiden überall, in unendlicher Vergangenheit, in unendlicher Zukunft'.
32 Ronald Peacock, p. 191.
33 Matthew Arnold, 'Spinoza and the Bible', *Essays in Criticism*, London, 1884, p. 333.
34 Goethe, 'Erster Entwurf einer allgemeinen Einleitung in die vergleichende Anatomie, ausgehend von der Osteologie', *Werke*, Hamburg edition, vol. 13, p. 171.
35 See above, pp. 64 ff.
36 Goethe, ed. cit., vol. 13, p. 560.
37 See above, note 23.
38 Strohl, 1935, p. 651: 'Was Goethe für den Bau der Pflanzen versucht, unternimmt Büchner am Wirbeltiergehirn.'
39 Helmig, p. 22: 'Als Axiom stellt er die Theorie Okens an den Anfang: "Der Schädel ist eine Wirbelsäule, das Hirn ein metamorphosiertes Rückenmark und die Hirnnerven sind Spinalnerven", um sich dann die Aufgabe zu stellen, den Beweis für den letzten Teil dieser Behauptung zu bringen' (cf. 2, 293).
40 Helmig, p. 22: 'Er hat versucht zu beweisen, daß es sechs Paar ursprüngliche Hirnnerven gibt, daß ihnen sechs Schädelwirbel entsprechen, und daß die Entwicklung der cerebralen Massen gemäß ihrer Herkunft vor sich geht, woraus sich ergibt, daß der Schädel und sein Inhalt nur das Produkt einer Umwandlung der Wirbel und der Medulla sind.'
41 *Über Schädelnerven*: 'Die einfachsten Formen leiten immer am Sichersten, weil in ihnen sich nur das Ursprüngliche, absolut Nothwendige zeigt' (2, 296).
42 Strohl, 1936, p. 59.
43 Ibid., pp. 50 f.
44 Helmig, p. 28: 'Wenn Büchner in einzelnen Fragen, zum Zwecke der generellen Beweisführung, über das Ziel hinausschoß, so bleibt doch die Tatsache bemerkenswert, daß ein Morphologe ein halbes Jahrhundert früher zu einer Theorie gelangt, die sich im wesentlichen, nämlich der Identifikation der Spinalnerven mit den Hirnnerven, mit einer der heutigen Ansichten deckt. Ganz besonders beachtenswert wird diese Leistung, wenn wir die Problematik, die dieses Gebiet auch heute noch bietet, berücksichtigen.'
45 See above, pp. 13 f.
46 It is evident here how unjust is the assertion of Robert Mühlher 'daß Georg

Büchners Weltbild das des *Wertnihilismus* ist, den Jaspers als "Bejahung der bloßen wert- und sinnlosen Realität" charakterisiert.' Büchner's patient and laborious effort to reveal the primal 'law of beauty' in his own particular field of natural science shows that for him nature – at least in its physical constitution – was not a 'valueless and meaningless reality'. Still less can his view of the world be said to involve an 'affirmation' of, or acquiescence in, such an empty reality. Cf. Mühlher, 'Georg Büchner und die Mythologie des Nihilismus', Martens, 1965, p. 263.

47 Strohl, 1935, p. 650: 'Deutlich zeigt sich hierbei, daß wenn auch Büchner zeitweise die Dinge nach Goethes Art sieht, er doch nie in pantheistische Vorstellungen gerät.'

48 Schelling, *Bruno oder über das göttliche und natürliche Prinzip der Dinge.* Cf. Goethe's letter to Schiller, 16 March 1802, and *Werke*, ed. cit., vol. 1, p. 614.

49 Strohl, 1935, p. 652: 'einerseits die Natur zu entgeistigen, sie von der Jahrtausende alten Schicht menschlicher Gefühls-, Gewohnheits- und Indifferenzmotive zu befreien, um so ihrem wahren Wesen immer näher- zukommen, und andererseits gerade dadurch den Nimbus des Gewaltigen, des in neuem Sinn *Wunder*baren zu verstärken, der ihr im tiefsten Grunde eigen ist.'

50 Cf. Camus, *Essais*, ed. cit., p. 426: 'Dans la révolte, l'homme se dépasse en autrui et, de ce point de vue, la solidarité humaine est métaphysique. Simplement, il ne s'agit pour le moment que de cette sorte de solidarité qui naît dans les chaînes.'

51 See above, p. 17.

52 Schopenhauer: 'die . . . Ableitung des Mitleids, als alleiniger Quelle der Handlungen von moralischem Wert' (*Preisschrift über die Grundlage der Moral*, § 16); 'das *Mitleid*, welches, wie ich dargetan habe, die Basis der Gerechtigkeit und Menschenliebe, *caritas*, ist' (*Die Welt als Wille und Vorstellung*, II. Teil, Kap. 47, ed. cit., p. 1409).

53 Schopenhauer: 'Das neutestamentliche Christentum, dessen ethischer Geist der des Brahmanismus und Buddhismus . . . ist' (*Die Welt als Wille und Vorstellung*, II, 46, ed. cit., p. 1383).

54 Martens, 'Zum Menschenbild Georg Büchners', Martens, 1965, pp. 384 f.: 'In der Zerstörung des idealistischen Bildes vom freien, harmonischen, seiner selbst mächtigen Menschen – und im Widerspruch zur aufklärerischen Anthropologie seiner Zeit – wird damit hier bei Büchner eine andere, "realistische", in Analogie zu christlicher Anschauung stehende Auffassung vom Menschen freigelegt, die die Gefährdungen und Abrgünde, das Triebhafte, das Böse im Menschen miteinbegreift und die trotzdem in den "leidenden, gedrückten Gestalten" [cf. 2, 423], den Mühseligen und Bela- denen das Menschliche sichtbar werden läßt.'

55 Müller-Seidel, p. 229: 'Aber die Leidenden, die sich darin erkennen, daß sie Leidende sind, sind keine Puppen mehr.'

56 See above, pp. 39 f.

57 Caroline Schulz (Bergemann, pp. 297 f.): 'Die Nacht war unruhig; der Kranke wollte mehrere Male fort, weil er wähnte, in Gefangenschaft zu

geraten, oder schon darin zu sein glaubte und sich ihr entziehen wollte. Den Nachmittag vibrierte der Puls nur, und das Herz schlug 160 mal in der Minute; die Ärzte gaben die Hoffnung auf. Mein sonst frommes Gemüte fragte bitter die Vorsehung: "Warum?" Da trat Wilhelm ins Zimmer, und da ich ihm meine verzweiflungsvollen Gedanken mitteilte, sagte er: "Unser Freund gibt dir selbst Antwort, er hat soeben, nachdem ein heftiger Sturm von Phantasieen vorüber war, mit ruhiger, erhobener, feierlicher Stimme die Worte gesprochen: "Wir haben der Schmerzen nicht zu viel, wir haben ihrer zu wenig, denn durch den Schmerz gehen wir zu Gott ein!"–"Wir sind Tod, Staub, Asche, wie dürften wir klagen?"' Mein Jammer löste sich in Wehmut auf, aber ich war sehr traurig und werde es noch lange sein.'

58 Viëtor, 1949, p. 258: 'daß Einsichten ihnen aufgehen, zu denen der im Rhythmus des ungestörten Lebens Wachsende Jahre, Jahrzehnte braucht'.

### 4. AESTHETIC REVOLT

1 'Büchner liebte vorzüglich Shakespeare, Homer, Goethe, alle Volkspoesie, die wir auftreiben konnten, Äschylos und Sophokles; Jean Paul und die Hauptromantiker wurden fleißig gelesen. Bei der Verehrung Schillers hatte Büchner doch vieles gegen das Rhetorische in seinem Dichten einzuwenden. Übrigens erstreckte sich der Bereich des Schönliterarischen, das er las, sehr weit; auch Calderon war dabei. Für Unterhaltungslektüre hatte er keinen Sinn; er mußte beim Lesen zu denken haben. Sein Geschmack war elastisch. Während er Herders "Stimmen der Völker" und "Des Knaben Wunderhorn" verschlang, schätzte er auch Werke der französischen Literatur ... Für die Antike und für das Seelenbezwingende in der Dichtung neuerer Zeiten hatte er gleiche Empfänglichkeit, übrigens so, daß er sich dem einfach Menschlichen mit Vorliebe zuwandte'–Bergemann, pp. 273 f.

2 Franzos, p. vii.

3 'Ich glaube, es ist von den erwähnten beiden Brüdern [Friedrich und Georg Zimmermann], die uns andere mit ihrer Begeisterung für Shakespeare ansteckten, ausgegangen, daß wir uns verabredeten, in dem schönen Buchwald bei Darmstadt an Sonntagnachmittagen im Sommer die Dramen des großen Briten zu lesen, die uns die anregendsten und teuersten waren, als den "Kaufmann von Venedig", "Othello", "Romeo und Julia", "Hamlet", "König Richard III" usw. Wir hatten Momente innigster und wahrster Hingerissenheit und Erhebung, z.B. beim Lesen der Stelle: "Wie süß das Mondlicht auf dem Hügel schläft ..." und "Der Mann, der nicht Musik hat in sich selbst – trau keinem solchen"'–Bergemann, pp. 276 f.

4 See above, p. 46 and p. 51.

5 Ludwig Büchner, p. 18: 'Nächst Shakespeare schlug Byron die meisten verwandten Saiten in seinem Geiste an.'

6 See above, p. 39.

7 See above, p. 39.

8 Aristotle, *Poetics*, 9: ἡ μὲν γὰρ ποίησις μᾶλλον τὰ καθόλου, ἡ δ' ἱστορία τὰ καθ' ἕκαστον λέγει.

9 Ibid., 25: Σοφοκλῆς ἔφη αὐτὸς μὲν οἵους δεῖ ποιεῖν, Εὐριπίδην δὲ οἷοι εἰσίν – Aristotle also recognized the kind of idealization which is simply embellishment, as when (ibid., 15) he advises the tragic dramatist to 'follow the example of good portrait-painters, who reproduce the distinctive features of a man, and at the same time, without losing the likeness, make him handsomer than he is' (Ingram Bywater's translation).

10 *Hamburgische Dramaturgie*, 94. Stück, Anm. 7.

11 Winckelmann, *Geschichte der Kunst des Altertums* (1764), Berlin/Wien, 1913, 161 f.: 'Es fällt Bernini ein sehr ungegründetes Urteil, wenn er die Wahl der schönsten Teile, welche Zeuxis an fünf Schönheiten zu Kroton machte, da er eine Juno daselbst zu malen hatte, für ungereimt und für erdichtet ansah, weil er sich einbildete, ein bestimmtes Teil oder Glied reime sich zu keinem andern Körper, als dem es eigen ist. Andere haben keine als individuelle Schönheiten denken können, und ihr Lehrsatz ist: die alten Statuen sind schön, weil sie der schönen Natur ähnlich sind, und die Natur wird alle Zeit schön sein, wenn sie den schönen Statuen ähnlich ist. Der vordere Satz ist wahr, aber nicht einzeln, sondern gesammelt (*collective*); der zweite Satz aber ist falsch: denn es ist schwer, ja fast unmöglich, ein Gewächs zu finden, wie der Vatikanische Apollo ist. – Der Geist vernünftig denkender Wesen hat eine eingepflanzte Neigung und Begierde, sich über die Materie in die geistige Sphäre zu erheben, und dessen wahre Zufriedenheit ist die Hervorbringung neuer und verfeinerter Ideen. Die großen Künstler der Griechen, die sich gleichsam als neue Schöpfer anzusehen hatten, ob sie gleich weniger für den Verstand als für die Sinne arbeiteten, suchten den harten Gegenstand der Materie zu überwinden, und wenn es möglich gewesen wäre, dieselbe zu begeistern; dieses edle Bestreben derselben auch in früheren Zeiten der Kunst gab Gelegenheit zu der Fabel von Pygmalions Statue. Denn durch ihre Hände wurden die Gegenstände heiliger Verehrung hervorgebracht, welche, um Ehrfurcht zu erwecken, Bilder von höheren Naturen genommen zu sein scheinen mußten.'

12 Lehmann, 1971, p. 69, suggests that Büchner's sentence in his letter of 28 July 1835: 'der dramatische Dichter ist in meinen Augen nichts, als ein Geschichtsschreiber' was written in demonstrative opposition to Lessing's sentence in the *Hamburgische Dramaturgie*, 11. Stück: 'Denn der dramatische Dichter ist kein Geschichtsschreiber' – though in some respects Büchner nevertheless appears to Lehmann to be an 'Aristotelier and Lessingianer' (ibid., p. 70).

13 Quoted by J. G. Robertson, *Lessing's Dramatic Theory*, Cambridge, 1939, p. 406. Cf. Lessing, op. cit., 94. Stück.

14 E. H. Gombrich, *Art and Illusion*, New York, 1960, p. 156.

15 Kant, *Kritik der Urteilskraft*, 1. Aufl., p. 54.

16 Ibid., p. 258.

17 Hegel, *Ästhetik* (1835), Berlin und Weimar, 1955, vol. 1, p. 77.

18 Ibid., vol. 1, p. 20.

19 Ibid., vol. 1, p. 20: 'Denn die Geschichtsschreibung hat auch nicht das unmittelbare Dasein, sondern den geistigen Schein desselben zum Elemente ihrer Schilderungen, und ihr Inhalt bleibt mit der ganzen Zufälligkeit der

gewöhnlichen Wirklichkeit und deren Begebenheiten, Verwickelungen und Individualitäten behaftet, während das Kunstwerk uns die in der Geschichte waltenden ewigen Mächte ohne dies Beiwesen der unmittelbar sinnlichen Gegenwart und ihres haltlosen Scheines entgegenbringt.'

20  Cf. Goethe's *Winckelmann* (1805), Hamburg edition, vol. 12, pp. 96 ff., especially p. 103: 'Ist es [das Kunstwerk] einmal hervorgebracht, steht es in seiner idealen Wirklichkeit vor der Welt, so bringt es eine dauernde Wirkung, es bringt die höchste hervor.'

21  Cf. Goethe's essay 'Einfache Nachahmung der Natur, Manier, Stil' (1789), ed. cit., vol. 12, p. 32: 'Wie die einfache Nachahmung auf dem ruhigen Dasein und einer liebevollen Gegenwart beruhet, die Manier eine Erscheinung mit einem leichten, fähigen Gemüt ergreift, so ruht der *Stil* auf den tiefsten Grundfesten der Erkenntnis, auf dem Wesen der Dinge, insofern uns erlaubt ist, es in sichtbaren und greiflichen Gestalten zu erkennen.' Art is for the classical Goethe, consequently, 'die wahre Vermittlerin' of the *Urphänomenen* (*Maximen und Reflexionen*, ed. cit., vol. 12, p. 367).

22  Goethe's *Tagebuch für Charlotte von Stein*, Bologna, 19 October 1786.

23  Goethe to Frau v. Stein, Apolda, 6 March 1779, ed. cit., vol. 5, p. 403.

24  Schiller, 'Über Bürgers Gedichte' (1789), Nationalausgabe, vol. 22, p. 253: 'Eine der ersten Erfordernisse des Dichters ist Idealisierung, Veredlung, ohne welche er aufhört, seinen Namen zu verdienen. Ihm kommt es zu, das Vortreffliche seines Gegenstandes (mag dieser nun Gestalt, Empfindung oder Handlung sein, *in* ihm oder *außer* ihm wohnen) von gröbern, wenigstens fremdartigen Beimischungen zu befreien, die in mehrern Gegenständen zerstreuten Strahlen von Vollkommenheit in einem einzigen zu sammeln, einzelne, das Ebenmaß störende Züge der Harmonie des Ganzen zu unterwerfen, das Individuelle und Lokale zum Allgemeinen zu erheben. Alle Ideale, die er auf diese Art im einzelnen bildet, sind gleichsam nur Ausflüsse eines innern Ideals von Vollkommenheit, das in der Seele des Dichters wohnt.'

25  Schiller was later inclined to free the concept 'idealization' from the moral implications with which the critique of Bürger is so heavily charged: 'Etwas idealisieren heißt mir nur, es aller seiner zufälligen Bestimmungen entkleiden und ihm den Charakter innerer Notwendigkeit beilegen. Das Wort veredeln erinnert immer an verbessern, an eine moralische Erhebung' (Zu Gottfried Körners Aufsatz über Charakterdarstellung in der Musik', 1795). And in the reprint of the review of Bürger's poems the word 'Veredlung' was omitted from the passage quoted above (cf. Schiller's *Werke*, Insel-Verlag, 1966, vol. 4, pp. 879 f.). Yet in Schiller's great treatise on aesthetics, *Über die ästhetische Erziehung des Menschen* (1795), art is still regarded as the 'instrument' (*Werkzeug*) by which 'Veredlung des Charakters' can be achieved (cf. the 9th letter).

26  Schiller, 'Über den Gebrauch des Chors in der Tragödie', *Werke*, Insel-Verlag, vol. 2, p. 243: 'daß die Kunst nur dadurch wahr ist, daß sie das Wirkliche ganz verläßt und rein ideell wird.'

27  Ibid., pp. 244 f.: 'dem Naturalism in der Kunst offen und ehrlich den Krieg zu erklären'.

28 Ibid., p. 248: 'Der alte Chor in das französische Trauerspiel eingeführt, würde es in seiner ganzen Dürftigkeit darstellen und zunichte machen; eben derselbe würde ohne Zweifel Shakespeares Tragödie erst ihre wahre Bedeutung geben.'

29 Ibid., pp. 244 f.: 'so sollte er [der Chor] uns eine lebendige Mauer sein, die die Tragödie um sich herumzieht, um sich von der wirklichen Welt abzuschließen, und sich ihren idealen Boden, ihre poetische Freiheit zu bewahren'.

30 *Über die ästhetische Erziehung*, Nationalausgabe, vol. 20, p. 388: 'Er [der *Künstler*] muß . . . den Krieg gegen die Materie in ihre eigene Grenze spielen, damit er es überhoben sei, auf dem heiligen Boden der Freiheit gegen diesen furchtbaren Feind zu fechten.'

31 Schiller, *Über Anmut und Würde*, Nationalausgabe, vol. 20, p. 254: 'Bewegungen, welche keine andere Quelle als die Sinnlichkeit haben, gehören bei aller Willkürlichkeit doch nur der Natur an, die für sich allein sich nie bis zur Anmut erhebet.' Contrast ibid., p. 299: 'wo findet man mehr Anmut als bei Kindern, die doch ganz unter sinnlicher Leitung stehen?'

32 Schiller, 'Gedanken über den Gebrauch des Gemeinen und Niedrigen in der Kunst', Nationalausgabe, vol. 20, p. 241: 'Einen gemeinen Geschmack haben in der bildenden Kunst die Niederländischen Maler, einen edlen und großen die Italiener, noch mehr aber die Griechen bewiesen. Diese gingen immer auf das Ideal, verwarfen jeden gemeinen Zug, und wählten auch keinen gemeinen Stoff.'

33 See above, p. 77.

34 Goethe, ed. cit., vol. 12, p. 13: 'Sie wollen euch glauben machen, die schönen Künste seien entstanden aus dem Hang, den wir haben sollen, die Dinge rings um uns zu verschönern. Das ist nicht wahr! . . . Die Kunst ist lange bildend, eh sie schön ist, und doch so wahre, große Kunst, ja oft wahrer und größer als die schöne selbst.'

35 Reinhold Lenz, *Werke und Schriften*, Stuttgart, 1966, vol. 1, p. 342: 'Nach meiner Empfindung schätz ich den charakteristischen, selbst den Karikaturmaler zehnmal höher als den idealischen, hyperbolisch gesprochen, denn es gehört zehnmal mehr dazu, eine Figur mit eben der Genauigkeit und Wahrheit darzustellen, mit der das Genie sie erkennt, als zehn Jahre an einem Ideal der Schönheit zu zirkeln, das endlich doch nur in dem Hirn des Künstlers, der es hervorgebracht, ein solches ist.'

36 Goethe, 'Von deutscher Baukunst', ed. cit., vol. 12, p. 14: 'Gesalbter Gottes'.

37 See above, p. 4.

38 Strohl, 1936, p. 53: 'Diese möglichste Annäherung an das Objekt – nie vollkommen erreichbar – ist aber auch, weit entfernt von literarischnaturalistischen Tendenzen, eines der vornehmsten Arbeitsprinzipien des um Naturgeschichte bemühten Forschers. In diesem, aller Konventionalität und allen Gewohnheitsmächten widerstrebenden Bemühen um Wahrhaftigkeit den Dingen gegenüber begegnen sich Künstler und Naturforscher.'

39 Landau, vol. 1, p. 120, Martens, 1965, p. 46.

40 Ludolf Wienbarg, *Ästhetische Feldzüge* (1834), Berlin/Weimar, 1964, p. 162: 'Das aber ist das Kennzeichen des echten Dramatikers wie jedes großen Dichters, daß er der Zeit ein Spiegel ist, worin sie sich selbst erkennen mag.'

41 Ibid., p. 56: 'Und so kommt uns von allen Seiten die Bestätigung zu, daß das Leben das Höchste ist und allem übrigen, wenn es gedeihen soll, zugrunde liegen muß, geschweige der Kunst, der Schönheit und der sich mit ihr beschäftigenden Ästhetik.'

42 Ibid., p. 55: 'Woher stammt diese Fülle von Leben und Kraft, die uns an Shakespeare entzückt und seine dichterischen Gebilde so lebensderb, so kühn, so unübertrefflich macht?'

43 Ibid., pp. 236 ff.: 'Nennen wir nun einen Dichter, der die gesamten Elemente, woraus die Nation gegenwärtig besteht, einigermaßen zu befrieden weiß, einen deutschen Nationaldichter, so machte keiner diesem Namen größere Ehre als eben Schiller . . . Wir, sollen wir jungen Dichtern den Rat geben, in Schillers Fußstapfen zu treten und gleich ihm nach dem Ruhm zu trachten, deutsche Nationaldichter zu heißen? Nimmer. Andere Stern winken der Zeit, andere Ziele tun sich ihr auf.'

44 Victor Hugo, *Cromwell* (1827), *Théâtre Complet de Victor Hugo*, 1963, vol. I, p. 416.

45 Ibid., vol. I, p. 416.

46 Ibid., vol. I, p. 441.

47 *La Chartreuse de Parme*, II, Chapitre XV.

48 *Le Rouge et le Noir*, II, Chapitre XIX: 'Eh, monsieur, un roman est un miroir qui se promène sur une grande route. Tantôt il reflète à vos yeux l'azur des cieux, tantôt la fange des bourbiers de la route. Et l'homme qui porte le miroir dans sa hotte sera par vous accusé d'être immoral!'

49 Mayer, 1946, p. 287: 'Man kann nur wünschen, zu bessern und zu verändern, wenn an die Möglichkeit geglaubt wird, durch freies Tun die Umstände umzugestalten . . . Büchner aber teilt solchen Glauben nicht. Ihm sind die menschlichen Verhältnisse rätselhaft festgelegt und unveränderlich.'

50 Cf. Stendhal, *Racine et Shakespeare* (1823), Paris, 1928, p. 52: 'Schiller a copié Shakespeare et sa rhétorique; il n'a pas eu l'esprit de donner à ses compatriotes la tragédie réclamée par leur mœurs.'

51 Landau, vol. I, p. 122, Martens, 1965, p. 48. Landau's conjecture that the picture of Christ at Emmaus in the Darmstadt gallery is the picture described by Büchner in *Lenz* has been confirmed by evidence adduced by Fischer (p. 39) from the diary of Alexis Muston: 'Muston, der in Darmstadt mit Büchner das Landesmuseum besucht hat, vermerkt in seinen Tagebuchheften: "Un Christ à Emmaüs m'a également frappé, mais je ne me souviens pas de l'auteur."'

52 Viëtor, 1949, p. 168. Nicolas Maes, 1634–93, also a pupil of Rembrandt, is known for his religious genre-pictures. His picture 'An old woman praying' in the Rijksmuseum, Amsterdam, is close in spirit to the picture described by Büchner but evidently not identical with it.

53 Mayer, 1954, p. 159: 'Bei Büchner steht hinter Lenzens Worten vor allem eine Abspiegelungslehre.'

54  See above, pp. 64 f.

55  See above, pp. 71 f.

56  Cf. Lessing, *Hamburgische Dramaturgie*, 14. Stück: 'Die Namen von Fürsten und Helden können einem Stücke Pomp und Majestät geben; aber zur Rührung tragen sie nichts bei. Das Unglück derjenigen, deren Umstände den unsrigen am nächsten kommen, muß natürlicher Weise am tiefsten in unsere Seele dringen; und wenn wir mit Königen Mitleiden haben, so haben wir es mit ihnen als mit Menschen, und nicht als mit Königen.'

57  Marx to Lassalle, 19 April 1859: 'Du hättest dann von selbst mehr *shakespearisieren* müssen, während ich Dir das *Schillern*, das Verwandeln von Individuen in bloße Sprachröhren des Zeitgeistes, als bedeutendsten Fehler anrechne.'

58  Peter Demetz, *Marx, Engels und die Dichter*, Stuttgart, 1959, p. 248: 'Mehring bemühte sich mit einigem Erfolg, seine liberalen Sympathien für Schiller zu einem integralen Element des marxistischen Literaturkanons zu erklären – in welchem Maße ihm dies gelang, erwiesen erst unlängst die von der Kommunistischen Partei geförderten Schiller-Feiern in der Sowjetunion und in den Satellitenstaaten, einschließlich Ost-Deutschlands. Marx und Engels hätten jeden Enthusiasmus für Schiller ironisch abgelehnt, wenn sie ihn nicht gar – wie im Jahre 1859 – als ästhetisch falsch und gegenrevolutionär empfunden hätten.'

59  See above, p. 13 and p. 40.

60  Werner Heisenberg, 'Abschluß der Physik?', *Universitas*, 26 (1971), p. 2: 'Man [wird] zunächst feststellen müssen, daß es sich bei den großen zusammenfassenden Formulierungen von Naturgesetzen, wie sie zum erstenmal in der Newtonschen Mechanik möglich gewesen sind, um Idealisierungen der Wirklichkeit handelt, nicht um die Wirklichkeit selbst.'

61  B. v. Wiese, 1963, p. 125.

62  Emil Staiger, *Friedrich Schiller*, Zurich, 1967, p. 367: 'in der "Braut von Messina", wo "idealische Masken" agieren'; p. 209: 'Indes, auch die Gestalten dieser Gedichte wandeln nicht unter dem Licht der Sonne, die zugleich wärmt und erhellt. Abgeschiedene sind sie gleichfalls, . . . "wie" lebendig, aber durch ein Geländer von uns getrennt.'

63  Eckermann, *Gespräche mit Goethe*, den 4. Januar, 1824: 'Schiller, der, unter uns gesagt, weit mehr ein Aristokrat war als ich . . .'

64  Carlyle, *Critical and Miscellaneous Essays*, London, 1869, vol. II, p. 38.

65  Schiller, *Über Bürgers Gedichte*, Nationalausgabe, vol. 22, p. 250.

## 5. 'DANTONS TOD'

1  'Büchner erklärte, für den *Danton*, der so hurtig zustande gekommen, wären "die darmstädtischen Polizeidiener seine Musen gewesen"' – Gutzkow's 'Nachruf', *Frankfurter Telegraf*, June 1837.

2  See above, p. 5.

3  A complete list of the books about the French Revolution borrowed by Büchner from the Darmstadt library is given by Jaspers, p. 15.

4   Cf. Beck, p. 346 ff., and Thieberger.
5   Cf. Jaspers, p. 35. The literary influences on *Dantons Tod* were first thoroughly studied by Landsberg.
6   Landau, vol. I, p. 75 (Martens, 1965, p. 17), affirms this influence in opposition to Landsberg.
7   Cf. Frenzel.
8   Viëtor, 149, p. 119.
9   Gundolf, p. 387: 'Von den vielen episodischen Figuren vertritt jede entweder einen Standpunkt oder einen Beruf oder ein Laster oder ein Leid.' See also ibid., p. 386.
10  Mignet (1824), Paris, 1875, vol. I, p. 294.
11  Anatole France, *La Vie littéraire*, vol. I, pp. 7 f., quoted by J. D. Wilson, *Hamlet*, Cambridge, 1957, p. 1.
12  Martens, 'Ideologie und Verzweiflung, Religiöse Motive in Büchners Revolutionsdrama' (1960), Martens, 1965, p. 412: 'Danton kapituliert in Wahrheit, er streicht die Segel, er gibt es auf. Sein tobender Widerstand vor dem Tribunal ist nur ein letztes, elementar physisches Sich-Aufbäumen, in dem die angeborene Farbe der Empfindung, Wut und empörter Stolz noch einmal durchschlagen. Geistig, in seinem Zentrum, ist er zerbrochen, vom Tode gezeichnet, – von der ersten Szene an.'
13  Höllerer, 1960, p. 68: 'Das Wirklich-Unwirkliche der kleinsten Handlung und individuellen Regung wird zum Richter über die Selbstverständlichkeit der heroice dicta. Noch immer war *die* Büchner-Aufführung die beste, in der Regie und Schauspieler dies in Spiel brachten.'
14  Viehweg, p. 66: 'Moissi war ein fast zartgliedriger Danton, voller Leichtigkeit, mit einem fernen Lächeln. Auf dem Kopf trug er eine hochgelockte Rokokoperücke. Er spielte und sprach leise und verhalten, bis er dann mit seinem ganzen Temperament in der Verteidigungsrede vor dem Revolutionstribunal losbrach. Bei einem Gastspiel in Basel am 3. Juni 1917 riß er das Publikum in dieser Szene so mit, daß es sich an den Demonstrationen der Zustimmung und den Sympathiekundgebungen der Volksmassen auf der Bühne durch lautes Händeklatschen und Zurufen beteiligte . . . Diese "Danton"-Inszenierung war ein gewaltiger Erfolg für Reinhardt. Jahrelang blieb sie auf dem Spielplan des Deutschen Theaters.'
15  Ibid., p. 215.
16  Bradley, *Shakespearean Tragedy*, London, 1964 (1st edition 1904), p. 34. As Bradley remarks, one might be tempted to see an exception to the rule in *Julius Caesar*, and the problem of this play is indeed very close to that of *Dantons Tod*. The deed he has had to do in the cause of liberty weighs heavily on Brutus's conscience likewise; but, surer of himself than Danton, he is 'armed so strong in honesty' that even the apparition of Caesar's ghost can only momentarily discomfit him.
17  Büchner was familiar with this proposition from the philosophy of Epicurus. Cf. his excerpts from Tennemann (2, 405): 'Aus Nichts wird Nichts; ebensowenig kann aus Etwas Nichts werden.'
18  Cf. Thieberger, p. 147.
19  Schopenhauer, *Die Welt als Wille und Vorstellung*, ed. cit., vol. I, pp. 537 f.

20  'Das hypnotische Nichts-Gefühl, die Ruhe des tiefsten Schlafes, *Leidlosig-keit* kurzum – das darf Leidenden und Gründlich-Verstimmten schon als höchstes Gut, als Wert der Werte gelten, das muß von ihnen als positiv abgeschätzt, als *das Positive* selbst empfunden werden. (Nach derselben Logik des Gefühls heißt in allen pessimistischen Religionen das Nichts *Gott*.)' – Nietzsche, *Zur Genealogie der Moral*, Leipzig, 1923, vol. 7, p. 444 (quoted by Jacobs, p. 132).

21  Cf. the article by Leonard Forster on *acedia* and Goethe's Faust in *The Discontinuous Tradition: Studies in German Literature in Honour of E. L. Stahl*, edited by P. F. Ganz, Oxford, 1971.

22  Cf. Walther Rehm, *Experimentum Medietatis*, Munich, 1947, p. 30: 'Dieses Jahrhundert kennt den Abgrund der Schwermut und des "alten Nichts" und die unselige Gemeinschaft derer, die ohne Hoffnung sind, die zweifelnd suchen, ohne zu finden. Die Krankheit wird von Kierkegaard beschrieben: es ist die Krankheit zum Tode, es ist neben der Schwermut, der Langeweile, die Verzweiflung . . .'

23  Thieberger, p. 54.

24  Viëtor, 1949, p. 118: 'Büchner ist voller Ehrfurcht, man möchte sagen: er ist fromm dem Wirklichen gegenüber; da müssen Änderungen am geschichtlichen Stoff in der freien Art, wie Goethe sie sich im *Egmont*, Schiller in der *Jungfrau von Orleans* gestattet, unerlaubt, ja vermessen scheinen. Er will den bestimmten, grade diesen geschichtlichen Augenblick und Charakter darstellen, in seiner ungemilderten, ursprünglichen Wirklichkeit.'

25  Cf. J. D. Wilson, *Julius Caesar*, Cambridge, 1967, pp. xxxi and xxxiii and *Antony and Cleopatra*, Cambridge, 1968, p. xiii.

26  Marcuse, p. 19: 'Büchners visionärer Realismus.'

27  Knight, p. 89, says of this passage: 'What is plainly said here is that, though our actions may be determined, our thoughts are not. For them, then, we have a sort of responsibility . . . It all seems highly illogical.' Where is it 'plainly said' that our thoughts are not determined? What Robespierre does say – in a perfect anticipation of Freud's theory of dreams – is that the evil thoughts and impulses which we repress during the day reveal themselves in our dreams. But are we responsible for our dreams? Are our dreams not determined? Hofmannsthal's Marschallin knew better: 'Ich schaff mir meine Träume nicht an.' Elsewhere (p. 82) Knight writes: 'A good deal of the conversation in *Dantons Tod*, obscene and other, is mere long-winded nonsense.' Such an assertion must be supported by evidence, or it remains a mere violence.

28  Thieberger, p. 141.

29  Lehmann, 'Robespierre – "ein impotenter Mahomet"?', *Euphorion*, 57 (1963).

30  *Unsere Zeit*, vol. 12, p. 242: 'Er mochte seine Schützlinge aufgeben oder verteidigen, so setzte er sich immer der Gefahr aus, als ein neuer Mahomed hingestellt zu werden, der seine Herrschaft auf Lügen und Betrug gründen wolle.' Cf. Mignet, ed. cit., vol. II, p. 73.

31  Tieck's *Schriften*, Berlin, 1828, vol. 7, p. 71. For other instances of the probable influence of *William Lovell* on *Dantons Tod* compare the discus-

sion of the theatre in the former (ibid., 6, 51: 'je mehr sich der Schauspieler von der Natur entfernt, je mehr wird er für einen großen Künstler gehalten' etc.) with Camille's remarks in *Danton* II. iii. 37. Also *William Lovell*, ibid., 6, 228: 'Der menschliche Geist ... hat wie ein Monochord nur sehr wenige Töne' and *Danton* II. i. 32: 'So ein armseeliges Instrument zu seyn, auf dem eine Saite immer nur einen Ton angiebt!'; *William Lovell*, ibid., 7, 27: 'In jedem Körper liegt die Seele, wie ein armer Gequälter in dem Stiere des Phalaris ... und die Töne verwandeln sich und dienen zur Belustigung der umgebenden Menge' and *Danton* IV. v. 72: 'Sind wir Kinder, die in den glühenden Molochsarmen dießer Welt gebraten und mit Lichtstrahlen gekitzelt werden, damit die Götter sich über ihr Lachen freuen?'

32  *Wirkendes Wort* 14 (1964), pp. 244–54.

33  Solzhenitsyn, *The First Circle*, translated by Michael Guybon, 1968, p. 112.

34  Thiers, *Histoire de la Révolution française*, Paris, 1845, v, 384. Mignet, ed. cit., vol. I, pp. 316 f.

35  See above, pp. 37–8.

36  See above, pp. 31 f.

37  Lukács, 'Der faschistisch verfälschte und der wirkliche Georg Büchner', Martens, 1965, p. 209: 'Danton widerlegt nämlich mit keinem Wort die *politische* Anschauung Robespierres. Er weicht im Gegenteil einer politischen Auseinandersetzung aus, er hat kein einziges Argument gegen den politischen Vorwurf, gegen die politische Konzeption Robespierres, die, wenn wir uns an die zuletzt angeführten Briefe Büchners erinnern, im wesentlichen die Konzeption des Dichters selbst ist.'

38  Thiers, op. cit., v, p. 300: 'Tous deux [Camille and Danton] pensaient que la république étant sauvée par ses dernières victoires, il était temps de mettre fin à des cruautés désormais inutiles; que ces cruautés prolongées plus longtemps ne seraient propres qu'à compromettre la révolution, et que l'étranger pouvait seul en désirer et en inspirer la continuation.' Cf. Mignet, ed. cit., vol. II, p. 36.

39  Cf. C. J. Burckhardt, *Begegnungen*, Zurich, 1958, p. 339: 'Als das Urteil [über die Girondisten] verkündet wurde, hat Desmoulins geweint, und diese Tränen ... sollten ihm bei seinem eigenen Prozeß von Saint-Just vorgeworfen werden.'

40  Hérault similarly addresses to Camille, as the person most likely to appreciate it, his remark about the Greeks and Romans (IV. v. 71): 'Griechen und Götter schrieen, Römer und Stoiker machten die heroische Fratze' – This appears to be a reminiscence of Lessing's *Laokoon*.

41  Camille's words 'Da liegen allein, kalt, steif in dem feuchten Dunst der Fäulniß' (III. vii. 60) are obviously influenced by Claudio's 'Da liegen, kalt und regungslos und faulen' (Wolf Graf von Baudissin's translation of *Measure for Measure* III. i. This translation must have been known to Büchner as it was included in Tieck's Shakespeare, 1825–33).

42  Cf. Majut's remark (Martens, 1965, p. 339) 'daß es mit der Gestalt des Camille Desmoulins, so wie Büchner sie konzipierte, unvereinbar ist, ein Buch wie die "Nachtgedanken" auszuwählen ... Camille ist alles andere als ein Moralist.'

43 Cf. C. J. Burckhardt, op. cit., p. 354.
44 It is true that the word *Weltgeist* was used by others before Hegel, notably by Herder and by Goethe; but it was mainly Hegel, in whose philosophy of history it is a key-term, who gave it currency in Büchner's time.
45 See above, pp. 6 f.
46 Martens, 1965, p. 433: 'Hier scheint uns – von der historischen Wirklichkeit angeregt (so wie Dostojewski seine Revolutionäre der russischen Wirklichkeit seiner Zeit nachzeichnete) – der Typus des fanatischen Revolutionärs, des besessenen Ideologen zum ersten Mal in der Literatur gültig erfaßt zu sein.' Cf. ibid., p. 428.
47 'Zum Menschenbild Georg Büchners', Martens, 1965, p. 380: 'Ihr Sein, auf dem Schuld am Tode des Freundes und der Mutter lastet, ist zutiefst tragisch.'
48 See Thieberger, p. 52.
49 Cf. *Unsere Zeit*, vol. 12, p. 156.
50 Marcuse, p. 27: 'die dramatische Sprache [ist] wenig nuanciert'.
51 Keller to Paul Heyse, 29 March 1880: '. . . nicht zu reden von dem nun vollständig erschienenen Danton, der von Unmöglichkeiten strotzt'.
52 Hermann Conrad, p. 137: 'Was in jeder gesitteten Familie undenkbar war, das sollte auf der Bühne erlaubt sein, das galt als Realismus. Es war das Gegenteil wenigstens für Deutschland, dessen herrschende, sittlich und geistig vornehme Gesellschaft niemals auf diesen niederen gallischen Standpunkt hinabgesunken ist.'
53 Jacobs, p. xv.
54 Viëtor, 1949, p. 117: 'Daß er aus den Zoten nicht herauskommt, verrät eine Lebensstufe, auf der das Geschlechtliche wichtiger erscheint als die anderen Lebensbereiche.'
55 Thiers, op. cit., v, p. 389.
56 Landau, vol. 1, p. 84, Martens, 1965, p. 26.
57 Jacobs, p. 121.
58 Beck, p. 365: 'der Jargon der Revolutionsideologie'.
59 Höllerer, 1960, p. 83: 'Dieser Satz überkreuzt die gewohnten Realitäten so, daß in einer surrealen Fügung eine neue, unheimlich eindringliche, bisher fremde und verborgene Wahrheit aufleuchtet.'
60 *William Lovell*, ed. cit., vol. 7, p. 185: 'Ach, noch weit entsetzlicher ist das einsame Krankenbette, in das der Tod nach und nach mit hineinkriecht, sich mit uns unter einer Decke verbirgt und so vertraulich tut.' See above, Ch. 5, n. 30.
61 For a systematic study of the 'open' form in the plays of Büchner and other dramatists see Volker Klotz, *Geschlossene und offene Form im Drama*, München, 1960.
62 Viëtor, 1949, p. 155: 'das *Prinzip des antipathetischen Gegensatzes*'.
63 Heyn, p. 30: 'Nirgends in den Dialogen des "Danton" sind die vorgetragenen Meinungen der Zündstoff der Handlung.'
64 Scheuer, p. 37: 'Die Menschen suchen gemeinsam Halt zu finden vor dem Abgrund, der sie alle bedroht.'
65 Viehweg, p. 102.

66 Ibid., p. 332.

67 Thieberger, p. 25.

68 Klotz, pp. 113 f.: 'Ein im Drama der offenen Form weit verbreitete Weise, den latenten Sinnzusammenhang, die verdeckte Grundkonzeption der scheinbar wirr und turbulent sich reihenden und häufenden Szenenflut explizite aufzuhellen, ist der *Integrationspunkt*. Hierin kommt das Bedeutungsfazit bündig zur Sprache.'

69 Krapp, p. 68, seeks to limit the nihilistic implications of this passage by arguing (a) that Danton's words 'Das Nichts ist der zu gebärende Weltgott' contradict his earlier utterance: 'Das Nichts hat sich ermordet . . . die Welt ist das Grab, worin es fault' (III. vii. 61); and (b) that the sentence 'Die Welt ist das Chaos' is metaphorical, not logical, and has therefore only the value of 'spontaneous expression' and no conclusive significance for the drama as a whole. But (a) there is no contradiction in saying that God has ceased to exist and that God has yet to be born. The idea of the death and rebirth of God is familiar to many religions, and inasmuch as both sentences assert our present separation from God they do not contradict but confirm each other. And (b) a proposition does not necessarily become less significant by being expressed in metaphorical rather than in logical language. One might as well deny the significance of Nathan's famous reply to Saladin because it is expressed in the form of a parable.

70 Höllerer, 1960, p. 81, writes: 'Die Hoffnung auf das Nichts wird wieder fallen gelassen . . . Vom Nichts ist in der Szene der Hinrichtung nicht mehr die Rede.' But the fact that Danton in his last few minutes of life does not speak of Nothingness is no proof that he has ceased to hope for it. He does not speak of it for the simple reason that he has already so insistently spoken of it, and Büchner does not expect his readers to have such short memories as Höllerer supposes. Nor is it possible to accept Höllerer's further suggestion: 'So sehnt er sich zunächst nach dem Nichts als Einheit, Ordnung und Weltgott.' Nothingness as 'unity and order' is a meaningless concept; and Danton thinks of nothingness as God only in the sense that it is 'devoutly to be wished'.

71 See above, p. 53.

72 Contrast Büchner's state of mind as described in his letter to Minna of 10 March 1834 (2, 425), in the period *before* he had found a channel of expression in literary productivity: 'Alles verzehrt sich in mir selbst; hätte ich einen Weg für mein Inneres, aber ich habe keinen Schrei für den Schmerz, kein Jauchzen für die Freude, keine Harmonie für die Seligkeit. Dies Stummsein ist meine Verdammniß.'

## 6. 'LEONCE UND LENA'

1 Ludwig Büchner, p. 37: 'Die Cotta'sche Buchhandlung hatte bis zum 1. Juli einen Preis auf das beste Lustspiel ausgesetzt.'

2 'In derselben Zeit und später zu Zürich vollendete er ein im Manuskript vorliegendes Lustspiel, Leonce und Lena, voll Geist, Witz und kecker Laune.'

3   This is according to Gutzkow's account of the matter (*Werke*, ed. by Reinhold Gensel, vol. 11, p. 90). Lehmann (*Textkritische Noten*, p. 29) suggests that Gutzkow may have received an original MS of *Leonce und Lena* and, having mislaid or lost it, may only have pretended to have received a copy in order to conceal his carelessness. It seems improbable that Gutzkow would have dared to publish a statement which, as he must have known, Minna Jaegle would immediately recognize to be false. There is no reason to suspect Gutzkow of dishonesty. Lehmann himself remarks (ibid., p. 29) that Gutzkow frankly confessed to Louise Büchner that he had lost some of her brother's papers.

4   Bergemann, 1922, p. 687: 'aus Prüderie oder Unachtsamkeit'.

5   Lehmann, *Textkritische Noten*, p. 34: 'die von politischer Vorsicht diktierte, von literarischem Unverständnis und schulmeisterlichem Hochmut zeugende Redaktion Ludwig Büchners'.

6   '. . . ein wunderlicher, wetterwend'scher Kerl, der alle Leute unterhält und immer Langeweile hat, witzig und verlegen, hart und wohltätig, geht immer wie ein Verliebter herum, hat alle Weiber nach der Reihe in sich vernarrt und quält sie mit Kälte'.

7   Gundolf, p. 390: 'Doch das Ganze kommt aus der literarischen Nachahmung Brentanos, Tiecks, Shakespeares.'

8   Mayer, p. 310: 'Leonce aber, Lena, Valerio und alle die anderen Gestalten des Märchenspuks haben vor allem sehr viele Bücher gelesen. Prinz und Vielfraß, Prinzessin und empfindsame alte Jungfer führen ein Leben aus zweiter Hand.'

9   Hölderlin, 'Über den Unterschied der Dichtarten', StA 4, p. 266.

10   Mayer, p. 311: 'Größerer Mißklang ist nicht denkbar als hier zwischen Büchners sonstiger Lehre, der Gesamtanlage seines Werks, und diesem ironisch-romantischen Spiel von den beiden Königskindern.'

11   Cf. Fink, 'Leonce und Lena', Martens, 1965, pp. 500 f.: 'Die nüchterne Wirklichkeit, wie er sie in seinen Dramen zeigte, war tieftraurig, ja tragisch, so daß sie keineswegs einer komischen Gattung hätte einverleibt werden können. Realismus und Komödie sind in seinen Augen unvereinbar . . . Diese pessimistische Auffassung von der Wirklichkeit bringt als Gegensatz dazu die Unwirklichkeit der Komödie mit sich.'

12   Viëtor, 1949, p. 177.

13   Majut, 1934, pp. 235 f., was mistaken in suggesting that Gautier's *Mademoiselle de Maupin* could have influenced *Dantons Tod*, for *Mademoiselle de Maupin* was not published till late in 1835. But Majut was right in thinking that Gautier's novel could have influenced *Leonce und Lena* and that the allusion to Nero and Caligula in particular could have been suggested by it. See *Mademoiselle de Maupin*, Paris, 1955, p. 141 and cf. my article 'Büchner and Gautier', *Seminar*, 1973.

14   Schröder, p. 159, says of this passage: 'Sie steht im Kontext wie vom Dichter hinsouffliert.' I do not share Schröder's opinion that the corresponding passage in *Lenz* (87, ll. 30–2) is open to the same objection.

15   Viëtor, 1949, p. 184: 'Aber ihr pessimistischer Gehalt löst sich hier auf in den hellen, gläubigen Klängen eines Mozartischen Opern-Finales.'

16 Bradley, op. cit., p. 161.

17 *Faust I*, v. 3102 f.: 'Ach, daß die Einfalt, daß Unschuld nie / Sich selbst und ihren heil'gen Wert erkennt!'

18 Beckers, p. 139 and p. 155.

19 Schröder, p. 79: '"Daß wir uns selbst erlösen *müssen* mit unserem Schmerz." Das furchtbare Verdammungswort "muß" erscheint hier in einer bei Georg Büchner einmaligen Schwebe zwischen Marionettenhaftigkeit und Freiheit, zwischen Fluch und Selbsterlösung.'

20 Camus, *L'Homme révolté*, ed. cit., p. 445: 'Les blasphémateurs, paradoxalement, font revivre le dieu jaloux que le christianisme voulait chasser de la scène de l'histoire. L'une de leurs audaces profondes a été justement d'annexer le Christ lui-même à leur camp, en arrêtant son histoire au sommet de la croix et au cri amer qui précéda son agonie.'

21 Cf. *Die Leiden des jungen Werthers*, Hamburg edition, vol. 6, p. 9: 'Wenn . . . ich dann im hohen Grase am fallenden Bache liege, und näher an der Erde tausend mannigfaltige Gräschen mir merkwürdig werden; wenn ich das Wimmeln der kleinen Welt zwischen Halmen . . . fühle, und fühle die Gegenwart des Allmächtigen, . . . der uns in ewiger Wonne schwebend trägt und erhält.'

22 Cf. *Dantons Tod* III. i. 47: 'Gott muß also nach dem er eine Ewigkeit geruht einmal thätig geworden seyn, muß also einmal eine Veränderung in sich erlitten haben, die den Begriff *Zeit* auf ihn anwenden läßt, was Beydes gegen das Wesen Gottes streitet.'

23 Renker, p. 124, n. 19.

24 Stylization can be either a means of exposing reality (as in the caricature of King Peter) or a means of attenuating reality (as in the grotesque representation of Valerio or the Governess). Cf. Höllerer, 1958, p. 422: 'Gogol z.B. gibt meistens nicht "ernsthafte" Darstellung alltäglicher Wirklichkeit. Dennoch ist sein "Revisor" nicht weniger Wirklichkeitsdichtung als Stendhals "Le Rouge et le Noir". Es gibt um diese Zeit auch ein die Wirklichkeit ernstnehmendes Lachen.'

25 Viëtor, 1949, p. 181.

26 Viëtor, 1949, p. 181: 'Wirklich, es ist nicht zu verkennen: dieser faselnde Märchenkomödien-König hat sich mit den Fragen der Hegel'schen Philosophie in einer Weise beschäftigt, die ebensoviel dilettantisches Vergnügen wie unglückliche Neigung verrät. Und er selbst steht da als eine leibhaftige Satire auf die Lehre dieser Philosophie, daß der Fürst die Spitze des Staates sei.'

27 Quoted above, pp. 29 f.

28 Lehmann, *Textkritische Noten*, p. 30.

29 Schröder, p. 136: 'Unübersehbar häufen sich zahlreiche rhetorische Stilfiguren und durchsetzen das ganze Lustspiel, sei es nun einfache Wiederholung, Variation, Häufung, Parallelismus, Zwei-, Drei-, bis Fünfgliedrigkeit oder die Anapher, der Chiasmus, das Oxymoron u.a.m.' See also ibid., p. 131.

30 *Much Ado about Nothing*, edited by A. Quiller-Couch and J. D. Wilson, Cambridge, 1969, p. xxi.

31 Lehmann, *Textkritische Noten*, pp. 9 ff.
32 See above, p. 167.
33 Renker, p. 46: 'Brentano hat im Grunde nur eine Farbe auf der Palette.'
34 Landau, vol. I, p. 136, Martens, 1965, p. 61: 'Im Ponce reden alle Personen die nämliche, geistreiche, gezierte Sprache.'
35 Lehmann, 1969, p. 11: 'Arthur Adamov, der französische Dramatiker, erklärt: Il n'y a rien entre Shakespeare et le Don Juan de Molière jusqu'à Brecht que Büchner. Das sagt ein Repräsentant der europäischen Avantgarde. Büchner erweist sich unversehens auch als Ahnherr des absurden Theaters. Für den Kenner seines Werks keineswegs unerwartet. Denn Büchner hat das erste Drama des absurden Theaters von hohem künstlerischen Range geschrieben: *Leonce und Lena*, die Tragikomödie des menschlichen Sinnverlustes, die absurde Komödie der Langeweile.'

### 7. 'LENZ'

1 'Ihre Novelle Lenz soll jedenfalls, weil Straßburg dazu anregt, den gestrandeten Poeten zum Vorwurf haben?' (2, 479)
2 'Geben Sie uns, wenn weiter nichts im Anfang, *Erinnerungen an Lenz*: da scheinen Sie Thatsachen zu haben, die leicht aufgezeichnet sind.' (2, 481)
3 'Dieser . . . Aufsatz bildet die Grundlage der leider Fragment gebliebenen Novelle "Lenz" meines verstorbenen Freundes Georg Büchner. Er trug sich schon in Straßburg lange Zeit mit dem Gedanken, Lenz zum Helden einer Novelle zu machen, und ich gab ihm zu seinem Stoffe alles, was ich an Handschriften besaß.'
4 There are inconsistencies in the indications of dates at the following places in the *Novelle*: p. 93, l. 11; 94, 12; 94, 17; 95, 34; 97, 27; 100, 11 (cf. Landau, vol. I, p. 108, Martens, 1965, p. 35). The grammar is strange or the text corrupt at 84, 29 ff.; and in the expression *leeres tiefes Bergwasser* (85, 26) one should probably read *reines* instead of *leeres*.
5 Cf. Höllerer, 1958, p. 423: 'Nach den Thesen von H. Friedrich ("Das antiromantische Denken im modernen Frankreich", München, 1935; "Die Klassiker des französischen Romans", Leipzig, 1939) entsteht Wirklichkeitsdichtung aus dem Absturz und als Gegenbild gegen alle Vollkommenheitsvorstellungen.'
6 Höllerer, ibid., pp. 134 f.: 'So wird Büchner, ein Vater des Realismus, gleichzeitig auch ein Ahnherr des sogenannten Surrealismus, sich stützend auf romantische Sprachbewegung.'
7 Camus, 'Hermann Melville', *Théâtre, Récits, Nouvelles*, 1962, p. 1901: 'Comme les plus grands artistes, Melville a construit ses symboles sur le concret, non dans le matériau du rêve. Le créateur de mythes ne participe au génie que dans la mesure où il les inscrit dans l'épaisseur de la réalité et non dans les nuées fugitives de l'imagination. Chez Kafka la réalité qu'il décrit est suscitée par le symbole, le fait découle de l'image, chez Melville le symbole sort de la réalité, l'image naît de la perception. C'est pourquoi Melville ne s'est jamais séparé de la chair ni de la nature, obscurcies dans l'œuvre kafkéenne.'

8 Stöber, *Vie de J.-F. Oberlin*, Strasbourg, 1831, pp. 116, 114, 182, 523, 547.
9 Ibid., pp. 533 f.
10 Voss, p. 6: 'Die Lebensgeschichte Oberlins, von Daniel Ehrenfried Stöber 1828 verfaßt, hat Büchner genau gekannt und ziemlich viele Einzelheiten in seine Novelle übernommen, um der Gestalt Oberlins die nötige Plastik zu geben und die religiöse Atmosphäre des Steintals besser zu zeichnen.'
11 Ludwig Büchner, p. 19.
12 Ibid., p. 47: 'In Lenzens Leben und Sein fühlte er verwandte Seelenzustände, und das Fragment ist halb und halb des Dichters eigenes Porträt.'
13 Landau, vol. I, p. 113, Martens, 1965, p. 41.
14 Cf. Lindenberger, p. 75: '*Lenz*, though it is his only non-theatrical work, has something of the same "dramatic" quality as his plays.'
15 Baumann, 1958, p. 169: 'Für Büchner ergibt sich eine lockere Fügung von in sich selbständigen Szenen, eine Dramatik des Parataktischen.'
16 Voss, p. 96: 'Im Gegensatz zur Klassik, die von der Form her das Leben sucht, gewinnt diese "barocke" Kunst vom Leben her die Form.'
17 Cf. Höllerer, 1958, pp. 131 f. and pp. 423 f.
18 See above, pp. 94 f.
19 Herrmann, p. 259: 'Büchner verändert beim Abschreiben seine Vorlage mit sicherstem Stilgefühl.'
20 Höllerer, 1958, p. 134: 'Seinem Realismus gesellen sich Einblicke und Ausblicke zu, die alles andere sind als "Mimesis".'
21 Hasubek, p. 42: 'Der Gebrauch der verbalen Dynamik durch Büchner ist ... als ein Rückgriff auf eine frühere Stiltradition zu erklären ... Er will mit diesem Stilmittel nicht nur den Dichter Lenz, sondern stärker noch den literarischen Epochenstil imitieren, dem Lenz' Werk angehörte.'
22 These figures are derived from the *Wortindex zu Georg Büchner Dichtungen und Übersetzungen*, bearbeitet von Monika Rössing-Hager, Berlin, 1970.
23 Gutzkow, introducing *Lenz* in the *Telegraph für Deutschland*, 1839; 'Wir müssen erstaunen über eine solche Anatomie der Lebens- und Gemütsstörung.'
24 W. Schulte: 'jene klassisch gewordene Schizophreniestudie' (Irle, *Der psychiatrische Roman*, Stuttgart, 1965, p. 8).
25 Irle, ibid., p. 75: 'Die Büchnersche Novelle ist in einer distanzierten, kühlen, "wissenschaftlichen" Weise geschrieben, die wie eine Chronik einzig das Geschehen heraustreten läßt. Die Phänomene der Geisteskrankheit stellen sich ohne alles Aufmerksamkeit heischende Pathos dar. In den ersten Sätzen, die Lenz auf dem Weg durch das Gebirge kennzeichnen, wird mit Gelassenheit beschrieben: "Müdigkeit spürte er keine, nur war es ihm manchmal unangenehm, daß er nicht auf dem Kopf gehen konnte." Oder, ein wenig später: "Es war ihm alles so klein, so nahe, so naß; er hätte die Erde hinter den Ofen setzen mögen." Das Ungeheuerliche einer psychischen Krankheit stellt sich in einer Nüchternheit und Sachlichkeit dar wie ein normales Phänomen, die Erwähnung eines Regenschauers beispielsweise.'
26 Irle, ibid., p. 82: 'Rümkes Forderung nach der Darstellung der "geformten Oberfläche", seine Feststellung, daß "Autoren, die die Oberfläche in allen Formen und Varianten nachzuzeichnen in der Lage sind" uns dabei "einen

tieferen Einblick in die menschliche Existenz" zu geben imstande sind, "als diejenigen, die uns eine Einsicht in die versteckten Tiefen zu geben" bemüht sind, scheint mir am Beispiel der Büchnerschen Novelle "Lenz" glänzend bestätigt.'

27  Höllerer, 1958, p. 135: 'Realismus in diesem Sinne ist nicht Abschilderung, sondern birgt stärkste Symbolkraft.'

28  Viëtor, 1949, p. 161: 'Ur-Angst vor dem Abgrund des Lebens.'

29  Cf. August Langen, 'Zum Problem der sprachlichen Säkularisation in der deutschen Dichtung des 18. und 19. Jahrhunderts', *Zeitschrift für deutsche Philologie*, 83 (1964), Sonderheft, S. 31: 'Beispielhaft für den Pietismus ist Wilhelm Hoffmanns 1735 erschienenes Erbauungsbuch "Der leidende Christ, wie er im Kreuz überwindet" . . . mit dem (später in Büchners "Lenz" aufgenommenen) Verse: "Leiden ist jetzt mein Gewinnst; . . . Leiden ist mein Gottesdienst."'

30  Cf. Viëtor, 1949, p. 167: 'Für Büchner ist, trotz der enthüllenden Skepsis seines Geschichtsbildes und dem verzweifelten Nihilismus seiner Weltanschauung, der Mensch über die Natur erhoben, weil er ein inneres Leben hat, Gefühl, Geist, Seele. Unbegreiflich für ihn nur, daß im Gang der Welt mit dem Menschen verfahren wird, als sei er ein bewußtloses, willenloses Stück der Natur nur, und nicht auch Übernatur.'

31  'Oberlins Aufzeichnungen' (Lehmann's edition of Büchner, vol. 1, p. 478): 'Denn fürchterlich und höllisch war es, was er ausstund, und es durchbohrte und zerschnitt mir das Herz, wenn ich an seiner Seite die Folgen der Principien, die so manche heutige Modebücher einflößen, die Folgen seines Ungehorsams gegen seinen Vater, seiner herumschweifenden Lebensart, seiner unzweckmäßigen Beschäftigungen, seines häufigen Umgangs mit Frauenzimmern, durchempfinden mußte.'

32  Irle, op. cit., p. 78: 'Man wird unterstellen können, daß Büchner . . . sehr wohl von den unglücklich endenden Beziehungen Lenzens zu Friederike gewußt hat. Er ist nicht dem Kurzschluß erlegen, die Geisteskrankheit als Folge dieses Erlebens darzustellen . . . Erst recht nicht hat er die Überlegungen Oberlins zur Genese der Lenzschen Krankheit übernommen.'

33  Voss, p. 29.

34  'ungläubig gegen Gott und Menschen', Schlosser to Oberlin, 2 March 1778, quoted by A. Stöber, op. cit., p. 32.

35  Cf. Fischer, pp. 41 ff.

## 8. 'WOYZECK'

1  Winkler, p. 181.

2  Krause, p. 161.

3  Winkler, p. 124: 'Büchner fühlte sich der Welt gegenüber verantwortlich; er wollte diese gegebene Außenwelt gestalten, nicht irgend eine in ihm lebende Phantasiewelt . . . So sind ihm die Clarusquelle und die andern Quellen ein Stück Natur und Geschichte; dieses Stück sucht er recht zu sehen, richtig zu deuten, dann in einem Werk zu verdichten.'

4  Vogt, op. cit., p. 77.

5 Ibid., p. 55: 'Der Glanzpunkt dieser anatomischen Vorlesung war die Demonstration der Ohrmuskeln. Der Sohn, der die Ohren brillant bewegen konnte, mußte dann erscheinen und man erzählte, daß die Szene in folgender Weise sich abspielte. Nach der Beschreibung der Ohrmuskeln sagte der Professor: "Diese Muskeln sind beim Mens-ken obsolet geworden. Der Mens-k kann die Ohren nicht bewegen, das können nur die Äffken. Jolios, mach's mal!" Der unglückliche Jolios mußte dann aufstehen und mit den Ohren wedeln!'

6 See above, Ch. 3, n. 21. The so-called 'folio MS' of *Woyzeck* includes H1 and H2, H4 is sometimes referred to as the 'quarto MS', while H3 consists of a separate sheet of paper. For a description of the MSS of the *Woyzeck* fragments, now in the Goethe–Schiller Archive in Weimar, see Lehmann, *Textkritische Noten*, p. 40.

7 Krause, pp. 76 f., suggests more or less the same dating for the four fragments: H1 – June–July (less probably August) 1836; H2, H3 – September–October; H4 – October 1836–February 1837.

8 Bornscheuer, *Woyzeck*, *Erläuterungen und Dokumente*, pp. 69 f.

9 See Ludwig Büchner, pp. 39 f.

10 Winkler, p. 55.

11 Elema (p. 140), Krause (p. 89) and Kanzog (p. 439) agree with Winkler in this respect.

12 Lehmann, *Textkritische Noten*, p. 54: 'Dieser sozial- und bewußtseinskritische Zug [in H2] wird durch die erste Szene des Quartblatts H3 (*Der Hof des Professors*) noch weiter vorangetrieben und radikalisiert.'

13 Richards (p. 57) rightly said of H3, 1: 'Szenen dieser Art gehören in die Exposition.' It is wrong, however, to place H3, 1 right at the beginning of the play, as in the recent production of the Berliner Ensemble, a position which clearly belongs to H4, 1. In general one must deplore the senseless liberties which the Berliner Ensemble, in its very disappointing production, permitted itself to take with Büchner's text.

14 Horn, *Archiv für medizinische Erfahrung* (etc.), March–April 1820, pp. 313 f. Quoted by Krause, pp. 178 f.

15 Horn, op. cit., p. 311. Quoted Krause, p. 178.

16 Martens, 1960, pp. 361 ff. Cf. Buch, p. 71: 'statt dessen weist alles darauf hin, daß der Barbier und Louis identisch sind'. The identity of the two figures was also assumed in the production of the play by the Berliner Ensemble in December 1973, and the scene H1, 10 was actually contaminated with H4, 14, so that we had the absurd spectacle of the hero behaving with the cowardice of the barber in the first half of the scene and with the courage of Woyzeck in the second half.

17 Cf. the remark of a critic on the acting of Eugen Klöpfer in this scene in a performance at the Vienna Raimundtheater (7 October 1921): 'Wundervoll, wie er das Weib tötet und dabei zugleich seine Liebe ausströmt' (quoted Strudthoff, p. 71).

18 Lehmann, 1, 514: 'Als in Gohlis die Kirmse gewesen, habe er Abends in Bette gelegen und an die Woostin gedacht, daß diese wohl dort mit einem anderen zu Tanze seyn könne. Da sey es ihm ganz eigen gewesen, als ob er

die Tanzmusik, Violinen und Bässe durcheinander, höre, und dazu im Takte die Worte: *Immer drauf, immer drauf!*'

19 Horn, op. cit., pp. 306 f. Quoted Krause, p. 176.

20 Cf. Scheuer, p. 62: 'die Landschaft scheint an dem Geschehen selbst in einer geheimnisvollen Weise beteiligt zu sein'.

21 Lehmann, *Textkritische Noten*, p. 53.

22 Klotz, p. 108: 'Die Textur übernimmt Aufgaben der Struktur.'

23 Landau, vol. I, p. 155 (Martens, 1965, p. 78): 'sie geben dem Stück etwas von der düsteren Einfalt der Volksdichtung, die Stimmung einer alten schaurigen Ballade.'

24 Cf. Scheuer, p. 61: 'Mit vollem Recht können wir hier also von einem "balladesken" Drama sprechen', and Elema, p. 137: 'eine kausal verbundene, teilweise aber auch schon ausgeführte balladeske Szenenfolge'.

25 The thought has evidently been suggested by Lenz's Hauptmann Pirzel in *Die Soldaten* II. ii: 'Denken, denken, was der Mensch ist, das ist ja meine Rede. (*Faßt ihn an die Hand.*) Sehen Sie, das ist Ihre Hand, aber was ist das, Haut, Knochen, Erde.' The words uttered by Büchner on his deathbed, though widely different in their emotional tone, are alike in substance: 'Wir sind Tod, Staub, Asche . . .', and the manner in which they are anticipated in *Die Soldaten* and in 'Woyzeck' is another reason for not regarding those words as a valid expression of Büchner's views. Writers such as Mautner, Viëtor, Oppel and Krause regard as the very summit of Büchner's wisdom a thought which is essentially the same as that expressed in *Die Soldaten* by the 'caricature' Pirzel and in 'Woyzeck' by the contemptible barber. Cf. above, pp. 115 ff.

26 Ursula Paulus (p. 241) comments on the grandmother's tale as follows: 'Übrig bleibt nichts als die stumme Geste des Leids, das ein Leiden am Ausgesetztsein, am Alleinsein, am Dasein überhaupt ist. Dieses Ende ohne Trost ist dennoch aller Nihilismus-Deutung entzogen, denn es erkennt das Leid, hat einen Ausdruck dafür, und dieser Ausdruck ist "*weinen*".' That the poor child *weeps* in its loneliness and forsakenness, in its absolute dearth of comfort and hope, is hardly a convincing reason for saying that the grandmother's tale is 'aller Nihilismus-Deutung entzogen'; one is again astonished at the slenderness of the grounds on which some critics deny Büchner's nihilism. Emrich (p. 21) rightly protests against the vain attempts of critics to read into this desperately gloomy tale 'irgendeine religiöse Intention im positiven Sinne'.

27 Winkler, p. 131.

28 Jean Paul, *Blumen-, Frucht- und Dornenstücke* (*Siebenkäs*), 2. Bändchen, 1. Blumenstück.

29 Ibid.: 'Da kamen, schrecklich für das Herz, die gestorbenen Kinder . . . und sagten: "Jesus! haben wir keinen Vater?" – Und er antwortete mit strömenden Tränen: "wir sind alle Waisen, ich und ihr, wir sind ohne Vater."'

30 Schmolling had given himself up (close to the scene of the murder when a number of people were standing by the corpse; cf. Krause, p. 177). Woyzeck had been arrested (Lehmann, I, 491).

31 Martens, 1960, p. 381.

32 Cf. Lehmann, 1971, p. 82: 'Aber warum in aller Welt soll denn auch nur mit dieser *Möglichkeit* gerechnet werden. Die Szene H1, 20 bietet doch keinen Hinweis, daß es sich um eine Selbstertränkung handeln könnte. Es handelt sich eindeutig um die Beseitigung von belastenden Indizien.' Similarly Kanzog, p. 18.

33 Lehmann, 1, 507 f.

34 Cf. Winkler, p. 154: 'Aus Büchners eigenem Erleben heraus ist auch die Liebe Woyzecks geworden. Wie allein die Braut in der Gießener Zeit Büchner einen Sinn für das Dasein gibt, so ist allein Marie und ihr Kind Lebenssinn Woyzecks.'

35 H2, 9 consists only of one line of text: 'Und ist kein Betrug in seinem Munde erfunden. Herr Gott!', which is preceded in the MS by the incomplete and cancelled sentence: 'La corruption du siècle est parvenue à ce point, que pour maintenir la moral...' Kanzog (p. 435) suggests that the corruption of the age referred to here consisted for Büchner in the fact that 'Glaubensinhalte von den Herrschenden als Mittel der Unterdrückung benutzt werden' and that Louise's religious impulses are merely a consequence of this method of oppression. Kanzog may well be right, but nothing can be inferred with certainty from a cancelled quotation (if it is a quotation) of unknown provenance and context.

36 Winkler, p. 160: 'Diese beiden Briefstellen sind fast das Programm für den Hauptmann und den Doktor.'

37 See above, pp. 10–11.

38 Knight, p. 118.

39 Nadler: 'Hauptmann und Regimentsarzt behandeln ihn gut, mit einer Art wohlwollenden Vertraulichkeit' (quoted by Höllerer, 1958, p. 136).

40 Cf. Lehmann, 1971, p. 76.

41 Cf. Klotz, p. 156: 'Das geschlossene Drama verlegt äußere Bewegungen weitgehend in den Bewußtseinsraum der Personen, das offene dagegen projiziert innere Bewegungen mimisch in den szenischen Raum. So wird denn Pantomime häufig zum Ausdrucksmedium für Vorgänge und Zustände, die den Personen sprachlich nicht faßbar sind.'

42 In my remarks on the style of *Woyzeck* I am much indebted to Winkler (especially pp. 82 and 225).

43 Adamov, 'Wozzeck', *Les Lettres françaises*, 28 November 1963.

44 Ibid.

45 Strudthoff, p. 70.

46 Lehmann, 1971, p. 77: 'Der Hauptmann zeigt sich von seiner besten Seite, ein gemütlicher jovialer Fettwanst.'

47 Knight (p. 136) writes: 'One of the salient characteristics of Büchner's Woyzeck is not sheer stupidity (though he appears stupid to his associates) ... but muddleheadedness.' There is no indication that Marie or Andres regards Woyzeck as stupid; they regard him as possibly insane, or as tending to insanity. Woyzeck is, in fact, neither stupid nor muddleheaded – his conversation with the captain shows him capable of acute insights – but he is uneducated, uninformed, consequently open to superstition; and his experiences are often of a kind that are scarcely communicable to others.

48 'Möge die heranwachsende Jugend bei dem Anblicke des blutenden
   Verbrechers, oder bei dem Gedanken an ihn, sich tief die Wahrheit ein-
   prägen, daß Arbeitsscheu, Spiel, Trunkenheit, ungesetzmäßige Befriedigung
   der Geschlechtslust, und schlechte Gesellschaft, ungeahnet und allmählich
   zu Verbrechen und zum Blutgerüste führen können' (Lehmann, 1, 490).

49 Nöllner, p. 423.

50 Hamann, p. 260.

51 Cf. *Die Soldaten* I. vi, where Lenz's Marie seeks to conceal her seducer's
   gift as Büchner's Marie does in H4, 4.

52 Cf. Viëtor, 1949, p. 205.

53 This is well expressed by Margaret Jacobs (p. xxi): 'Woyzeck's social
   circumstances are organically part of it [the tragedy] because they underline
   the cardinal factor that he possesses nothing but Marie and the child and
   relies upon this possession alone for meaning in life.' Richards supports
   the wrong view when he writes (p. 56): 'Aus der letzten Fassung geht klar
   hervor, daß die soziale Thematik, die Büchner in die zweite Handschrift
   eingeführt hatte, nicht von Woyzecks Tragödie ablenken sollte.' Two
   things must be observed here: (1) It is not true that Büchner's alleged
   intention to subordinate 'die soziale Thematik' emerges clearly from the
   last version of the play. Our analysis has shown, on the contrary, that
   'die soziale Thematik' is much more strongly emphasized in the last
   version than in any of the earlier ones. (2) It is evident that on Richards'
   view the play disintegrates into two basically unrelated parts: (a) 'die
   soziale Thematik'; (b) 'Woyzecks Tragödie'. Like Kurt May (p. 269),
   Ursula Paulus (p. 242) and many other critics, Richards fails to see that
   Büchner is not concerned with an abstract entity called 'human nature'
   which is supposed to exist independently of social circumstances. He is
   concerned with particular human beings in a concrete social situation, and
   the tragedy results from the combination and conflict of *all* the factors, individual and social, in that specific constellation.

54 Cf. the valuable article by J. Elema, 'Der verstümmelte Woyzeck',
   *Neophilologus* 49 (1965), especially pp. 151–3.

55 Elema, p. 153.

56 Cf. Emrich, p. 12: 'Vielmehr ist die Katastrophe bereits vor Beginn des
   Dramas da, das Ende ist schon im Anfang anwesend', and Klotz, p. 110:
   'Die Handlungsbewegung ist hier . . . ein Kreisen. Die siebte Szene beim
   Doktor im "Woyzeck" ist dem Ende nicht näher als die zweite, im "Freien
   Feld".'

57 Kanzog, p. 433, objects to 'die einseitige Festlegung des *Woyzeck* auf das
   offene Drama' and favours, instead of this typology, a 'Funktionslehre . . .
   die das im "offenen Drama" gewonnene Eigengewicht der einzelnen
   Szenen neuen dramaturgischen Gesetzen (mit einer gegenüber dem
   "geschlossenen Drama" differenzierteren Behandlung von Exposition,
   Peripetie und Katastrophe) zuordnet'. The concepts 'open' and 'closed'
   form, popularized by Wölfflin in his *Renaissance und Barock*, have the relative validity and real, though limited, usefulness of other such hermeneutic
   concepts; they are as useful, for example, as Brecht's distinction between

'epic' and 'dramatic' theatre, and we may note that Kanzog does not avoid them in the statement of his own position. But one has to remember that within such categories there are infinite possibilities of variety and originality, and that this is true also of the 'closed' form of drama; so that it seems rather bold and questionable to suggest that the particular modification or development of the 'open' form in *Woyzeck* is more 'differentiated' than all the actual or possible modifications or developments of the 'closed' form'.

58  Fink, 'Volkslied und Verseinlage', Martens, 1965, p. 481: 'eine gewisse stereometrische, letzthin allgemein menschliche Tiefe'.

59  Krause, p. 27.

60  Krause, p. 220: 'Es fragt sich nun, ob Büchner in den Szenen H4, 12 und H4, 13 mit den Übernahmen aus H1 und mit der neugeschaffenen Szene H4, 15 Unstimmigkeiten innerhalb der letzten Fassung erzeugt, indem er Dinge darin einbaut, die nicht mehr hineinpassen.'

61  Krause, p. 225: 'Die Frage bleibt bestehen, ob die Figur Woyzeck innerhalb dieser fragmentarischen, sprunghaften und keineswegs widerspruchsfreien, ja nicht einmal klaren, sondern nur sehr schwer faßbaren Gestaltung nicht überladen wurde.'

62  Lehmann, 1971, p. 69.

63  Cf. Lehmann, 1971, p. 81. Mautner, arguing that the testament scene (H4, 17) represents a profound religious change in Woyzeck, suggests that the unique significance of the scene is indicated by the absence of the key-words otherwise associated with Woyzeck ('Wortegewebe, Sinngefüge und "Idee" in Büchners "Woyzeck"', Martens, 1965, p. 538): 'Diese Testamentszene ist nicht nur christlich getönt in der Gesinnung, sie ist buchstäblich als einzige frei von den Wortmotiven, die sonst jedes Auftreten Woyzecks begleiten.' But this is inaccurate. The important key-words *rot* and *arm* occur in this scene, and a link with the murderous impulses of H4, 13 is established by the words 'Armer du mußt Schnaps trinke und Pulver drin das tödt das Fieber'; while the last sentence: 'wenn der Schreiner die Hobelspän sammlet, es weiß niemand, wer sein Kopf drauf lege wird' recalls Woyzeck's very first speech in the play (H4, 1): 'Drei Tag und drei Nächt und er lag auf den Hobelspänen.' The neglect of these facts is a serious fault in an essay specifically concerned with 'Wortgewebe' in *Woyzeck*.

64  Jacobs, p. 144.

65  Elema, p. 153.

66  Cf. Elema, p. 150: 'Büchner hatte ja, wie die Woyzeck–Doktor–Hauptmann-Szenen beweisen, noch etwas ganz anderes vor als die Darstellung dieses persönlichen Leides. Er muß, wie bestürzend es auch sein mag sich das auszudenken, noch eine grausige Steigerung des Geschehens im Sinne gehabt haben.'

67  Buch, p. 14: 'Die seit längerem schon erkannte Abwendung Büchners "von der materialistischen Zynik, von radikalem Nihilismus", ereignete sich nicht, wie bisher angenommen, zwischen "Dantons Tod" und "Woyzeck" sondern innerhalb der "Woyzeck"-Entwürfe.'

NOTES TO PP. 254-66

68  Cf. Krause, pp. 207 f. and p. 171: 'Woyzeck [wird] immer stärker auf . . .
    Überwindung des Leids hin angelegt.'
69  Mautner, 'Wortgewebe . . . in Büchners "Woyzeck"', Martens, 1965,
    p. 550: 'Die stärkste Änderung einer moralphilosophischen oder meta-
    physischen Tendenz finden wir in H in der Einfügung des Abschieds
    Woyzecks von Andres. Sie deutete eine positivere Einstellung zum Leiden
    der Welt an, verglichen mit der in den Entwürfen . . . Sie ist religiös und
    kommt der christlichen nahe.'
70  Mautner, ibid., p. 551: 'Überhaupt findet sich in Woyzecks Reden trotz
    aller Angst, Traurigkeit, Verdammung der sündigen Welt kein einziges
    Wort der Anklage Gottes oder der Verzweiflung über die Leitung der Welt.'
71  Mautner, ibid., p. 536.
72  See above, p. 205.
73  Höllerer, 1958, p. 136: 'Lukács . . . hat übersehen, daß Büchner sich gerade
    deswegen von der Politik ab- und zur Dichtung hingewendet hat, weil sich
    ihm dort eine Spiel und Gegenspiel vereinigende Möglichkeit darbot.'
74  Stern, p. 99.
75  See above, p. 155.
76  See above, p. 91.
77  Fink, 'Volkslied und Verseinlage', Martens, 1965, p. 482: 'Aber zeugt
    nicht diese Anklage für die Sehnsucht nach einer wahren Gemeinschaft, die
    der Liebe ihren Platz einräumt?'
78  Toller, letter to Stefan Zweig, 13 June 1923 (Prosa, Briefe, Dramen,
    Gedichte, Hamburg, 1961, pp. 228 f.): 'Nur der Schwache resigniert, wenn er
    sich außerstande sieht, dem ersehnten Traum die vollkommene Verwirk-
    lichung zu geben. Dem Starken nimmt es nichts von seinem leidenschaft-
    lichen Wollen, wenn er wissend wird. Not tun uns heute nicht die Menschen,
    die blind sind im großen Gefühl, not tun uns, die wollen – obwohl sie
    wissen.'
79  Cf. Carl Zuckmayer: 'Eigentliche Vorbilder habe ich nicht gehabt, wenn
    man nicht gerade das große Vorbild aller modernen Dramatik nennen will...
    Georg Büchner' (Horst Bienek, Werkstattgespräche mit Schriftstellern,
    Munich, 1965, p. 213).
80  Adamov, 'Wozzeck', Les Lettres françaises, 28 November 1973: 'De quoi
    s'agit-il cette pièce qui me touche si profondément, dans cette pièce
    dont Brecht me dit, quelques mois avant sa mort, qu'elle marquait pour lui
    aussi le début du théâtre moderne?'

9. CONCLUSION

1  Viëtor, 1949, p. 189: 'das kühnste und revolutionärste von Büchners
   Werken: die Tragödie des armen Woyzeck'.
2  Golo Mann's essay on 'Georg Büchner und die Revolution', Neue Rundschau,
   80 (1969), is a good example of the condescension and superficiality with
   which Büchner's political views and activity are commonly treated by modern
   scholars. It is inaccurate and misleading to say of Büchner, as Mann does
   (p. 3): 'Als die Bauern auf sein Manifest nicht so reagierten, wie er gehofft

hatte, verlor er das Interesse an der Sache.' And where, in the *Landbote*, does Büchner advocate a 'primitiven Bauernsozialismus' (Mann, p. 6)?

3  Ludwig Feuerbach an Wilhelm Bolin, den 15. Februar 1862: 'Trotz Schopenhauer ist Glückseligkeit der letzte Zweck und Sinn alles menschlichen Tuns und Denkens' (*Ausgewählte Briefe von und an Ludwig Feuerbach*, 11, Leipzig, 1904, p. 283).

4  Spinoza, *Ethices* Pars III . . . 'Laetitia est hominis transitio a minore ad majorem perfectionem . . . Tristitia est hominis transitio a majore ad minorem perfectionem.' Cf. Hölderlin, 'Reflexionen' (StA 4, 235): 'Aus Freude must du das Reine überhaupt, die Menschen und andern Wesen verstehen . . . aus Freude, ehe die Noth eintritt, der Verstand, der blos aus Noth kommt, ist immer einseitig schief.'

5  'Prometheus, der Held einer der schönsten Tragödien, ist gewissermaßen das Sinnbild der Tragödie selbst' – Quoted by Benno v. Wiese, *Die deutsche Tragödie von Lessing bis Hebbel*, 1955, p. 281.

6  E.g. Knight, p. 5: 'It is quite wrong to treat Büchner as if he were a fully matured, fixed character, with opinions finally crystallized . . . Admittedly Büchner was not merely an unusually gifted young man, but also unusually mature, but, even so, the most enthusiastic admirer must bear his youth continually in mind, and must treat his opinions with great reserve and a continually exercised sense of proportion.' Against the presumptuous claim to be wiser than Büchner merely by virtue of being older, one must insist that opinions are to be judged on their merits, not by the age of the persons who hold them.

# CHRONOLOGICAL TABLE

1813    17 October. Birth of Georg Büchner in Goddelau, near Darmstadt, then *Residenzstadt* in the Grand Duchy of Hesse. Georg is the first child of Dr med. Ernst Büchner (1786–1861) and Caroline, née Reuss (1791–1858).

1814    18 September. Beginning of the Congress of Vienna (concluded 9 June 1815).

1815    Birth of Mathilde, Georg's eldest sister.

1816    The Büchner family moves to Darmstadt.

1817    Birth of Wilhelm, Georg's eldest brother. Pharmacist, factory owner, member of the Hessian Landtag and the Reichstag (died 1892).

1818    'Allgemeine deutsche Burschenschaft' founded.

1819    23 March. Kotzebue assassinated by Karl Ludwig Sand (executed 20 May 1820).

August. The Carlsbad decrees, further restricting the freedom of the press and of the universities.

1821    Birth of Louise Büchner, poet and novelist, publicist, feminist (*Die Frauen und ihr Beruf*, 1855).

Georg Büchner receives first tuition from his mother.

1822    Georg enters the private school of Dr Carl Weitershausen.

1824    Birth of Ludwig Büchner. Physician and author of the famous book *Kraft und Stoff* (1855).

1825    26 March. Georg admitted to the second class of the Darmstadt *Gymnasium*.

1827    Christmas. Georg dedicates a poem to his father.

1828    Christmas. Georg dedicates to his parents the poem 'Die Nacht'.

1830    Birth of Alexander Büchner (who later became professor of literature in Caen).

July revolution in Paris.

Death of Ludwig I, Grand Duke of Hesse-Darmstadt; accession of Ludwig II (1830–48).

September. The 'bloodbath of Södel', a rising of the starving peasants, brutally suppressed by troops, near the village of Södel in Upper Hesse.

29 September. A public speech by Büchner in the Darmstadt *Gymnasium* on Cato and in defence of his suicide.

1831    30 March. Speech by Büchner in Latin at the end of term ceremony in the *Gymnasium*.

9 November. Büchner is enrolled as a student of medicine in the University of Strasbourg.

November. He becomes one of the regular guests (*hospites perpetui*) of the students' club 'Eugenia' in Strasbourg.

4 December. Büchner witnesses and participates in the enthusiastic reception in Strasbourg of Polish freedom-fighters under General Ramorino. (2, 413)

1832    24 May. Büchner speaks in the 'Eugenia' on the corruption of the German governments and the coarseness of the students.

27 May. 'Das Hambacher Fest', a popular demonstration against the

reactionary governments of Austria and the German states.
August–September. Büchner spends holidays in Darmstadt.
1833  3 April. The Frankfurt *Putsch*.
July. Büchner wanders over the Vosges mountains. (2, 418 f.)
Büchner and Minna Jaegle become secretly engaged.
31 October. Enrolment as student of medicine in the University of Giessen.
November. Büchner sick with meningitis.
Early December. Returns to Darmstadt to complete convalescence.
1834  Early January. Büchner returns to Giessen. Becomes acquainted with Friedrich Ludwig Weidig (1791–1837), then rector in Butzbach and anonymous author of the illegal journal *Leuchter und Beleuchter für Hessen*.
March. Büchner founds in Giessen the 'Gesellschaft der Menschenrechte'.
End of March (?). Büchner begins to write the original version of *Der Hessische Landbote*.
Early April. Journey to Strasbourg to visit fiancée.
April. Büchner's engagement to Minna made public.
Returns to Darmstadt for remainder of Easter holidays.
Founds Darmstadt branch of the 'Gesellschaft der Menschenrechte'.
Second half of May. Büchner again in Giessen.
End of May. Becker and Clemm bring the complete MS of the *Landbote* to Weidig.
Early June. Becker brings the altered MS of the *Landbote* back to Büchner.
3 July. Meeting of the conspirators and sympathizers on the Badenburg by the Lahn.
July. The first edition of *Der Hessische Landbote* printed in Offenbach.
31 July. Minnigerode and Zeuner fetch the printed copies of the *Landbote* from Offenbach. Zeuner and Becker convey part of the edition to Weidig for distribution in Upper Hesse.
31 July. The conspiracy is betrayed by J. K. Kuhl to the government in Darmstadt.
1 August. Minnigerode is arrested as he is entering Giessen with part of the edition of the *Landbote*.
Büchner immediately sets out to warn his fellow conspirators in Butzbach and Offenbach.
His room is searched in his absence by *Universitätsrichter* Georgi (later *Untersuchungsrichter* in the case against Weidig).
September. Weidig transferred to Ober-Gleen, a village near Alsfeld.
September. Many members of the 'Gesellschaft der Menschenrechte' arrested.
September. Büchner returns to Darmstadt.
October. His father refuses to let him return to Giessen.
October. Minna Jaegle visits Büchner and his parents in Darmstadt.
November. Weidig publishes a second (modified) edition of *Der Hessische Landbote*.
December. Büchner attempts to organize the escape of Minnigerode from the Friedberg fortress. Plan defeated by Minnigerode's weak health.

# CHRONOLOGICAL TABLE

1835   January. Further arrests of members of the 'Gesellschaft der Menschenrechte'.

Büchner summoned to give evidence before the investigating judges in Offenbach and Friedberg.

*Ca.* 15 January–*ca.* 21 February. Composition of *Dantons Tod*.

1 March. Büchner, in danger of arrest, leaves Darmstadt and makes for Strasbourg, crossing the French border at Weißenburg (9 March).

22 April. August Becker arrested.

24 April. Weidig arrested.

April–May. Fragmentary publication of *Danton* in the *Phönix*.

13 June. Warrant issued in Darmstadt for the arrest of Büchner.

July 1835. *Dantons Tod* published complete but with many unauthorized alterations by Eduard Duller, under the title *Dantons Tod. Dramatische Bilder aus Frankreichs Schreckensherrschaft, von Georg Büchner*.

Summer–autumn. Translation of two dramas by Victor Hugo, *Lucretia Borgia* and *Maria Tudor*.

November–December (?). Probable date of composition of *Lenz*.

10 December. The Federal Diet bans all works by Heine and 'Young Germany', including Gutzkow's and Wienbarg's projected *Deutsche Revue*, to which Büchner had been invited to contribute.

1835–6  Winter. Philosophical studies ('Ich werde ganz dumm in dem Studium der Philosophie' – 2, 450). Biological studies (*Mémoire sur le système nerveux du barbeau*).

1836   3 February. The publisher Cotta announces a prize for the best German comedy.

13 April, 20 April, 4 May. Büchner reads his *Mémoire* at three meetings of the *Société d'histoire naturelle de Strasbourg*. He is made a corresponding member of the society, which resolves to include his *Mémoire* among its publications.

April–June (?). Probable date of composition of *Leonce und Lena*.

June–July (?). Probable date of the first 'Woyzeck' fragment (H1).

July. The MS of *Leonce und Lena* is returned to Büchner unopened, as it had arrived two days after the deadline for Cotta's competition (1 July).

August–September. Further scientific and philosophical studies (Descartes and Spinoza) in preparation for a course of lectures on natural science and a course on philosophy in Zurich.

September–October (?). Probable date of second and third *Woyzeck* fragments (H3 and H2).

September. Büchner receives doctorate of the University of Zurich for his *Mémoire*.

18 October. Büchner moves to Zurich.

November. Büchner gives a trial lecture in Zurich *Über Schädelnerven*. Begins regular course of lectures on the comparative anatomy of fishes and Amphibia.

November 1836–February 1837 (?). Probable date of last *Woyzeck* fragment (H4).

1837   2 February. Beginning of the fatal illness (typhus).

# CHRONOLOGICAL TABLE

19 February. Büchner dies.

23 February. Weidig, still in *Untersuchungschaft* in Darmstadt, commits suicide.

1838  *Leonce und Lena* published by Gutzkow in *Telegraph für Deutschland* (first Act incomplete).

1839  *Lenz* published by Gutzkow in *Telegraph für Deutschland*.

1850  Büchner's *Nachgelassene Schriften* edited by Ludwig Büchner (without *Woyzeck*).

1879  Büchner's *Sämtliche Werke* edited by Karl Emil Franzos (including first attempt to publish *Woyzeck*).

1895  3 May. First performance of *Leonce und Lena*, Munich (Theaterverein 'Intimes Theater').

1902  5 January. First performance of *Dantons Tod*, Berlin ('Neue Freie Volksbühne').

1913  8 November. First performance of *Woyzeck*, Munich (Residenztheater).

# BIBLIOGRAPHY

In references to *Dantons Tod* and *Leonce und Lena* the numbers of the Act and Scene are given, as well as the page number in the first volume of Lehmann's edition. In references to *Lenz* only the page number of Lehmann's edition is given. *Woyzeck* is referred to by the number of the MS (H1, H2, H3 or H4) and the number of the Scene. In references to books and articles specifically concerned with Büchner only the name of the author and the page number are given. If an author has made more than one contribution, these are distinguished by their dates.

## I. EDITIONS

Büchner, Ludwig: *Nachgelassene Schriften von Georg Büchner*, Frankfurt a. M., 1850.

Franzos, Karl Emil: *Georg Büchners Sämtliche Werke und handschriftlicher Nachlaß*, Frankfurt a. M., 1879.

Landau, Paul: *Georg Büchners Gesammelte Schriften*, 2 Bände, Berlin, 1909 (Landau's comments on *Dantons Tod*, *Lenz*, *Leonce und Lena* and *Woyzeck* reprinted in Martens, 1965, pp. 16 ff.).

Witkowski, G.: *Georg Büchner, Woyzeck*, nach den Handschriften des Dichters herausgegeben, Leipzig, 1920.

Bergemann, Fritz: *Georg Büchner, Sämtliche Werke und Briefe*, Leipzig, 1922 (with critical apparatus omitted in later editions of this work).

*Georg Büchner, Werke und Briefe*, 6. Aufl., Wiesbaden, 1953. (Unless otherwise indicated, references to Bergemann are to this edition.)

Thieberger, Richard: *La Mort de Danton de Georges Büchner et ses sources*, Paris, 1953.

Jacobs, Margaret: *Georg Büchner, Dantons Tod and Woyzeck*, Manchester, 1968 (1st edition 1954).

Meinerts, H. J.: *Georg Büchner, Sämtliche Werke*, Gütersloh, 1963.

Benn, M. B.: *Georg Büchner, Leonce und Lena and Lenz*, London, 1972 (first published 1963).

Krause, Egon: *Georg Büchner, Woyzeck*, Frankfurt a. M., 1969.

Lehmann, Werner R.: *Georg Büchner. Sämtliche Werke und Briefe*. 4 Bände. Historisch-kritische Ausgabe mit Kommentar. 1. Band, Dichtungen und Übersetzungen mit Dokumentation zur Stoffgeschichte, Hamburg, 1967. 2. Band, Vermischte Schriften und Briefe, Hamburg, 1971. (The third and fourth volume of this edition had not appeared at the date of the completion of the present work.)

Bornscheuer, Lothar: *Woyzeck. Kritische Lese- und Arbeitsausgabe*, Stuttgart, 1972.

311

## 2. BIBLIOGRAPHY

Schlick, Werner: *Das Georg Büchner Schrifttum bis 1965.* Eine internationale Bibliographie, Hildesheim, 1968.

## 3. CRITICAL LITERATURE

Adamov, Arthur: 'Wozzeck ou la fatalité mise en cause', *Les Lettres françaises*, 28 November 1963.

Auger-Duvignaud, Jean: *Georg Büchner dramaturge*, Paris, 1954.

Bach, Anneliese: 'Verantwortlichkeit und Fatalismus in Georg Büchners Drama "Dantons Tod"', *Wirkendes Wort*, 6 (1955).

Baumann, Gerhart: *Georg Büchner. Die dramatische Ausdruckswelt*, Göttingen, 1961.

Beck, Adolf: 'Unbekannte französische Quellen für "Dantons Tod" von Georg Büchner', *Forschung und Deutung. Ausgewählte Aufsätze zur Literatur*, Frankfurt/Bonn, 1966.

Beckers, Gustav: *Georg Büchners 'Leonce und Lena'. Ein Lustspiel der Langeweile*, Hamburg, 1955 (dissertation).

Benn, M. B.: 'Anti-Pygmalion: an Apologia for Georg Büchner's Aesthetics', *MLR*, 64 (1969).

'Büchner and Gautier', *Seminar*, IX (1973).

Bornscheuer, Lothar: *Woyzeck. Erläuterungen und Dokumente*, Stuttgart, 1972.

Brinkmann, Donald: *Georg Büchner als Philosoph*, Zurich, 1958.

Brunn, W. L. v.: 'Georg Büchner', *Deutsche medizinische Wochenschrift*, 89 (1964).

Buch, Wilfried: *Woyzeck. Fassungen und Wandlungen*, Dortmund, 1970.

Büchner, Anton: *Die Familie Büchner*, Darmstadt, 1963.

Büchner, Louise: *Nachgelassene belletristische und vermischte Schriften*, 2 Bände, Frankfurt a. M., 1878.

Büchner-Preis: *Die Reden der Preisträger, 1950–1962*, eingeleitet von Carl Zuckmayer, Heidelberg/Darmstadt, 1963.

Büttner, Ludwig: *Georg Büchner. Revolutionär und Pessimist*, Nürnberg, 1948. *Büchners Bild vom Menschen*, Nürnberg, 1967.

Camus, Albert: *L'Homme révolté* (1949), *Essais*, Bibliothèque de la Pléiade, Paris, 1965.

Conrad, Hermann: 'Dantons Tod von Georg Büchner', *Preußische Jahrbücher*, 167 (1917).

Cruickshank, John: *Albert Camus and the Literature of Revolt*, London, 1959.

Dam, Hermann van: 'Zu Georg Büchners Woyzeck', *Akzente*, 1 (1954) (reprinted Martens, 1965, pp. 305 ff.).

Dietze, Walter: '"Dantons Tod" – Georg Büchner und Aleksej Tolstoy', *Weimarer Beiträge*, 15 (1969).

Dymschitz, A. L.: 'Die ästhetischen Anschauungen Georg Büchners', *Weimarer Beiträge*, 8 (1962).

Edschmid, Kasimir: 'Georg Büchner', *Die Großen Deutschen*, Bd. 3, Berlin, 1956.

Elema, J.: 'Der verstümmelte Woyzeck', *Neophilologus*, 49 (1965).

Emrich, Wilhelm: 'Von Georg Büchner zu Samuel Beckett. Zum Problem einer literarischen Formidee', *Aspekte des Expressionismus*, hrsg. von Wolfgang Paulsen, Heidelberg, 1968.

Enzensberger, Hans Magnus: *Georg Büchner, Ludwig Weidig, Der Hessische Landbote, Texte, Briefe, Prozeßakten*, Frankfurt a. M., 1965.

Esslin, Martin: *The Theatre of the Absurd*, London, 1966.

Fink, Gonthier-Louis: 'Léonce et Léna. Comédie et réalisme chez Büchner', *Études Germaniques*, 16 (1961) (German translation in Martens, 1965, pp. 488 ff.).

'Volkslied und Verseinlage in den Dramen Büchners', *DVjs*, 35 (1961) (reprinted Martens, 1965, pp. 443 ff.).

Fischer, Heinz: *Georg Büchner. Untersuchungen und Marginalien*, Bonn, 1972.

Frenzel, E.: 'Mussets Lorenzaccio – ein mögliches Vorbild für Dantons Tod', *Euphorion*, 58 (1964).

Friedrich, Eva: *Georg Büchner und die Französische Revolution*, Winterthur, 1956 (dissertation).

Gravier, M.: 'Georg Büchner et Alfred de Musset', *Orbis Litterarum*, 19 (1954).

Gundolf, Friedrich: 'Georg Büchner', *Romantiker*, Berlin, 1930 (reprinted Martens, 1965, pp. 82 ff.).

Hamann, Holger: 'Zum Namen der weiblichen Hauptperson in Büchners "Woyzeck"', *Orbis Litterarum*, 25 (1970).

Hasubek, Peter: '"Ruhe" und "Bewegung". Versuch einer Stilanalyse von Georg Büchners "Lenz"', *Germanisch-Romanische Monatsschrift*, 19 (1969).

Helmig, Hermann: *Der Morphologe Georg Büchner*, Basel, 1950 (dissertation).

Herrmann, Hans Peter: '"Den 20. Jänner ging Lenz durchs Gebirg". Zur Textgestalt von Georg Büchners nachgelassener Erzählung', *Zeitschrift für deutsche Philologie*, 85 (1966).

Heyn, Fritz: *Die Sprache Georg Büchners*, Marburg, 1955 (dissertation).

Hinck, Walter: 'Georg Büchner', *Deutsche Dichter des 19. Jahrhunderts*, hrsg. von Benno v. Wiese, Berlin, 1969.

Höllerer, Walter: 'Georg Büchner', *Zwischen Klassik und Moderne*, Stuttgart, 1958.

'Dantons Tod', *Das deutsche Drama*, hrsg. von Benno v. Wiese, Bd. 2, Düsseldorf, 1960.

Honigmann, Georg: *Die sozialen und politischen Ideen im Weltbild Georg Büchners* Giessen, 1929 (dissertation).

Hoyer, Walter: *Stoff und Gestalt bei Georg Büchner*, Leipzig, 1922.

Irle, Gerhard: *Der psychiatrische Roman*, Stuttgart, 1965.

Jansen, J.: *Dantons Tod. Erläuterungen und Dokumente*, Stuttgart, 1969.

Jaspers, Anna: *Georg Büchners Trauerspiel 'Dantons Tod'*, Marburg, 1921 (dissertation).

Jens, Walter: 'Schwermut und Revolte. Georg Büchner', *Von deutscher Rede*, München, 1969.

Johann, Ernst: *Georg Büchner in Selbstzeugnissen und Bilddokumenten*, Hamburg, 1958.

Kanzog, Klaus: 'Wozzeck, Woyzeck und kein Ende', *DVjs*, 47 (1973).

Kerner, Dieter: 'In memoriam Georg Büchners', *Deutsches medizinisches Journal*, Berlin, 14 (1963).

# BIBLIOGRAPHY

Klotz, Volker: *Geschlossene und offene Form im Drama*, München, 1960.

Knight, Arthur, H. J.: *Georg Büchner*, Oxford, 1951.

Koopmann, Helmut: '"Dantons Tod" und die antike Welt. Zur Geschichts-philosophie Georg Büchners', *Zeitschrift für deutsche Philologie*, 84 (1965) [Sonderheft].

Krapp, Helmut: *Der Dialog bei Georg Büchner*, Darmstadt, 1958.

Kreuder, Ernst: *Georg Büchner. Existenz und Sprache*, Mainz, 1955.

Lamberechts, L.: 'Zur Struktur von Büchners "Woyzeck". Mit einer Darstellung des dramaturgischen Verhältnisses Büchner–Brecht', *Amsterdamer Beiträge zur Germanistik*, 1 (1972).

Landsberg, Hans: *Georg Büchners 'Dantons Tod'*, Berlin, 1900 (dissertation).

Lehmann, Werner R.: 'Robespierre – "ein impotenter Mahomet"?', *Euphorion*, 57 (1963).

*Textkritische Noten. Prolegomena zur Hamburger Büchner-Ausgabe*, Hamburg, 1967.

*'Geht einmal euren Phrasen nach . . .': Revolutionsideologie und Ideologiekritik bei Georg Büchner*, Darmstadt, 1969.

'Beiträge zu einem Streitgespräch über den "Woyzeck"', *Euphorion*, 65 (1971).

Lindenberger, H.: *Georg Büchner*, Carbondale, Southern Illinois University Press, 1964.

Lipmann, Heinz: *Georg Büchner und die Romantik*, München, 1923.

Lukács, Georg: 'Der faschistisch verfälschte und der wirkliche Georg Büchner', *Deutsche Literatur in zwei Jahrhunderten*, Neuwied, 1964 (reprinted Martens, 1965, pp. 197 ff.).

McGlashan, Leonard: *Sinn und Form des realistischen Dramas bei Georg Büchner*, Münster, 1955 (dissertation).

Majut, Rudolf: *Studien um Büchner. Untersuchungen zur Geschichte der problema-tischen Natur*, Berlin, 1932.

'Büchner und Gautier', *Archiv für das Studium der neueren Sprachen*, 165 (1934).

'Georg Büchner and some English Thinkers', *MLR*, 48 (1953) (German translation in Martens, 1965, pp. 334 ff.).

Mann, Golo: 'Georg Büchner und die Revolution', *Neue Rundschau*, 80 (1969).

Marcuse, L.: *Georg Büchner und seine besten Bühnenwerke*, Berlin, 1921.

Martens, Wolfgang: 'Zum Menschenbild Georg Büchners. "Woyzeck" und die Marionszene in "Dantons Tod"', *Wirkendes Wort*, 8 (1957/58) (reprinted Martens, 1965, pp. 373 ff.).

'Zur Karikatur in der Dichtung Büchners (Woyzecks Hauptmann)', *Ger-manisch-Romanische Monatsschrift*, 8 (1958).

'Ideologie und Verzweiflung. Religiöse Motive in Büchners Revolutions-drama', *Euphorion*, 54 (1960) (reprinted Martens, 1965, pp. 406 ff.).

'Der Barbier in Büchners "Woyzeck"', *Zeitschrift für deutsche Philologie*, 79 (1960).

*Georg Büchner*, hrsg. von Wolfgang Martens, Wege der Forschung, Bd. LIII, Darmstadt, 1965.

Mautner, Franz H.: 'Wortgewebe, Sinngefüge und "Idee" in Büchners

# BIBLIOGRAPHY

"Woyzeck"', *DVjs*, 35 (1961) (reprinted Martens, 1965, pp. 507 ff.).

May, Kurt: 'Büchners "Woyzeck"', *Form und Bedeutung: Interpretationen deutscher Dichtung des 18. und 19. Jahrhunderts*, Stuttgart, 1957 (reprinted Martens, 1965, pp. 241 ff.).

Mayer, Hans: *Georg Büchner und seine Zeit*, Wiesbaden, 1946. (Neue, erweiterte Auflage, Frankfurt a. M., 1972.)

'Georg Büchners ästhetische Anschauungen', *Studien zur deutschen Literaturgeschichte*, 2. Aufl., Berlin, 1955.

Mühlher, Robert: 'Georg Büchner und die Mythologie des Nihilismus', *Dichtung der Krise*, Wien, 1951 (reprinted Martens, 1965, pp. 252 ff.).

Müller-Seidel, Walter: 'Natur und Naturwissenschaft im Werk Georg Büchners', *Festschrift für Klaus Ziegler*, Tübingen, 1968.

Neuse, E. K.: 'Büchners "Lenz". Zur Struktur der Novelle', *German Quarterly*, 43 (1970).

Nöllner, Friedrich: *Actenmäßige Darlegung des wegen Hochverraths eingeleiteten gerichtlichen Verfahrens gegen Pfarrer D. Friedrich Ludwig Weidig*, Darmstadt, 1844.

Oppel, Horst: *Die tragische Dichtung Georg Büchners*, Stuttgart, 1951.

Paulus, Ursula: 'Georg Büchners "Woyzeck". Eine kritische Betrachtung zu der Edition Fritz Bergemanns', *Jahrbuch der deutschen Schillergesellschaft*, 8 (1964).

Peacock, Ronald: 'A Note on Georg Büchner's Plays', *German Life and Letters*, 10 (1956–7) (German translation in Martens, 1965, pp. 360 ff.).

Petersen, J. H.: 'Die Aufhebung der Moral im Werk Georg Büchners', *DVjs*, 47 (1973).

Plard, Henri: 'A propos de *Leonce und Lena*. Musset et Büchner', *Études Germaniques*, 9 (1954) (German translation in Martens, 1965, pp. 241 ff.).

'L'Ennui dans *Leonce und Lena*', *Études Germaniques*, 17 (1962).

Poschmann, Henri: 'Das künstlerische Werk Georg Büchners', *Weimarer Beiträge*, 17 (1971).

Pütz, Heinz Peter: 'Büchners "Lenz" und seine Quelle. Bericht und Erzählung', *Zeitschrift für deutsche Philologie*, 84 (1965) [Sonderheft].

Renker, Armin: *Georg Büchner und das Lustspiel der Romantik. Eine Studie über Leonce und Lena*, Berlin, 1924.

Richards, David G.: 'Zur Textgestaltung von Georg Büchners "Woyzeck". Anmerkungen zur Hamburger Büchner-Ausgabe, den "Woyzeck" betreffend', *Euphorion*, 65 (1971).

Ritscher, Hans: *Georg Büchner, Dantons Tod*, Frankfurt a. M., 3. Aufl., 1969.

Roche, Reinhard: 'Stilus demagogicus. Beobachtungen an Robespierres Rede im Jakobinerklub', *Wirkendes Wort*, 13 (1964).

Rössing-Hager, Monika: *Wortindex zu Georg Büchners Dichtungen und Übersetzungen*, Berlin, 1970.

Scheuer, Erwin: *Akt und Szene in der offenen Form des Dramas dargestellt an den Dramen Georg Büchners*, Berlin, 1929.

Schmid, Peter: *Georg Büchner. Versuch über die tragische Existenz*, Bern, 1940.

Schmidt, Henry J.: *Satire, Caricature and Perspectivism in the Works of Georg Büchner*, The Hague/Paris, 1970.

Schröder, Jürgen: *Leonce und Lena. Das Lustspiel als Kehrform des Büchnerschen Dramas*, München, 1965.

Stern, J. P.: 'A World of Suffering: Georg Büchner', *Re-Interpretations*, London, 1964.

Strohl, Jean: *Lorenʒ Oken und Georg Büchner*, Zürich, 1935.

    *Lorenʒ Oken und Georg Büchner. Zwei Gestalten aus der Übergangsʒeit von Naturphilosophie und Naturwissenschaft*, München, 1936.

Strudthoff, Ingeborg: *Die Reʒeption Georg Büchners durch das deutsche Theater*, Berlin, 1957.

Szondi, Peter: 'Büchners "Dantons Tod"', *Deutsche Dramen von Gryphius bis Brecht*, hrsg. von J. Schillermeit, Frankfurt a. M., 1966.

Tennemann, W. G.: *Geschichte der Philosophie*, Bd. 10, Leipzig, 1817.

Ullman, Bo: *Die soʒiale Thematik im Werk Georg Büchners und ihre Entfaltung im 'Woyʒeck'*, Stockholm, 1970 (dissertation).

    'Der unpolitische Georg Büchner. Zum Büchner-Bild der Forschung, unter besonderer Berücksichtigung der "Woyzeck"-Interpretationen', *Studier i modern språkvetenskap*, 4 (1972).

Viehweg, Wolfram: *Georg Büchners 'Dantons Tod' auf dem deutschen Theater*, München, 1964.

Viëtor, Karl: *Georg Büchner als Politiker*, Bern, 1939.

    *Georg Büchner. Politik, Dichtung, Wissenschaft*, Bern, 1949.

Vogeley, Heinrich: *Georg Büchner und Shakespeare*, Marburg, 1934 (dissertation).

Vogt, Karl: *Aus meinem Leben*, Stuttgart, 1896.

Voss, Kurt: *Georg Büchners 'Lenʒ'. Eine Untersuchung nach Gehalt und Formgebung*, Bonn, 1922 (dissertation).

Wessell, L. P.: 'Eighteenth-century theodicy and the death of God in Büchner's "Dantons Tod"', *Seminar*, VIII (1972).

Wiese, Benno v.: 'Georg Büchner. Lenz', *Die deutsche Novelle von Goethe bis Kafka. Interpretationen*. II. Düsseldorf, 1962.

    'Die Religion Büchners und Hebbels', *Studien ʒur deutschen Literatur*, Düsseldorf, 1963.

Winkler, Hans: *Georg Büchners 'Woyʒeck'*, Greifswald, 1925 (dissertation).

Zabeltitz, Max Zobel v.: *Georg Büchner, sein Leben und sein Schaffen*, Berlin, 1912.

Zweig, Arnold: *Lessing, Kleist, Büchner. Drei Versuche*, Berlin, 1925.

#### 4. TRANSLATIONS INTO ENGLISH

Büchner, Georg: *Lenʒ*. Translated by Michael Hamburger, London, 1966.

    *Woyʒeck*. Translation with notes and supplementary material by Henry J. Schmidt, New York, 1969.

    *Danton's Death*. Translation with notes and supplementary material by Henry J. Schmidt, New York, 1971.

    *The Plays of Georg Büchner (Danton's Death, Leonce and Lena, Woyʒeck)*. Translated by Victor Price, London, 1971.

# INDEX

## INDEX

# INDEX